OKANAGAN UNIV/COLLEGE LIBRARY

01954700

D0712888

BF 575 .W8 W67 1994
Worrying : perspectives on
195470

DATE DUE

APR 2 6 1995	
NOV 17 1995	
FEB – 3 1998 FEB 1 8 1998	
NOV 5 1998	
NOV 3 0 1998	
DEC – FEB due Dec 9/99	
FEB – 6 2001	
NOV 3 0 2001	

BRODART   Cat. No. 23-221

WORRYING

*Perspectives on
Theory, Assessment
and Treatment*

THE WILEY SERIES IN CLINICAL PSYCHOLOGY

Series Editor

J. Mark G. Williams *Department of Psychology, University College of North Wales, Bangor, UK*

Paul Dickens Quality and Excellence in Human Services

Graham C.L. Davey and Frank Tallis (Editors) Worrying: Perspectives on Theory, Assessment and Treatment

Further titles in preparation

Full list of series titles on back end-papers

Edited by

GRAHAM C.L. DAVEY
The City University, London, UK and

FRANK TALLIS
The Charter Nightingale Hospital, London, UK

WORRYING

Perspectives on Theory, Assessment and Treatment

JOHN WILEY & SONS
Chichester · New York · Brisbane · Toronto · Singapore

Copyright © 1994 by John Wiley & Sons Ltd,
Baffins Lane, Chichester,
West Sussex PO19 1UD, England

Telephone (+44) 243 779777

All rights reserved.

No part of this book may be reproduced by any means,
or transmitted, or translated into a machine language
without the written permission of the publisher.

Other Wiley Editorial Offices

John Wiley & Sons, Inc., 605 Third Avenue,
New York, NY 10158-0012, USA

Jacaranda Wiley Ltd, 33 Park Road, Milton,
Queensland 4064, Australia

John Wiley & Sons (Canada) Ltd, 22 Worcester Road,
Rexdale, Ontario M9W 1L1, Canada

John Wiley & Sons (SEA) Pte Ltd, 37 Jalan Pemimpin #05-04,
Block B, Union Industrial Building, Singapore 2057

Library of Congress Cataloging-in-Publication

Worrying : perspectives on theory, assessment, and treatment / edited
  by Graham C.L. Davey, Frank Tallis.
      p. cm. — (The Wiley series in clinical psychology)
    Includes bibliographical references and index.
    ISBN 0-471-94114-X (cased)
    1. Worry.   2. Anxiety.   I. Davey, Graham.   II. Tallis, Frank.
III. Series.
    [DNLM: 1. Anxiety—diagnosis.   2. Anxiety—therapy.   WM 172 W929
1994]
    BF575.W8W67   1994
    152.4'6—dc20
    DNLM/DLC
    for Library of Congress   93–21368
                                                                        CIP

British Library Cataloguing in Publication Data

A catalogue record for this book is available from the British Library

ISBN 0-471-94114-X

Typeset in 10/12 Palatino by Inforum, Rowlands Castle, Hants.
Printed and bound in Great Britain by Biddles Ltd, Guildford, Surrey

CONTENTS

LIST OF CONTRIBUTORS

David H. Barlow   *Center for Stress and Anxiety Disorders, University at Albany, State University of New York, 1535 Western Avenue, Albany, NY 12203, USA*

Kirk R. Blankstein   *Erindale College, University of Toronto in Mississuaga, 3359 Mississuaga Road North, Mississuaga, Ontario L5L 1C6, Canada*

Alyson Bond   *Department of Psychology, Institute of Psychiatry, De Crespigny Park, London SE5 8AF, UK*

T.D. Borkovec   *The Stress and Anxiety Disorders Institute, Department of Psychology, Penn State University, University Park, PA 16802, USA*

Timothy A. Brown   *Center for Stress and Anxiety Disorders, University at Albany, State University of New York, 1535 Western Avenue, Albany, NY 12203, USA*

Gillian Butler   *Department of Psychology, Warneford Hospital, Headington, Oxford OX3 7JX UK*

Nicola Capuzzo   *Department of Psychology, Institute of Psychiatry, De Crespigny Park, London SE5 8AF, UK*

Guylaine Côté   *Center for Stress and Anxiety Disorders, University at Albany, State University of New York, 1535 Western Avenue, Albany, NY 12203, USA*

Eric L. Daleiden   *Department of Psychology, The Ohio State University, 1885 Neil Avenue, Columbus, Ohio 43210, USA*

Graham C.L. Davey   *Psychology Division, Department of Social Sciences, City University, Northampton Square, London EC1V 0HB, UK*

Deborah J. Dowdall   *Center for Stress and Anxiety Disorders, University at Albany, State University of New York, 1535 Western Avenue, Albany, NY 12203, USA*

Gordon L. Flett   *Department of Psychology, York University, 4700 Keele Street, North York, Ontario M3J 1P3, Canada*

Andrew K. MacLeod   *Royal Holloway, University of London, Egham Hill, Egham, Surrey TW20 0EX, UK*

Silvia Molina   *The Stress and Anxiety Disorders Institute, Department of Psychology, Penn State University, University Park, PA 16802, USA*

Frank Tallis   *The Charter Nightingale Hospital, 11–19 Lisson Grove, London NW1 5SH, UK*

Michael W. Vasey   *Department of Psychology, The Ohio State University, 1885 Neil Avenue, Columbus, Ohio 43210, USA*

Adrian Wells   *Department of Psychiatry, Warneford Hospital, University of Oxford, Oxford OX3 7JX, UK*

Patricia A. Wisocki   *Department of Clinical Psychology, University of Massachusetts, Tobin Hall, Amherst, MA 01003, USA*

SERIES PREFACE

Almost all clients who come into contact with health professionals report "worry" as a primary or secondary component of their problem. Worry is now the most common problem in people who consult their family practitioners with psychological problems, and it features in all the anxiety disorders, especially in the "General Anxiety Disorders" where it is the central aspect. Despite this, until the early 1980s, worry was considered to be an epiphenomenal accompaniment of anxiety; not thought worthy of separate study. Since then, the pioneering work of cognitive clinical psychologists has shown how worry is a serious problem in its own right. They have identified the need to understand the psychological processes that render people vulnerable to, precipitate, and maintain worry. In this book, Graham Davey and Frank Tallis have brought these clinical researchers together for the first time. A decade after worry was placed firmly on the agenda, this book takes stock; outlines how worry may be assessed; shows how worry may affect people throughout the lifespan—in children, adults and the elderly; and shows what new developments in treatment exist. Finally, it places all this in the context of the latest developments in cognitive and behavioural theory. The book provides a comprehensive guide to the burgeoning literature on the topic, written by the experts themselves. It will be useful for all health care professionals, especially those of us who find our patients and clients burdened by persistent worry. The Wiley Series in Clinical Psychology is pleased to offer this landmark book as a contribution to the field.

J.M.G. Williams
Series Editor

PREFACE

You cannot prevent the birds of worry and care from flying over your head. But you can stop them from building a nest in your head. (Chinese Proverb)

Worry must be the only mental state described in DSM-III-R (American Psychiatric Association, 1987) which also features in such diverse media as an ancient Chinese proverb, a recent popular song (Bobby McFerrin's "Don't worry, be happy") and the Thoth deck of Tarot cards (Wasserman, 1978). Although academic interest in worry is relatively recent, the lay construct of worry has been recognised for centuries. This delay in academic interest is commonly attributed to methodological and conceptual problems. Firstly, an internal process does not lend itself readily to experimental study and secondly, the independence of worry from anxiety was considered questionable. Both of these problems have now been, to a greater or lesser extent, addressed. The rise of contemporary cognitive clinical psychology has given legitimacy to self-report measures (Beck, Rush, Shaw & Emery, 1979) circumventing the necessity of direct observation. Moreover, worry and anxiety can now be considered separate constructs, each relating independently to different life event measures (Davey, Chapter 2, this volume).

The suggested DSM-IV draft criteria for generalised anxiety disorder (GAD; American Psychiatric Association, 1993) include worry as a cardinal feature. Moreover, reference in this document to factors such as difficulty of control, indicate that the inclusion of worry in DSM-III-R has been fully accepted, and a process of consolidation and refinement has begun. The continued presence of worry in an internationally accepted diagnostic scheme would not be significant in itself, were it not for the complementary growth of interest in academic and clinical circles. Already, there is a considerable body of evidence suggesting that worry is more common than previously thought, and that worry is relevant not only to GAD, but to psychological health status in general

From 1957 to 1976, a large-scale study conducted in the USA showed that worry was a psychological problem of increasing prevalence (Veroff, Douvan & Kulka, 1981). This finding is reflected in the clinic, where worry is now known to be the most frequent symptom reported by patients with psychological problems consulting doctors in family practice (Goldberg, Bridges, Duncan-Jones & Grayson, 1987). There is some evidence to suggest a link between worrying and poor psychological health in general (Hodgson, Tallis & Davey, submitted), and more specifically, worry is known to be a feature of all the anxiety disorders (Brown, Antony & Barlow, 1992; Brown, Dowdall, Côté & Barlow, Chapter 9, this volume).

Fortunately, recognition of the importance of worry has resulted in practical and clinically relevant developments. Several measurement instruments have been devised, for the assessment of worry at all points along the developmental continuum; in children (Vasey & Daleiden, Chapter 7, this volume), adults (Molina & Borkovec, Chapter 11, this volume; Tallis, Davey & Bond, Chapter 12, this volume), and the elderly (Wisocki, Chapter 10, this volume). Further, specific management and treatment strategies have begun to emerge. These include the modification of existing techniques, such as stimulus control (Borkovec, Wilkinson, Folensbee & Lerman, 1983) and problem-solving (Tallis, 1990), in addition to relatively fresh approaches. For example, Butler (Chapter 8, this volume) and Wells (Chapter 4, this volume), identify novel targets for behavioural programmes and cognitive restructuring in worriers; respectively, "demoralisation" and meta-cognition (e.g. worry about worry). Although quite different, both concepts could profitably guide therapeutic practice. Finally, MacLeod (Chapter 5, this volume) has developed a particularly useful strategy for modifying pessimism in worriers: "counterexplanation". This technique has evolved from a thorough understanding of the experimental literature on explanation-based processes in future judgements and represents an imaginative marriage of theory and clinical practice.

The modern worry literature has been precipitated largely by the work of Thomas Borkovec (Borkovec, Robinson, Pruzinski & DePree, 1983), who began investigating worry after observing that psychogenic insomnia was associated with uncontrollable cognitive intrusions. Borkovec and colleagues' 1983 paper "Preliminary exploration of worry" marks something of a watershed. Before this date, a literature search would have produced several articles mentioning worry within the context of test anxiety (Flett & Blankstein, Chapter 6, this volume), but only a handful of articles from outside that rather specialised tradition. After only 10 years, a present day student of worry can expect a literature search to yield a plethora of articles reflecting the construct's dramatic change in status.

Attempting to document the history of worry research before 1983 is certainly beyond the scope of this brief preface; however, it is interesting to note that one contemporary preoccupation, namely the function of worry (Borkovec, Chapter 1, this volume), has received attention in several contexts prior to the last decade. Although Sigmund Freud did not use the term worry as such, he had emphasised the role of "anxious expectation" in the maintenance of anxiety states as early as 1885. He discusses how the preservation of fear in individuals who have "experienced a thunderstorm in the open" cannot be explained in terms of the "persistence of strong impressions" alone; rather, emotionally disturbing "impressions remain powerful only in people with *anxious expectation*". His account bears a remarkable similarity to contemporary accounts of anxiety maintenance such as that proposed by Barlow (1988, p. 274), who suggests that "Only when learned alarms become associated with a strong cycle of *anxious apprehension* is a clinical anxiety disorder manifested". For Barlow, "intense worry" is a central feature of the process of anxious apprehension (p. 250).

Unlike many other processes closely associated with psychopathology, worry is unique in that the negative state engendered by worry may have adaptive consequences. The first psychologist to articulate this idea formally was Irving Janis, who in the 1950s introduced the concept of the "work of worrying". He suggested that the work of worrying "enables the person to cope more effectively in the long run with a painful reality situation" (Janis, 1958, pp. 374–388). The process is triggered by an appraisal of impending danger and represents a form of "inner preparation" that increases the individual's tolerance for subsequent "threat or danger stimuli". Avoidant individuals who fail to engage in mental rehearsal experience compromised coping. As with Freud, these precocious ideas relating to the function of worry bear interesting comparison with current thinking; especially if the term "mental rehearsal" is interpreted as an attempt to engage in mental problem-solving (Davey, Chapter 2, this volume).

When studying a relatively undocumented phenomenon, it is wise to learn something of its occurrence in normal populations before examining its occurrence in abnormal populations. Without doing so, it is virtually impossible to elucidate the important processes that contribute to the development of a clinical disorder. Obsessive–compulsive disorder (OCD) serves as an instructive example. Until recently, OCD was largely defined according to the presence of intrusive and bizarre thoughts. However, in 1978, Rachman & de Silva demonstrated that obsessional-type cognition is relatively common in non-clinical groups. This finding has had a profound impact on contemporary models of OCD, which now emphasise an individual's response to obsessional thoughts, rather than the presence of the thoughts alone (Salkovskis, 1985). Studies of non-pathological worry (Tallis, Davey & Capuzzo, Chapter 3; Tallis, Davey & Bond, Chapter 12, this volume), and consideration of process variables that transform it into a pathological condition (Davey, Chapter 2, this volume), will hopefully ensure that a comprehensive picture of the phenomenon emerges at an early stage of study.

Worry is an apparently ubiquitous experience. Moreover, it is relevant throughout the course of an individual's life, from childhood (Vasey & Daleiden, Chapter 7, this volume), to old age (Wisocki, Chapter 10, this volume). The contributions in this volume represent work conducted largely over the past 10 years. As such, modern worry research is barely out of its infancy. If the next 10 years of worry research are as productive as the last, then we anticipate an eventful adolescence.

REFERENCES

American Psychiatric Association (1987). *Diagnostic and Statistical Manual of Mental Disorders III Revised* (DSM-III-R). Washington: American Psychiatric Association.

American Psychiatric Association (1993). *Diagnostic and Statistical Manual of Mental Disorders IV. Draft Criteria* (DSM-IV). Washington: American Psychiatric Association.

Barlow, D. (1988). *Anxiety and its Disorders: The Nature and Treatment of Anxiety and Panic*. New York: Guilford Press.

Beck, A., Rush, A., Shaw, B. & Emery, G. (1979). *Cognitive Therapy of Depression*. New York: Guilford Press.

Borkovec, T.D., Robinson, E., Pruzinsky, T. & DePree, J.A. (1983). Preliminary exploration of worry: some characteristics and processes. *Behaviour Research and Therapy*, **21**, 9–16.

Bortovec, T.D., Wilkinson, L., Folensbee, R. and Lerman, C. (1983). Stimulus control applications to the treatment of worry. *Behavior Research and Therapy*, **21**, 247–251.

Brown, T.A., Antony, M.M. & Barlow, D.H. (1992). Psychometric properties of the Penn State Worry Questionnaire in a clinical anxiety disorders sample. *Behaviour Research and Therapy*, **30**, 33–37.

Freud, S. (1895). Uber die Berechtigung, von der Neurasthemie einen bestimmten Symptomencomplex als' Angstneurose' abzutrennen. *Neurologische Centralblatt*, **14**, 50–66.

Goldberg, D.P., Bridges, K., Duncan-Jones, P. & Grayson, D. (1987). Dimensions of neurosis seen in primary-care settings. *Psychological Medicine*, **17**, 461–470.

Hodgson, S., Tallis, F. & Davis, G.C.L. (submitted) Worried sick: The relationship between worrying and psychological and physical health status.

Janis, I. (1958). *Psychological Stress*. New York: Wiley.

Rachman, S. & de Silva, P. (1978). Abnormal and normal obsessions. *Behaviour Research and Therapy*, **16**, 233–248.

Salkovskis, P. (1985). Obsessional–Compulsive problems: a cognitive-behavioural analysis. *Behaviour Research and Therapy*, **25**, 571–583.

Tallis, F. (1990). *How to Stop Worrying*. London: Sheldon Press.
Veroff, J., Douvan, E. & Kulka, R.A. (1981). *The inner American: A Self-portrait from 1957 to 1976*. New York: Basic Books.
Wasserman, J. (1978). *Instructions for Aleister Crowley's Thoth Tarot Deck*. New York: US Games Systems Inc.

Graham C.L. Davey
Frank Tallis

London, August 1993

SECTION I   Theoretical perspectives

INTRODUCTION

Research on worrying has been conducted in earnest only in the last 10–15 years. Traditionally, worrying had been considered as a relatively insignificant cognitive correlate of anxiety rather than a psychological phenomenon in its own right. However, recent research has propelled worrying to a relatively prominent role in the description of cognitive pathology, and it is likely to remain an important feature of a number of anxiety disorders with the advent of DSM-IV.

A discussion of the theoretical aspects of worrying requires that a variety of important questions be addressed. These include

1 *Elaborating the construct of worry*, especially with respect to related constructs such as anxiety and depression, and in particular, in terms of its role in the various anxiety disorders.
2 *Describing the phenomenology of worrying.* Worrying is an activity that almost everyone indulges in to some degree; what are its defining features in terms of the experiences of the worrier, and in terms of the things that people worry about?
3 *Describing the cognitive processes which characterise worrying.* This question will be central to our eventual understanding of the process of worrying and how it might evolve from a normal, constructive activity to a pathological process which underlies a number of anxiety disorders.
4 *Elucidating the function of worrying.* Since worrying appears to be so pervasive, what are the factors that maintain it and does it have a particular psychological function?
5 *Defining the features and processes which distinguish normal and pathological worrying.* Most people worry at some time, but only some people find it such an uncontrollable and emotionally disturbing experience that it interferes with their ability to live a normal life. What factors underlie this difference?
6 *Discovering the origins of pathological worrying.* Can pathological worrying be explained solely in terms of discrete cognitive processes or will

a fuller explanation allude to factors in the developmental experiences of the worrier?

The chapters in this introductory section attempt to address these various questions.

There is now some evidence that worrying can be considered as a construct that is independent of anxiety and has its own explanatory value. Davey (Chapter 2) outlines the evidence which shows that measures of worrying possess sources of variance that are independent of measures of anxiety. These independent sources of variance relate primarily to problem-oriented activities, and this suggests that whilst worrying might have a pathological side to its nature, it also has constructive, task-oriented features. In the context of test anxiety, Flett & Blankstein (Chapter 6) also emphasise the independence of the construct of worrying from a variety of other related psychological processes.

The chapters by Tallis, Davey & Capuzzo (Chapter 3), Borkovec (Chapter 1) and Wells (Chapter 4) all provide further information that enables us to construct a fuller picture of the phenomenology of worrying for both normal and pathological worriers. Tallis et al. provide an extensive overview of the phenomenology of normal worry, including such details as the duration of the normal worry episode, its temporal focus (on past, present, or future events), the time of day it is most likely to occur, the factors that trigger worrying, its narrative characteristics, its effect on everyday functioning, and its perceived consequences. Most worry content appears to be related to current concerns, and is considered a response to real rather than imaginary problems. Wells reports that the content of worry can be grouped under three headings: worry about social factors, worry about health factors, and meta-worry (i.e. worrying about worrying). Interestingly, there tends to be very little difference in the content of worry between normal and pathological worriers (see Tallis, Davey & Bond, Chapter 12). The chapter by Borkovec (Chapter 1) contains detailed descriptions of the experience of worrying in generalised anxiety disorder (GAD) clients. These subjective reports indicate that, even though GAD clients find their worrying uncontrollable and a source of chronic anxiety, they still believe that the worry process has beneficial effects when it comes to dealing with imminent threats and stressors.

All of the chapters in this section have something to say about the cognitive processes that either characterise or underlie worrying. Worrying is seen largely as composed of thoughts rather than images (Borkovec, Chapter 1). However, in the case of pathological worrying, these thoughts tend to be overwhelmingly negative, characterised by obsessive ruminating and catastrophising, and are often initiated by negative intrusive thoughts (Wells, Chapter 4). The chapter by MacLeod (Chapter 5) emphasises that worry involves beliefs that worried-about future events are likely, and this chapter describes some of the cognitive processes that enable worriers to more readily access reasons why a future negative event will happen, rather than reasons why it will not. Davey (Chapter 2) considers worrying as exacerbated problem-solving, and suggests that worriers may be characterised by a variety of cognitive predispositions which thwart effective problem-solving; these include a preponderance of negative cognitions, a tendency to interpret ambiguous events as threats, and poor personal problem-solving confidence. Similarly, Flett & Blankstein provide extensive evidence that test-anxious worry reflects evaluative concerns about failure that stem largely from a negative view of the self (Chapter 6). Wells discusses a number of attentional processes that may contribute to worrying. He proposes a cognitive–attentional model of pathological worry which emphasises that worriers may have dysfunctional meta-cognitive plans which specify ruminative and preservative appraisal, self-monitoring of cognition, and frequent use of cognitive–behavioural thought control strategies.

There are a number of hypotheses emerging as to the psychological function of worry. Borkovec (Chapter 1) gives a detailed account of the evidence which suggests that worrying prevents the emotional processing of phobic imagery. In this respect worrying functions to avoid those threatening images that evoke physiological arousal and anxiety. While this function has a reinforcing effect on worrying, it also has the maladaptive effect of preventing the emotional processing of phobic images and thus preventing their extinction. In contrast, Davey (Chapter 2) emphasies the potential problem-solving function of worrying. At least some worrying is viewed as constructive and task-oriented and acts to help solve potential life problems. Davey argues that pathological worrying occurs when this constructive function is thwarted by cognitive features of the pathological worrier which prevent closure of the problem and gives rise only to further unproductive worrying. There are some other theories of the function of worrying which are mentioned tangentially in these chapters; for example, the adaptive role of worrying in enhancing the appraisal of threats (see Wells, Chapter 4). It is perhaps worth emphasising that none of these differing hypotheses as to the function of worry are necessarily mutually exclusive. Worrying may directly or indirectly serve a number of psychological functions, each of which can be described as influencing different psychological and physiological outcomes.

Arguably, the question of most clinical relevance in this section is "What distinguishes normal and pathological worriers?" Descriptively, normal and pathological worrying can be distinguished on the basis of the frequency, intensity and uncontrollability of worrying (Tallis et al., Chapter 3). However, the important theoretical breakthrough will arrive when we are able to specify clearly the cognitive processes that characterise pathological worriers, and how these processes interact to generate pathological worrying. Some initial attempts to indicate the relevant processes are outlined in the chapters by Wells, Borkovec, MacLeod and Davey.

Finally, where does pathological worrying originate? At the level of process one can already identify a number of dysfunctional cognitions that contribute to worrying, but what in turn gives rise to these dysfunctional cognitions? The chapter by Borkovec gives some intriguing insights into the possible developmental factors that may influence subsequent pathological worrying. These include a history of traumatic experiences, and also a parenting style that promotes insecure attachment in childhood. Both developmental factors may generate a tendency to view the world as a dangerous place that fosters anxiety and worry.

CHAPTER 1   The nature, functions, and origins of worry

T.D. Borkovec*

Worry is an intriguing phenomenon whose nature has only recently come under experimental scrutiny. It is a pervasive human activity: Nearly everyone is periodically aware of its occurrence, and for some it is a constant but unwanted and severe companion. Indeed, in a 20-year cross-sectional study in the United States, worry was only one of two mental health indicators to show a significant increase among eight such measures (Veroff, Douvan & Kulka, 1981). The purpose of the present chapter is to review some of the empirically determined characteristics of worry and to suggest theoretical perspectives that may account for the functions and origins of this ubiquitous process.

THE IMPORTANCE OF WORRY

The present volume arrives at a moment when attempts to understand the phenomenon of worry are becoming increasingly important. First, in 1987, DSM-III-R (American Psychiatric Association, 1987) created generalized anxiety disorder (GAD) and defined its central feature as chronic worry. This was a significant event: The field of psychiatry had agreed to the existence of a disorder whose cardinal characteristic was clearly a psychological process. Reconsideration of that decision by the DSM-IV Task Force has resulted in intense debate within the field of psychiatry, with some arguments currently being offered in favor of eliminating the disorder altogether. At the time of this writing, the second draft of the DSM-IV criteria (American Psychiatric Association, 1993) still retains GAD, with worry as its defining feature.

Second, investigation of worry has generated some fascinating results leading to the tentative conclusion that the process may be a highly

*Penn State University, University Park, USA

Worrying: Perspectives on Theory, Assessment and Treatment. Edited by G.C.L. Davey and F. Tallis.
© 1994 John Wiley & Sons Ltd.

significant contributor to the maintenance of anxiety, not only for GAD but possibly for all of the other anxiety disorders as well. If this is the case, then significant information is being acquired in the context of worry research that will have implications for understanding anxiety and its disorders and for the development of increasingly effective interventions for their amelioration.

Third, it is becoming increasingly clear that human movement through space and time is usefully considered to be a function of rapid interactions among multiple information processing systems in a nonlinear dynamical fashion. For example, moment-to-moment affect influences what information is retrieved from memory, what interpretation is given to ongoing external events, and what content and form exists in thought. What an individual believes and thinks, on the other hand, also affects how he or she feels on a moment-to-moment basis. All of these processes contribute to choices of behaviors that constantly interact with a constantly changing environment and the consequences that world provides to the chosen responses. Worry appears to involve such intriguing interactions among several human systems: conceptual, imaginal, affective, attentional, memory representational, behavioral, and physiological. Its study thus offers opportunities for developing an integrated understanding of human process, both psychopathological and normal.

As recently as 1980, the extant literature on worry was very sparse. The only focused tradition came from the test anxiety area, wherein systematic attempts to distinguish between worry (defined as self-evaluative negative thinking) and emotionality (awareness of physiological and emotional states) by questionnaire method revealed a stronger relationship of the former than the latter to actual test performance, task-generated attentional interference, and grade-point average (cf. Deffenbacher, 1980). (See Chapter 6, this volume.) Although numerous anxiety researchers had begun to suggest functional differences between cognitive and somatic subcomponents in anxious process (e.g. Davidson & Schwartz, 1976), the test anxiety studies already had empirically established the separateness of worry as well as its crucial relationship to behavioral disruption. Since 1980, a rapidly growing experimental literature has arisen on the topic of worry, and the results are beginning to tell a rather remarkable story.

THE NATURE OF WORRY

When the Penn State program began its research on worry, a tentative definition was offered (Borkovec, Robinson, Pruzinsky & Depree, 1983):

Worry is a chain of thoughts and images, negatively affect-laden and relatively uncontrollable; it represents an attempt to engage in mental problem-solving on an issue whose outcome is uncertain but contains the possibility of one or more negative outcomes; consequently, worry relates closely to fear process. Research since that time has supported several features of that definition but has encouraged further elaborations and significant modifications.

Conceptual and Imaginal Cognitive Activity

Cognitive intrusion and incubation

If worriers are asked to focus on a simple monotonous task (e.g. focus on breathing), they will report lower ability to remain focused and more frequent distractions by negative thoughts than will nonworriers (Borkovec et al., 1983). If all subjects then spend 15 minutes worrying about their greatest concern, both worriers and nonworriers will show an increase in the number of negative thought intrusions during an immediately subsequent period. Thirty minutes of worry, on the other hand, will produce a reduction in subsequent negative thoughts. It appears, then, that worry process shows some evidence of acting like fear, displaying habituation with long exposures and incubation with briefer exposures. And the incubation phenomenon indicates that worrisome thinking can be self-perpetuating under certain temporal conditions. The chronic presence of negative thought intrusions among worriers and the incubating effects of brief periods of worry are not due to the somatic aspects of anxious experience that accompany the worrisome state: briefly induced worry yields perpetuation of negative thinking to a significantly greater degree than neutral states, whereas somatic anxiety induction does not (York, Borkovec, Vassey & Stern, 1987).

The predominance of thought

Perhaps the most important, fundamental characteristic of worry is that it involves a type of internal verbal–linguistic activity, i.e. thinking. When asked what proportion of their worrisome experience is predominantly thought, imagery, or a mixture of these two cognitive events, 900 community women indicated 51%, 3%, and 46%, respectively; when asked in a format forcing a choice between thoughts and images, 300 college students of both genders reported 70% and 30%, respectively (Borkovec & Lyonfields, 1993). Somewhat more valid data came from GAD clients and their matched, nonanxious control counterparts during laboratory periods of self-relaxation and worry (Borkovec & Inz, 1991). Thought samples indicated that relaxing controls reported a vast majority of imagery and little thinking, whereas GAD clients reported equal amounts of each. During a period during which they were asked to worry about their currently most pressing concern, both groups showed a shift to heightened frequency of thought and lowered frequency of imagery. Valence ratings revealed greater anxiety associated with sampled mentations for the clients, during both relaxation and worry, than the comparison group, and increased anxiety for both groups during worry. Significantly, at a post-therapy laboratory retest, the clients showed a normalization of both thought/imagery percentages and the degree of anxiety associated with them.

This predominance of thought in worry was not discovered until recently, but its determination is significantly influencing theoretical perspectives on the nature and functions of the phenomenon. The distinction between thought and image among the variety of processes called "cognitive" is of fundamental importance, especially as it relates to affective systems and emotional processing, as will be described later.

The Affective Experience of Worry

Connection to anxiety

Worry was expected to be highly related to the emotions of fear and anxiety, and indeed this appears to be the case (Borkovec et al., 1983). Worry (defined as the percentage of the day spent worrying) correlates significantly with the Beck Depression Inventory but even more highly with trait anxiety, and it did so to a greater degree than did reports of general tension. Among a variety of emotion scales, anxiety, tension, and apprehensiveness were the most highly rated when subjects were asked to characterize the feeling states that they typically experienced when worrying. The majority of their worries (46.9%) related to the future, implying anticipated threat, as opposed to the past (20.9%). Awareness of somatic activity was not as intense as has been found for fear. However, among somatic experiences, muscle tension was the most highly rated when worrying. Good reason exists for predominance of this physiological channel: muscle tension is the only system significantly distinctive of GAD.

If there is a central source of the anxious experience of worriers and GAD clients, it resides in social evaluative issues. Worry correlates most highly with social evaluative concerns on a fear survey schedule and very little with nonsocial items (Borkovec et al., 1983). Fear of making mistakes, of being criticized, and of meeting people rank among the highest, specific, anxiety-provoking events. Moreover, worriers score significantly higher on public self-consciousness (Pruzinsky & Borkovec, 1990), and social phobia is the most frequent comorbid diagnosis for principal GAD cases (Brown & Barlow, 1992). There may be a very fundamental basis for this connection between worry and social concerns. Worry primarily involves thought. From an evolutionary perspective, thought has its origins in verbal–linguistic communication. Speculatively, the prototype for worrisome thinking might then be found developmentally in verbal attempts to express one's anxious feelings to significant others (cf. Borkovec, Shadick & Hopkins, 1991). Why this perpetuates into adulthood in pathological form for GAD is considered later when speculations about the origins of chronic worry and GAD are discussed.

Connection to depression

The above results, based primarily on global trait-like and retrospective reports, indeed suggested a close relationship between worry and fear. Questionnaire results also suggested a connection between worry and depression. Given the customarily high correlations between anxiety and depression measures, such a relationship was hardly surprising. However, it turns out that worry may be more intimately associated with both depression and anxiety than the latter two are to each other. A study contrasting induced worry and somatic anxiety conditions for their affective effects included a depression induction condition in the design (Andrews & Borkovec, 1988). Somatic anxiety induction yielded the highest degree of reported state-anxiety on the Multiple Affect Adjective Checklist (Zuckerman, Lubin & Rinck, 1983), followed in turn by worry and then depression induction. Depression induction produced the greatest amount of reported state-depression, followed by worry and then somatic anxiety inductions. More strikingly, whereas no overlap existed among the most highly rated affect items between depression and somatic anxiety conditions, worry resulted in a non-unique mixture, with 60% of the most frequently endorsed items coming from the top somatic anxiety items and 40% from the depression items. Moreover, correlations of the three resulting profiles of mood found the strongest relationships between worry and each of the other two states, significantly greater than the mood relationship between somatic anxiety and depression. Thus, unlike anxiety and depression, worry involves moderate levels of both states and to a less intense degree than the most salient affective experience for each of the other two.

The implications of the possibility that depressive, in addition to anxious, process is also contained within the experience of worry may be highly significant. It would mean that worry variously involves the functions and associated effects of both moods. Mathews (1990) has argued that depression involves elaboration of associated material in memory, whereas anxiety is characterized by avoidance of further elaboration. What then would be the functional properties of a phenomenon that includes each of these processes? Whatever the answer is to this intriguing question, it would no doubt implicate a considerable richness and complexity in the nature and functions of worry beyond what has been so far learned from experimental pursuit of its anxiety-related functions. It will perhaps be necessary to wed depressive functions with those of anxiety before a thorough understanding of worrisome process emerges.

Attentional Activity and Memory Retrieval

Clinical experience as well as empirical results paint a picture of the chronic worrier as one who is constantly engaging in negative thinking, even during resting states in the laboratory (Borkovec et al., 1983; Borkovec & Inz, 1990; Pruzinsky & Borkovec, 1990) and in daily daydreaming (Pruzinsky & Borkovec, 1990). If so much attention is devoted to this activity, then less attentional resource would remain for other information processing tasks. Certainly, less processing will occur of immediately available environmental information. As a consequence, the worrier may not be experiencing the present moment or learning from experience to the degree that he/she might. Thus far no empirical data on this hypothetical implication have been acquired, and it remains for future research. Considerable experimental information does exist, however, for certain effects of worry on attentional mechanisms, interpretation of the environment, and memory retrieval, comprehensively reviewed by Mathews (1990) and summarized below.

GAD clients show interference of threat-related material in dichotic listening tasks, even outside of awareness (Mathews & MacLeod, 1986). They display the same effect on the Stroop color-naming task, and the degree to which this occurs relates to the degree to which the client is currently worried about the topic associated with the threat (Mogg, Mathews & Weinman, 1989). Indeed, both positive and negative Stroop words show this effect, but only if the words are related to the client's current worry topics (Mathews & Klug, 1993). More dramatically, GAD clients display a preattentive bias to immediately available threatening information, in contrast to depressed individuals (MacLeod, Mathews &

Tata, 1986; Gotlib, McLachlan & Katz, 1988). Subjective risk is significantly inflated among GAD clients (Butler & Mathews, 1983), and such inflation has been found to relate to topics of current concern in another anxiety disorder, i.e. panic (Clark et al., 1988). Trait-anxious subjects and GAD clients will also interpret ambiguous external information in a more threatening manner (Eysenck, MacLeod & Mathews, 1987; Eysenck et al., 1990). Unlike depression, however, GAD does not involve a spread of activation throughout the associative network surrounding worry topics. Retrieval of threat-related information is not biased by mood congruent memory effects among clinically anxious subjects; indeed, anxious subjects recalled significantly fewer threat words than nonanxious subjects, a demonstration that anticipates recent findings presented later that indicate poorer recall of childhood experiences for GAD clients despite evidence that their early years involved more insecure attachment.

The combination of results indicating preattentive bias to threat but absence of biased recall has led Mathews (1990) to suggest that worry involves a cognitive avoidance of elaboration of the associative network surrounding anxious material. Threat information is encoded, however, despite rapid avoidance upon detection; implicit memory tests indicate that GAD clients will significantly more often complete word stems with previously seen (but not recalled) threat words than will nonanxious controls (Mathews, Mogg & Eysenck, 1989).

Many of these results document the cognitive avoidant function of worry, suggest the consequences of continuous mental rehearsal of worrisome thoughts for strengthening threat-related information in memory, and provide experimental foundation for some of the other observed or inferred characteristics of GAD clients. For example, GAD clients report significantly greater interference of their worries in daily life when compared to other anxiety disorder groups and nonanxious individuals (Borkovec et al., 1991). Furthermore, if threat cues are detected preattentively outside of awareness on the basis of primed anxiety-related memory structures, are immediately avoided upon detection rather than elaborated, and are not recalled, then it makes sense that GAD clients are constantly in an anxious state and that they report that their worries emerge vaguely from within themselves rather than being triggered by external stimuli (Craske, Rapee, Jackel & Barlow, 1989).

The above data contrasting GAD to depression also suggest that, despite the earlier mentioned co-occurrence of anxiety and depression in worry, in many preparations anxious process is predominating. Whether the depressive elements of worrisome process have an impact in other ways remains as yet uncertain.

Behavioral Responding

One of the features that distinguishes GAD from other anxiety disorders is the absence of obvious, circumscribed phobic stimuli that are motorically avoided. Clinical experience suggests, however, that clients often engage in more subtle avoidance to a wide variety of environmental circumstances (Butler et al., 1988), and GAD clients in therapy in the Penn State program have often reported problems with procrastination. Neither of these observations has been as yet documented with valid measures. Those disrupted behaviors that have been demonstrated tend to be reflections of characteristic cognitive processing difficulties described earlier (e.g. poor test performance, preattentive bias, task disruption by threat material). Two further studies exemplify a similar effect that is perhaps more obviously related to procrastination. In one (Metzger et al., 1990), worriers took longer than nonworriers to make decisions about whether or not an ambiguous stimulus matched a pretrained target, and the degree of this effect related to the degree of ambiguity. Moreover, nonworriers will show the same effect after an incubating period of worry. So task disruption does not necessarily have to relate only to immediately presented, specific threat cues. A neutral task can lead to indecision, even among nonworriers subsequent to worry induction. Such an effect suggests the priming of general, social evaluative, threatening meanings. Fear of making a mistake, chronically present in worriers or tonically elicited in individuals who are induced into a worrisome state, would reasonably lead to hesitant behavior. In the second study, Tallis, Eysenck & Mathew (1991) determined that the slower decision rates of worriers may be due to elevated evidence requirements: They took longer than nonworriers to decide whether a target letter was present or absent when a random-letters display did not contain the target, whereas latencies were not significantly different when the target was present.

Physiological activity

The physiological domain of research has yielded some of the most exciting and illuminating data that have emerged for understanding the nature and functions of worry and its clinical GAD prototype. Preliminary work failed to identify any cardiovascular differences between worriers and nonworriers, between GAD clients and matched nonanxious controls, or even between resting states and worrisome states (Borkovec et al., 1983; Elliott, 1990). This was initially surprising, given that fight-or-flight reactions are customarily viewed to involve sympathetic activation and that robust cardiovascular effects are routinely found in much of the anxiety literature. The publication of a review of psychophysiological research on the anxiety disorders by Hoehn-Saric & McLeod (1988) provided a possible answer. GAD clients do show elevated muscle tension during rest and in response to challenge (providing a physiological basis for their reports of the predominance of this system, as mentioned earlier), but they otherwise do not display the usual sympathetic activation response so typical of other anxiety disorders. Rather, their peripheral physiology (heart rate and skin conductance) reveals a restriction in range of variability. From these results, the authors concluded that GAD is typified by some degree of sympathetic *inhibition* and a resulting autonomic inflexibility. Such a physiological substrate makes sense in conjunction with what else is known about GAD. The stimuli that they fear have to do less with immediately present threat that requires motoric avoidance and more to do with internally generated thoughts about a currently nonexistent future threat. In other words, their fear involves fight-or-flight with no place to go. The best animal learning analog is the "freezing" response when no effective avoidance response is available. Such freezing directly implicates increased muscle tension. As for reductions in peripheral physiological variability, not only has increased muscle tension via isometric hand-drip been found to reduce autonomic variability, but other experimental tasks that elicit such an effect are easily related to demonstrated or reasonably assumed characteristics of GAD and worry, e.g. threat of shock, recall of past aversive events, and engagement in attempts to solve mental arithmetic problems (Grossman & Svebak, 1987; Grossman, Stemmler & Meinhardt, 1990).

Given that excessive conceptual activity is the hallmark of GAD, one could speculate that it is the predominance of worrisome thinking that is particularly causative of their autonomic inflexibility. Lyonfields (1991) recently compared GAD and non-GAD analog subjects during rest, a 4-minute period of aversive imagery related to a topic of greatest concern, and a 4-minute period of worrying about that topic. The central dependent measure of interest was Mean Successive Difference of heart rate interbeat interval, a preferred method for assessing cardiovascular variability that reflects degree of parasympathetic tone. He found the GAD subjects displayed very little variabilty throughout the experiment. Nonanxious subjects, on the other hand, showed a significant reduction in variability from rest to aversive imagery, and a further significant reduction from imagery to worrisome thinking. In terms of subjective affective state during these tasks, worry generated greater report of anxious feelings than did aversive imagery for all subjects, and they reported greater ease of generating and maintaining the worrisome thinking than the aversive images. Thus, worry can restrict autonomic variability and increase negative affect to a degree greater than aversive imagery. The high frequency of negative thinking that occurs irrespective of task and so effortlessly for GAD subjects hypothetically yields their chronic states of both distressing subjective affect and restrictive psychophysiology.

Two methodological features prevent unequivocal conclusions from the Lyonfields study, however. First, reduced variability during worry among control subjects may have been due to order effects; the aversive imagery period always preceded the worry period. Most importantly, the tonically reduced variability among GAD subjects and reductions during worry among controls may have been caused merely by the predominance of thinking but not necessarily *worrisome* thinking. Although evidence for the functional distinctiveness of worrisome thinking in affecting cardiovascular response does exist from another study described later, Lyonfields is currently contrasting neutral vs. aversive imagery vs. thinking in a 2×2 within-subject design with control for order effects. The results should help to determine whether the autonomic inflexibility of the GAD subject is associated with excessive thinking *per se* or excessive negative thinking in particular.

More recently, exciting data are beginning to emerge from psychophysiological assessments of GAD clients and matched, nonanxious control subjects at the Penn State program. Data from only six subjects in each group have been analyzed so far, but the results are striking (Friedman, Thayer, Borkovec & Lyonfields, 1993). Collapsing over all of the phases of the assessment session (baseline, self-relaxation, and worry periods), the data showed that GAD clients had a significantly greater restriction in heart rate variability, as expected. More importantly, spectral analysis of interbeat interval, which provides a valid estimate of degree of parasympathetic control of cardiovascular functioning independent of sympathetic activity, has revealed a significant deficiency in parasympathetic tone among the clients. Furthermore, these clients displayed significant increases in variability and parasympathetic tone subsequent to successful therapy and no longer differed from the nonanxious subjects on these variables. Not all subjects have yet been analyzed, and statistical evaluation of the differential effects of the two experimental phases has not yet been performed, so it will be a few months before confident assertions can be made about the implications of these results. The preliminary outcomes are encouraging, however.

If excessive or worrisome conceptual processing produces restricted autonomic functioning, then it should at the same time yield distinctive electroencephalographic activity. Indeed, engaging in worry has been found to increase frontal cortical activation, and this activation is greater in the left hemisphere for worriers than for nonworriers (Carter, Johnson & Borkovec, 1986). Tucker (1981) has hypothesized on the basis of extant physiological literature that the processing and organization of information in routinized, repeatable, and redundant sequences of operation should be the specialized function of the analytic left hemisphere. Such information processing certainly does characterize chronic worriers, so the finding of left hemisphere predominance makes sense. Preliminary evidence also indicates that the same inflexibility of process characteristic of autonomic activity exists at the cortical level for GAD. Inz (1990) found reduced EEG variability for GAD clients contrasted with matched non-anxious control subjects. Rigidity in peripheral physiological responding appears then to be paralleled by rigidity in higher cortical physiology. Hypothetically, the GAD client is stuck in repetitious and habitual thought patterns as well.

Given the distinctiveness of the physiological activity associated with GAD and/or worry process, one might expect a similarly distinctive phenomenological experience of centrally and autonomically mediated somatic activity, and this has recently been demonstrated to be the case. In two separate investigations, Noyes and colleagues, comparing GAD and panic disorder clients on the Hamilton Anxiety Rating Scale items, found that panic is characterized by autonomic symptoms, whereas GAD shows symptoms predominantly mediated by the central nervous system (Noyes et al., 1987, 1992). More recently, a multi-site investigation involving four separate samples of GAD clients and assessing somatic complaints on the DSM-III-R 18-item GAD checklist found remarkable consistency across sites in the rank-ordered predominance of the symptoms, with central nervous system symptoms (restlessness or feeling keyed up or on edge, being easily fatigued, difficulty concentrating or mind going blank, irritability, muscle tension, and sleep disturbance) clearly occurring with highest frequency and autonomic symptoms being less prevalent (Marten et al., in press). Because of these empirical demonstrations, proposed DSM-IV criteria will eliminate the 18-item checklist and replace it with these six most characteristic somatic symptoms.

THE FUNCTIONS OF WORRY

Cognitive Avoidance of Threat

Evidence has been reviewed supporting the hypothesis that worry is closely related to anxiety, and preliminary experimental evidence using methods from cognitive psychology suggests that it may function as a cognitive avoidance response to threatening information. The present section will elaborate on this theme, showing that there may be a variety of avoidant functions involved and that these functions have significant implications for emotional processing (Rachman, 1980), a construct that may well reside at the very heart of attempts to understand the maintenance and amelioration of anxiety.

Consider the situation of chronic worriers. They are frequently afraid that bad events are going to occur in the future. Their constant worry is being triggered, often outside of awareness, by numerous internal cues and external reminders of an upcoming event. But the actual threat exists only in their minds, i.e. in thoughts and images about what the future might hold. There is no place to run, no place to hide, and nothing to fight. Consequently, conceptual activity is one of the few remaining devices left available for them in their attempts to avoid predicted catastrophe.

It seems likely that, regardless of how effective worry might actually be for avoiding threat, worriers might well believe that it serves this function and would thus be motivated to do it for that reason. There is evidence that GAD subjects do indeed so believe. In the course of therapy at the Penn State program, GAD clients have been asked what benefits they derive from their worrying. Although individual differences exist, the five reasons most commonly offered have at their base a clear reference to the avoidance of threat. By their descriptions, then, sufficient functional conditions exist for the strengthening of worry by the same type of negative reinforcement present in any avoidance paradigm. The first two reasons that the clients have offered focus on attempts to control the external environment and likely involve delayed negative reinforcement of the worrying, whereas the remaining three have to do with attempts to control oneself (emotions and/or behaviors) and likely provide more immediate reinforcement.

1 Superstitious avoidance of catastrophe: "Worrying makes it less likely that the feared event will occur." Although the clients largely recognize that no logical connection exists between worry and the ultimate outcome, it still feels to them as if this were the case. However, the vast majority of negative outcomes that GAD clients fear have a low probability of actual occurrence. Thus, constant worry about anticipated outcomes is most often negatively reinforced by the nonoccurrence of the feared catastrophe.

2 Actual avoidance of catastrophe: "Worrying helps to generate ways of avoiding or preventing catastrophe." Worry is thus viewed as a method of problem solving in order to determine actions that might

prevent the occurrence of the event. Whether or not solutions actually are discovered in the process of worry has not been empirically assessed, but to the degree that a client believes this to be true, a further source of negative reinforcement upon event nonoccurrence is generated.

3   Avoidance of deeper emotional topics: "Worrying about most of the things I worry about is a way to distract myself from worrying about even more emotional things, things that I don't want to think about." This is an intriguing possibility and suggests a dynamical cognitive–affective process that may serve internally to maintain worrisome activity.

4   Coping preparation: "Worrying about a predicted negative event helps me to prepare for its occurrence." The perceived reinforcement from this perspective resides in the expected mitigation of emotional reaction to a catastrophe, should it actually happen. It is an example of attempts at internal control as opposed to attempts to control the external environment exemplified by the first two reasons.

5   Motivating device: "Worry helps to motivate me to accomplish the work that needs to be done." A system of aversive control of adaptive behavior is thereby established, and the occurrence of any actual accomplishment reinforces worry as a motivational strategy.

Rating scales representing each of the above reasons for worrying have been administered to college students who met all, some, or none of the diagnostic criteria for GAD (Roemer et al., 1991). The responses indicated that each of the five is perceived to be a beneficial reason for worrying by different subsets of subjects, but significant differences were found between the groups on three of the scales. More so than the other two groups, GAD subjects believed that their worrying distracts them from more disturbing emotional topics. Research reviewed later on trauma histories and early childhood experiences supports the possibility that this might actually be functionally true. The GAD subjects also think that worry is an effective problem-solving method, to a significantly greater degree than either partial GAD or non-GAD subjects, and superstition plays a graeter role for GAD than non-GAD subjects.

These subjective reports are, of course, not a convincing vehicle for demonstrating veridical relationships. The reasons an individual generates to explain his or her behavior are often *post hoc* and unrelated to true causative relationships. But they do provide a view of how chronic worriers and GAD clients perceive their worrying, and these perceptions clearly relate to threat avoidance with the inherent functional possibility for negative reinforcement of worrisome process. Moreover, empirical evidence does support a foundational function for worry from which these client reports may well emerge. That function has to do the inhibiting effects of worry on emotional processing.

Inhibition of Emotional Processing

Perhaps the most exciting and important discovery about worry is that it is negatively reinforced by its suppressing effects on autonomic activity and by this function results in a prevention of emotional processing. The former provides a basis for understanding what is probably its most crucial, temporally immediate function: worry involves cognitive avoidance of the autonomic features of anxious experience. The latter gives rise to its most critical implication: worry perpetuates threatening meanings and guarantees the maintenance of anxiety.

Relative isolation of the abstract system

The foundation for this reasoning derives from the earlier mentioned demonstration that worry principally involves verbal–linguistic thinking (Borkovec & Inz, 1990). Verbal articulation of emotional material has been found to have very little cardiovascular effect when compared to imagery of the same material (Vrana, Cuthbert & Lang, 1986). Abstract conceptual activity has fewer connections to efferent command into physiological and behavioral channels. Such isolation from efferent command, somatic aspects of affect, and overt behavior is evolutionarily of greater significance to the adaptive value of the conceptual system. Because thought is not immediately expressed in efferent channels, humans are able to delay overt responding, search memory for usable information, manipulate symbols, deploy logical analysis and problem-solving tactics, and freely experiment with possibilities in the absence of any environmental consequences during such processing. The importance of such a capability for survival and adaptive creation and control of the environment hardly needs mention. But this same system also provides opportunities for defensive processes that are similarly distinctively human but contributory to maladaptive conditions.

Worry: Avoidance of imagery to avoid physiologically-based affect

The literature reviewed above demonstrating the suppressing effect of worrisome thinking on physiological activity supports the hypothesis that worry is constantly and immediately reinforced by reductions in certain aspects of autonomically based affective experience: "*Cogito, ergo,* I can suppress affect.*"* More speculatively, worry may do this by functioning as a conceptual avoidance response to aversive imagery related to threatening topics. As one moves sequentially from relaxed nonanxious subjects through relaxed GAD clients, worrying nonanxious subjects, and worrying GAD clients, there are decreasing degrees of reported imagery and increasing amounts of reported thinking (Borkovec & Inz, 1990). Consequently, worry may function to avoid imagery in order to avoid affect. The dilemma for the chronic worrier is that worrying is likely to prime easier retrieval of aversive images that now need to be immediately avoided, and a vicious cycle is created.

The theoretical picture painted above differs little from Mowrer's (1947) two-stage theory of fear maintenance, except that the conditioned stimuli and avoidance response are posited to be taking place primarily within the individual in imaginal and conceptual channels. As long as one rapidly detects and then avoids threatening information, threatening meaning is preserved; no extinction can take place. The modern neo-behavioristic view of Mowrer's theory, built on Lang's (1985) work on the bio-informational view of anxious imagery, suggests that extinction will occur upon repeated exposure to feared stimuli only if the entire fear structure stored in memory is accessed and fully processed (Foa & Kozak, 1986). A critical element of that associative network involves response propositions. For exposure to yield changed meaning, it is important that all aspects of meaning, including the physiological/affective features, be accessed and experienced; only then can emotional processing truly take place. Because worry involves primarily the verbal–linguistic processing of material, the likelihood of accessing all meaning elements in the fear structure during repeated exposures is minimized. If it is essential, or even merely important, for the sake of change that the individual (a) access the aversive images related to the threatening theme fully and for long durations and (b) emotionally process the associated affect, then worry would effectively preclude both processes and thus contribute to the maintenance of anxiety.

Preceding worry: preclusion of extinction

The first demonstration that worry precludes emotional processing came from a study of speech anxious subjects (Borkovec & Hu, 1990). All subjects were given 10 repeated exposures to the same public speaking scene that included both stimulus and response propositions. Three groups differed in what type of thinking they generated just prior to each scene presentation: relaxed thinking, neutral thinking, and worrisome thinking. The former two conditions produced effects analogous to those found previously in phobic imagery research that had used deeply relaxed and neutral states (e.g. Borkovec & Sides, 1979). Greater cardiovascular response occurred to the initial image for the relaxed thinking group with a trend toward habituation upon repeated exposure, whereas the neutral condition showed significantly less reaction to the initial image and no change over repeated exposures. Most importantly, the worry condition showed no cardiovascular response at all to the first and subsequent images, indicating a complete failure to process the emotional material contained in the image. A replication and extension of this study (Borkovec, Lyonfields, Wiser & Diehl, 1993) recently found that it is worrisome thinking and not merely thinking *per se* that is specifically causing this inhibition of processing. Analysis of subject reports of the ratio of amount of thinking to the amount of imagery during the crucial first-image trial indicated a significant positive correlation with cardiovascular response within the relaxed thinking condition and a significant negative correlation within the worry condition. To the extent that one is thinking *relaxed* thoughts, the onset of a threatening image will be more fully processed. To the degree that one is engaging in *worrisome* thinking just before image presentation, emotional processing is prevented. These demonstrations further support the hypothesis that worry functions to avoid autonomically based aspects of affective experience. It also provides a basis for understanding why people in general feel that one of the benefits from worrying is that it prepares them for the worst (Girodo & Stein, 1978; Roemer et al., 1991). Indeed, worrying does dampen some of the somatic reactions to feared events when they do occur. It does so, however, at a significant cost: emotional processing fails to take place, threatening meanings maintain, and consequently the individual remains anxious and worried in response to thematically related stimuli.

A second study involving the effects of preceding worry on a process relevant to emotional processing was conducted in the context of unconditioned stimulus (UCS) evaluation research. Jones & Davey (1990) previously determined that merely imagining the UCS from prior classical conditioning trials leads to a maintenance of fear during subsequent CS-only trials, in contrast to intervening periods of neutral imagery or aversive imagery unrelated to the UCS, both of which were associated with extinction effects. In a replication and extension (Davey & Matchett, 1992), the incubating effect of UCS rehearsal was found to be (a) associated with high levels of trait anxiety, (b) facilitated by the preceding period of induced somatic anxiety, and most importantly (c) eliminated by the preceding period of worry. Subjects in the worry condition did report greater thinking during the induction period, whereas subjects in the somatic anxiety condition reported more imagery. The authors concluded that these outcomes provide further evidence for the mitigation of emotional processing through the process of worrisome thinking.

One of the intriguing possibilities mentioned by Davey and his colleagues in discussion of this line of investigation is that the maintenance of anxiety disorders could be facilitated merely by the periodic imagination of the past traumas underlying the disorder (as in the case of post-traumatic stress disorder) or of future feared catastrophes (as in the case for any anxiety disorder). They have also raised the paradoxical implication that worry might actually facilitate extinction. The present author would have to agree on the basis of their results that whatever catastrophic images do occur during a worrisome episode may not play a role in the further strengthening of anxiety. The several avoidant functions of worry described earlier appear to provide a basis for failure of emotional processing of critical aspects of anxious meaning. So sufficient maintaining processes inherent in worry make up for the possible absence of UCS evaluation contributions to anxiety maintenance.

Subsequent worry: preservation of emotional disturbance

Another investigation relevant to emotional processing has demonstrated the consequences of worrying *after* the occurrence of a stressful event. Butler, Wells & Dewick (1992) showed a highly aversive film to subjects and then asked them to either worry verbally about the film, visualize images from the film, or merely "settle down" during a 4-minute period after the film. Anxiety decreased significantly for the worry and control conditions by the end of the latter manipulation, whereas the imagery group remained anxious, significantly more so than the control condition. These results provide another demonstration that worry partially avoids and therefore mitigates aspects of aversive affect in the present moment and may thus be immediately negatively reinforced. More importantly, intrusive thoughts about the film during the subsequent 3 days were significantly more frequent for the worry group than either of the other two groups on a daily diary measure. Thus, hypothetically, worry prevented subsequent emotional processing of the film content, unlike the imagery, and produced a maintenance of its disturbing meaning. Manipulation checks also revealed that the worry and imagery groups reported equivalent amounts of thoughts and images during post-film manipulation, leading the authors to argue that the differential immediate and long-term impacts of the two conditions may have more to do with attentional deployments to ongoing thinking and imagery rather than actual predominance of one type of mentation over another. Thus, differential focus of attention to the verbal channel among the worry group, rather than suppression of imagery, may underlie the prevention of emotional processing revealed by the increased negative thought intrusions during the days after the film.

Mechanisms for inhibition of emotional processing

The mechanisms by which worry prevents emotional processing remain unverified. Several candidates present themselves, however. First, if one is excessively focused on conceptual activity of any type, fewer attentional resources are available for processing other external or internal information.

Second, but in a related vein, it may be difficult deliberately to shift attention from excessive and habitual thought activity to some other stimulus, and this may be particularly true if it is negatively valanced (worrisome) thinking. Negative, intrusive thoughts are known to be more difficult to dismiss than aversive images, even when the latter are more disturbing than the former (Parkinson & Rachman, 1981), and the uncontrollability of worry is such a hallmark of the phenomenon in GAD that DSM-IV will add this feature to its diagnostic criteria.

Third, conceptual worry may eliminate one of the conditions that create anxiety in Gray's (1982) neuropsychological theory. By his perspective, anxiety will occur when information received is aversive and/or when a mismatch occurs between information expected and information received. Worry at the conceptual level reduces the likelihood that newly presented information regarding the threat is unexpected; there is a lessened mismatch between external and internal information. Indeed, there may be two dimensions of possible match or mismatch, as exemplified by the phobic imagery studies reported earlier. One has to do with the channel of information processing (conceptual vs. imaginal), and the other involves emotional valence (pleasant, neutral, and negative). The greatest anxiety is likely to be experienced (and therefore more fully processed) if one experiences the greatest mismatch between internal and external information. In this instance, an internal state involving thought and positive affect (e.g. relaxed thinking) is most mismatched with an aversive image. In worrisome thinking, on the other hand, only the channel of processing is mismatched (thought vs. image), even then the content is thematically matched (both have to do with the threat), and no mismatch exists in the affective valence. It is as if the individual is operating on the basis that the environmental information (in this case, the phobic image) contains no new information and thus does not need to be processed.

Fourth, one of the interesting properties of the semantic system is that repetition of a word results in its isolation from the rest of its associative network (Smith, 1984). If this is the case for its associations within the semantic domain, it is all the more likely that its connections with associative meaning in different domains (most importantly, the affective domain, efferent command, or response propositions) are even more thoroughly weakened. The implication for conceptual worry is that the inherent, constant repetition of verbal linguistic meaning of the threat contains within its process the very mechanism by which access to other levels of meaning is inhibited.

Although these possible mechanisms have obvious relevance to understanding the effects of worry that just precedes or occurs contemporaneously with the presentation of threatening information, as in the phobic imagery and UCS evaluation studies, they may also apply to the effects of worry on emotional processing of material after the stressful event has occurred, as in the Butler et al. (1992) investigation. This would require the assumption that after an emotional event, some degree of adaptive processing of its content continues and thereby ultimately allows for a resolution of its disturbing effects, unless worrisome thinking intervenes and inhibits such processing.

Implications of inhibited emotional processing for exposure therapy

If worry does have an inhibiting effect on emotional processing, then significant applied implications exist for its potentially damaging influence on change process in exposure therapies. To the extent that a client engages in worry before, during, or after therapeutic exposures, extinction process will be mitigated. It is reasonable to speculate that slow progress in, or complete failure of, exposure treatment with particular clients may be indicative of ongoing, excessive worry. This is potentially true for any anxiety disorder and not just GAD. Indeed, there is good reason to suspect the possible presence of significant worry in the other disorders, wherein 40% to 60% report worrying just about minor things (Barlow, 1988). As yet, no one has assessed the extent to which such clients also worry about topics specifically related to their particular disorder (but it is likely to be quite high), nor have assessments of the occurrence of worry in the context of exposure therapy been obtained from them to evaluate the extent to which extant worrisome process may interfere with therapeutic effects. Hypothetically, to the degree that such worrying does occur, reduced emotional processing and therefore retardation of extinction are likely to be the consequences.

THE ORIGINS OF CHRONIC WORRY AND GAD

That human beings would use the abstract verbal–linguistic system for anticipating the future and for planning coping responses to maximize good events and minimize bad events is not surprising. Indeed, a recent cognitive theory proposed by McGuire & McGuire (1991) suggests that this is precisely the purpose of thinking: "Our basic assumption is that thought systems develop around the person's anticipation of significant core events that might befall him or her and that these systems help the person cope realistically or autistically with these possible events" (p. 1). Furthermore, these authors suggest that such coping methods are based on thoughts about the likelihood of an event and/or the event's perceived desirability (i.e. its pleasantness or unpleasantness). Most human beings experience fear and anxiety under some circumstances, most engage in worry periodically, and the use of thought in attempts to resolve these difficulties would be a natural recourse, given that thought is hypothetically designed to function for just such purposes. It is of interest in this regard that available evidence indicates that virtually all of the effects of worry found in research with chronic worriers and GAD clients can be observed in nonworriers when they are asked to worry about their most pressing concerns (Borkovec et al., 1991). The earlier analysis of the functions of worry provides a basis for understanding why worrisome thinking specifically might develop as a coping response to perceived threat in humans in general.

The empirical literature indicates that the main differences between pathological and nonpathological groups reside in the frequency, intensity, and uncontrollability of the phenomenon. A remaining question then is why certain people develop pathological levels of worry. This question can be broken into two such sub-questions, one having to do with individual differences in how dangerous the world is perceived to be and how incapable the person feels he or she is in coping with it and the other surrounding the issue of why the thought system becomes the principal but maladaptive and excessive method of coping with such a generalized perception.

The latter question finds a possible, though speculative, answer in a description of the conditions the chronic worrier faces. As mentioned earlier, because worries commonly refer to the future, a proximal threat does not exist in the present. Moreover, even those things feared in the future commonly have a low probability of occurring. For both reasons, the threat does not exist in reality. How to avoid what does not exist certainly presents the individual with an insolvable problem. Given that he or she perceives a problem for which action cannot be the solution, few resources other than constant mental attempts to remove the perceived threat are available; excessive thinking wins by default. This result is not unique to worrisome thinking. In the classic Zeigarnik (1927) effect, people mentally ruminate about problems that have not been solved rather than about those successfully solved. Given the engagement of the abstract system under these default circumstances, the functional effects of worry in suppressing somatic aspects of anxious experience, as described earlier, provide a maintaining device through negative reinforcement and without solving the insolvable problem. One could readily speculate that the same process would be elicited even among anxious but non-GAD clients under analogous conditions wherein their ordinarily effective motor avoidance is blocked. Worry would be predicted to increase significantly during such moments in an attempt to determine how to remove the threat (and incidentally would contribute to the maintenance of fear by preventing the emotional processing that would otherwise occur during the ongoing exposure to the environmental threat cues). By this analysis, no special principles need to be invoked to explain the development of worry. Whether individual differences in developmental history may contribute to excessive use of the thought system in general or worrisome thinking in particular remains an intriguing question.

If the above reasoning is correct, then it is the first question about individual differences in threat perception that holds the key to the emergence of chronic worry. The Penn State program has concentrated on two possible developmental pathways to GAD in an effort to understand why so much generalized threat is perceived and/or why the person feels that he or she is not prepared to cope with whatever comes down the road of life. One route may reside in a history of past traumatic events. If one has valid evidence that the world is indeed a dangerous place because of actual experience, there is good reason to be fearful about the future. The other route may find its origin in early childhood attachment (Bowlby, 1973). If one has not had a secure base in a loving care-giver, moving out into the world is a constantly threatening prospect because of the absence of a safe place to which to return.

History of Trauma

Preliminary information on trauma history has so far come only from analog GAD subjects and awaits replication with clients. Overall in three separate questionnaire studies involving over 1000 participants, subjects meeting GAD criteria have reported a significantly greater frequency of past traumatic events as defined by the post-traumatic stress disorder section of DSM-III-R than have non-GAD subjects. The former group has also indicated more frequent trauma (significantly so in one study) than a control group composed of subjects meeting only some of the GAD criteria. Similar results emerged on a measure of the frequency of intrusive thoughts about such events during the preceding week.

Content analysis of the types of past trauma experienced by subsets of GAD and non-GAD subjects (Molina, Roemer, M. Borkovec & Posa, 1992) has also revealed a very interesting picture, especially in conjunction with content analysis of the types of topics about which GAD subjects currently worry. Four categories of trauma were used: (a) death of significant other and/or illness/injury events involving self or other, (b) physical or sexual assault, (c) emotional events involving family or friends, and (d) miscellaneous. The vast majority of traumas among nonanxious subjects fell into the first category (80%) with the remainder distributed evenly (6–8%) over the other three categories. The pattern was significantly different for the GAD subjects by χ-square analysis. Although the illness/injury/death category was also their most dominant, only 50% of their traumas were so categorized. Assault was the second highest (21%), with the remainder involving emotional events (17%) and miscellaneous (11%). Although trauma involving illness/injury/death had occurred one-and-a-half times more often for GAD than nonanxious subjects, the former group also had experienced traumas related to miscellaneous events, assault, and emotional events at a rate four to six times greater.

Combining assault with illness/injury/death into a single category related to physical threat accounted for 71% of GAD traumas. This is in striking contrast to other research that has categorized the topics of current worry content obtained from diagnostic interview (Borkovec et al., 1991; Craske et al., 1989; Sanderson & Barlow, 1990; Shadick, Roemer, Hopkins & Borkovec, 1991). Categories of worries typically included in these studies have related to interpersonal/family, occupational, financial, illness/injury, health, and miscellaneous issues. For nonanxious controls as well as GAD clients and analog GAD subjects, interpersonal/family issues have been found to be the area of most frequent concern. The remarkable difference among groups occurs on the illness/injury/health category. For GAD clients and analog subjects, it is typically the most infrequent area of current worry (3% and 0%, respectively); for nonanxious subjects, it is the second most frequent (25%). These interview-based outcomes lead to the hypothesis that GAD subjects under some circumstances avoid thinking about those past events that they consider to be traumatic. Such a notion fits well with the most significant difference previously found between GAD and non-GAD analog subjects on their ratings of reasons for worrying (i.e. "Worrying about most of the things I worry about is a way to distract myself from worrying about even more emotional things, things that I don't want to think about."). Hypothetically, it appears the GAD may be more closely related to post-traumatic stress disorder than was previously thought. Trauma may provide a basis for continuing feelings that the world is in fact dangerous, leading to generalized worrying about the future, but to think about those particular memories is too anxiety-provoking. Once again, the cognitive avoidance function of worry is implicated. In this instance, however, it may not be completely effective. In one study (Craske et al., 1989) using self-monitoring of daily worry episodes, a complete reversal occurred: nonanxious subjects reported the fewest worries about illness/injury/ health relative to their other topics, whereas GAD clients reported them to be the most frequent.

Although the trauma data support the possibility that chronic worry can develop from actual experiences with a dangerous world, rival interpretations exist. It may be that GAD was present prior to the occurrence of the reported traumatic events, that chronic anxiety influenced the GAD subject's perception of, reaction to, or later reports of the events, and that no actual difference in frequency of objectively defined trauma exists. If so, then the etiology of GAD would reside even earlier in the developmental history of the individual.

Insecure Attachment in Childhood

Bowlby's (1973) description of insecure attachment in childhood appears to be a virtual prototype for the development of adult GAD. Recent data support this hypothesis. In one of the GAD analog studies mentioned earlier (Roemer et al., 1991), 65 GAD, 65 non-GAD, and 53 somatically anxious but non-GAD subjects completed a questionnaire designed to assess recollections of attachment related memories about the primary care-giver (Lichtenstein & Cassidy, 1991). Among the six factors of the measure, the GAD group was found to be significantly more insecurely attached than both other groups on two scales: (a) enmeshment/role-reversal, i.e. the need to protect, and fear of losing, the primary care-giver, and (b) preoccupying anger and oscillating feelings toward care-giver. They also felt significantly more rejected as children by the primary care-giver than did the non-GAD group on a third scale.

The Penn State program has so far collected data on the same questionnaire from 25 GAD clients and their matched controls under the direction of Dr Jude Cassidy. Although the full sample has not yet been obtained

and the data are not fully analyzed, preliminary results provide an interesting view of the childhood recollections and current state of mind of
this more clinically severe group. The clients reported more en-
meshment/role-reversal and rejection than the control subjects, but the
differences between the groups were only marginally significant. The
GAD clients were, however, experiencing significantly greater anger/
oscillation (e.g. "My mother can make me feel really good, but when she
is not nice to me, she can really tear me apart"), balance/forgiveness (e.g.
"For all our past problems, my mother and I can still enjoy a good laugh
together"), and lack of childhood memory (e.g. "It's hard to remember
my early relationship with my mother"). Discriminant function analysis
indicated that the lack of memory scale had the highest loading in distinguishing the two groups. Inner conflict is well depicted by the
simultaneous relevance of both anger and forgiveness in their current
feelings toward mother, hinting at a distressed and insecure childhood
history. But direct evidence of such a history is less clear because memories of that childhood in general are absent. Once again, cognitive avoidance appears to be operating. Just as the current worries of GAD subjects
do not include topics related to their previous traumas, so they seem to
have suppressed memories of their insecure childhoods. Moreover, the
fact that such insecurity existed in the context of the earliest and most
significant interpersonal relationship may provide the basis for the cen-
trality of social evaluative fears so characteristic of chronic worry in
adulthood.

It is essential in future research that trauma and attachment histories be
obtained from other anxiety disorder groups in addition to GAD and
nonanxious control groups. Although good theoretical reasons exist for
the likely role of such histories in the development of a generalized,
anxiety-provoking view of self and the world, as yet no evidence directly
supports the notion that either of these histories specifically leads to this
particular disorder.

SUMMARY AND CONCLUSIONS

Worry is a predominantly verbal–linguistic attempt to avoid future aversive events. Its chronic and severe forms emerge in individuals who
diffusely perceive the world to be a dangerous place and who are afraid
that they will not be able to cope with the events that their future holds
for them. These perceptions may find their origin in frequent traumas that
have actually provided evidence in support of their validity and/or in a
childhood that was characterized by insecure attachment to the primary

care-giver. The occurrence of worry is negatively reinforced in a variety of ways, the most immediate of which involves its suppressing effects on some aspects of somatic anxious experience. Although the avoidant functions provide the short-term gain of reducing anxiety, similar to all types of avoidance, the long-term consequences of this process include the inhibition of emotional processing and the maintenance of anxious meanings.

Despite the considerable progress made in the past 10 years of experimental research on worry, much remains to be discovered. The implications of its association with depression need to be elaborated. Given its connections to attentional, conceptual, and memory representational processes, additional, creative applications of cognitive psychology methods and theory are required to elucidate more precisely the functional interconnectedness of these systems in worrisome thinking. Expansion of assessments of possible historical or developmental antecedents and comparisons to other psychological disorders must be implemented.

Perhaps most importantly, therapy methods need to be developed that are rigorously based on what is known about chronic worry. The outcome literature is relatively sparse for GAD. What has so far been determined is that cognitive behavioral strategies that include applied relaxation combined with cognitive therapy and/or imaginal rehearsal techniques such as self-control desensitization yield significant and long-lasting change (cf. Borkovec & Whisman, in press; Chambless & Gillis, 1993). However, the degree of clinically significant change for chronic and severe GAD has been relatively moderate, perhaps because none of the therapy applications to date has incorporated methods specifically grounded in extant basic knowledge of worry process. Attempts toward such applications at the Penn State therapy program include: (a) emphasis on the development of multiple, flexibly deployed relaxation and cognitive strategies to combat the characteristically rigidity psychophysiological and conceptual patterns of GAD clients (cf. Borkovec & Costello, 1993) and more recently (b) use of childhood and past trauma experiences, in addition to current life circumstances, as targets for imaginal exposure and cognitive therapy.

If the striking increase in research on worry over the last decade and the creation of this volume are accurate indications of the importance of this phenomenon and its susceptibility to experimental scrutiny, then we can expect many more fascinating results concerning the nature and functions of worry in the future and an increased likelihood that more systematic applications of such results to the development of more efficacious treatments will occur.

ACKNOWLEDGEMENT

Preparation of this chapter was supported in part by Grant MH-39172 from the National Institute of Mental Health.

REFERENCES

American Psychiatric Association. (1987). *Diagnostic and Statistical Manual of Mental Disorders*, 3rd edn–Rev. Washington, DC: American Psychiatric Association.

American Psychiatric Association. (1993). *DSM-IV Draft Criteria*. Washington, DC: American Psychiatric Association.

Andrews, V.H. & Borkovec, T.D. (1988). The differential effects of inductions of worry, somatic anxiety, and depression on emotional experience. *Journal of Behavior Therapy and Experimental Psychiatry*, **19**, 21–26.

Barlow, D.H. (1988). *Anxiety and its Disorders*. New York: Guilford.

Borkovec, T.D. & Costello, E. (1993). Efficacy of applied relaxation and cognitive behavioral therapy in the treatment of generalized anxiety disorder. *Journal of Consulting and Clinical Psychology*, **61**, 611–619.

Borkovec, T.D. & Hu, S. (1990). The effect of worry on cardiovascular response to phobic imagery. *Behaviour Research and Therapy*, **28**, 69–73.

Borkovec, T.D. & Inz, J. (1990). The nature of worry in generalized anxiety disorder: A predominance of thought activity. *Behaviour Research and Therapy*, **28**, 153–158.

Borkovec, T.D. & Lyonfields, J.D. (1993). Worry: Thought suppression of emotional processing. In H. Krohne (Ed.), *Vigilance and Avoidance*, pp. 101–118, Toronto: Hogrefe and Huber Publishers.

Borkovec, T.D., Lyonfields, J.D., Wiser, S.L. & Diehl, L. (1993). The role of worrisome thinking in the suppression of cardiovascular response to phobic imagery. *Behaviour Research and Therapy*, **31**, 321–324.

Borkovec, T.D., Robinson, E., Pruzinsky, T. & DePree, J.A. (1983). Preliminary exploration of worry: Some characteristics and processes. *Behaviour Research and Therapy*, **21**, 9–16.

Borkovec, T.D., Shadick, R. & Hopkins, M. (1991). The nature of normal versus pathological worry. In R. Rapee & D.H. Barlow (Eds.), *Chronic Anxiety and Generalized Anxiety Disorder*. New York: Guilford Press.

Borkovec, T.D. & Sides, J.K. (1979). The contribution of relaxation and expectancy to fear reduction via graded, imaginal exposure to feared stimuli. *Behaviour Research and Therapy*, **17**, 529–540.

Borkovec, T.D. & Whisman, M.A. (in press). Psychosocial treatment for generalized anxiety disorder. In M. Mavissakalian & R. Prien (Eds.), *Anxiety Disorders: Psychological and Pharmacological Treatments*. Washington, DC: American Psychiatric Association.

Bowlby, J. (1973). *Attachment and Loss: Vol. 2. Separation*. New York: Basic Books.

Brown, T.A. & Barlow, D.H. (1992). Comorbidity among anxiety disorders: Implications for treatment and DSM-IV. *Journal of Consulting and Clinical Psychology*, **60**, 835–844.

Butler, B., Cullington, A., Hibbert, G., Klimes, I. & Gelder, M. (1988). Anxiety management for persistent generalized anxiety. *British Journal of Psychology*, **151**, 535–542.

Butler, B. & Mathews, A. (1983). Cognitive processes in anxiety. *Advances in Behaviour Research and Therapy*, **5**, 51–62.

Butler, G., Wells, A. & Dewick, H. (1992, June). Differential effects of worry and imagery after exposure to a stressful stimulus. Paper presented at the World Congress of Cognitive Therapy, Toronto.

Carter, W.R., Johnson, M.C. & Borkovec, T.D. (1986). Worry: An electrocortical analysis. *Advances in Behaviour Research and Therapy*, **8**, 193–204.

Clark, D.M., Salkovskis, P.M., Gelder, M., Koehler, C., Martin, M., Anastasiades, P., Hackmann, A., Middleton, H. & Jeavons, A. (1988). Tests of a cognitive theory of panic. In I. Hand & H.U. Wittchen (Eds.), *Panic and Phobias*, Vol. 2, pp. 149–158. Berlin: Springer.

Chambless, D.L. & Gillis, M.M. (1993). Cognitive therapy of anxiety disorders. *Journal of Consulting and Clinical Psychology*, **61**, 248–260.

Craske, M.G., Rapee, R.M., Jackel, L. & Barlow, D.H. (1989). Qualitative dimensions of worry in DSM-III-R generalized anxiety disorder subjects and nonanxious controls. *Behaviour Research and Therapy*, **27**, 397–402.

Davey, G.C.L. & Matchett, G. (1992). UCS rehearsal and the incubation and retention of differential "fear" conditioning: Effects of worrying and trait anxiety. Unpublished manuscript.

Davidson, R.J. & Schwartz, G.E. (1976). The psychobiology of relaxation and related states: A multi-process theory. In D.I. Mostofsky (Ed.), *Behavior Control and Modification*. Englewood Cliffs, NJ: Prentice-Hall.

Deffenbacher, J.L. (1980). Worry and emotionality in test anxiety. In I.G. Sarason (Ed.), *Test Anxiety: Theory, Research and Application*. Hillside, NJ: Erlbaum.

Elliott, T.K. (1990). The role of autonomic arousal in generalized anxiety disorder. Unpublished doctoral dissertation, Pennsylvania State University, University Park, PA.

Eysenck, M.W., MacLeod, C. & Mathews, A. (1987). Cognitive functioning in anxiety. *Psychological Research*, **49**, 189–195.

Eysenck, M.W., Mogg, K., May, J., Richards, A. & Mathews, A. (1990). Bias in interpretation of ambiguous sentences related to threat in anxiety. *Journal of Abnormal Psychology*, **100**, 144–151.

Foa, E.B. & Kozak, M.J. (1986). Emotional processing of fear: Exposure to corrective information, *Psychological Bulletin*, **99**, 20–35.

Friedman, B.H., Thayer, J.F., Borkovec, T.D. & Lyonfields, J. (1993, May). Psychophysiological assessment of generalized anxiety disorder. Paper presented at the Midwestern Psychological Association, Chicago.

Girodo, M. & Stein, S.J. (1978). Self-talk and the work of worrying in confronting a stressor. *Cognitive Therapy and Research*, **2**, 305–307.

Gotlib, I.H., McLachlan, A.L. & Katz, A.N. (1988). Biases in visual attention in depressed and nondepressed individuals. *Cognition and Emotion*, **2**, 185–200.

Gray, J.A. (1982). Precis of "The neurophysiology of anxiety: An enquiry into the functions of the septo-hippocampal system." *Behavioral and Brain Sciences*, **5**, 469–534.

Grossman, P., Stemmler, G. & Meinhardt, E. (1990). Paced respiratory sinus arrhythmia as an index of cardiac parasympathetic tone during varying behavioral tasks. *Psychophysiology*, **27**, 404–416.

Grossman, P. & Svebak, S. (1987). Respiratory sinus arrhythmia as an index of parasympathetic cardiac control during active coping. *Psychophysiology*, **24**, 228–235.

Hoehn-Saric, R. & McLeod, D.R. (1988). The peripheral sympathetic nervous system: Its role in normal and pathologic anxiety. *Psychiatric Clinics of North America*, **11**, 375–386.

Inz, J. (1990). EEG activity in generalized anxiety disorder. Unpublished doctoral dissertation, Pennsylvania State University, University Park, PA.

Jones, T. & Davey, G.C.L. (1990). The effects of cued UCS rehearsal on the retention of differential "fear" conditioning: An experimental analogue of the "worry" process. *Behaviour Research and Therapy*, **28**, 159–164.

Lang, P.J. (1985). The cognitive psychophysiology of emotion: Fear and anxiety. In A.H. Tuma & J.D. Maser (Eds.), *Anxiety and the Anxiety Disorders*, pp. 131–170. Hillsdale, NJ: Erlbaum.

Lichtenstein, J. & Cassidy, J. (1991, April). The inventory of adult attachment (INVAA): Validation of a new measure. Paper presented at the Society for Research in Child Development, Seattle.

Lyonfields, J.D. (1991, November). *An examination of image and thought processes in generalized anxiety*. Paper presented at the Association for the Advancement of Behavior Therapy, New York.

MacLeod, C., Mathews, A. & Tata, P. (1986). Attentional bias in emotional disorders. *Journal of Abnormal Psychology*, **95**, 15–20.

Marten, P.A., Brown, T.A., Barlow, D.H., Borkovec, T.D., Shear, K.M. & Lydiard, R.B. (in press). Evaluation of the ratings comprising the associated symptom criterion of DSM-III-R generalized anxiety disorder. *Journal of Nervous and Mental Disease*.

Mathews, A. (1990). Why worry? The cognitive function of anxiety. *Behaviour Research and Therapy*, **28**, 455–468.

Mathews, A. & Klug, F. (1993). Emotionality and interference with color-naming in anxiety. *Behaviour Research and Therapy*, **31**, 57–62.

Mathews, A.M. & MacLeod, C. (1986). Discrimination of threat cues without awareness in anxiety states. *Journal of Abnormal Psychology*, **95**, 131–138.

Mathews, A., Mogg, K., May, J. & Eysenck, M. (1989). Implicit and explicit memory bias in anxiety. *Journal of Abnormal Psychology*, **98**, 236–240.

McGuire, W.J. & McGuire, C.V. (1991). The content, structure, and operation of thought systems. In R.S. Wyer, Jr & T.K. Srull (Eds.), *Advances in Social Cognition*, Vol. IV, pp. 1–78. Hillsdale, NJ: Erlbaum.

Metzger, R.L., Miller, M.L., Cohen, M., Sofka, M. & Borkovec, T.D. (1990). Worry changes decision making: The effect of negative thoughts on cognitive processing. *Journal of Clinical Psychology*, **46**, 78–88.

Mogg, K., Mathews, A. & Weinman, J. (1987). Memory bias in clinical anxiety. *Journal of Abnormal Psychology*, **96**, 94–98.

Mogg, K., Mathews, A. & Weinman, J. (1989). Selective processing of threat cues in anxiety states: A replication. *Behaviour Research and Therapy*, **27**, 317–323.

Molina, S., Roemer, L., Borkovec, M. & Posa, S. (1992, November). Generalized anxiety disorder in an analogue population: Types of past trauma. Paper presented at the Association for the Advancement of Behavior Therapy, Boston.

Mowrer, O.H. (1947). On the dual nature of learning – a re-interpretation of "conditioning" and "problem-solving." *Harvard Educational Review*, **17**, 102–148.

Noyes, R., Clarkson, C., Crowe, R.R., Yates, W.R. & McChesney, C.M. (1987). A family study of generalized anxiety disorder. *American Journal of Psychiatry*, **144**, 1019–1024.

Noyes, R., Woodman, C., Garvey, M.J., Cook, B.L., Suelzer, M., Chancy, J. & Anderson, D.J. (1992). Generalized anxiety disorder vs. panic disorder: Distinguishing characteristics and patterns of comorbidity. *Journal of Nervous and Mental Disease*, **180**, 369–379.

Parkinson, L. & Rachman, S. (1981). The nature of intrusive thoughts. *Advances in Behaviour Research and Therapy*, **3**, 101–110.

Pruzinsky, T. & Borkovec, T.D. (1990). Cognitive and personality characteristics of worriers. *Behaviour Research and Therapy*, **28**, 507–512.

Rachman, S. (1980). Emotional processing. *Behaviour Research and Therapy*, **18**(1), 51–60.

Roemer, L., Borkovec, M., Posa, S. & Lyonfields, J. (1991, November). Generalized anxiety disorder in an analogue population: The role of past trauma. Paper presented at the Association for the Advancement of Behavior Therapy, New York.

Sanderson, W.C. & Barlow, D.H. (1990). A description of patients diagnosed with DSM-III revised generalized anxiety disorder. *Journal of Nervous and Mental Disease*, **178**, 588–591.

Shadick, R.N., Roemer, L., Hopkins, M.B. & Borkovec, T.D. (1991, November). *The nature of worrisome thoughts*. Paper presented at the Association for the Advancement of Behavior Therapy, New York.

Smith, L.C. (1984). Semantic satiation affects category membership decision time but not lexical priming. *Memory and Cognition*, **12**, 483–488.

Tallis, F., Eysenck, M. & Mathews, A. (1991). Elevated evidence requirements and worry. *Personality and Individual Differences*, **12**, 21–27.

Tucker, D.M. (1981). Lateral brain function, emotion, and conceptualization. *Psychological Bulletin*, **87**, 380–383.

Veroff, J., Douvan, E. & Kulka, R.A. (1981). *The inner American: A self-portrait from 1957 to 1976*. New York: Basic Books.

Vrana, S.R., Cuthbert, B.N. & Lang, P.J. (1986). Fear imagery and text processing. *Psychophysiology*, **23**, 247–253.

York, D., Borkovec, T.D., Vasey, M. & Stern, R. (1987). Effects of worry and somatic anxiety induction on thoughts, emotion, and physiological activity. *Behaviour Research and Therapy*, **25**, 523–526.

Zeigarnik, B. (1927). On finished and unfinished tasks. *Psychologische Forschung*, **9**, 1–85.

Zuckerman, M., Lubin, B. & Rinck, C.M. (1983). Construction of new scales for the Multiple Affect Adjective Checklist. *Journal of Behavioral Assessment*, **5**, 119–129.

CHAPTER 2   Pathological worrying as exacerbated problem-solving

*Graham C.L. Davey**

INTRODUCTION: THE RAMIFICATIONS OF DEFINING WORRY

In a book of this kind there will almost certainly be some considerable debate even over a definition of worrying, let alone over the processes that contribute to and characterise worrying. Nevertheless, how one defines worrying is of critical importance to our understanding of the process, especially since we are still at a relatively young age in the scientific study of worry. The definition that one adopts is important because it delineates the bounds of the phenomenon, and this will (either rightly or wrongly) tend to focus the search for the causes of the phenomenon.

It is instructive to look at some definitions of worrying that have appeared in the literature in the recent past, and to consider how these definitions may have guided research on this topic.

MacLeod, Williams & Bekerian (1991) summarise a number of definitions of worry, and conclude that common to all of the definitions are several characteristics: "Worry is a cognitive phenomenon, it is concerned with future events where there is uncertainty about the outcome, the future being thought about is a negative one, and this is accompanied by feelings of anxiety" (1991, p. 478). Much the same contemporary definition is outlined by Borkovec & Lyonfields (1992) who describe worrying as an unwanted, uncontrollable, aversive cognitive activity associated with negative thoughts and some sense of emotional discomfort. It is perhaps not so surprising that this is the kind of definition that is now common in the clinical literature, since much of the current research on worrying has been driven by clinical research which has highlighted pathological

*The City University, London, UK

Worrying: Perspectives on Theory, Assessment and Treatment. Edited by G.C.L. Davey and F. Tallis.
© 1994 John Wiley & Sons Ltd.

worrying as a central feature of a number of anxiety-based disorders (e.g. Barlow et al., 1986; Brown, Antony & Barlow, 1992). Hence, within this rather specific clinical domain, worrying is clearly dysfunctional and clearly associated with anxiety—yet it is a definition that marginalises non-clinical worry, and begs the question of whether pathological worrying is the same theoretical beast as the worrying that occurs in the absence of major affective dysfunction.

The clinically-oriented definition of worrying outlined above has important ramifications for two reasons. First, it assumes that all worrying is anxiety-related. In the extreme, it has been argued that worry and anxiety are simply different manifestations of the same underlying process (e.g. O'Neill, 1985; Mathews, 1990). Later in this chapter, however, I will attempt to argue that they can be considered as quite different constructs, each possessing their own unique sources of variance, and possibly representing orthogonal psychological processes.

Second, early definitions of worrying often alluded to a putative problem-solving function of worrying. For example, in 1983 Borkovec and colleagues wrote "the worry sequence seems to be initiated by a fear stimulus (environmental and/or imaginal) which elicits mental problem-solving activity designed to prevent the occurrence of traumatic future events and/or devise coping strategies for such events" (1983, p. 10). Over the years, however, the idea that one of the functions of worrying may be to help solve potential problems has tended to be omitted from contemporary definitions. The reasons for this are not too difficult to discern. As the focus of worry research shifted increasingly towards the clinical end of the continuum, it became clear that pathological worrying seemed to have quite the opposite effect to solving problems—it actually appeared to exacerbate them. Pathological worrying appeared to define more problems than it solved (Borkovec, 1985), to lead to a "danger being constantly rehearsed without a solution ever being found" (Mathews, 1990, p. 457), to lead to "catastrophising" a problem into being worse than it was first perceived (Vasey & Borkovec, 1993), or to vacillation over the solution to a problem (Tallis, 1990; Tallis, Eysenck & Mathews, 1991a).

However, simply because pathological worrying does not contribute to effective problem-solving does not logically imply that it is therefore not a part of a problem-solving process—only that, if it is to do with problem-solving, it is extremely inefficient and ineffective. The concentration on clinically pathological worrying and its exacerbation rather than amelioration of problems has tended to distract attention from the possible problem-solving origins of the worrying process. I will attempt to argue in this chapter that pathological worrying can be conceived of as a problem-solving activity that may be thwarted by a variety of factors. This approach is theoretically different from other purely "pathological" approaches because it implies that pathological worrying has a number of underlying features that it shares in common with effective problem-solving; it also provides some insight into how those features of pathological worrying that are considered dysfunctional (e.g. negative cognitions, catastrophising, high levels of anxiety, etc.) exacerbate worrying through disruption of effective problem-solving.

THE TWO EXTREMES OF THE WORRYING CONTINUUM

Worrying means different things to different people, and in its common usage the word can have a range of connotations.

At the pathological end of the continuum it is clear that worrying refers to unwanted, intrusive cognitions that are associated with potentially stressful events and accompanied by distressing mood states such as anxiety. At this end of the continuum worrying has been identified as an important characteristic of psychological dysfunction. It is currently a cardinal diagnostic feature of generalised anxiety disorder (GAD) (Barlow et al., 1986), and has been hypothesised to be present to some extent in all of the DSM-III-R anxiety disorders (Barlow, 1988). Using the Penn State Worry Questionnaire (PSWQ) as a measure of the frequency and intensity of worry, Meyer, Miller, Metzger & Borkovec (1990) found that GAD subjects scored significantly higher on the PSWQ than subjects who met only some of the criteria for GAD diagnosis, and GAD subjects scored significantly higher than those subjects who met the criteria for post-traumatic stress disorder (PTSD). In a more detailed analysis, Brown, Antony & Barlow (1992) found that scores on the PSWQ distinguished GAD subjects from all other anxiety disorder patients, and also that subjects diagnosed as suffering from a variety of other anxiety disorders (panic disorder, panic disorder with agoraphobia, social phobia, simple phobia, obsessive–compulsive disorder) also scored higher on worry than normal control subjects. In addition, we have also found that worrying is a significantly better predictor of scores on the Fear Survey Schedule (FSS) (a measure of simple phobias) than measures of trait anxiety (Davey, 1992).

All of this evidence clearly indicates that pathological worrying does appear to be a central feature of anxiety-based psychological disorders. This is supported by the fact that measures of worrying are also highly correlated with measures of anxiety (Davey, Hampton, Farrell & David-son, 1992; Meyer et al., 1990; Tallis, Eysenck & Mathews, 1991a; Metzger et al., 1990; Wisocki, Handen & Morse, 1986) and depression (Meyer et al., 1990; Metzger et al., 1990).

However, apart from its pathological associations, worrying is often seen as a constructive occupation that helps to solve potential problems in living. It may even be viewed as a necessary activity in these circum-stances. For example, the student who is approaching final examinations may consider it appropriate and necessary to worry about them. This may have the dual benefit of motivating the individual and helping him or her to define and think through any potential problems in good time (see Chapter 3, this volume). For these individuals worrying has an event-ual anxiety-reducing consequence rather than an anxiety-enhancing effect, and anxiety reduction appears to be dependent on the success with which worrying enables the individual to cope with the specific life prob-lem. In this context, worrying can be regarded as a part of a problem-focused approach to life problems, in which task-oriented activities such as logical analysis, problem-solving, information-seeking, and active be-havioural coping play a central part (cf. Lazarus & Folkman, 1984; Endler & Parker, 1990; Billings & Moos, 1981, 1984; Pearlin & Schooler, 1978).

The critical differences between these two extremes of the worry con-tinuum seem to be that (i) the pathological end appears to be associated with anxiety enhancement and the constructive end with anxiety reduc-tion, and (ii) the pathological end tends to be associated with the exacer-bation of problems (and hence perpetuates worrying) and the constructive end with the amelioration of problems.

WORRYING AS A CONSTRUCTIVE PROBLEM-SOLVING ACTIVITY

If at least some worrying is constructive and task-oriented, then we ought to be able to identify this in a variety of ways. The first approach would be to investigate whether measures of worrying are in some way associ-ated with measures of problem-focused coping. Davey et al. (1992) and Davey (1993a) approached this question by attempting to discover whether there was any relationship between measures of worrying and problem-focused coping as measured by the subscales of the Health and Daily Living Form (Moos, Cronkite, Billings & Finney, 1986).

Using an *ad hoc* instrument designed to measure the frequency of worry-ing in students (the Student Worry Scale, SWS), Davey et al. (1992) ini-

Table 2.1   Partial correlation of worry or trait anxiety (TA) while holding the other constant (Davey, Hampton, Farrell & Davidson, 1992, Study 2)

Method of coping	Worry	Trait anxiety
Active cognitive coping	.22*	−.25*
Active behavioural coping	.37**	−.25
Avoidance coping	.05	.30**
Focus of coping		
Logical analysis	.17	−.25*
Information seeking	.21*	−.00
Problem-solving	.26**	−.21*
Affective regulation	.38**	−.31**
Emotional discharge	.14	.18

* $p < .05$; ** $p < .01$.

tially found no significant correlations between frequency of worrying and the frequency of problem-focused coping activities. However, when levels of trait anxiety had been partialled out, worrying was subsequently significantly associated with a range of problem-focused coping activities including active cognitive coping, active behavioural coping, information-seeking and problem-solving (see Table 2.1). This suggested that worrying does exhibit a significant relationship to a variety of problem-focused activities, but this relationship is disrupted or masked in some way by factors associated with trait anxiety.

Essentially similar results were reported by Davey (1993a) using a variety of validated worry measures. When levels of trait anxiety were partialled out, scores on the SWS and the Worry Domains Questionnaire (WDQ, Tallis, Eysenck & Mathews, 1992) were significantly related to a number of problem-focused activities. However, similar findings were not reported with the PSWQ, where—even when trait anxiety was partialled out—scores on the PSWQ remained unrelated to problem-focused activities. Davey (1993a) explained this anomaly by suggesting that, because of the way in which it was developed, the PSWQ is an instrument that is unlikely to tap the constructive end of the worry continuum. For instance, the pool of items used to construct the PSWQ contained references to clinical experiences and statements from GAD patients (cf. Meyer et al., 1990), and some of the PSWQ items actually contain explicit references to pathological worrying. Therefore, the PSWQ appears to be essentially a measure of pathological worrying and has yet to be shown to be independent of measures of trait anxiety (see Chapter 11, this volume).

These findings show that content-based measures of worrying (such as the SWS and the WDQ) do tap into some of the features of constructive, task-oriented worrying, but that this relationship between worrying and problem-focused activities is obscured unless trait anxiety is partialled out.

WORRYING AND TRAIT ANXIETY AS INDEPENDENT CONSTRUCTS

One other interesting feature of the partial correlation data shown in Table 2.1 is that worrying and trait anxiety possess their own unique sources of variance. This is shown at its most dramatic in the case of active cognitive coping and problem-solving, where these variables contribute significant variance to both worrying and trait anxiety, but in quite different directions: worrying is significantly positively correlated with these variables and trait anxiety is significantly negatively correlated (see also Davey, 1993a).

These data suggest that worrying is not simply the cognitive manifestation of anxiety as some writers have argued (e.g. O'Neill, 1985; Mathews, 1990), but that it can be considered as an independent construct which possesses its own unique sources of variance. The sources of this independent variance appear primarily to be measures of problem-focused coping activities, which reinforce the view that worrying is directly associated with problem-solving strategies.

SOURCES OF VARIANCE CONTRIBUTING TO MEASURES OF WORRY AND TRAIT ANXIETY

Using the partial correlation analysis described above, Davey et al. (1992) investigated some of the significant sources of variance for measures of worry and trait anxiety respectively. While measures of the frequency of worrying appeared to be significantly and independently related to measures of problem-focused activities, measures of trait anxiety were independently associated with psychological processes that would normally be considered to result in poor psychological outcomes. Table 2.1 shows that trait anxiety is negatively related to a variety of problem-focused activities, and Table 2.2 shows that trait anxiety is significantly and independently related to measures of poor self-perceived problem-solving efficacy (poor problem-solving confidence and poor perceived personal control over the problem-solving process) and responsibility for negative but not positive outcomes.

Thus, although almost all studies which have measured trait anxiety and worrying have reported high levels of correlation between the two vari-

Table 2.2   Partial correlations of worry and trait anxiety while holding the other constant (Davey, Hampton, Farrell & Davidson, 1992, Study 1)

	Worry	Trait anxiety
Problem-Solving Inventory (PSI)		
Problem-solving confidence	.03	.40**
Approach–avoidance style	−.07	.17
Personal control	.12	.43**
Locus of control		
Responsibility for positive outcomes	.15	−.16
Responsibility for negative outcomes	.00	.33**

*$p < .05$; ** $p < .01$.

Note that high scores on the PSI denote poor perceived problem-solving efficacy.

ables, a partial correlation analysis reveals that the two measures possess important and independent sources of variance. Worrying is associated with constructive, task-oriented activities which should lead to good psychological outcomes, while trait anxiety is independently related to a variety of processes that would normally be considered to result in poor psychological outcomes.

A HYPOTHESIS: PATHOLOGICAL WORRYING AS THWARTED PROBLEM-SOLVING

Since two psychological measures that are normally highly correlated can on more detailed analysis be seen to be independently associated with quite different psychological processes, perhaps it is an interaction between these opposing processes that gives rise to exacerbated or pathological worrying.

Davey et al. (1992) outlined a number of processes that might thwart active attempts to solve potential life problems, but these can be conveniently drawn into two categories.

Situational Factors

Worrying is associated with problem-focused activities which include active behavioural coping, problem analysis, and information-seeking, yet these strategies are only likely to reduce anxiety and stress and actively remove the stressor if the problem is potentially controllable. For instance, worrying has been shown to be independently associated with the information-seeking coping strategy of "monitoring" (Davey et al.,

1992, Study 3; Davey, 1993a), and monitoring appears to be an attempt to seek out threat-relevant information which may help to ameliorate the threat (e.g. Miller, 1987). However, there is clear evidence that those individuals who adopt a monitoring coping style actually become more stressed when the situation is an uncontrollable one (such as an untreatable illness) (Miller & Mangan, 1983; Phipps & Zinn, 1986; Sparks, 1989; Sparks & Spirek, 1988), and in such circumstances monitoring is significantly related to hypertension (Miller, Leinbach & Brody, 1989).

Clearly, persisting with problem-focused activities in circumstances in which the problem is not easily soluble or controllable can have detrimental psychological consequences. Such activities may persist in bringing to conscious awareness the fact that the situation is threatening without providing any obvious means of dealing with it (Breznitz, 1971; Mechanic, 1962). This is likely to maintain or facilitate anxious arousal and to perpetuate further bouts of worrying or attempted problem-solving.

Of course, the factors which define a problem as controllable or uncontrollable are not entirely situation-specific, and also reside in the individual's own appraisal of the problem and an assessment of their own coping resources. As Lazarus & Folkman (1984) have argued, an individual's assessment of the ability to cope with a stressor will be dependent not only on their primary appraisal of the stressor as a threat, but on the coping resources that they feel they can effectively recruit to deal with the stressor. This interactive appraisal process is likely to continually define and redefine the controllability of a stressor. Thus, while some problems may be intrinsically less controllable than others (e.g. a terminal illness, versus, say, resolving a minor argument with a relative or colleague), even the perceived controllability of these events will be modulated by personality factors and individual appraisal processes.

Personality Factors

While some problems have intrinsic characteristics which make them resistant to solution, other factors associated with the individual may render the problem-solving process ineffective or inefficient. Davey et al. (1992) hypothesised that the high correlation between worrying and anxiety may be a result of certain cognitive predispositions acting to thwart or exacerbate the problem-solving function of worrying. This activates a vicious circle of more worrying which generates more anxiety, and so on. Some putative examples of the kinds of cognitive predispositions that may thwart effective problem-solving are the following.

Poor personal problem-solving abilities

Some individuals may be unable to arrive at acceptable solutions to a personal problem because of deficiencies in their own social problem-solving skills. This may give rise to perpetual rumination over the features of the problem without generating any effective solution. There is considerable evidence that a range of clinical groups are characterised by deficits in problem-solving abilities and these include maladjusted adolescents (Platt et al., 1974), alcoholics (Intagliata, 1978), and heroin addicts (Platt, Scura & Hannon, 1973). In particular, problem-solving deficits are regularly found to be associated with depression (Nezu & Ronan, 1985; Zemore & Dell, 1983; Marx, Williams & Claridge, 1992), and both depression (Metzger et al., 1990; Borkovec et al., 1983) and a bias towards pessimistic subjective probabilities (MacLeod, Williams & Bekerian, 1991) are known to be significantly correlated with measures of worrying.

Poor personal problem-solving confidence/Poor perceived personal control over the problem-solving process

It may be that pathological worriers may not be lacking in specific social problem-solving skills, but may have less faith either in the solution that they have arrived at, or their ability to implement that solution. For instance, the partial correlation analyses reported by Davey et al. (1992) suggest that poor problem-solving confidence is not related to worrying *per se*, but appears to be independently related to levels of trait anxiety. This would be predicted if worrying is primarily a constructive problem-solving process that is thwarted by cognitive predispositions that are essentially orthogonal to the worry process. The possibility that exacerbated worrying may be generated by poor problem-solving confidence is supported by evidence from a study by Tallis, Eysenck & Mathews (1991a). They found that worriers had a significant tendency towards elevated evidence requirements for a successful solution to a variety of stimulus categorisation tasks, and defining elevated evidence requirements would essentially be one consequence of poor problem-solving confidence.

Predisposition to negative cognitions or pessimistic thought patterns during problem-solving

It is now well established that negative cognitions are a prominent feature of both anxiety and depression (e.g. Beck et al., 1987), and a cognitive predisposition to think negatively could well frustrate successful problem-solving. It is also clear that negative cognitions are a significant feature of pathological worrying. For instance, chronic worriers exhibit more negative cognitions than non-worriers during relaxed wakefulness, during a single monotonous task, and during a problem-solving task (Pruzinsky & Borkovec, 1990); chronic worriers also construct more negative mental models in response to stimuli generic to their primary worry domain (Tallis, Eysenck & Mathews, 1991b) and show an increased accessibility of explanations for why a negative event should occur combined with a reduced accessibility of explanations for why it should not (MacLeod, Williams & Bekerian, 1991). Periods of induced worrying have been shown to result in increased levels of negative thought intrusions (Borkovec et al., 1983; York, Borkovec, Vasey & Stern, 1987) which can result in slower response latencies in ambiguous concept categorisation tasks (Metzger et al., 1990). Self-labelled worriers appear to be distinguished from non-worriers by the reported uncontrollability of negative cognitive intrusions once worrying has been initiated (Borkovec et al., 1983). All of this evidence is consistent with the hypothesis that chronic worriers may have a cognitive predisposition towards negative thinking and negative thought intrusions, and that negative thoughts can effectively retard successful problem-solving (cf. Pruzinsky & Borkovec, 1990; Metzger et al., 1990).

Predispositions to define events as threats

One traditional problem with conceiving of worrying as a problem-solving process was that it appeared to raise more problems than it actually solved (e.g. Borkovec, 1985), and indeed, the frequency of worrying is significantly correlated with the tendency to define events as threats (Davey et al., 1992, Study 2; Russell & Davey, 1993). Davey et al. (1992) devised an ambiguous/unambiguous situations diary in which some entries were ambiguous and could be interpreted as either threatening or non-threatening (e.g. "I phoned the doctor today and was surprised to hear the results of last weeks check up") and other entries were either unambiguously threatening or non-threatening. Subjects had to indicate whether each entry would be a cause for concern or not. Not only was the frequency of worrying significantly correlated with the tendency to interpret ambiguous events as threats (Davey et al., 1992), but it was also significantly correlated with the tendency to define unambiguous events as threats (Russell & Davey, 1993). Thus, worriers even had a tendency to find cause for concern in diary entries that independent assessors had unanimously agreed should be classified as non-threatening! Using a subsequent recognition–memory test, Mathews, Richards & Eysenck (1989) have found similar results in a subject population diagnosed as clinical worriers. They found that subjects diagnosed as GAD were more likely than normal controls to interpret ambiguous sentences in a threatening fashion. The source of this tendency of chronic worriers to interpret events as threatening is unclear, although it could reside in information processing biases associated with anxiety. These might include attentional predispositions to threatening cues (e.g. Mathews & MacLeod, 1985), or the tendency of anxious mood to facilitate the activation of anxiety-related information in memory. This would result in differentially rapid accessing of threat-relevant information during the appraisal of events with essentially ambiguous components (e.g. Bower, 1981; Eysenck, 1983).

One extreme form of the tendency to define events as threats is the process known as "catastrophising". This is a common feature of the thought processes of chronic worriers, who, when entering a bout of worrying, tend to define increasingly worse and worse outcomes to a potential problem (cf. Tallis, 1990). This is characterised by the "What if . . .?" question that worriers perpetually ask about a problem. Chronic worriers tend to define significantly more catastrophic consequences for a worry topic than non-worriers, and worriers report a significant increase in subjective discomfort as catastrophising progresses (Vasey & Borkovec, 1993).

Clearly, having a tendency to define events as threats is likely to severely disrupt any problem-solving activities that are directed towards a potential problem. It is likely to lead to the rejection of potential solutions because they may also be perceived as having problematic features. It is also likely to exacerbate the problem-solving process by inflating the severity of the problem (e.g. through catastrophising). Both of these effects will prolong problem-oriented worrying, significantly reduce the likelihood of arriving at an acceptable solution, and maintain or increase anxiety and emotional discomfort.

Relationship Between Factors Which Might Lead to Thwarted Problem-solving

The previous section discusses four cognitive factors which may thwart effective problem-solving, yet these four factors need not be mutually exclusive but may be separately identifiable features of a more global and integrated psychological predisposition. For example, a tendency to define events as threats may be mediated by a predisposition to negative cognitions, and a predisposition to negative cognitions may be the legacy of poor problem-solving skills generating a history of failure to deal successfully with problems, and so on. The causal relationships between these cognitive factors are in clear need of some mapping in controlled experimental settings, and this is something that has only recently begun to be tackled (e.g. Borkovec et al., 1983; York et al., 1987).

SOME PRELIMINARY TESTS OF THE THWARTED PROBLEM-SOLVING HYPOTHESIS

Worrying, Social Problem-solving Abilities, and Social Problem-solving Confidence

One prediction from the thwarted problem-solving scenarios outlined above is that if pathological worrying results from either poor problem-solving skills or poor problem-solving confidence, then measures of either or both should be significantly correlated with measures of the frequency of worrying.

In a study designed to investigate these relationships (Davey, 1993b), normal non-clinical subjects were given a questionnaire which measured, amongst other things, social problem-solving ability (the Means–Ends Problem Solving inventory, MEPS; Platt & Spivack, 1975), problem-solving confidence (the Problem-Solving Inventory, PSI; Heppner & Petersen, 1982), the frequency of worry (WDQ and PSWQ), and trait anxiety (the STAI Y-2; Spielberger, 1983).

The MEPS provides a measure of real-life problem-solving ability by examining the individual's ability to conceptualise step-by-step means (strategies) to achieve a goal, and subjects' responses are scored on two dimensions: (i) relevant means (discrete steps which are effective in enabling the resolution of a problem to be reached), and (ii) effectiveness (i.e. a problem-solving strategy is considered to be effective if it maximizes positive and minimizes negative short- and long-term consequences, D'Zurilla & Goldfried, 1971). The PSI measures three problem-solving constructs: (i) problem-solving confidence (the individual's confidence in engaging in a wide range of problem-solving activities), (ii) approach–avoidance style (whether an individual approaches or avoids different problem-solving activities), and (iii) personal control (the individual's perception of their degree of control over their emotions and behaviours while problem-solving).

Table 2.3 shows the correlation coefficients between MEPS and PSI scores and scores on the Coping Inventory for Stressful Situations (CISS, Endler & Parker, 1990), the WDQ and PSWQ (measures of worry), the STAI Y-2 (trait anxiety), and the Miller Behavioural Style Scale (MBSS, Miller,

Table 2.3 Correlations between MEPS and PSI scores and scores on the CISS, WDQ, PSWQ, STAI Y-2, and MBSS (Davey, 1993b)

	MEPS		PSI		
	Relevant means	Effectiveness	Problem-solving confidence	Approach–Avoidance style	Personal control
CISS					
Task oriented	.29*	.12	−.35**	−.30*	−.15
Emotion-oriented	.11	.05	.47**	.25	.56**
Avoidance coping	.02	−.09	.20	.45**	
Worry questionnaires					
WDQ	.18	.05	.47**	.24	.45**
PSWQ	.08	.05	.58**	.31*	.49**
Anxiety					
STAI Y-2	.09	.07	.57**	.32*	.59**
MBSS					
Monitoring	.15	.12	.18	.05	.23
Blunting	.04	.02	.03	.08	.09
M–B difference	.08	.06	.17	.10	.10

* $p < .01$; ** $p < .001$.

Note that high scores on the PSI denote poor perceived problem-solving efficacy.

1987). This shows that the only significant relationship between MEPS scores and the other scales was between relevant means and task-oriented coping. There were no significant correlations between MEPS scores and either worry or trait anxiety scores. The correlation between relevant means and task-oriented coping is one that would be intuitively expected and provides some degree of confidence in the validity of the MEPS scores as a measure of problem-solving ability.

Despite these negative results it is possible that at least two factors might have been masking any simple relationship between worrying and MEPS scores. First, the relationship between worrying and problem-solving might not be monotonic. For instance, at relatively low levels of worrying there may be a positive relationship between worrying and problem-solving ability which reflects the task-oriented nature of worrying. However, higher levels of worry may in fact be counterproductive by generating anxiety and negative cognitions that may interfere with effective problem-solving. In order to test this possibility both PSWQ and WDQ scores were subjected to a median split and correlations with MEPS scores calculated separately for the high and low groups. Nevertheless, partitioning worry scores into high and low worrying groups still failed to result in any significant correlations with MEPS scores.

In contrast, there was a variety of significant correlations between PSI scores and worrying and trait anxiety. Table 2.3 shows that worrying was significantly associated with poor problem-solving confidence and poor personal control over problem-solving activities—results similar to those reported by Davey et al. (1992).

Interestingly, MEPS scores were not significantly related to any of the sub-scale scores of the PSI. This suggests that the factors which determine the confidence an individual has in their problem-solving abilities are largely independent of that individual's actual ability to produce effective solutions.

These results indicate that, while there is a strong relationship between worrying and poor problem-solving confidence, there is no significant association between worrying and problem-solving ability *per se*. Indeed, while not significant, most correlations between MEPS scores and worry scores were in fact positive, implying better problem-solving ability with increased worrying. This suggests that pathological worrying is not generated by poor problem-solving skills exacerbating the problem-solving process, but the findings are consistent with the hypothesis that worrying may be generated by an individual's lack of belief in the adequacy of their problem-solving abilities and their ability to implement solutions.

These results are also consistent with some theorising by Marx, Williams & Claridge (1992) on the relationships between problem-solving capabilities and anxiety and depression. Marx et al. (1992) found that a group of clinically anxious subjects scored significantly better on problem-solving skills than clinically depressed patients (although the anxious group performed marginally worse than the non-clinical controls). They hypothesised that anxiety and depression may cause problem-solving deficiencies at different levels: depressed subjects appear to have difficulties in the early stages of problem-solving which leads to ineffective solutions, whereas anxious subjects seem to have difficulties in the later stages—possibly at the level of implementation of the solution.

However, these results are only consistent with that part of the thwarted problem-solving hypothesis which suggests that pathological worrying is generated by poor problem-solving confidence thwarting effective problem-solving. It must be stressed that this preliminary study is only correlational and does not indicate causal direction. For instance, it is possible that poor problem-solving confidence may be the result of ineffective chronic worrying rather than a cause of it. Only studies manipulating the relevant variables will determine the causal influences involved in this relationship.

Worrying and the Controllability of the Stressor

When worrying is perceived as a problem-solving process, then one factor which may thwart effective problem-solving and exacerbate worrying is the controllability of the problem. If the problem is intrinsically uncontrollable, or the individual believes it to be so, then solutions which remove or deal effectively with the problem will be difficult to arrive at, and task-oriented activities such as worrying will be perpetuated.

Davey (1993c) reported a study which investigated some of the factors that predicted the frequency and perceived outcomes of worrying about significant life stressors in a normal non-clinical population. Among the factors that were investigated in this study were the effect that the subjectively- and objectively-rated controllability of the stressor had on both the frequency and perceived outcomes of worrying about the stressor.

Table 2.4. shows the correlations between frequency of worrying about the stressor and a variety of situational and trait factors. This shows that both the objectively- and subjectively-estimated controllability of the stressor was unrelated to the frequency of worrying about it (objective controllability was estimated by two independent raters; interrater reliability was .82). However, a number of trait measures, including levels of trait anxiety and trait worry, were all significantly correlated with the reported frequency of worrying about the stressor.

Table 2.5 shows the correlations between controllability of the stressor and trait factors and ratings of the perceived consequences of worrying. This indicates that the more controllable the stressor, the more that worrying was perceived to have constructive benefits such as helping the individual feel more in control and helping to solve the problem. In

Table 2.4 Correlations between frequency of worrying about the stressor, and controllability of the stressor and trait factors

	Objective controllability	Subjective controllability	Trait anxiety (STAI Y-2)	WDQ	PSWQ
Frequency of worrying (Stressor 1)	−.01	.05	.30**	.21	.35**
Frequency of worrying (Stressor 2)	−.04	.00	.24*	.16	.24*

$* p < .01; ** p < .001.$

Table 2.5 Correlations between the perceived consequences of worrying about the stressor, and controllability of the stressor and trait factors

	Objective controllability	Subjective controllability	Trait anxiety (STAI Y-2)	WDQ	PSWQ
Stressor 1					
Felt more in control	.03	.21	.03	.04	.04
Felt more anxious	−.03	.01	.17	.02	.25*
Helped to solve problem	.17	.28*	−.11	−.12	−.10
Stressor 2					
Felt more in control	.07	.14	.04	.13	−.01
Felt more anxious	.08	.10	.24*	.11	.30*
Helped to solve problem	.33**	.36**	−.03	.06	.00

* $p < .01$; ** $p < .001$.

contrast, trait measures such as trait anxiety and trait worrying were only significantly related to worrying making the individual feel more anxious.

This study appears to show that the controllability of the stressor only predicts the degree of benefit obtained from worrying (in terms of feelings of control and help in solving problems), but is not significantly related to either the frequency of worrying or the perception of worrying as increasing anxiety about the stressor. If the uncontrollability of the problem acts to thwart effective problem-solving and exacerbate worrying, then we would have predicted a significant inverse relationship between ratings of controllability and both the frequency of worrying and ratings of worrying being perceived as increasing anxiety: only measures such as trait anxiety and trait worrying consistently predict these latter two pathological outcomes.

These findings suggest that the uncontrollability of the stressor may not be a factor which directly promotes thwarting-generated worry. While controllability may be a factor which does influence the perceived benefits of worrying, descent into the worry–anxiety spiral when an uncontrollable stressor is encountered may be determined by other factors such as those related to high trait anxiety or the perceived upsetting impact of the stressor. An individual low in trait anxiety who encounters an uncontrollable stressor may avoid the worry–anxiety spiral by adopting alternative coping strategies which have a dampening effect on anxiety and worry (e.g. positive reappraisal of the threat, cognitive devaluation of the threat, cf. Davey, 1993d, and below for further discussion of this possibility). In this sense, an assessment of the controllability of the stressor may be equivalent to Lazarus & Folkman's (1984) primary appraisal stage, in which the threatening nature of the stimulus is evaluated. This appraisal then informs the feelings of control and also expectations of success at dealing with the stressor that the individual reports. The subsequent, secondary appraisal stage is the one at which the individual decides on the appropriate strategies to cope with the stressor. It is at this stage that those factors associated with trait anxiety and trait worrying (e.g. poor problem-solving confidence, catastrophising, negative cognition, etc.) may thwart the problem-solving process and spark the worry–anxiety spiral. Within this scenario, the uncontrollability of the stressor does not contribute to worrying *per se*, but only to perceptions of the possible beneficial effects of worrying.

Summary

These two preliminary studies provide data which permit some refinement of the thwarted problem-solving scenarios outlined earlier in this chapter. They suggest that poor problem-solving confidence is related to the frequency and intensity of worrying, whereas poor problem-solving abilities and the controllability of the problem do not appear to be factors which are significant predictors of levels of worrying.

While these studies have begun to investigate only some of the implications of the thwarted problem-solving hypothesis, they begin to suggest that chronic worrying may be critically associated with those psychological factors that affect the acceptability and implementation of solutions rather than those factors which thwart effective problem-solving. In this respect, psychological factors which might contribute to thwarted problem-solving may do so only to the extent that they facilitate doubt about the acceptability and implementation of a solution. For example, negative cognitions may facilitate worrying only by generating a lack of confidence in a solution: they would, according to this account, not necessarily facilitate worrying by interfering with effective problem-solving *per se*. In any case, what is likely to be of primary importance for the worrier is not the actual objective effectiveness of a solution to the problem, but whether they themselves find it acceptable as an effective solution: an individual may have very poor social problem-solving skills and arrive at what are likely to be relatively ineffective solutions to problems, but if they are convinced that the solution is satisfactory then both worrying and anxiety will be alleviated (at least in the short term). Poor problem-solving skills are only likely to lead to exacerbated worrying if the individual is aware that they possess these poor skills and that this is likely to lead to ineffective solutions.

One direction in which research on this topic should move is towards studies of the effect of putative thwarting factors on levels of worrying. Given that we may be able to experimentally manipulate the frequency of some of the central cognitive features supposed to cause thwarting (e.g. negative cognitions, tendency to define events as threats, catastrophising, problem-solving confidence, etc.), we ought to be able to predict the effect they might have on subsequently monitored periods of worrying and problem-solving.

ADDITIONAL CONSEQUENCES OF CONCEIVING PATHOLOGICAL WORRY AS EXACERBATED PROBLEM-SOLVING

If pathological worrying results from certain cognitive biases and predispositions which thwart ongoing problem-solving, then why not simply describe worrying in terms of these biases and predispositions? What additional heuristic consequences might there be to implying that there is a problem-solving process which underlies pathological worrying?

What Motivates Worrying?

When considered in isolation, those cognitive factors that characterise chronic worrying do not provide a means of explaining the persistence of the activity of worrying. For example, a tendency to define events as threats and a predisposition towards negative cognitions do not provide a reason to persevere with the act of worrying—they merely influence the nature of the content of worry. Assuming that worrying represents a problem-solving process provides some insight into the possible factors that motivate worrying (but note that there are alternative accounts of the function of worrying; cf. Borkovec & Lyonfields, 1992; Borkovec, this volume). The fact that in certain analyses the frequency of worrying is significantly related to problem-focused activities supports this view (Davey et al., 1992; Davey, 1993a). That chronic worriers find the act of worrying uncontrollable is not inconsistent with the problem-solving approach (Borkovec et al., 1983), since a desire to ameliorate stressors need not necessarily be a conscious nor actively controllable process. A problem-solving view of worrying merely assumes that there is an underlying motivation to remove threatening stressors.

What Characterises Non-worriers?

Defining chronic worrying as the result of thwarted problem-solving has a number of implications for identifying individuals whom we would describe as non-worriers.

First, there are those who can arrive at acceptable solutions to their life problems relatively efficiently. These would be the individuals who possess psychological characteristics which are the antithesis of those postulated to cause thwarted problem-solving, and, indeed, possession of these characteristics has been shown to enhance successful adaptation to stressful encounters and to reduce the incidence of dysfunctional mood such as depression and anxiety. These characteristics include a predominance of positive rather than negative beliefs (Heppner, Reeder & Larson, 1983); good rather than poor self-appraised problem-solving confidence (MacNair & Elliott, 1992; Elliott et al., 1991; Heppner, Kampa & Brunning, 1987); an optimistic disposition which facilitates the use of potentially successful problem-focused coping strategies (Taylor et al., 1993; Scheier & Carver, 1985; Scheier, Weintraub & Carver, 1986); and an attentional predisposition to orient away from, rather than towards, threatening cues (MacLeod & Mathews, 1988; Alloy & Abramson, 1979).

Second, there are those who can cognitively neutralise potential threats or problems before they are appraised as requiring problem-oriented activities, and these individuals would also be classed as primarily non-worriers. There are a variety of cognitive appraisal strategies that can devalue or neutralise potential stressors before they require detailed attention, and these include denial (denying the existence of the threat; Breznitz, 1983; Sjöbäck, 1973), positive reappraisal (attempting to bestow positive value on a threat; Folkman et al., 1986), and threat devaluation (attempting to devalue the personal importance of a threat; Davey, 1993d). Both positive reappraisal and threat devaluation are strategies that are used significantly less by anxious individuals (Davey, 1993d) and patients suffering clinical anxiety disorders (Davey, Burgess & Rashes,

1993) than by non-anxious control subjects. Similarly, individuals characterised as deniers display greater self-esteem, optimism, and less short-term depression and anxiety (Dinardo, 1971; Hackett, Cassem & Wishnie, 1968; Wolff, Friedman, Hofer & Mason, 1964; Stern, Pascale & McLoone, 1976; Cohen & Lazarus, 1983).

Third, there are those who use primarily avoidance coping strategies which allow them to distract from rather than tackle potential threats (e.g. Endler & Parker, 1990). These are individuals who accept that a threat is significant and problematic, but who attempt to alleviate anxiety and avoid worrying by distracting. However, identifying this group of non-worrying avoiders is potentially problematic since avoidance strategies are also used by chronic worriers as they attempt to distract themselves from their worries (Davey et al., 1992; Davey, 1993a; Meyer et al., 1990). Presumably, non-worrying avoiders will be distinguished from worrying avoiders by significantly lower levels of trait anxiety. Nevertheless, even this is not certain because avoidance coping strategies will not be effective tactics in the face of problems that objectively do require some practical intervention; hence, avoidance coping may always be associated with some psychological distress if individuals are unable to switch successfully from avoidance to problem-focused strategies when necessary.

What Would be the Effects of Successfully Alleviating Pathological Worrying?

If pathological worrying results from thwarted problem-solving, then successfully alleviating pathological worrying and, in particular, those psychological factors which are postulated to cause thwarting should have beneficial effects not only on affect and cognitive content, but also on problem-solving success. There is some indirect evidence that bears on this question.

A number of studies have shown that inducing positive affect facilitates creative problem-solving in a variety of conceptual and real-life tasks (e.g. Isen, Daubman & Nowicki, 1987; Carnevale & Isen, 1986). While the exact mechanisms that mediate this relationship between positive affect and creative problem-solving are still unclear, one possibility is that induced positive affect may facilitate access to cognitive and memory structures which are incompatible with the cognitive and memory structures which may cause thwarted problem-solving (e.g. facilitated access to positive rather than negative cognitions, facilitated access to optimistic rather than pessimistic subjective probabilities, etc., cf. MacLeod, Williams & Bekerian, 1991).

What Types of Treatment might be Appropriate for Pathological Worrying?

While the present approach clearly defines a number of psychological factors that are postulated to generate pathological worrying, successful therapy need not require attention to these factors individually (e.g. decatastrophising—Kendall & Ingram, 1987; cognitive restructuring of negative subjective probability levels—MacLeod, Williams & Bekerian, 1991).

If pathological worrying is the result of thwarted problem-solving, then constructive problem-solving therapy may well be a useful approach to ameliorating a variety of the cognitive factors which facilitate thwarting (Tallis, 1990). Nevertheless, chronic worriers do not appear to have deficits in problem-solving skills *per se* (see above), but do have deficits in problem-solving confidence. Any problem-solving therapeutic approach adopted to deal with chronic worrying would need to specifically address this latter factor.

CONCLUSIONS

There appear to be a number of heuristic benefits to conceiving of pathological worrying as exacerbated problem-solving. The construct of worrying has been shown to be significantly associated with problem-focused activities (Davey et al., 1992; Davey, 1993a), and the failure of pathological worrying to deal successfully with life problems can then be conceived as the result of a number of possible psychological and cognitive predispositions thwarting successful problem-solving. While chronic worriers do not appear to possess poor problem-solving skills *per se*, they do possess poor problem-solving confidence, and this may be one factor which thwarts successful problem-solving. This chapter has discussed a variety of other possible psychological and cognitive processes that may result in thwarted problem-solving. What are now required are some controlled experimental studies which investigate the effects of these variables on both the frequency of worrying and successful problem-solving.

ACKNOWLEDGEMENTS

The author is grateful to Frank Tallis and Mark Williams for comments on earlier versions of this chapter.

REFERENCES

Alloy, L.B. & Abramson, L.Y. (1979). Judgment of contingency in depressed and non-depressed students: Sadder but wiser? *Journal of Experimental Psychology*, **108**, 441–485.

Barlow, D.H. (1988). *Anxiety and its Disorders*. New York: Guilford.

Barlow, D.H., Blanchard, E.B., Vermilyea, J.A., Vermilyea, D.B. & DiNardo, P.A. (1986). Generalized anxiety and generalized anxiety disorder: Description and reconceptualization. *American Journal of Psychiatry*, **143**, 40–44.

Beck, A.T., Brown, G., Steer, R.A., Eidelson, J.I. & Riskind, J.H. (1987). Differentiating anxiety and depression: A test of the cognitive content-specificity hypothesis. *Journal of Abnormal Psychology*, **96**, 179–183.

Billings, A.G. & Moos, R.H. (1981). The role of coping responses and social resources in attenuating the impact of stressful life events. *Journal of Behavioral Medicine*, **4**, 139–157.

Billings, A.G. & Moos, R.H. (1984). Coping, stress, and social resources among adults with unipolar depression. *Journal of Personality and Social Psychology*, **46**, 877–891.

Borkovec, T.D. (1985). Worry: A potentially valuable concept. *Behaviour Research and Therapy*, **23**, 481–482.

Borkovec, T.D. & Lyonfields, J.D. (1992). Worry: Thought suppression of emotional processing. In H.W. Krohne (Ed.), *Vigilance and Avoidance*. Toronto: Hogrefe & Huber.

Borkovec, T.D., Robinson, E., Pruzinsky, T. & Dupree, J.A. (1983). Preliminary exploration of worry: Some characteristics and processes. *Behaviour Research and Therapy*, **21**, 9–16.

Bower, G.H. (1981). Mood and memory. *American Psychologist*, **36**, 129–148.

Breznitz, S. (1983). A study of worrying. *British Journal of Social and Clinical Psychology*, **10**, 271–299.

Brown, T.A., Antony, M.M. and Barlow, D.H. (1992). Psychometric properties of the Penn State Worry Questionnaire in a clinical anxiety disorders sample. *Behaviour Research and Therapy*, **30**, 33–37.

Carnevale, P.J.D. & Isen, A.M. (1986). The influence of positive affect and visual access on the discovery of integrative solutions in bilateral negotiation. *Organizational Behavior and Human Decision Processes*, **37**, 1–13.

Cohen, F. & Lazarus, R.S. (1983). Coping and adaptation in health and illness. In D. Mechanic (ed.), *Handbook of Health, Health Care, and the Health Professions*. New York: The Free Press.

Davey, G.C.L. (1992). Worrying and trait anxiety as predictors of scores on the Fear Survey Schedule. Submitted.

Davey, G.C.L. (1993a). A comparison of three worry questionnaires. *Behaviour Research and Therapy*, **31**, 51–56.

Davey, G.C.L. (1993b). Worrying, social problem-solving abilities, and social problem-solving confidence. *Behaviour Research and Therapy* (in press).

Davey, G.C.L. (1993c). Trait and situational factors predicting worrying about significant life stressors. *Personality and Individual Differences* (in press).

Davey, G.C.L. (1993d). A comparison of three cognitive appraisal strategies: The role of threat devaluation in problem-focussed coping. *Personality and Individual Differences*, **14**, 535–546.

Davey, G.C.L., Burgess, I. & Rashes, R. (1993). Coping strategies and phobias: The relationship between fears, phobias and methods of coping with stressors. Submitted.

Davey, G.C.L., Hampton, J., Farrell, J. & Davidson, S. (1992). Some characteristics of worrying: Evidence for worrying and anxiety as separate constructs. *Personality and Individual Differences*, **13**, 133–147.

Dinardo, Q.E. (1971). Psychological adjustments to spinal cord injury. Unpublished doctoral dissertation. University of Houston, Texas.

D'Zurilla, T.J. & Goldfried, M.R. (1971). Problem-solving and behavior modification. *Journal of Abnormal Psychology*, **78**, 107–126.

Elliott, T.R., Godsall, F.J., Herrick, S.M., Witty, T.E. & Spruell, M. (1991). Problem-solving appraisal and psychological adjustment following spinal cord injury. *Cognitive Therapy and Research*, **15**, 387–398.

Endler, N.S. & Parker, J.D.A. (1990). Multidimensional assessment of coping; A critical evaluation. *Journal of Personality and Social Psychology*, **58**, 844–854.

Eysenck, M. (1983). *Attention and Arousal: Cognition and Performance.* Berlin: Springer.

Folkman, S., Lazarus, R.S., Dunkel-Schetter, C., DeLongis, A. & Gruen, A.R. (1986). Dynamics of a stressful encounter: Cognitive appraisal, coping, and encounter outcomes. *Journal of Personality and Social Psychology*, **50**, 992–1003.

Hackett, T.P., Cassem, N.H. & Wishnie, H.A. (1968). The coronary-care unit: An appraisal of its psychological hazards. *New England Journal of Medicine*, **279**, 66–75.

Heppner, P.P., Kampa, M. & Brunning, L. (1987). The relationship between problem-solving self-appraisal and indices of physical and psychological health. *Cognitive Therapy and Research*, **11**, 155–168.

Heppner, P.P. & Petersen, C.H. (1982). The development and implications of a personal problem-solving inventory. *Journal of Consulting Psychology*, **29**, 66–75.

Heppner, P.P., Reeder, B.L. & Larson, L.M. (1983). Cognitive variables associated with personal problem-solving appraisal: Implications for counseling. *Journal of Counseling Psychology*, **30**, 537–545.

Intagliata, J.C. (1978). Increasing the inter-personal problem-solving skills of an alcoholic population. *Journal of Consulting and Clinical Psychology*, **46**, 489–498.

Isen, A.M., Daubman, K.A. & Nowicki, G.P. (1987). Positive affect facilitates creative problem solving. *Journal of Personality and Social Psychology*, **52**, 1122–1131.

Kendall, P.C. and Ingram, R.E. (1987). The future for cognitive assessment of anxiety: Let's get specific. In L. Michaelson & L.M. Ascher (Eds.), *Anxiety and Stress Disorders: Cognitive-behavioral Assessment and Treatment.* New York: Guilford.

Lazarus, R.S. & Folkman, S. (1984). *Stress, Appraisal and Coping.* New York: Springer.

MacLeod, A.K., Williams, J.M.G. & Bekerian, D.A. (1991). Worry is reasonable: The role of explanations in pessimism about future personal events. *Journal of Abnormal Psychology*, **100**, 478–486.

MacLeod, C. and Mathews, A. (1988). Anxiety and the allocation of attention to threat. *Quarterly Journal of Experimental Psychology*, **40**, 653–670.

McNair, R.R. and Elliott, T.R. (1992). Self-perceived problem-solving ability, stress appraisal, and coping over time. *Journal of Research in Personality*, **26**, 150–164.

Marx, E.M., Williams, J.M.G. and Claridge, G.C. (1992). Depression and social problem solving. *Journal of Abnormal Psychology*, **101**, 78–86.

Mathews, A. (1990). Why worry? The cognitive structure of anxiety. *Behaviour Research and Therapy*, **28**, 455–468.

Mathews, A. & MacLeod, C. (1985). Selective processing of threat cues in anxiety states. *Behaviour Research and Therapy*, **23**, 563–569.

Mathews, A., Richards, A. & Eysenck, M. (1989). Interpretation of homophones related to threat in anxiety states. *Journal of Abnormal Psychology*, **98**, 31–34.

Mechanic, D. (1962). *Students under Stress: A Study in the Social Psychology of Adaptation*. New York: The Free Press.

Metzger, R.L., Miller, M.L., Cohen, M., Sofka, M. and Borkovec, T.D. (1990). Worry changes decision making: The effect of negative thoughts on cognitive processing. *Journal of Clinical Psychology*, **48**, 76–88.

Meyer, T.J., Miller, M.L., Metzger, R.L. & Borkovec, T.D. (1990). Development and validation of the Penn State Worry Questionnaire. *Behaviour Research and Therapy*, **28**, 487–495.

Miller, S.M. (1987). Monitoring and blunting: Validation of a questionnaire to assess styles of information-seeking under threat. *Journal of Personality and Social Psychology*, **51**, 345–353.

Miller, S.M., Leinbach, A. & Brody, D.S. (1989). Coping style in hypertensives: Nature and consequences. *Journal of Consulting and Clinical Psychology*, **57**, 333–337.

Miller, S.M. and Mangan, C.E. (1983). The interacting effects of information and coping style in adapting to gynaecologic stress: Should the doctor tell all? *Journal of Personality and Social Psychology*, **45**, 223–236.

Moos, R.H., Cronkite, R.C., Billings, A. & Finney, J.W. (1986). *Health and Daily Living Form*. Social Ecology Laboratory, Veterans Administration of Stanford University Medical Centers.

Nezu, A.M. & Ronan, G.F. (1985). Life stress, current problems, problem-solving, and depressive symptoms: An integrative model. *Journal of Consulting and Clinical Psychology*, **53**, 693–697.

O'Neill, G.W. (1985). Is worry a valuable concept? *Behaviour Research and Therapy*, **23**, 479–480.

Pearlin, L.E. & Schooler, C. (1978). The structure of coping. *Journal of Health and Social Behavior*, **19**, 2–21.

Phipps, S. & Zinn, A.B. (1986). Psychological response to amnioscentesis: II. Effects of coping style. *American Journal of Medical Genetics*, **25**, 143–148.

Platt, J.J., Scura, W.C. & Hannon, J.R. (1973). Problem-solving thinking of youthful incarcerated heroin addicts. *Journal of Community Psychology*, **1**, 278–281.

Platt, J.J. & Spivack, G. (1975). Unidimensionality of the Means–Ends Problem-solving (MEPS) procedure. *Journal of Clinical Psychology*, **31**, 15–16.

Platt, J.J., Spivack, G., Altman, N., Altman, D. & Peizer, S.B. (1974). Adolescent problem-solving thinking. *Journal of Consulting and Clinical Psychology*, **42**, 787–793.

Pruzinsky, T. & Borkovec, T.D. (1990). Cognitive and personality characteristics of worriers. *Behaviour Research and Therapy*, **28**, 507–512.

Russell, M. & Davey, G.C.L. (1993). The relationship between life event measures and anxiety and its cognitive correlates. *Personality and Individual Differences*, **14**, 317–322.

Scheier, M.F. & Carver, C.S. (1985). Optimism, coping, and health: Assessment and implications of generalized outcomes expectancies. *Health Psychology*, **4**, 219–247.

Scheier, M.F., Weintraub, J.K. & Carver, C.S. (1986). Coping with stress: Divergent strategies of optimists and pessimists. *Journal of Personality and Social Psychology*, **51**, 1257–1264.

Sjöbäck, H. (1973). *The Psychoanalytic Theory of Defensive Processes*. New York: Wiley.

Sparks, G.G. (1989). Understanding emotional reactions to a suspenseful movie: The interactions between processing and preferred coping style. *Communications Monographs*, **56**, 325–340.

Sparks, G.G. & Spirek, M.M. (1988). Individual differences in coping with stressful mass media: An activation-arousal view. *Human Communication Research*, **15**, 325–340.

Spielberger, C.C. (1983). *State–trait Anxiety Inventory*. Palo Alto, CA.: Consulting Psychologists' Press.

Stern, M.J., Pascale, L. & McLoone, J.B. (1976). Psychosocial adaptation following an acute mytocardial infarction. *Journal of Chronic Diseases*, **29**, 513–516.

Tallis, F. (1990). *How to Stop Worrying*. London: Sheldon Press.

Tallis, F., Eysenck, M. & Mathews, A. (1991a). Elevated evidence requirements and worry. *Personality and Individual Differences*, **12**, 21–27.

Tallis, F., Eysenck, M. & Mathews, A. (1991b). The role of temporal perspective and ego-relevance in the activation of worry structures. *Personality and Individual Differences*, **12**, 909–915.

Tallis, F., Eysenck, M. & Mathews, A. (1992). A questionnaire for the measurement of nonpathological worry. *Personality and Individual Differences*, **13**, 161–168.

Taylor, S.E., Kemeny, M.E., Aspinall, L.G., Schneider, S.G., Rodriguez, R. & Herbert, M. (1993). Optimism, coping, psychological distress and high-risk sexual behavior among men at risk for Acquired Immunodeficiency Syndrome (AIDS). *Journal of Personalty and Social Psychology*, **63**, 460–473.

Vasey, M. & Borkovec, T.D. (1993). A catastrophizing assessment of worrisome thoughts. *Cognitive Therapy and Research* (in press).

Wisocki, P.A., Handen, B. & Morse, C.K. (1986). The worry scale as a measure of anxiety among homebound and community elderly. *Behavior Therapist*, **5**, 91–95.

Wolff, C.T., Friedman, S.B., Hofer, M.A. & Mason, J.W. (1964). Relationship between psychosocial defenses and mean urinary 17-hydroxycorticosteroid excretion rates, Parts I and II. *Psychosomatic Medicine*, **26**, 576–609.

York, D., Borkovec, T.D., Vasey, M. & Stern, R. (1987). Effects of worry and somatic anxiety induction on thoughts, emotion and physiological activity. *Behaviour Research and Therapy*, **25**, 523–526.

Zemore, R. & Dell, L.W. (1983). Interpersonal problem-solving skills and depression-proneness. *Personality and Social Psychology Bulletin*, **9**, 231–235.

CHAPTER 3 The Phenomenology of non-pathological worry: a preliminary investigation

Frank Tallis, Graham C.L. Davey†
and Nicola Capuzzo‡*

INTRODUCTION

When people say that they are "worrying" what do they mean exactly? Without at least a modest understanding of phenomenology it is difficult to ascertain how worry is similar to, and different from, other mental phenomena. Presumably, the presence of the word "worry" and its equivalent in English and other languages provides *prima facie* evidence for the existence of a relatively unique mental state. Moreover, this mental state can be distinguished from those that are semantically near relatives. For example, to "brood", "ponder", or "ruminate". Recourse to the Oxford English Dictionary suggests that worry is a "repetitive" phenomenon, "continuously or intermittently troublesome" that allows "no rest or peace of mind"; however, through worry, one might obtain a solution to problems. It is also associated with "anxiety". These excerpts from the OED are remarkably consistent with the first working definition of worry provided by Borkovec, Robinson, Pruzinsky & DePree (1983), who emphasised the uncontrollable nature of worry, its problem-solving function, and its relationship with affective variables.

It is widely recognised that consigning all mental phenomena to a single category, under the rubric "cognitive factors", fails to capture the diversity of mental events. In the clinical literature, obsessions (Wartburg, 1799 (cited in Monserrat-Esteve, 1971)), fixed ideas (Buccola, 1880), morbid

*Charter Nightingale Hospital, London, †The City University, London and ‡Institute of Psychiatry, London, UK

Worrying: Perspectives on Theory, Assessment and Treatment. Edited by G.C.L. Davey and F. Tallis.
© 1994 John Wiley & Sons Ltd.

preoccupations (Rachman, 1973), ruminations (Beech, 1974), negative automatic thoughts (Beck, 1976), dysfunctional assumptions (Kovacs & Beck, 1978; Fennell, 1989), and intrusive thoughts (Rachman, 1981), are all evidence of an evolving and more discriminating vocabulary. To some extent, this evolving vocabulary reflects the subtle distinctions already present in everyday language. If worry has a legitimate place in this evolving clinical lexicon, it is necessary to demonstrate the existence of a cohesive lay construct, with unique features, that might be refined through academic study.

To date, there has only been one substantial phenomenological investigation of worry (Craske, Rapee, Jackel & Barlow, 1989). This examined qualitative dimensions of worry in generalised anxiety disorder (GAD) and non-anxious controls. The findings of this study indicated that clinical and non-clinical worriers differed in several respects. Firstly, GAD patients worried more about threats to physical safety (i.e. illness and injury) and miscellaneous "minor" issues than controls. Consistent with other work (Sanderson & Barlow (cited in Barlow, 1988); Tallis, Eysenck & Mathews, 1992; Eysenck & van Berkum (cited in Eysenck, 1992)), worries volunteered by both groups could be categorised according to several domains (e.g. relationships, finances, work and illness). Sixty-four per cent of the GAD group and 88% of the non-clinical control group worried in response to recognisable precipitants. GAD patients considered their worry to be less controllable, less realistic, and less successfully reduced by corrective action. Approximately 65% of worries were "resisted" in both groups. Moreover, 53% of the GAD group and 71% of the non-clinical group engaged in preventative or ritualistic action as a result of worrying. The worries recorded by the two groups "did not differ in terms of level of maximum anxiety, level of maximum aversiveness, degree to which the content of the worry was considered likely or probable, and level of anxiety when attempting to resist worrying" (p. 400).

Unlike other types of intrusive thinking (e.g. obsessions and negative automatic thoughts), worry can be regarded, at least in part, as adaptive. The dictionary definition of worry, as well as the first working definition of worry proposed by Borkovec et al. (1983), both emphasise a problem-solving component. An adaptive dimension to worrying was also emphasised by Janis (1958) and Janis & Leventhal (1965), who describe "the work of worrying"; a form of inner preparation for imminent trauma. Recent research on non-clinical populations is consistent with a functional account of worry. For example, Davey, Hampton, Farrell & Davidson (1992) have demonstrated that worrying is associated with problem-focused coping strategies and an information-seeking coping style.

Perhaps the most distinctive feature of worry is its narrative quality. Borkovec and colleagues originally described worry as a "chain of thoughts and images" (Borkovec et al., 1983; Borkovec, Metzger & Pruzinsky, 1986), usually linked by conditional propositions (i.e. "What if? . . . then" statements). Worry is not simply a string of negative and largely automatic thoughts but a dynamic process in which themes develop and are duly elaborated. Schonpflug (1989) has suggested that worries can be analysed in a similar way to stories, and proposes that the technique of "story representation" should be adopted for this purpose. He suggests that three formal features determine the structure of worry plots: (i) time perspective, (ii) branching, and (iii) concreteness. Moreover, he makes a distinction between condensed and elaborated stories. Condensed stories can be very brief (e.g. "A truck will hit me"), providing a means of including "fleeting" worries within his system of analysis. Although the narrative quality of worry has been described in the literature, there have been no attempts to establish its existence in a systematic way using self-report measures.

The remainder of this chapter reports the results of a preliminary investigation into the phenomenology of worrying in a non-clinical population. When studying a relatively undocumented psychological phenomenon, it is wise to investigate its normal parameters first. Without doing so it is virtually impossible to elucidate the important processes that contribute to the development of an abnormal manifestation. Even though the present study focuses on non-pathological worry, comparisons between "normal" high and low worriers are reported. It may be the case that continuities exist between non-clinical and clinical populations. If a dimensional model of psychopathology is endorsed, then inferences with respect to the phenomenology of worry within GAD can be made with some legitimacy.

METHOD

Subjects

One hundred and twenty-eight subjects took part in the study. Fifty-two were male (40.6%) and 76 female (59.4%). Eighty-one (65.3%) subjects were undergraduates. Forty-seven (36.7%) subjects were largely in employment but attending an undergraduate summer school. Ages for the total sample ranged from 18 to 59; however, 58.6% of the sample were aged 22 years or less. Seventy per cent of the sample were single, 5% divorced, and 25% married.

Procedure

Each subject completed the Penn State Worry Questionnaire (PSWQ) (Meyer, Miller, Metzger & Borkovec, 1990) and the Worry Domains Questionnaire (WDQ) (Tallis, Eysenck & Mathews, 1992). In addition, each subject completed a 56 item questionnaire designed to elicit information on the phenomenology of worry. The majority of questions required answers in the form of ratings on 0–8 point scales or endorsement of a given statement given a multiple choice. However, 10 questions required subjects to provide answers in their own words. The purpose of these questions was to gather qualitative information that would supplement responses given on 0–8 point scales. Qualitative data were analysed in two ways: an arbitrary method of categorisation or factor analysis. Arbitrary categorisation was undertaken in the following way. If any one subject produced two responses that might be included in the same category, only one response was recorded. However, if a single response could legitimately be placed in more than one category then this was done. Any ambiguous responses were omitted. Only the most salient features of this analysis are reported with respect to most frequently endorsed categories. When factor analysis was considered appropriate, qualitative data were condensed into questionnaires, where each item could be rated on a Likert-type scale. These questionnaires were distributed to different student populations, and data matrices subjected to factor analysis. A relatively large number of subjects did not complete qualitative sections of the phenomenology questionnaire (mostly between 25% and 50% of the total sample).

The phenomenology questionnaire provided information with respect to the following areas.

1   Self-perceived worry status
2   The content of worry
3   Frequency and duration of worry
4   The formal qualities of worry (e.g. narrative)
5   The precipitants of worry (e.g. environmental triggers)
6   The temporal focus of worry (i.e. past, present, future) and associated mood disturbance
7   Perceived justification and subsequent accuracy of worry
8   Acceptability of worry
9   Uncontrollability of worry, control strategies and their consequences
10   Negative consequences of worry (e.g. work impairment, health impact)
11   Positive consequences: perceived function and adaptivity
12   Behavioural concomitants of worry
13   Coping style

14 Exacerbating and associated factors
15 Meta-worry (i.e. worry about worry)

It should be noted that the above scheme is not arbitrary and was devised in order to investigate issues and phenomena previously discussed in the worry literature. It is impossible to mention all of the studies which provided a rationale for this scheme; however, the reader is referred to the discussion section of this chapter where some of the relevant studies are cited with respect to our results.

RESULTS

The number of missing cases for questions rated on 0–8 point scales was small, mostly between two and seven. The maximum number of missing cases was 13.

Questionnaire Measures

The mean WDQ and PSWQ scores were 29.40 (SD 12.97) and 44.07 (SD 12.56) respectively.

Self-perceived Status

Subjects were requested to indicate on a 0–8 point scale the degree to which they would describe themselves as worriers. The scale ranged from "Not at all" to "Always". The mean for the sample was 3.06 (2.22), which falls between value labels of "Rarely" and "Sometimes". The frequency histogram generated from these data was skewed favouring relatively low self-perceived worry status. For example, 54.8% of the sample endorsed values including and between "Not at all" and "Rarely" on the scale. Only 11.9% of subjects endorsed values in the range corresponding with "Definitely" to "Always".

Self-perceived worry status was significantly correlated ($p < .001$) with the WDQ ($r = .51$) and PSWQ ($r = .70$) measures.

The Content of Worry

Respondents were asked to write down (i) their most frequent and (ii) their most upsetting worries. "Most frequent" worries could be divided into two superordinate categories, those that were self-relevant (i.e. of direct personal concern) and those that were self-irrelevant (e.g. environmental or altruistic concerns). Percentages were calculated using the total number of individual endorsements as the base. Only 2% of worries were not directly relevant to respondents. The most frequently endorsed themes were those pertinent to competence at work (17%), academic performance (11%), health issues (10%), financial circumstances (10%), and intimate relationships (9%). Clearly the conspicuous presence of "academic" worries reflects the composition of the sample. All of the "most upsetting" worries were self-relevant; however, fewer were volunteered than above. The most frequently endorsed themes were those pertinent to intimate relationships (20%), physical threats, for example accidents (18%), death of self or significant others (17%), and health issues (15%).

Frequency and Duration of Worry

Frequency. Subjects were asked to endorse statements reflecting varying frequencies of the occurrence of worry ranging from "I never worry" to "I worry continuously"; 19.4% suggested that they worried "Maybe once every 2 or 3 days". The next most endorsed statement was "About once a month" (15.3%). However, collapsing categories revealed that 38% of the sample worried at least everyday and more.

Duration. Subjects were then given a multiple choice of 20 time durations ranging from "fleeting" to "more than 12 hours" on which to indicate the average length of a worry episode. The average duration of a worry episode for the sample was "five to 10 minutes'; 48.2% reported worrying between 1 and 30 minutes and 10.8% of the sample reported that worry could be fleeting. Similarly, 10.8% suggested that worry could last between 1 and 2 hours (see Figure 3.1).

The Formal Qualities of Worry

Thoughts vs. imagery. The difference between thoughts and images was described before subjects were requested to indicate the composition (with respect to these two components) of their worry on a 0–8 point scale. The mean was 2.39 (1.85), corresponding with "Mostly thoughts and some images" on the scale; 71.3% of the sample reported a predominance of thought, rather than images, with 14.8% reporting thoughts only. No respondents reported worry in the form of images only.

Figure 3.1   Duration of average worry episode

Narrative quality. Three descriptions of worry were given, each reflecting an increasing degree of narrative and elaboration. Subjects were requested to endorse the description which best reflected their experience of worry; 19.3% of respondents suggested that their worry consisted of a single repeated phrase whereas 33.6% reported that their worry consisted of a few phrases; however, 47.1% suggested that their worry consisted of several phrases resembling a story.

Sensitisation and habituation. Subjects were given a range of descriptions, each reflecting a different pattern of worrying with respect to sensitisation and habituation parameters. For example: "I start worrying, but my worry doesn't get better or worse", or, "I start worrying, it builds up for a while, but then usually gets considerably better". No clear pattern emerged from the frequency histogram generated by this data. However, the most endorsed statement was: "I start worrying, it builds up to a maximum level, but then it usually gets a little better" (27.2%).

The Precipitants of Worry

Time of day. Subjects were asked if there were particular times of the day in which they worried. Forty-two per cent were aware of specific times. These subjects were then given a multiple choice of 3-hour time periods (e.g. noon–3 p.m.) on which to indicate their principal worry times. The most endorsed time periods were 9 p.m. to midnight (32.8%) and midnight to 3.00 a.m. (25.9%: Figure 3.2).

Location. Subjects were asked to describe the location where they worried most.

Responses could be divided into two superordinate categories: "at home" (65%) or "outside home" (35%). A number of locations were described outside the home, for example "at work", "at the dentists", and "while travelling"; however, no one location was endorsed particularly more than any other. Percentages were calculated using the total number of individual endorsements as the base. With respect to worry in the home, 57% of subjects endorsed the bedroom. Other locations were reported with low and approximately equal frequency. It is worth noting that many respondents stressed that worry was a solitary activity.

Situations. Subjects were requested to indicate on a 0–8 point scale the degree to which their worrying was triggered by particular events or people. A frequency histogram was skewed favouring environmental

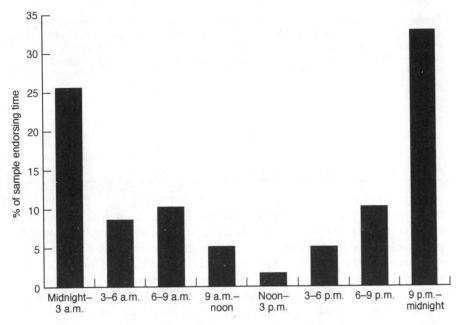

Figure 3.2   Respondents' most frequent worry times of the day

triggers; 71.4% of the sample suggested that worry was triggered by events or people, with 65.3% of these suggesting that this occurred from "sometimes" to "often".

Subjects were then asked to describe the situations that most often triggered worry. Percentages were calculated using the total number of individual endorsements as the base. The most endorsed situations were social situations (20%), situations at work (14%), relationship situations (12%) and academic situations (11%). The presence of academic situations clearly reflects the composition of the sample. Other situations were varied (e.g. "travelling", "new situation") with uniformly low levels of endorsement.

The Temporal Focus of Worry and Associated Mood Disturbance

Subjects were requested to indicate the temporal focus of worry on a percentage scale, and then to rate on 0–8 point scales associated "depression" and "anxiety/tension". The mean percentage estimates for past, present, and future concerns were 27.94%, 49.60%, and 38.95% respectively. Results are displayed in Table 3.1. It was predicted that worry over

Table 3.1   Temporal focus of worry and associated mood disturbance. Subjects were requested to indicate the temporal focus of worry on a percentage scale, and then to rate on 0–8 point scales associated "depression" and "anxiety/tenstion". Standard deviations accompanying mood scale means are in parenthesis

	Temporal focus		
	Past	Present	Future
Mean % estimates	27.94%	49.60%	38.95%
Depression	2.96 (2.03)	3.09 (1.79)	2.66 (1.92)
Anxiety/tension	2.51 (1.83)	3.66 (1.88)	3.17 (1.87

past events would be associated with more depression than worry over expected events. Conversely, worry about future events was predicted to be associated with more anxiety/tension than worry about past events. Although the data are consistent with predictions, mean ratings cluster around 3 on the 0–8 point scales. This corresponds with a data point that is "more than slightly" but "less than definitely". Therefore worry-associated mood disturbance appears to be relatively minor in a non-clinical population.

Perceived Justification and Subsequent Accuracy of Worry

Response to real vs. imagined problems. Subjects were requested to indicate on a 0–8 point scale the degree to which they understood their worry to be a response to real problems as opposed to imagined. The frequency histogram generated from these data was skewed, favouring worrying as a response to real problems; 34.9% of respondents suggested that this was "sometimes" the case and 24.6% suggested that this was "often" the case. Less than 8.7% responded in such a way as to indicate that their worry was related to imaginary, or largely imaginary, problems.

Realistic vs. unrealistic worry. Subjects were requested to indicate on a 0–8 point scale the likelihood of worries about unpleasant events actually occurring. Only 3.2% believed that they worried about things which had no likelihood of occurring; 59.5% reported that their worry content reflected negative outcomes that were between "a little likely" and "quite likely" to happen.

Accuracy. Subjects were requested to indicate on a 0–8 point scale the degree to which past worries were accurate, with 0 representing outcomes "No where near as bad" as expected and 8 representing outcomes

"Much worse" than expected. The mean for the sample was 2.68 (1.70), corresponding roughly with "Not as bad as expected" on the scale (a data point endorsed by 40.5% of the sample). The frequency histogram was skewed favouring outcomes being less negative than expected; however, 12.7% claimed that their worry was accurate. Those who reported negative outcomes being worse than expected were in a very small minority.

The effect of worry on appraisal. Subjects were requested to indicate on a 0–8 point scale whether they thought that worrying made things seem worse than they actually were. Zero corresponded with "Strongly disagree" while "8" corresponded with "Strongly agree". The mean for the sample was 5.73 (1.66), representing "Agree" on the scale. Indeed, 67.6% of responders felt that worry had the effect of making things seem worse.

Acceptability of Worry

Subjects were required to rate the degree to which they found their worries unacceptable on a 0–8 point scale ranging from "Not at all unacceptable" to "Completely unacceptable". The frequency histogram generated for these data was skewed, favouring the general acceptability of worries. The mean for the sample was 2.08 (1.89), corresponding with only "A little unacceptable" on the scale; 44.7% of the sample reported feeling that their worries were within the range from "Not at all unacceptable" to only "A little unacceptable".

Uncontrollability of Worry, Control Strategies, and Their Consequences

Termination of worry. Subjects were required to indicate on a 0–8 point scale the frequency with which they attempted to stop a worry episode: the scale ranged from "Not at all" (0) to "Always" (8). The mean for the sample was 4.96 (1.99), falling between "Sometimes" and "Often". It is interesting to note that although 33.1% tried "Often" to stop themselves from worrying, as many as 20.2% only tried "Sometimes" and 13.7% never or "Rarely" attempted to stop.

Difficulty stopping. Subjects were required to rate the degree to which they found their worry difficult to stop on a 0–8 point scale ranging from "Not at all difficult" to "Extremely difficult". The mean for the sample was 2.68 (1.76), falling roughly between "Slightly difficult" and "Quite difficult" on the scale. The majority of the sample endorsed points between and including these value labels (61.4%). However, 7.3% had "No difficulty" stopping worry, while only 0.8% had "Extreme difficulty".

Control strategies. Subjects were asked to write in their own words what strategies they employed to stop worrying. Cognitive strategies were the most frequently endorsed, in particular "problem solving" (36%) and "distraction" (27%). A strategy within the problem-solving domain that featured quite significantly was attempting to impose a realistic perspective on worry content. "Relaxation" (9%) and "Talking to others" (10%) were the only other clearly discernable and cohesive strategies. The remaining strategies were varied (e.g. "crying", "sleeping", "praying") and showed low levels of endorsement.

The affective consequences of successful control. Subjects were required to indicate on a 0–8 point scale the degree to which successful termination of a worry episode resulted in increased discomfort. The value labels ranged from "Not at all" (0) to "Always" (8). The mean for the sample was 1.69 (1.85), corresponding with "Rarely" on the scale. However, 78.8% reported that termination of a worry episode never or only "Rarely" results in increased discomfort; 33.9% of these endorsed "Not at all".

Paradoxical effects of thought control. Subjects were asked if successful termination of a worry episode resulted in the return of worry at a later time (cf. Wegner, Schneider, Carter & White, 1987). Answers were requested on a 0–8 point scale ranging from "Not at all" to "Always". The mean of the sample was 4.20 (1.85) corresponding with "Sometimes" on the scale; 25% reported that terminated worries often return, and approximately 75% reported at least some degree of return.

Severity of rebound. Subjects were required to indicate on a 0–8 point scale the degree to which "rebound" worries were more troublesome, intrusive, or upsetting. The value labels ranged from "Not at all" (0) to "Always" (8). The mean for the sample was 2.56 (1.93), corresponding most closely with "Rarely" on the scale; 54.1% experienced returning worries as no more, or rarely more troublesome after termination of a worry episode. However, 18% suggested that returning worries could "Sometimes" be more upsetting. Only 10.7% found them "Often" to "Always" more upsetting.

Reparative and preventive behaviour. Subjects were given a description of reparative and preventive behaviour. Irrational and superstitious qualities were emphasised. It was necessary for subjects to indicate on a 0–8 point scale the degree to which they engaged in behaviours "to make things right" when worrying. Value labels ranged from "Not at all" (0) to "Always" (8). The mean for the sample was 2.00 (2.14) corresponding with "Rarely" on the scale. In terms of percentages, 63.7% reported no engagement or rare engagement in reparative and preventive behaviours; 39.5% described none at all.

Typology of reparative and preventive behaviour. Subjects who reported reparative and preventive behaviours in response to worry were asked to describe them. Again, irrational, superstitions and habitual qualities were stressed. It should be noted that a large number of respondents either interpreted this question literally with respect to superstitious practices, or simply reported unremarkable control strategies.

This latter group are not worthy of comment. A wide range of irrational reparative and preventive behaviours were reported. The majority simply reflected traditional superstitious practices (e.g. "touching wood" (23.3% for the sub-sample), "use of lucky charms" (17%), and "crossing fingers" (7%)). However, several individual respondents reported habits that were clearly of a more obsessional nature (e.g. "not saying things to tempt fate", "adding up numbers", "throwing pen in the air several times", "having a bath", "changing coats"). Nevertheless, it should be recognised that this latter group represented a tiny minority of the total sample (4%).

Efficacy of reparative and preventive behaviour. Subjects were required to indicate on a 0–8 point scale the degree to which reparative and preventive behaviours were effective, i.e. with respect to whether or not they made respondents feel any better. The mean for the sample was 3.47 (2.53), indicating that subjects felt "No different" after their behaviour was executed. The frequency histogram generated by this data did not show any marked trends; however, the most endorsed data point on the scale was 2, indicating that behaviours made respondents feel "A little better' (26.4%). Only 72 subjects responded to this question (56.25% of the total sample). It should be noted that qualitative descriptions of reparative and preventive behaviours suggest that these findings do not reflect the presence of obsessional rituals.

Duration of relief after reparative and preventive behaviour. Subjects were given a multiple choice of 20 time durations ranging from "fleeting" to "more than 12 hours" on which to indicate the average length of relief associated with reparative and preventive behaviour. The average duration of relief was "46 to 60 minutes". However, this data point was only endorsed by 10.5% of the sample. No clear trend emerged from inspection of the frequency histogram. However, 26.3% of respondents suggested that their behaviours could be effective in providing relief for 12 hours or more, whereas 10.5% suggested that effectiveness was fleeting. As suggested above, it is unclear whether the concept of irrational reparative and preventative behaviours was understood by the sample. No conclusions can be drawn with respect to the presence of obsessional phenomena.

Negative Consequences of Worry

Negative Consequences. Subjects were asked whether or not they felt that worrying made things worse in general: 71.1% thought that this was so. These responders were then asked to describe in their own words how worry made things worse. Responses were then placed on a 50 item Likert scale (0–5 point) type questionnaire. All synonyms were rejected. This was then distributed to a sample of 127 undergraduate students. Results were factor analysed using the SPSS pc Factor package. This analysis provided a four factor solution. Factor 1 accounted for 48.6% of the variance. It captured seven items reflecting themes of "Pessimism and negative outlook". The most discriminatory items were "Continued worry makes me lose track of all the good things that happen" (.77), "Worrying stops me living for the moment" (.73), and "I think about all the possible outcomes but I believe the worst scenario will happen causing me to have a negative attitude, diminished self-confidence and low self-esteem" (.67). Unfortunately this was the least semantically cohesive factor. Factor 2 accounted for 4.8% of the variance, and captured eight items, largely about "Problem exaggeration". The most discriminating items were "Worrying blows situations out of proportion" (.70), "Worrying exaggerates reality" (.65), and "Worrying puts things out of perspective" (.62). Factor 3 captured seven items and accounted for 3.9% of the variance. These items reflected the theme of "Performance disruption". The most discriminating items were "Worrying stalls decisive action" (.72), "Worrying stops me from thinking straight" (.66), and "Worrying stops me from dealing with certainsituations" (.66). Finally, Factor 4 accounted for 3.4% of the variance and captured six items. These were largely related to "Emotional discomfort". The most discriminating items were "Worrying makes me focus on the wrong things" (.62), "Worrying gets me worked up" (.61), and "worrying increases my anxiety" (.51). All items are shown in Table 3.2.

Impairment of everyday functioning. Subjects were required to rate the degree to which worrying caused impairment in three domains: work,

Table 3.2 Perceived costs of worrying. Items captured by Factors 1–4 (loadings > .45)

Factor 1 (48.6% of variance)

Pessimism and negative outlook

1. Continued worry makes me lose track of all good things that happen (.77).
2. Worrying stops me living for the moment (.73).
3. I think about all the possible outcomes but I believe the worst scenario will happen causing me to have a negative attitude, diminished self-confidence and low self-esteem (.67).
4. Worrying makes me expect the worst and therefore prevents me from solving the problem (.62).
5. Worrying distorts the problem I have so I am unable to solve it (.61).
6. Worry weakens me by affecting my levels of energy in response to those events that worry me (.57).
7. Deep down I know I do not need to worry that much but I can't help it (.53).

Factor 2 (4.8% of variance)

Problem exaggeration

1. Worrying blows situations out of proportion (.70).
2. Worrying exaggerates reality (.65).
3. Worrying puts things out of perspective (.62).
4. Problems are magnified when I dwell on them (.61).
5. Worrying makes me think things are getting on top of me (.60
6. I become paranoid when I worry (.57).
7. Worrying makes me obsessed with the problem and makes it worse (.56).
8. Worrying gives me a pessimistic and fatalistic outlook (.54).

Factor 3 (3.9% of variance)

Performance disruption

1. Worrying stalls decisive action (.72).
2. Worrying stops me from thinking straight (.66).
3. Worrying stops me from dealing with certain situations (.66).
4. Worrying obscures my thoughts (.55).
5. Worrying causes depression therefore making it harder to concentrate and get on with things (.55).
6. Worry decreases my self-confidence (.53).
7. Worrying increases my anxiety and so decreases my performance (.52).

Factor 4 (3.4% of variance)

Emotional discomfort

1. Worry makes me focus on the wrong things (.62).
2. Worrying gets me worked up (.61).
3. Worrying increases my anxiety (.51)
4. Worrying causes me stress (.50).
5. Worrying makes me tense and irritable (.46).
6. Worrying makes me nervous and irrational (.45).

domestic and social/leisure. A 0–8 point scale was used for each, ranging from "Not at all" (0) to "Severe" (8). All three frequency histograms were skewed favouring "Slight" to "No impairment", with 62.1%, 75.4%, and

54.8% of respondents endorsing this range for work, domestic and social domains respectively.

The effect of worry on health. Subjects were requested to indicate on a 0–8 point scale the degree to which excessive worry had caused their health to suffer. The mean for the sample was 4.54 (2.19), between the "Neither agree nor disagree" and "Agree" value labels. The frequency histogram was skewed favouring the belief that worry does indeed have an adverse effect on health; 47.2% of the sample responded within the range "Agree" to "Strongly agree".

Nature of health problems. Subjects were then requested to list health problems that they had experienced in the past which were associated with excessive worry. Percentages were calculated using the total number of symptom endorsements as the base. The most frequently reported problems were anergia (19%), headaches (12%), insomnia (11%), colds (9%), loss of appetite/weight loss (8%), and stomach ache (7%). A wide range of other problems were reported (e.g. dermatological, respiratory); however, these received relatively few endorsements.

Positive Consequences: Perceived Function and Adaptivity

Worry as problem-solving. Subjects were required to indicate on a 0–8 point scale the degree to which they believed that when worrying, they were in fact problem-solving. Value labels ranged from "Not at all" (0) to "Always" (8). The mean for the sample was 5.02 (1.84), falling between "Sometimes" and "Definitely" on the scale. It is interesting to note that 46% of respondents suggested that worrying was an attempt to solve problems, occupying the range between "Definitely" and "Always" on the scale. Inspection of the frequency histogram for this data is clearly skewed favouring worry as an attempt to engage in problem-solving.

The efficacy of worry as problem solving. Subjects were required to indicate on a 0–8 point scale the frequency with which worrying resulted in the production of "a reasonable" solution to a recognised problem. Value labels ranged from "Not at all" (0) to "Always" (8). The mean for the sample was 4.66 (1.32), falling roughly between "Sometimes" and "Definitely" on the scale; 83.3% of the sample endorsed value labels in this range. The frequency histogram generated for these data is clearly skewed favouring the efficacy of worry as a problem-solving activity. Only 0.8% suggested that their worry was totally unproductive and only 6.3% of the sample endorsed data points in the "Rarely" to "Not at all" productive range.

The nature of helpful worry. Subjects were asked to explain how worry was a helpful process, in particular with respect to solving problems: responses were then placed on a 50 item Lickert scale (0–5 point) type questionnaire. All synonyms were rejected. This was then distributed to a sample of 86 undergraduate students. Note that this sample was different to that used for the negative consequence factor analysis. Results were factor analysed using the SPSS pc Factor package. This analysis provided a two factor solution. Factor 1 accounted for 42.6% of the variance. It captured six items reflecting worry as a source of "Motivation". The most discriminatory items were "Worrying acts as a stimulant" (.71), "Worrying challenges and motivates me, without them I would not achieve much in life" (.71), and "In order to get something done I have to worry about it" (.69). Factor 2 accounted for 6.9% of the variance and captured six items. These items reflected "Preparatory and analytic thinking". The most discriminating items were "Worrying makes me reflect on life by asking questions I might not usually ask when happy" (.68), "Worrying gives me the opportunity to analyse situations and work out the pros and cons" (.64), and "Worrying starts off a process of preparing me to meet new situations" (.59). All items are shown in Table 3.3.

Table 3.3 Perceived benefits of worrying. Items captured by Factors 1 and 2 (loadings > .5)

Factor 1 (42.6% of variance)

Motivation

1. Worrying acts as a stimulant (.71).
2. Worrying challenges and motivates me, without them I would not achieve much in life (.71).
3. In order to get something done I have to worry about it (.69).
4. Worrying increases my awareness thus increasing my performance (.62).
5. Worrying makes me do things by increasing my adrenaline levels (.57).
6. Worrying clarifies thoughts and concentration (.51).

Factor 2 (6.9% of variance)

Preparatory and analytic thinking

1. Worrying makes me reflect on life by asking questions I might not usually ask when happy (.68).
2. Worrying gives me the opportunity to analyse situations and work out the pros and cons (.64).
3. Worrying starts off as a process of preparing me to meet new situations (.59).
4. Worrying allows me to work through the worst that can happen, so when it doesn't happen things are better (.57).
5. Worrying adds to the problems and as such leads me to explore different possibilities (.53).
6. By worrying I reorganise and plan my time better—if I stick to it, it makes me feel better, if I don't I worry more (.51).

Insoluble problems. Subjects were requested to indicate on a 0–8 point scale the frequency with which they worried about insoluble problems (e.g. death, serious illness), ranging from "Not at all" (0) to "Always" (8). The mean for the sample was 3.06 (2.22), falling between "Rarely" and "Sometimes". Although 25.4% endorsed the "Sometimes" value label, the frequency histogram was skewed suggesting relatively rare worry about insoluble problems.

Behavioural Concomitants of Worry

Subjects were asked to describe in their own words any behaviour that they engaged in while worrying. A few examples were given as a rough guide (e.g. pacing, smoking and biting lower lip). Percentages were calculated using the total number of individual endorsements as the base. A broad class of mildly self-injurious behaviours accounted for most of the responses (36%). These included scratching, biting, picking, and pulling various parts of the body. However, "nail biting" was the most significant activity in this subgroup (17% of responses for this section). These behaviours are perhaps closely related to a second cluster of items reflecting physical restlessness, in particular, pacing and general fidgeting (15%). A group of addictive or appetitive behaviours (i.e. smoking, drinking and eating) also received a large number of endorsements (29%). A few subjects reported more adaptive behavioural responses (e.g. relaxation, talking to others, reading); however, these seem to reflect control strategies rather than immediate behavioural consequences.

Coping Style

Information seeking coping style. Subjects were asked to indicate on a 0–8 point scale the degree to which they attempted to find out as much as possible about worrisome problems. The scale ranged from "Not at all" (0) to "Always" (8). The mean for the sample was 5.37 (1.76), falling between "Sometimes" and "Definitely"; 89.7% of subjects endorsed data points within the range from "Sometimes" to "Always".

Avoidance coping. Subjects were required to indicate on a 0–8 point scale the degree to which they avoided anything that reminded them of a worrisome problem. The mean for the sample was 3.09 (1.96), falling between "Rarely" and "Sometimes". The frequency histogram generated from these data did not indicate the presence of significant levels of avoidance coping. In fact, 41.3% of the sample suggested that they did not avoid, or only rarely avoided, worry relevant information. However, 25.4% did endorse the "Sometimes" value label.

Worry as active prevention. Subjects were asked to indicate on a 0–8 point scale the degree to which their worry was an attempt to prevent something bad from happening. The mean for the sample was 4.03 (2.19), corresponding with the "Sometimes" value label. The frequency histogram showed no discernable pattern; roughly equal numbers agreed and disagreed.

Exacerbating and Associated Factors

Uncertainty of outcome. Subjects were required to rate on a 0–8 point scale the degree to which uncertainty of outcome was a feature of their worry. The scale ranged from "Not at all" (0) to "Always" (8). The mean for the sample was 4.76 (1.80) corresponding to a value between "Sometimes" and "Definitely"; 31.5% of the sample endorsed the value corresponding with the value label "Sometimes". However, 85.5% of the sample endorsed values ranging from "Sometimes" to "Always", skewing the frequency histogram with respect to the presence of uncertainty.

Personal relevance. Subjects were requested to indicate on a 0–8 point scale the degree to which they worried more about things if they were of greater personal relevance. An example was given of "job" as opposed to "starvation in the third world". The scale ranged from "Not at all" to "Always". The mean for the sample was 6.06 (1.63) corresponding with "Definitely" on the scale, which was also the most endorsed value label (47.6%); 81.8% of respondents endorsed values within the value-label range of "Definitely" to "Always", skewing the distribution of the frequency histogram in favour of personal relevance.

Imminence. Subjects were requested to indicate on a 0–8 point scale the reliability with which imminence of anticipated events increased worry. The scale ranged from "Not at all" (0) to "Always" (8). The mean for the sample was 5.33 (1.96), falling between "Sometimes" and "Definitely" on the scale; 53.2% of the sample endorsed values including and between "Definitely" and "Always". Only 9.5% of the sample endorsed values from "Not at all" to "Rarely".

Indecisiveness and doubt. Subjects were requested to indicate on a 0–8 point scale the degree to which their worry is usually associated with indecision and doubt. The scale ranged from "Not at all" (0) to "Always" (8). The mean for the sample was 4.34 (1.90) corresponding with

"Sometimes", a value label endorsed by 31.5% of respondents. However, 76.6% of the sample endorsed values including and between "Sometimes" and "Always", skewing the frequency histogram in favour of the presence of indecision and doubt.

Meta-worry

Worry about not worrying. Subjects were requested to indicate on a 0–8 point scale the degree to which they worried about not worrying. The scale ranged from "Not at all" (0) to "Always" (8). The mean for the sample was 1.21 (1.83), a data point between the value labels "Not at all" and "Rarely"; 59.5% of the sample suggested that they never worry about not worrying. Indeed, 79.4% of the sample endorsed values including and between "Not at all" and "Rarely".

THE CHARACTERISTICS OF HIGH AND LOW WORRIERS

In addition to examining the characteristics of the total sample, a series of pairwise comparisons, between high and low worriers, were undertaken with respect to quantitative data. The two groups were determined according to a median split using WDQ scores. The low worry group were those subjects scoring 27 and below, while the high worry group were those subjects scoring 28 and above. The WDQ was favoured over the PSWQ as it is primarily a measure of non-pathological worry and is associated with more of the adaptive components of worry (Davey, 1993). A median split and pairwise comparisons were also conducted on the sample using the PSWQ. However, fewer significant differences between groups were found using this method and all of these were captured by the WDQ analysis. There was only one significant difference between groups captured by the PSQW analysis that failed to reach significance in the WDQ analysis; this was with respect to avoidance coping ($p < .001$). Inspection of means showed that PSWQ high worriers "Sometimes" avoided information relevant to their worries, whereas PSWQ low worriers "Rarely" did so.

Forty-six pairwise comparisons were undertaken; because of the statistical problems associated with establishing significance using multiple t-tests, a conservative alpha level of $p < .002$ was determined. All tests were two-tailed. The maximum number of cases missing for any single comparison was 16; however, most analyses rarely exceeded the loss of five or six cases.

Self-perceived Worry Status

High and low worry groups differed significantly on this measure ($p <$ .001).

Frequency and Duration of Worry

Frequency. High and low worriers differed significantly with respect to the frequency of self-reported worry episodes ($p <$ .001). The mean for high worriers corresponded with the value label "About once a day", whereas the mean for low worriers corresponded with the value label "About once a week".

Temporal Focus and Associated Mood Disturbance

High worriers suffered significantly more mood disturbance (depression and anxiety/tension) than low worriers with respect to worrying with past, present, and future temporal foci ($p <$ .001).

Uncontrollability of Worry, Control Strategies and their Consequences

Difficulty stopping. High worriers reported significantly more difficulty stopping worry compared to low worriers ($p <$ .001). The mean for high worriers corresponded with the value label "Quite", whereas the mean for low worriers corresponded with the value label "Slight".

Paradoxical effects of thought control. Higher worriers reported significantly more return of worry after successful termination than low worriers ($p <$ .001). Means corresponded with value labels "Sometimes" and roughly between "Sometimes" and "Often" for low and high worriers respectively. The PSQ did not reach significance on this comparison.

Negative Consequences of Worry

Impairment of everyday functioning. High worriers differed from low worriers significantly ($p <$ .001) with respect to perceived impairment in work, domestic and social domains.

The effect of worry on health. High worrier and low worriers differed significantly ($p < .001$) with respect to perceived negative consequences of excessive worry on health. The PSWQ did not show significant differences on this comparison.

Exacerbating and Associated Factors

Indecisiveness and doubt. High worriers reported more indecision and doubt while worrying compared to low worriers ($p < .002$). The PSWQ did not show significant differences on this comparison.

DISCUSSION

It is now possible to provide a description of the phenomenological features of non-pathological worry. Worry content tends to focus on everyday problems arising in a number of domains. These domains largely correspond with those already evident in content based worry measures (see Tallis, Davey & Bond, Chapter 12, this volume). Particularly upsetting worries tend to focus on uncontrollable outcomes (e.g. accident and death). For a large percentage of the normal population, worry is a relatively routine activity, occurring more or less every day. The average worry episode lasts between 5 and 10 minutes; however, roughly 50% of individuals will worry, on average, within the range 1–30 minutes. Approximately a third of respondents describe an increase and decrease of worry activity comparable with the sensitisation and habituation curve described in the anxiety literature (Stone & Borkovec, 1975). Although some theorists have attributed the self limitation of worry to habituation effects (Borkovec et al., 1983), it may well be the case that 30 minutes is a sufficient time in which to reach an acceptable solution to problems causing worry.

Worry takes the form of thoughts, rather than images, and follows a predominantly narrative course. Worry is most likely to occur in either the latter part of the evening or the early hours of the morning. Subsequently, many individuals worry in bed. This might be attributable to a lack of competing stimuli (Borkovec et al., 1986) and further underscores the well attested relationship between worry and insomnia (Borkovec, 1979).

Most respondents suggest that worry is triggered, to a greater or lesser extent, by either events or people. Conflict at work, and conflict within intimate relationships, are particularly pertinent triggers.

Most worry content is related to current concerns; however, the temporal focus of worry can also be past and future. This is slightly inconsistent with earlier work suggesting that worry content is primarily concerned with future events (Borkovec et al., 1983). Perhaps a distinction needs to be made between proximal and distal future events for data to be meaningfully interpreted. If worry is considered a response to perceived threat (Mathews, 1990) then worry must always be oriented towards future events; threats, by definition, are always located in the future. Clearly, when respondents suggest that most worry content is focused on events "happening in the present", they do not mean that their worry is focused on events happening in the "here and now". It is far more likely that a present temporal focus refers to ongoing problems and their immediate negative consequences than events expected to occur some distance in the future (e.g. an exam in a year's time). Irrespective of temporal focus, worry is always associated with a slight to moderate degree of mood disturbance.

Worry is considered a response to real rather than imaginary problems. Moreover, expected negative events are viewed as having a moderate likelihood of actual occurrence. However, worry has the effect of inflating the perceived magnitude of expected negative events. This is consistent with laboratory evidence demonstrating how cognitive rehearsal of an aversive unconditioned stimulus (UCS) can influence the strength and evaluation of UCS representations (Jones & Davey, 1990).

Worries are largely ego-syntonic; nearly 50% of the sample reporting only negligible levels of unacceptability. Although worries are mostly acceptable, about a third of the sample attempted to terminate worry episodes "often". However, an equal number of respondents only attempted to stop worrying "Sometimes" or "Rarely". If a decision is made to "stop worrying", this may prove moderately difficult to achieve. However, only a tiny proportion of the sample reported extreme difficulty. Cognitive strategies such as problem-solving and distraction are common means of worry control.

Successful termination of a worry episode rarely results in affective disturbance; however, the majority of respondents report at least some degree of return of worry content. It is impossible, given present data, to determine whether the return of worry is best attributed to a suppression/rebound effect (cf. Wegner, Schneider, Carter & White, 1987), or more simply, the reallocation of attention to an unnresolved problem.

Previously terminated worries are not associated with increased levels of intrusiveness or affect. Moreover, only a minority of individuals engage in reparative and preventive behaviour as a result of worrying. This is inconsistent with the results of Craske et al. (1989), who suggest that a very high proportion of normal worriers (70.6%) engage in corrective, preventative, or ritualistic actions in response to worry. There is no obvious reason for this discrepancy, save the different demand effects associated with two different questionnaires. The minority of respondents admitting ritualistic type behaviours in the present study reported that they were effective to the extent that they afforded moderate levels of relief. However, the duration of this relief was extremely variable, ranging from minutes to hours. It is important to note that the reparative and preventive behaviours described by respondents were not comparable to obsessional type behaviours.

Worry causes slight impairment of everyday functioning in work, domestic, and social domains. Further, most individuals have a tendency to believe that excessive worry has a deleterious effect on health. This is consistent with other work (Hodgson, Tallis & Davey, submitted), which has demonstrated a relatively close association between excessive worry and psychological health status, independent of somatic anxiety, depression, and other related phenomena (e.g. negative life experiences). Inspection of qualitative data shows that worry can be associated with a number of negative psychological and somatic sequelae relevant to an individual's health status. Fatigue, headaches, stomach aches, colds and insomnia are problems particularly well represented. It is interesting to note that awareness of tension and upset stomach were found to be more associated with worry than other somatic variables by Borkovec et al. (1983).

Factor analysis of items reflecting the negative consequences of worry produced a four factor solution: "Pessimism and negative outlook", "Problem exaggeration", "Performance disruption" and "Emotional discomfort". Unfortunately, the first factor, which accounted for most of the variance, was not as semantically cohesive as the other factors.

The immediate behavioural consequences of worry involve a general state of restlessness, characterised by mild self-injurious behaviours. There are three ways in which these behaviours might be explained. Firstly, they may represent an attempt to control worry through self-inflicted pain. The use of pain to halt uncontrollable cognition has several clinical antecedents in the obsessional literature. For example faradic stimulation (Kenny, Solyom & Solyom, 1973), and thought stopping procedures (Stern, 1970). Secondly, these behaviours could be considered as self-inflicted punishment. Indeed, the psychoanalytic formulation of worry suggests that the worry process is an attempt at redemption through suffering in the form of self-punishment (Challman, 1974). Finally, mild self-injurious behaviours might represent the release of fixed action patterns triggered in anxiety states. This notion is comparable to the ethological account of obsessional behaviour. For example, Rapoport (1990) suggests that excessive washing represents the inappropriate activation of grooming programmes in the basal ganglia. Clearly, the endorsement of any of these putative explanations will very much depend on the individual's theoretical orientation, be it cognitive, analytic, or biological. Notwithstanding the exigencies of theoretical prejudice, the fact that so many respondents endorsed mildly self-injurious behaviours is intriguing.

Although worry is associated with several negative consequences, it is also perceived, at least in part, as having an adaptive function. It is associated with problem-solving and the vast majority of individuals (83.3%) suggest that worry episodes can produce reasonable solutions. Indeed, inspection of qualitative data shows that worry can help individuals to focus on problems and generate alternative approaches to problem solution. The adaptive component of worry is further underscored by the fact that respondents rarely avoid reminders of problems, favouring instead the gathering of relevant information. This is consistent with previous work showing non-pathological worrying to be associated with problem-focused coping strategies and an information seeking cognitive style (Davey, Hampton, Farrell & Davidson, 1992). Problem-focused coping is exercised appropriately, in that relatively few individuals worry over insoluble problems such as death. Perhaps the most important aspect of worry revealed in the present study is its ability to motivate individuals. Factor analysis of qualitative data produced a grouping of items clearly linked by a recognition of worry as a motivating force. Of less importance, but nevertheless relevant, was a second factor comprised of items stressing the preparatory and analytic function of worry. Taken together, the motivational and preparatory functions of worry share much in common with Janis's (1958) early concept of the "Work of worrying".

A number of general features of worry discussed in the literature were found to be consistent with self report. The majority of individuals worry when an outcome is uncertain (cf. Borkovec et al., 1983) and worry is likely to increase with respect to the imminence of an expected negative event and its personal relevance (cf. Tallis & Eysenck, cited in Eysenck, 1992; Tallis, Eysenck & Mathews, 1991b). Finally, worry is strongly associated with the subjective feelings of indecision and doubt (cf. Tallis, Eysenck, & Mathews, 1991a; Tallis & de Silva, 1992). The present sample rarely worried about "not worrying".

When the total sample was divided into high and low worriers, some interesting differences emerged. High worriers experienced significantly more worry episodes which, once started, are perceived as more difficult to terminate. This suggests that high worriers experience episodes of longer duration than low worriers. Although the duration comparison did not prove significant, it certainly approached significance ($p = .004$). High worriers report a greater likelihood of worries returning after the successful termination of a worry episode compared to low worriers. This suggests the presence of a suppression/rebound effect or, perhaps more plausibly, the failure to achieve "closure" after attempted problem-solving. High worriers experience a greater degree of mood disturbance when worrying compared with low worriers and the act of worrying is more strongly associated with indecision and doubt. It is possible that these mood and trait variables have a disruptive effect on problem-solving and thus maintain the worry state (cf. Tallis, Eysenck & Mathews, 1991a; see Davey, Chapter 2, this volume). High worriers experience a greater degree of impairment with respect to everyday functioning compared with low worriers and perceive themselves as suffering more ill effects with respect to psychological and physical health.

As suggested in the introduction, the differences found between non-clinical high and low worriers may give some indication as to what variables are important with respect to the development of pathological worry. Notwithstanding the very real problems of discontinuities between clinical and non-clinical populations, the comparison analysis between high and low worriers deserves some comment.

The significant differences emerging with respect to frequency, impact on health, and interference with everyday functioning might be considered as secondary to poor cognitive control and personality traits such as indecisiveness. Clearly, an inability to control worry will result in its more frequent occurrence and subsequent negative consequences. Similarly, indecision and doubtfulness might retard the selection of an appropriate coping strategy, block the progress of systematic problem-solving, and thus preserve the worry state (cf. Tallis, Eysenck & Mathews, 1991a). Unfortunately, both lack of cognitive control and indecisiveness might be attributed to mood differences between the two groups, thus compromising their explanatory value. In order to clarify mechanisms, a series of *post hoc* regression and partial correlation analyses were undertaken which are briefly reported here. Measures of depression and tension/anxiety associated with current worry were the independent mood variables, whereas worry status, determined by WDQ scores, represented the dependent variable. When entered initially, mood variables accounted for 29% of the WDQ variance (R Square $= .29$; $p < .0001$). However, degree of control accounted for an additional 10% of the WDQ variance when the effect of mood variables was partialled out ($r = .38$; $p < .0001$). The partial correlation employing indecision scores did not reach significance; however, a trend is clearly evident ($r = .17$; $p = .07$). From these analyses we can conclude that frequent worry and subsequent negative consequences are closely associated with mood disturbance. Nevertheless, an inability to exercise effective cognitive control strategies makes a significant contribution to determining worry status. These results bear interesting comparison with those of Craske et al. (1989), who found that GAD patients differed significantly from normal controls with respect to perceived control over worrying. Interestingly, the GAD group did not differ from the normal control group with respect to level of anxiety experienced while worrying, and level of anxiety experienced when attempting to resist worry. It is tentatively suggested that one of the critical differences between normal and pathological worry may be accounted for in terms of poor cognitive control strategies. This suggests that techniques employed to enhance thought control in patients suffering from obsessional thoughts (e.g. thought stopping, thought switching, thought control) might be usefully incorporated in worry management programmes for GAD patients.

REFERENCES

Barlow, D.H. (1988). *Anxiety and its Disorders*. New York, London. Guilford Press.
Beck, A.T. (1976). *Cognitive Therapy and the Emotional Disorders*. New York: International University Press.
Beech, H.R. (ed.) (1974). *Obsessional States*. London: Methuen.
Borkovec, T.D. (1979). Pseudo (experimental)-insomnia and idiopathic (objective) insomnia: theoretical and therapeutic issues. In H.J. Eysenck & S. Rachman (Eds.), *Advances in Behavior Research and Therapy*, pp. 27–55. London: Pergamon Press.
Borkovec, T.D., Metzger, R.L. & Pruzinsky, T. (1986). Anxiety, Worry, and the Self. In L. Hartman & K.R. Blankstein (Eds.), *Perception of Self in Emotional Disorder and Psychotherapy*. New York: Plenum Publishers.
Borkovec, T.D., Robinson, E., Pruzinsky, T. & DePree, J.A. (1983). Preliminary exploration of worry: some characteristics and processes. *Behaviour Research and Therapy*, **21**, 9–16.
Buccola, G. (1880). Les idées fixées et leurs conditions physiopathol. *Revue. Sper. Freniatria*, **6**, 155–181.
Challman, A. (1974). The empirical nature of worry. *American Journal of Psychiatry*, **131**(10), 1140–1141.
Craske, M., Rapee, R., Jackel, L. & Barlow, D. (1989). Qualitative dimensions of worry in DSM III-R generalised anxiety disorder subjects and nonanxious controls. *Behaviour Research and Therapy*, **27**, 397–402.
Davey, G.C.L. (1993). A comparison of three worry questionnaires. *Behaviour Research and Therapy*, **31**, 51–56.

Davey, G.C.L., Hampton, J., Farrell, J. & Davidson, S. (1992). Some characteristics of worrying: Evidence for worrying and anxiety as separate constructs. *Personality and Individual Differences*, **13**, 133–147.

Eysenck, M. (1992). *Anxiety: The Cognitive Perspective*. Hove, UK: LEA.

Fennell, M. (1989). Depression. In K. Hawton, P. Salkovskis, J. Kirk & D. Clark (Eds.) *Cognitive Behaviour Therapy for Psychiatric Problems*. Oxford: Oxford Medical Publications.

Hodgson, S., Tallis, F. & Davey, G.C.L. (Submitted). Worried sick: The relationship between worrying and psychological and physical health status.

Janis, I. (1958). *Psychological Stress*. New York: Wiley.

Janis, I. & Leventhal, H. (1965). Psychological aspects of physical illness and hospital care. In B. Wolman (Ed.), *Handbook of Clinical Psychology*. New York: McGraw-Hill.

Jones, T. & Davey, G.C.L. (1990). The effects of cues UCS rehearsal on the retention of differential "fear" conditioning: An experimental analogue of the "worry" process. *Behaviour Research and Therapy*, **28**, 159–164.

Kenny, F., Solyom, L. & Solyom, C. (1973). Faradic disruption of obsessive ideation in the treatment of obsessive neurosis. *Behavior Therapy*, **4**, 448–457.

Kovacs, M. & Beck, A.T. (1978). Maladaptive cognitive structures in depression. *Archives of General Psychiatry*, **135**, 525–533.

Mathews, A. (1990). Why worry? The cognitive function of anxiety. *Behaviour Research and Therapy*, **28**, 455–468.

Meyer, T., Miller, M., Metzger, R. & Borkovec, T.D. (1990). Development and validation of the Penn State Worry Questionnaire. *Behaviour Research and Therapy*, **28**, 487–495.

Monserrat-Esteve, S. (1971). Patologia Obsesiva, S. Monserrat-Esteve, J.M. Costa Molinari, and C. Ballus (ess), chap. 1, pp. 21, XI Congresso Nacional de Neuropsiquiatria, Graficasa, Malaga (Spain).

Rachman, S. (1973). Some similarities and differences between obsessional ruminations and morbid preoccupations. *Canadian Psychiatric Association Journal*, **18**, 71–73.

Rachman, S. (1981). Unwanted intrusive cognitions. *Advances in Behaviour Research and Therapy*, **3**, 89–99.

Rapoport, J. (1990). Obsessive compulsive disorder and basal ganglia dysfunction. *Psychological Medicine*, **20**, 465–469.

Schonpflug, W. (1989). Anxiety, worry, prospective orientation, and prevention. In C. Spielberger, I. Sarason and J. Strelau (Eds.), *Stress and Anxiety*, Vol. 12. Washington, DC: Hemisphere.

Stern, R. (1970). Treatment of a case of obsessional neurosis using thought-stopping technique. *British Journal of Psychiatry*, **117**, 441–442.

Stone, N.M. & Borkovec, T.D. (1975). The paradoxical effect of brief CS exposure on analogue phobic patients. *Behaviour Research and Therapy*, **13**, 51–54.

Tallis, F. & de Silva, P. (1992). Worry and obsessional symptoms: A correlational analysis. *Behaviour Research and Therapy*, **30**, 103–105.

Tallis, F., Eysenck, M.W. & Mathews, A. (1991a). Elevated evidence requirements and worry. *Personality and Individual Differences*, **12**, 21–27.

Tallis, F., Eysenck, M.W. & Mathews, A. (1991b). The role of temporal perspective and ego-relevance in the activation of worry structures. *Personality and Individual Differences*, **12**, 909–915.

Tallis, F., Eysenck, M.W. & Mathews, A. (1992). A questionnaire for the measurement of nonpathological worry. *Personality and Individual Differences*, **13**, 161–168.

Wegner, D., Schneider, D., Carter, S. & White, T. (1987). Paradoxical effects of thought suppression. *Journal of Personality and Social Psychology*, **53**, 5–13.

CHAPTER 4   Attention and the control of worry

*Adrian Wells**

Cognitive models of anxiety propose that dysfunctional patterns of thinking are involved in the maintenance of anxiety (Beck, 1976; Beck, Emery & Greenberg, 1985). These patterns of thinking are manifest, according to Beck (1976), at the surface level as negative automatic thoughts in the stream of consciousness. Worry, a variety of negative thinking, is a feature of a wide range of emotional disorders, and since the advent of DSM-III-R (American Psychiatric Association, 1987) it has become associated in particular with generalised anxiety disorder (GAD) of which it is a central feature. Specific models of the function and maintenance of worry have recently emerged such as those of Borkovec and colleagues (e.g. Borkovec & Inz, 1990) and of Tallis & Eysenck (cited in Eysenck, 1992). These approaches, presented in detail elsewhere in this volume, have begun to view worry in terms of a more general cognitive-processing framework. Borkovec, Shadick & Hopkins (1991) assert that worry serves an avoidance function by diverting attention from other forms of intrusive thought which may be more closely associated with somatic activation. However, it contributes significantly to the maintenance of anxiety. Worry is reinforced by its somatic-anxiety reducing effects and it is therefore difficult to change. It may also maintain anxiety by preventing emotional information from being fully processed because fear structures are not completely accessed. In addition to cognitive avoidance, Borkovec et al. (1991) also propose that worry serves to anticipate threat and enhance avoidance of threats which may be encountered in the future. Tallis & Eysenck (cited in Eysenck, 1992) propose that worry acts as an alarm by introducing threat material into consciousness. It also re-presents threat related thoughts into awareness which serves to prompt the individual. Finally, worry allows the individual to anticipate future threats and it therefore serves a preparation function.

*University of Oxford, UK

Worrying: Perspectives on Theory, Assessment and Treatment. Edited by G.C.L. Davey and F. Tallis.
© 1994 John Wiley & Sons Ltd.

The impetus for this chapter is the belief that advances in the study, theory and treatment of worry are likely to arise from a more detailed information-processing analysis of the phenomenon. An initial problem for such an analysis is taxonomic. There is no single class of cognitive event in anxiety but several which may not function in the same way. Part of this chapter, therefore concerns the discrimination between worry and other varieties of thought in anxiety. For the type of analysis proposed, an exploration of the relationship between attention and worry may be particularly useful for locating worry in an information-processing framework, for determining which characteristics, if any, differentiate between worry and other forms of negative thought, and for conceptualising the control of worry in information processing.

The concept of attention is broad, but it has been most commonly used to refer to selectivity of information processing and the degree of dependence of processing on conscious effort (e.g. Posner & Snyder, 1975; Kahneman, 1973). At any one time an individual is bombarded with external and internal information, and there are limits in the amount of information which can be simultaneously processed; only some information is processed and allowed into consciousness. Such limits have led to the use of a "capacity" metaphor to account for attention phenomena, in which attention has been viewed as a limited processing resource required for some cognitive operations.

Clearly some processing activities can be combined without encountering problems of limited processing capacity or attention. In this context cognition has been classified in terms of "automatic" or "controlled" processing (Posner & Snyder, 1975). Generally, automatic processes occur without intention, unconsciously, rapidly, and do not interfere with ongoing cognitive activity. These processes are viewed as requiring few attentional resources. Controlled processing in contrast is synonymous with conscious attention, it requires large quantities of resources (Shiffrin & Schneider, 1977; Schneider & Shiffrin, 1977) and is typically applied to activities which are not overly practised and involve more complex cognitive operations. Schneider, Dumais & Shiffrin (1984) propose that controlled processing is driven by a deliberate plan or strategy, whereas automatic processing is reflexively triggered by fixed inputs. In daily life, the focus of processing shifts between and combines levels frequently. Stimuli continuously trigger automatic processing, but controlled processing will be initiated when a breakdown in automatic performance is detected or when a stimulus of special importance is encountered. This differentiation between levels of processing can be problematic, however. For example, the criteria specified can dissociate. Processing activities commonly considered to be involuntary can interfere with performance

(Paap & Ogden, 1981), and automatic processing can be affected by the presence of other stimuli (Kahneman & Treisman, 1984) suggesting some reliance on attention.

VARIETIES OF THOUGHT IN ANXIETY

Worry is one of several labels which has been applied to the content of attention in anxiety. Other labels such as appraisal (Lazarus & Folkman, 1984), self-statements (Ellis, 1962), negative automatic thoughts (NATs; Beck, 1976), intrusive thoughts (Rachman, 1981) and catastrophic misinterpretations (Clark, 1986) dominate different anxiety literatures. It is not clear if these labels refer to a single or limited class of cognitive events, or the extent to which these cognitions are discriminable.

Experimental and descriptive analyses support at least some distinction between particular varieties of thought in anxiety. Moreover, it may be useful to make such a distinction because different types of thought may not be related to anxiety in the same way (e.g. Borkovec & Inz, 1990). In this section distinctions between worry and automatic thoughts and worry and intrusive thoughts are considered.

In early work Borkovec, Robinson, Prunzinsky & DuPree (1983) defined worry as: "a chain of thoughts and images, negatively affect-laden and relatively uncontrollable" (p. 10). The worry process was viewed as a problem-solving activity used in circumstances where outcomes are uncertain but contain the possibility of negative outcomes. The work of Borkovec and colleagues has evolved more recently to suggest that worry is predominantly a verbal conceptual activity which is used by some individuals, especially patients with generalised anxiety disorder, as a coping strategy (Borkovec, Shadick & Hopkins, 1991).

Beck (1967) first used the term "automatic thoughts" to refer to the thoughts which seemed to characterise consciousness in depressed patients. This term has also been used to refer to thinking in anxiety (Beck, 1976). The term was intended to reflect the nature of these thoughts, which occur without deliberation and seem involuntary. Beck, Emery & Greenberg (1985) describe negative automatic thoughts as intrusive, repetitive, and intuitively plausible at their time of occurrence. These thoughts may occur rapidly and the individual may be unaware of their occurrence. Nevertheless these thoughts are amenable to awareness and they may occur in verbal or imagery form (e.g. Beck, Laude & Bohnert, 1974).

The description of negative automatic thoughts presented by Beck et al. (1985) suggests that they are different from worry as defined by Borkovec et al. (1983, 1991). Whilst worry is described as a chain of thoughts, negative automatic thoughts seem to be more telegraphic and less consciously mediated. Kendall & Ingram (1987) argue that in anxiety many of the thoughts take the form of "What if . . ." questions. Perhaps automatic thoughts represent well rehearsed negative answers to "What if" questions whilst worry is an attempt to explore different answers and formulate particular coping responses. If worry is a problem-solving activity we would expect it to be relatively non-automatic and to rely on attentionally demanding controlled processing. Controlled processes can be readily modified by external or internal feedback and this would be an important characteristic of problem-solving activity. In contrast, automatic processes are not readily amenable to modification. We discuss later evidence from performance and attention manipulation studies which indicates that worry is an attentionally demanding process which can be displaced by concurrent controlled processing activity, suggesting it relies on attention.

Another class of cognitive product is intrusive thoughts, the clinical variety of which we may term obsessions (Parkinson & Rachman, 1981). Rachman (1981) defines intrusive thoughts as "repetitive thoughts, images or impulses that are unacceptable and/or unwanted. They are generally accompanied by subjective discomfort" (p. 89). Rachman (1981) specified criteria which are necessary and sufficient for defining a thought as intrusive: (1) the subjective report that the thought interrupts ongoing activity; (2) the thought is attributed to an internal origin; (3) the thought is difficult to control. Unfortunately these criteria are of limited use for distinguishing between varieties of anxious thought, since worry and automatic thoughts also satisfy these criteria. However, a feature of obsessions which perhaps sets them apart from worry and automatic thoughts is that they are experienced (at least initially) as senseless (DSM-III-R, American Psychiatric Association, 1987), as for example, having the thought of harming one's child whilst knowing that one would not want to do so.

Turner, Beidel & Stanley (1992) reviewed the literature on worry and obsessions and concluded that there were several differences. Whilst worry relates typically to normal daily experiences, obsessions include themes of dirt, contamination, etc. Worry most often occurs as a thought whereas obsessions can occur as thoughts, images and impulses. In addition, worry does not appear to be resisted as strongly as obsessions and it is perceived as less intrusive. A further difference seems to be that worry, at least in patient groups, is more often perceived as triggered by an internal or external event compared with obsessions. Finally the content of clinical worries is not perceived as unacceptable as is typical of intrusive thoughts in obsessive–compulsive disorder. These conclusions are, however, rather tentative because of the lack of empirical data using direct comparison between worry and intrusive thoughts. Wells and Morrison (in press) have investigated the characteristics of normal worry and intrusive thoughts. In their study 30 subjects were asked to keep a diary over a 2 week period and to record the first two worries and intrusive thoughts which occurred during that time. Subjects were also asked to rate each thought on a number of dimensions important for conceptualising the form of such thinking: degree of verbal/imagery involved; intrusiveness; realism; involuntariness; controllability; dismissibility; how distracting the thought was; how attention grabbing; amount of distress; degree of compulsion to act; resistance; and success at control.

Subjects were provided with general definitions of worry and intrusive thoughts in order to faciliate their discrimination. Significant differences emerged between the two varieties of thought on several dimensions. Worry was rated as predominantly verbal rather than imaginal, while the converse was true for intrusive thoughts. Worry was also rated as more realistic, less involuntary, harder to dismiss, more distracting and of longer duration (mean = 15.40 minutes) than intrusive thoughts (mean duration = 1.94 minutes). An unexpected finding was that worry was associated with a greater compulsion to act compared with intrusive thoughts.

In general, descriptive accounts and studies of worry, automatic thoughts and intrusive thoughts suggest particular differences between these types of event. An analysis of these features allows us to formulate some general conclusions concerning the attentional basis for negative thoughts. That is, the relationship between subjectivity experienced characteristics of thoughts and information-processing. The three types of negative thought considered seem to possess some attributes of automatic processing and some of controlled processing. The spontaneous nature of some of the thoughts, predominantly intrusive and automatic thoughts, and the difficulty in controlling all of these thoughts implies a degree of automaticity. However, the accessibility of the thoughts to consciousness indicates a link with controlled processing. Wells & Matthews (in press) review these data in more detail and conclude that whilst these thoughts may be initiated automatically, evidence for their continued processing being automatic is weak, particularly in the case of worry. However, the evidence is no more than suggestive in addressing the automaticity issue. In the next two sections evidence is reviewed suggesting that worry interferes with tasks requiring attention and is itself affected by attention manipulations, further implying that worry relies on attention.

EFFECT OF WORRY ON ATTENTIONAL PERFORMANCE

Anxiety is associated with performance decrements on a wide range of attentional tasks (e.g. Eysenck, 1992 for review). The concept of impaired task performance in anxiety has a long tradition in test-anxiety research (Wine, 1971). In this context the cognitive worry component of anxiety is considered to *interfere* with task processing by diverting attentional resources from the task at hand (Wine, 1971, 1982). Consistent with this assertion questionnaire items measuring worry and intrusive thoughts predict reduced performance more strongly than items which assess the physiological aspects of anxiety (Morris, Davis & Hutchings, 1981; Deffenbacher, 1978).

In evaluative situations the high-test-anxious individual is conceptualised as in a divided attention situation in which attention is split between processing task relevant information and negative self-evaluative processing or worry. This diversion of processing resources or attention results in decreased performance. However, not all studies show performance decrements in anxiety; anxiety may actually facilitate performance on easy tasks (Eysenck, 1982).

Dual attention tasks have been used to assess the impact of anxiety on performance; these studies tend to show that anxiety is associated with a slower reaction time to the detection of secondary probe stimuli even when high- and low-anxious groups are equated for the efficacy of performance on the primary task (Eysenck, 1992). Whilst studies of this type are suggestive of a capacity-mechanism underlying the association between anxiety and performance, there is theoretical disagreement over the nature of decrements. For example, high-test-anxious subjects may show motivational deficits because of a general expectancy of negative outcome in the testing situation (Carver, Peterson, Follansbee & Scheier, 1983). In addition, worry may affect the performance strategy adopted in situations, with anxious subjects tending to be more cautious and thus slower at responding (Green, 1987), or in other circumstances they may sacrifice accuracy of performance for increased speed (Leon & Revelle, 1985).

Worry is not unique in affecting task performance since other forms of cognition seem to have a similar effect. From a clinical standpoint it is interesting to note that the use of self-regulation and self-control strategies, which might normally be considered desirable, can also have a deleterious effect on performance. Kanfer & Stevenson (1985) asked subjects to perform a self-regulatory (self-monitoring of performance and goal setting for subsequent trials), or a maths task which was interspersed with continuous performance on a paired associates task. These conditions were compared with a condition in which there was a brief time delay in place of the secondary task. Within each group the attentional demands of the primary task was varied by varying the number of paired associates to be rehearsed. Both self-regulation and the maths task produced disruptions on the more demanding version of the primary task. These results imply that the use of self-control strategies by some individuals in anxiety-provoking situations could be deleterious for performance. In evaluative anxieties, such as social phobia, patients report self-monitoring of their performance, worry about negative evaluation, and coping strategies such as mental rehearsal. These cognitive processing activities are likely to drain attentional resources from the social task at hand, so that worry may not be the only deleterious influence on performance observed in situations.

Sarason, Sarason & Pierce (1990) suggest that a distinction should be made between worry, preoccupation and self-preoccupation since their performance effects may differ. Preoccupation and self-preoccupation are not necessarily negative in content and preoccupation is not always related to the self. Evaluation worries and anxious self-preoccupation on the other hand are specifically related to appraisal of personal inadequacy. Three questionnaires have been derived by Sarason et al. (1986) to measure different types of trait and state ideation in test situations. The Cognitive Interference Questionnaire (CIQ) is a state measure of interfering thoughts that occur in a recent situation. It assesses both task-relevant and task-irrelevant "worries". The thought occurrence questionnaire (TOQ) is a trait measure of the frequency of task-relevant and task-irrelevant intrusions. The other questionnaire is the Reaction to Tests questionnaire (RTT) and is a development of earlier test-anxiety scales, with cognitive (worry and test-irrelevant thinking) and non-cognitive scales (tension and bodily sensations). In a series of studies the worry scale of the RTT was related to poorer performance on a variety of tasks such as anagram solution and digit-symbol substitution (Sarason & Turk, 1983; Sarason, 1984, Study 2). However, scales like the test-irrelevant thinking scale of the RTT related poorly to performance (Sarason et al., 1986, Study 3). These results show that not all intrusive thoughts have the same deleterious effect on performance. As Wells & Matthews (in press) point out, theoretical accounts of performance decrements must make reference to the role of thought content. Task-relevant worry appears to be particularly detrimental to performance perhaps because it generates self-evaluative processing which has a higher priority than task processing.

Capacity explanations similar to the test-anxiety account of performance deficits have also been used to account for performance decrements in depressives. Hasher & Zacks (1979) account for attention and memory deficits in depression in terms of a disruption in controlled processing produced by depressive preoccupations. However, these effects may not only be the result of resource limitation but may result from choice of attentional strategy. Brand & Jolles (1987) experimentally demonstrated that depressives tended to use controlled processing strategies in automatic-detection tasks. However, these data could also be explained in terms of depressives adopting a more cautious performance strategy. It is possible that the adoption of a more controlled and cautious attentional strategy represents an attempt to compensate for the reduced attentional capacity produced by negative self-preoccupation.

EFFECT OF ATTENTIONAL MANIPULATIONS ON WORRY

If focusing attention on negative thinking is responsible for task decrements it follows that task-focusing instructions or other cognitive activity that blocks worry should have an ameliorative effect on performance.

Studies of depression show that adding a secondary task to the performance of a primary task improves the speed of primary task performance (Foulds, 1952). Foulds' accounts for this effect in terms of the primary task blocking depressive worries, thereby freeing up attentional resources for performance of the primary task. The problem with this explanation is that it does not account for why the secondary task does not reduce performance in the same way as worry. There are two possibilities: first the secondary task may be less attentionally demanding than worry and therefore drain fewer resources; second the secondary task may increase the effort of depressives on the primary task as they attempt to compensate for the negative effects of worry. Although the secondary task improves speed of performance on a maze task (Foulds, 1952) it increases the number of errors made. Williams, Watts, MacLeod & Mathews (1988, pp. 36–37) suggest that depressives may adopt a conservative performance strategy which sacrifices speed for accuracy but with increased attentional demands speed may be increased at the expense of accuracy.

In test-anxiety, attempts have been made to counteract deleterious performance effects of self-preoccupational worry with distraction techniques and instructions designed to increase task-focused attention. Distraction studies have produced mixed findings (Doleys, 1976). The high variability of distraction effects on performance have been attributed to the heterogeneous nature of samples, performance measures and instructions used in studies (Doleys, 1976). In a study by Thyer et al. (1981) two groups of test-anxious subjects were compared. Both groups received a common cognitive–behavioural treatment of progressive muscle relaxation plus biofeedback and training in positive self-statement and imagery. Subjects in one group were also trained in directing their attention to the task, through practice, instruction and modelling. Both treatments produced significant reductions in anxiety and improved anagram performance under distracting conditions. There were no significant differences between the groups. The failure of added attentional instructions to improve the cognitive-intervention may have been due to the redundancy of the procedure within a multi-component treatment which used other strategies to affect worry. Wise & Haynes (1983) compared cognitive restructuring with attentional training in which subjects were instructed to focus on task-relevant variables. Both treatments were superior to a no treatment wait list condition but there were no differences between the groups on outcome measures of anxiety and digit span performance. Performance studies only offer indirect support for an effect of attentional strategies on worry. More direct evidence is discussed next.

Effect of Distraction on Negative Thinking and Affect

Cognitive–behavioural treatments of depression and anxiety often use distraction-based strategies to facilitate symptom relief. These techniques are typically taught as coping or control skills and are thought to distract from negative rumination. Beck, Rush, Shaw & Emery (1979) refer to such techniques in the treatment of depression as "diversion" techniques (pp. 171–172) in which patients are instructed to focus on and describe in detail items in the consulting room, and are also encouraged to practise these techniques for homework.

Empirical studies of the effect of distraction show that it can reduce negative-thought frequency and depressed affect. In one study, Fennel & Teasdale (1984) asked one group of depressed patients to describe in detail slides of outdoor scenes whilst the control group were instructed to sit quietly looking at a square of white light projected on a wall. At intervals during the task a tone sounded which prompted the patients to report whether or not their thinking was depressed. On three occasions they reported their thoughts aloud so that the content could be rated by independent judges. Depressed mood was also rated before and after the task. Distracted patients reported fewer depressive thoughts than controls but the difference was non-significant. However, the data were examined separately for patients at or below the median depression level. In the low-depressed subgroup the distracted patients reported significantly fewer depressive thoughts compared with control patients. These findings were replicated in a within-subject study by Fennel, Teasdale, Jones & Damle (1987). In this study distraction significantly reduced the frequency of depressing thoughts articulated in low-endogenous depressed patients. These patients also reported feeling significantly less depressed following distraction than following the control condition.

In summary, the studies reviewed in the preceding sections imply that worry is a conscious controlled processing activity requiring large amounts of attentional capacity. Whilst the initiation of worry may be automatic and involuntary its continued processing requires allocation of attention. Since controlled activity is viewed as driven by plans in long-term memory (Schneider et al., 1984), individuals who experience perseverative worry can be conceptualised as having self-knowledge which specifies negative perseverative processing in response to particular stimuli. The challenge in developing a cognitive model therefore becomes one of identifying the types of self-knowledge contributing to the development of pathological worry.

PROCESS DIMENSIONS OF WORRY

The content of normal and generalised anxiety disorder worries are highly similar, and they tend to differ more in terms of process dimensions such as their controllability (Craske, Rapee, Jackel & Barlow, 1989; Turner et al., 1992). Craske et al. (1989) found that worries of GAD patients were rated as significantly less controllable, less realistic and less successfully reduced by corrective attempts than the worries for control subjects. In view of the importance of process dimensions, Wells (1992b) developed the Anxious Thoughts Inventory (AnTI) to measure individual differences in proneness to multiple content and process dimensions of worry.

Items for the initial AnTI were derived from interviews with 33 patients with generalised anxiety. Preliminary factor analysis of student responses to these ($n = 101$) items produced a six-factor solution based on the Scree test (Cattell, 1978). Subsequent revisions of the scale and two further factor analyses ($n = 110$ and $n = 239$) of student responses produced a final three factor solution. Factor 1 reflected *social worry* (e.g. "I worry about making a fool of myself"), factor 2 reflected health worry (e.g. "If I experience unexpected physical symptoms I have a tendency to think the worst possible thing is wrong with me"). The third factor reflected a preoccupation with *meta-cognition*, that is, worrying about worry and experiencing thoughts as uncontrollable and involuntary. (e.g. "I worry that I cannot control my thoughts as well as I would like to"). This dimension was termed *meta-worry*.

The AnTI subscales show good psychometric properties as summarised in Table 4.1. The internal consistency of the meta-worry subscale is lower than that of the other subscales, probably reflecting the fact that the subscale consists of items relating to more than one class of process dimension, and also items relating to the negative appraisal of thought itself. This dimension and its constituents warrant further investigation since it is likely to prove important in the development of information-processing models of worry. Meta-worry appears to reflect both a negative appraisal of the significance of thought and also difficulties with thought regulation. Meta-worry may represent dysfunctional self-knowledge about one's own cognition, and/or deficits or excesses in strategies directed at controlling thought. For example, evidence from a different line of research on the use of thought suppression suggests that particular thought control strategies may be counterproductive (e.g. Wegner, Schneider, Carter & White, 1987; Wenslaff, Wegner & Roper, 1988; Clark, Ball & Pape, 1991). In the next section we consider the uncontrollability of worry in more detail.

THE UNCONTROLLABILITY OF WORRISOME THOUGHT

In view of its controlled processing characteristics it is intriguing that worry is appraised by patients as uncontrollable. There have been few attempts to link uncontrollability of worry to an underlying mechanism

Table 4.1 Psychometric properties of the AnTI subscales

	Intercorrelations ($n = 239$)		Alpha reliability ($n = 239$)	Test retest (6 weeks) ($n = 64$)	Correlation with selected personality measures ($n = 96$)	
	Health	Meta			Trait anxiety	EPI neuroticism
Subscale:						
1. Social	.30*	.54*	.84	.76**	.63**	.62**
1. Health	—	.39*	.81	.84**	.36**	.52**
3. Meta	—	—	.75	.77**	.68**	.60**

* $p < .001$; ** $p < .0001$.
EPI: Eysenck Personality Inventory.

although this is likely to be crucial in understanding abnormal worry. Borkovec et al. (1991) suggest that worry distracts from other forms of thought (imagery) which have unpleasant physiological–affective consequences; as a result of these reinforcing properties worry becomes uncontrollable. In information-processing terms, however, it may be useful to distinguish between the initiation of processing associated with worry and the maintenance of such processing in conceptualising the controllability issue. We have seen that worry possesses characteristics of both automatic and controlled processing. Whilst worry may be initiated involuntarily it seems to require controlled processing for its continued execution. It is conceivable that the involuntary initiation of worry is appraised by some subjects as indicating that worry is generally uncontrollable, even though it can be displaced by concurrent controlled processing activities.

Aside from perceptions of uncontrollability arising from the automatic initiation of worry, uncontrollability might arise from certain self-control processes. Particular strategies aimed at controlling thoughts appear to have a paradoxical effect (Wegner et al., 1987; Clark et al., 1991). For example, Wegner et al. (1987) asked subjects not to think of a "white bear" but to report their stream of conscious thought for 5 minutes and ring a bell each time the target thought occurred. Subjects were unable to suppress the thought as instructed and when subsequently asked to think about a white bear for 5 minutes, the subjects who suppressed reported significantly more thoughts about the bear than subjects asked to think about the bear from the outset. In subsequent studies, Wenzlaff et al. (1988) demonstrated that college students with high depression scores, although initially successful at suppressing negative material, showed a delayed resurgence of unwanted negative thoughts. These subjects used more negative than positive thoughts as distracters, although they acknowledged that positive distracters were more effective than negative ones. These data imply that certain thought-control strategies could contribute to a "loss of control" of unwanted thought. In particular, a choice of negative distracter material which is closely associated with the to-be-suppressed thought may maintain activation of unwanted thought representations in memory. It is also possible that the use of distracting thoughts or distracting neutralising behaviours for thought control contribute to a generalisation of triggers for unwanted thought and thereby strengthen uncontrollability appraisals. This is clearly illustrated in the case of S., an obsessional patient recently treated by the author. The patient was a 41-year-old married woman. Her primary problem concerned the occurrence of distressing intrusive images in which she saw her husband's body mangled in the wreckage of his car. This image tended to occur whilst her husband was away at work. When this image occurred she engaged in neutralising responses consisting of repeating the action she was currently engaged in until the thought stopped. For example, when the thought occurred whilst dusting the house she would repeatedly dust, when it occurred during gardening she would repeatedly dig-up the garden. This led to a generalization of triggers such that the mere sight of a duster or the thought of tending to the garden was sufficient to activate the unwanted thoughts. The patient subsequently attempted to avoid these "triggers".

In summary, several processes may underlie the appraised uncontrollability of negative thoughts. However, in order to conceptualise the problem we need to look beyond response factors such as choice of control strategies, to the level of self-knowledge which directs processing, shapes appraisals and thus provides the motive for thought control. In particular, we are concerned with "thinking about thinking", which appears to be an important dimension of worry (Wells, 1992b; Wells & Hackmann, 1993) and obsessions (Salkovskis, 1985). Thus meta-cognitive self-knowledge is important.

Meta-cognitive Dimensions

Meta-cognition refers to self-knowledge about cognitive processes (Brown, 1978). There are a number of ways in which this knowledge could be dysfunctional and contribute to chronic worry, and general distress associated with intrusive thoughts. First, individuals may believe that their thoughts are uncontrollable when this is not the case. In particular, some individuals may have negative beliefs about the efficiency of their cognitive processes such as their ability to control thought, even though efficiency is not objectively impaired. Beliefs of this type might also contribute to doubting, checking and cognitive rehearsal. Second, some individuals may have dysfunctional beliefs about the significance of their worries. For example, some worriers believe that their negative thoughts predict the future, that thinking bad thoughts can make bad things happen and so on (e.g. Wells & Hackmann, 1993). In these cases individuals may monitor their worries and make more control attempts which are counterproductive. In contrast, there also appear to be positive beliefs concerning worry which could account for the use of worry as a predominant mode of emotional self-regulation in some subjects. Wells & Hackmann (1993) showed that 3 out of a sample of 10 patients with hypochondriasis who reported intrusive images and worry about health believed that worrying about health kept them safe. An individual may believe that worrying keeps them safe from the harmful effects of optimism. This could work in two ways. First, anticipating the negative might buffer against disappointment. Second, the individual may avoid optimistic thinking for fear of "tempting fate" or annoying God. In this context worry is a default self-regulation strategy which is intended to keep the individual "safe".

If we return to the case of S, the meta-cognitive beliefs were particularly evident. The patient believed that having the intrusive thought could make the accident happen, and because the thought occurred this meant that she was "willing the accident to happen". These beliefs account for her feelings of anxiety, guilt and appraisal of responsibility. In tracing potential origins of these beliefs the patient disclosed that her parents had been very superstitious, and as a child she worried about bad things happening to them. At that time her parents would leave her at home whilst they went out for an evening. On these occasions she repeated prayers in order to keep them safe and ensure their return home.

Clearly these types of belief, and certain cognitive–behavioural thought control strategies are likely to be important in transforming normal unwanted thought into a focus for anxiety and continued preoccupation. However, there is an aspect of worry itself which may contribute to uncontrollability appraisals. The distracting nature of worry may drain resources necessary for emotional processing of traumatic material and this may lead to increased intrusion of trauma material into consiousness.

Attention, Worry and Emotional Processing

Memory-network models of anxiety assert that anxiety results from the activation of particular memory structures containing information in propositional form about feared stimuli interconnected with information about physiological, affective, and behavioural responses. Activation is considered to spread between interconnected "nodes" representing this information (Bower, 1981). Lang (1977) suggests that images which accompany fear are constructed from propositional information stored in memory. Foa & Kozak (1986) have adopted the fear-network model to explain fear reduction in the treatment of anxiety disorders. They maintain that in order for treatment to be effective fear structures have to be accessed and incongruent information incorporated in them. A number of factors might actually prevent this "emotional processing" (Rachman, 1980), including cognitive–behavioural avoidance and high arousal. Rachman suggests that symptoms such as intrusive thoughts are examples of a failure to emotionally process.

Since worry is an attentionally demanding cognitive activity which has distracting qualities, it follows that it may affect "emotional processing". More specifically, if worry distracts from unpleasant imagery and somatic activation, as proposed by Borkovec & Inz (1990), it may interfere with both the accessing of fear structures and the encoding of new information in these structures. Clearly not only worry could have this effect; any demanding controlled processing activity could affect processing in a similar way. Moreover, some patients might adopt affect-regulation strategies typified by rumination and strategically driven compulsive activities which deviate attention away from activation of negative self-knowledge. Evidence on individual differences in coping strategies shows that some individuals do tend to use more passive and ruminative coping strategies (Wood et al., 1990), although the causal mechanism may not be cognitive–affective avoidance but may be general resource limitations or appraisal of general inefficacy of coping resources (Wells & Matthews, in press). There is some indirect clinical evidence that patients might use ruminative activities resembling worry to avoid affective activation more generally (e.g. Wells & Dattilio, 1992; Wells & Hackmann, 1993).

Worrying appears to have an effect on somatic arousal. More, specifically it reduces responsiveness to phobic imagery (Borkovec & Hu, 1990). It could be argued that worry should enhance rather than impair emotional processing since it reduces physiological responses during confrontation with a feared stimulus, and provides new information about reduced arousal which is inconsistent with the pre-existing fear structure. It is possible therefore that under some conditions worry is useful for emotional processing whilst under others it is not. For example, if worry drains off attentional resources to a high degree there may be insufficient resources for encoding fear incongruent information of either interoceptive or external origins. If worry reduces arousal, full network activation may be compromised and thus emotional processing may be rendered less efficient.

In a pilot study on the effect of worry on anxiety responses following exposure to a traumatic stimulus, Butler, Wells & Dewick (1992) demonstrated that worry might have some benefits in the short term, such as reducing anxiety, but not in the longer term. Butler et al. (1992) exposed three groups of subjects (11 subjects per group) to a gruesome film about a workshop accident. Subjects were then asked to: (1) worry in verbal form about what they had seen and its implications, or (2) image about the events in the film and the implications, or (3) "settle down" after the film. These manipulation periods lasted for 4 minutes. Subjects rated their anxiety level before and after the film and after the manipulation period.

All groups showed significant increments in anxiety during the film and there were no differences between groups in post-film anxiety level. Anxiety scores following the manipulation period showed that subjects who had imaged were the most anxious with subjects who had settled down least anxious. These differences were nevertheless non-significant. However, within group changes in anxiety across the manipulation period demonstrated significant decrements in anxiety for subjects in the worry and control conditions, whilst the decrement was non-significant for subjects in the imagery group. This anxiety change score was significantly greater for the control group than the imagery group. No other significant difference in change score were found. Following the film subjects were asked to keep a diary of intrusive images and worries, and distress associated with these thoughts during the following week. No significant differences were initially obtained between groups on these dimensions. However, it was apparent that most images and worries had been reported for the three day period following the film and so data for this period were analysed separately. The results showed that worry-group subjects reported significantly more intrusive thoughts (mean = 9) (but not worries or distress) than subjects in the imagery group (mean = 3.8) or control group (mean = 3.63). These preliminary data are interesting since they suggest that worrying might actually increase negative thought intrusion following exposure to traumatic stimuli. However, we must suspend confidence in these findings until they have been replicated with a larger sample of subjects. A post-experimental questionnaire used in the study showed that all subjects experienced images and worries about the film during the manipulation and there were no significant differences in the amount of time spent worrying or imaging during this period. Thus it may not be the proportion of time worrying or imaging which accounts for the pattern of results obtained, but the *amount of attention* devoted to worry versus imaginal processing. If replicated these data imply that some individuals may be disadvantaged at emotional processing because of the attentional strategy they employ after threat. Allocating attention to verbal worry activity may lead to a subsequent increase in intrusive thoughts and thus contribute to subjective appraisals of the uncontrollability of cognitive events.

SELF-FOCUSED ATTENTION AND WORRY

Specific individual differences in attentional style are associated with state and trait worry. One particular style concerns the degree of attention focused internally on the self versus the external world. Self-focused attention is positively associated with a wide range of psychopathological reactions (Ingram, 1990; Wells & Matthews, in press), such as depression anxiety and alcohol abuse (Smith & Greenberg, 1981; Ingram & Smith, 1984; Hull, 1981; Wells, 1987).

Individual differences in the tendency to self-focus attention are measured with the self-consciousness scale (Fenigstein, Scheier & Buss, 1975). The self-consciousness scale has three empirically distinct subscales: private self-consciousness, public self-consciousness and social anxiety. Private self-consciousness measures the extent to which people focus inwardly on their thoughts, feelings, moods and attitudes. Public self-consciousness measures the extent to which the focus of attention tends to be on publicly displayed aspects of self such as appearance. Social anxiety measures the individual's reaction to being focused on by others. Fenigstein et al. (1975) consider public self-consciousness to be a necessary antecedent for social anxiety. Other trait-measures of self-focus also exist. For example, the body-consciousness scale (Miller, Murphy & Buss, 1985) has independent subscales which assess individual tendencies to focus on bodily aspects of self. Most of the research on self-focus and worry has, however, used the self-consciousness scale.

Private and public self-consciousness are reliable predictors of various measures related to stress, including trait-anxiety, neuroticism, and cognitive failures (Dickstein, Wang & Whitaker, 1981; Wells, 1985, 1991; Matthews & Wells, 1988). Private and public self-consciousness also correlate positively with trait measures of worry. Meyer, Miller, Metzger & Borkovec (1990) report significant correlations of .26–.38 for the three self-consciousness scales with Penn State Worry scores. Stepwise regression of a series of personality predictors revealed that the significant predictors of worry in order of entry into the equation were: general time urgency, private self-consciousness, desire for control, perfectionism and the speech patterns subscale of the time urgency measure (a measure of time urgency characteristics of type A personality). All of these measures were positively related to worry apart from desire for control and speech patterns, which were negatively related to worry (Meyer et al., 1990). Wells (1992b) also demonstrated significant positive correlations between self-consciousness scores and worry proneness measured by the AnTI in a sample of undergraduate students ($N = 96$). Private self-consciousness correlated significantly with the three AnTI subscales of social (.39), health (.28) and meta-worry (.37). Public self-consciousness correlated significantly with social (.57) and meta-worry (.33) but not health worry (.14). These data imply that habitual self-focus may be a marker for proneness to emotional disturbance and intensified worry. Consistent with this proposal Wells (1985) reported a significant positive correlation of $r = .23$ between private self-consciousness measured immediately prior to an examination and a retrospective state worry-measure administered at the end of the examination in 64 undergraduate subjects. In two further studies, Wells (1991) explored self-attentional and appraisal influences on anxiety scores during exposure to traumatic film stimuli. In the first study private self-consciousness significantly predicted the degree of worry experienced during exposure to a gruesome film. In the second study, which also involved exposure to a gruesome film, subjects high in private body-consciousness reported significantly more worry than subjects low in private body consciousness. However, a manipulation of state self-focus used in the study did not produce significant differences in worry. In summary, these results show that self-attention tendencies are associated with worry at both a trait and state level. Whilst this effect appears reliable these data do not provide information concerning the mechanisms underlying this association and it does not address the issue of causality. Further studies are needed to elucidate the causal significance of attentional strategies in worry.

CONCLUSION AND INTEGRATION: A COGNITIVE–ATTENTIONAL MODEL OF PATHOLOGICAL WORRY

Several conclusions concerning the attentional characteristics and correlates of worry can be drawn from the present review. First, worry can be differentiated from other varieties of intrusive thought or obsessional thoughts. However it is likely that all of these cognitive events rely on some attention. Whilst the continued processing of worry relies on attention the initiation of worry may be involuntary and preceded by automatic precessing which issues a call for controlled processing involvement. Within an information-processing framework worry is not only initiated by low-level automatic processing activities, it may be initiated by top-down influences of self-knowledge. This knowledge will guide and shape activities of the controlled processing system in which worry is executed. We saw, for example, how some individuals may use worry as a coping strategy for reducing threats such as those believed to be associated with optimism. Moreover, the attentionally demanding nature of worry means that the process is capable of draining resources which could be used for processing other types of intrusion. Thus, as Borkovec & Inz (1990) suggest, worry may contribute to cognitive–emotional avoidance in some subjects.

It is proposed that meta-cognitive dimensions are important in conceptualising the psychopathology of intrusive thoughts. In this domain we may distinguish between particular self-beliefs (and the appraisal of worry associated with them), and regulatory strategies, which have been collectively termed "meta-worry" (Wells, 1987, 1992b). In particular, dysfunctional meta-cognitive self-knowledge concerning: (1) inefficacy of personal cognitive-control strategies; (2) the dangerous nature of certain varieties of cognition; (3) the advantages of worry as a threat reduction strategy; and (4) lack of knowledge about the functioning of the cognitive system, increase the likelihood of pathological worry. Wells & Matthews (in press) specify that dysfunctional meta-cognitive self-knowledge may be procedural rather than declarative, and represents general purpose plans stored in memory which direct the activity of the controlled processing system responsible for self-relevant processing. Whilst these plans may not be conscious their specifications can be inferred from the content of appraisals and cognitive processes. Worriers can be conceptualised as having meta-cognitive plans which, in response to specific stimulus configurations, specify ruminative and perseverative appraisal, self-monitoring of cognition and frequent use of cognitive–behavioural thought control strategies. Wells & Matthews (in press) suggest that high self-focused attention tendencies are a marker for the development of a specific cognitive–attentional syndrome which underlies proneness to emotional dysfunction. Part of this syndrome comprises perseverative appraisal (active worry).

Aside from influences of meta-cognitive self-knowledge on the maintenance of worry and negative appraisal of worry, cognitive regulation strategies arising from this self-knowledge also seem important. More specifically, we saw that the content of worry may not be especially useful in distinguishing normal and pathological worry processes. In contrast, dimensions such as uncontrollability are more relevant. Whilst uncontrollability appraisals may be based on inaccurate self-knowledge of the type already discussed, uncontrollability may also be a direct consequence of the use of certain control strategies. First, distraction from other internal events (thoughts or sensations) by ruminative worry may lead to generalisation of triggers for the unwanted internal event. Second, it may block the encoding of belief incongruent information in memory and thus maintain intrusion of negative material in consciousness. Third, attempts to suppress thoughts by distraction may lead to a perpetuation of unwanted thought, especially if the distracters used are associated with the unwanted material in memory. In general some attempts to regulate cognition are likely to maintain preoccupation with, and lower thresholds for, intrusion of worries in the longer term. These effects are likely to contribute to an increasing sense of loss of control over the worry process thereby establishing new or reinforcing existing dysfunctional meta-cognitive beliefs.

The cognitive model presented here is capable of unifying the somewhat diverse theoretical accounts of worry by Borkovec et al. (1991) and Tallis & Eysenck (1992). Their models attribute contrasting functions to worry of avoidance of threat versus enhanced appraisal of threat. On one level, perhaps different types of worry associated with different functions should be distinguished. Wells & Matthews (in press) suggest that we might discriminate between maladaptive worry associated with ruminative appraisal (and avoidance) and adaptive worry associated with efforts at active coping. Both worry functions can be explained in the present model in which selection of worry strategy is determined by the nature of self-knowledge activated under particular threat conditions. Under some circumstances the knowledge will specify orientation of attention to threat, active coping and reappraisal. In other circumstances perseverative processing, avoidance and control strategies may be specified; under these latter conditions worry may become subjectively "uncontrollable".

In conclusion, a better understanding of the phenomenology of worry and advances in treatment are likely to emerge from a detailed cognitive–attentional processing model of worry like the one suggested here. Future efforts are clearly required in exploring the process dimensions of worry so that mechanisms underlying uncontrollability may be investigated. Aside from the experimental approach important gains may also be made through the development of self-report measures of meta-worry (e.g. Wells, 1987, 1992b) which assess dimensions of worry about worry, the subjective form of worry processes, and also eventually include assessment of meta-cognitive beliefs and preference for particular thought control strategies.

For some individuals the locus of the worry problem appears not to be at the level of worry but at the level of factors responsible for "worry about worry" and also "worry about not worrying". Cognitive–behavioural treatment approaches may be better placed if they de-emphasise teaching active worry-control strategies and aim to modify dysfunctional meta-cognitive beliefs, and reduce the frequency with which the individual attempts unnecessary control.

REFERENCES

American Psychiatric Association (1987). *Diagnostic and Statistical Manual of Mental Disorders,* 3rd edn—rev. Washington DC: American Psychiatric Association.
Beck, A.T. (1967). *Depression: Causes and Treatment.* Philadelphia: University of Pensylvania Press.
Beck, A.T. (1976). *Cognitive Therapy and the Emotional Disorders.* New York: International Universities Press.

Beck, A.T., Emery, G. & Greenberg, R.L. (1985). *Anxiety Disorders and Phobias: A Cognitive Perspective*. New York: Basic Books.

Beck, A.T., Laude, R. & Bohnert, M. (1974). Ideational components of anxiety neurosis. *Archives of General Psychiatry*, **32**, 319–325.

Beck, A.T., Rush, A.J., Shaw, B.F. & Emery, G. (1979). *Cognitive Therapy of Depression*. New York: Guilford Press.

Borkovec, T.D. & Hu, S. (1990). The effect of worry on cardiovascular response to phobic imagery. *Behaviour Research and Therapy*, **28**, 69–73.

Borkovec, T.D. & Inz, J. (1990). The nature of worry in Generalised Anxiety Disorder: A predominance of thought activity. *Behaviour Research and Therapy*, **28**, 153–158.

Borkovec, T.D., Robinson, E., Prizinsky, T. & Depress, J.A. (1983). Preliminary exploration of worry: some characteristics and processes. *Behaviour Research and Therapy*, **21**, 9–16.

Borkovec, T.D. Shadick, R.N. & Hopkins, M. (1991). The nature of normal and pathological worry. In R.M. Rapee & D.H. Barlow (Eds.), *Chronic Anxiety: Generalised Anxiety Disorder and Mixed Anxiety-Depression*, pp. 29–51. New York: Guilford Press.

Bower, G.H. (1981). Mood and memory. *American Psychologist*, **36**, 129–148.

Brand, N. & Jolles, J. (1987). Information processing in depression and anxiety. *Psychological Medicine*, **17**, 145–153.

Broadbent, D.E. & Broadbent, M.H.P. (1986). Anxiety and attentional bias: State and trait. *Cognition and Emotion*, **2**, 165–183.

Brown, A. (1978). Knowing when, where and how to remember: A problem of metacognition. In R. Glaser (Ed.), *Advances in Instructional Psychology*. Hillsdale, NJ: Erlbaum.

Butler, G., Wells, A. & Dewick, H. (1992). Differential effects of worry and imagery after exposure to a stressful stimulus. Paper presented at the World Congress of Cognitive Therapy, Toronto, June 1992.

Carver, C.S., Peterson, L.M., Follansbee, D.J. & Scheier, M.F. (1983). Effects of self-directed attention on performance and persistence among persons high and low in test-anxiety. *Cognitive Therapy and Research*, **7**, 333–354.

Cattell, R.B. (1978). *The Scientific Use of Factor Analysis in Behavioural and Life Sciences*. New York: Plenum Press.

Clark, D.M. (1986). A cognitive model of panic. *Behaviour Research and Therapy*, **24**, 461–470.

Clark, D.M., Ball, S. & Pape, D. (1991). An experimental investigation of thought suppression. *Behaviour Research and Therapy*, **29**, 253–257.

Craske, M.G., Rapee, R.M., Jackel, L. & Barlow, D.H. (1989). Qualitative dimensions of worry in DSM-III-R Generalised Anxiety Disorder subjects and non-anxious controls. *Behaviour Research and Therapy*, **27**, 397–402.

Deffenbacher, J.L. (1978). Worry, emotionality and task generated interference in test anxiety: An empirical test of attention theory. *Journal of Educational Psychology*, **70**, 248–254.

Dickstein, L.S., Wang, N. & Whitaker, A. (1981). Private self-consciousness, public self-consciousness and trait-anxiety. *Psychological Reports*, **41**, 518.

Doleys, D. (1976). Distractibility and distracting stimuli: inconsistent and contradicting results. *Psychological Record*, **26**, 279–287.

Ellis, A. (1962). *Reason and Emotion in Psychotherapy*. New York: Lyle Stuart.

Eysenck, M.W. (1982). *Attention and Arousal: Cognition and Performance*. New York: Springer.

Eysenck, M.W. (1992). *Anxiety: The Cognitive Perspective.* Hillsdale, NJ: Erlbaum.

Fenigstein, A., Scheier, M.F. & Buss, A.H. (1975). Public and private self-consciousness: Assessment and theory. *Journal of Consulting and Clinical Psychology,* **43**, 522–527.

Fennell, M.J.V. & Teasdale, J.D. (1984). Effects of distraction on thinking and affect in depressed patients. *British Journal of Clinical Psychology,* **23**, 65–66.

Fennell, M.J.V., Teasdale, J.D., Jones, S. & Damle, A. (1987). Distraction in neurotic and endogenous depression: An investigation of negative thinking in major depressive disorder. *Psychological Medicine,* **14**, 441–452.

Foa, E.B. & Kozak, M.J. (1986). Emotional processing and fear: Exposure to corrective information. *Psychological Bulletin,* **99**, 20–35.

Foulds, G.A. (1952). Temperamental differences in maze performance II: The effect of distraction and electroconvulsive therapy on psychomotor retardation. *British Journal of Psychiatry,* **43**, 33–41.

Green, R.G. (1987). Test anxiety and behavioural avoidance. *Journal of Research in Personality,* **21**, 481–488.

Hasher, L. & Zacks, R.T. (1979). Automatic and effortful processes in memory. *Journal of Experimental Psychology: General,* **108**, 346–388.

Hull, J.G. (1981). A self-awareness model of the causes and effects of alcohol consumption. *Journal of Abnormal Psychology,* **90**, 586–600.

Ingram, R.E. (1990). Self-focused attention in clinical disorders: Review and a conceptual model. *Psychological Bulletin,* **107**, 156–176.

Ingram, R.E. & Smith, T.W. (1984). Depression and internal versus external focus of attention. *Cognitive Therapy and Research,* **8**, 139–152.

Kahneman, D. (1973). *Attention and Effort.* Englewood Cliffs, NJ: Prentice-Hall.

Kahneman, D. & Treisman, A. (1984). Changing views of attention and automaticity. In R. Parasuraman and D.R. Davies (Eds.), *Varieties of Attention.* New York: Academic Press.

Kanfer, F.H. & Stevenson, M.K. (1985). The effects of self-regulation on concurrent cognitive processing. *Cognitive Therapy and Research,* **9**, 667–684.

Kendall, P.G. & Ingram, R.E. (1987). The future for cognitive assessment of anxiety: Let's get specific. In L. Michaelson & L.M. Ascher (Eds.), *Anxiety and Stress Disorders: Cognitive-Behavioural Assessment and Treatment.* New York: Guilford Press.

Lang, P.J. (1977). Imagery in therapy: An information processing analysis of fear. *Behaviour Therapy,* **8**, 882–886.

Lazarus, R.S. & Folkman, S. (1984). *Stress, Appraisal and Coping.* New York: Springer.

Leon, M.R. & Revelle, W. (1985). Effects of anxiety on analogical reasoning: a test of three theoretical models. *Journal of Personality and Social Psychology,* **49**, 1302–1315.

Matthews, G. & Wells, A. (1988). Relationships between anxiety, self-consciousness, and cognitive failure. *Cognition and Emotion,* **2**, 123–132.

Meyer, T.J., Miller, M.L., Metzger, R.L. & Borkovec, T.D. (1990). Development and validation of the Penn State Worry Questionnaire. *Behaviour Research and Therapy,* **28**, 487–495.

Miller, L.C., Murphy, R. & Buss, A.H. (1981). Consciousness of body: Private and public. *Journal of Personality and Social Psychology,* **41**, 397–406.

Morris, L.W., Davis, M.A. & Hutchings, C.H. (1981). Cognitive and emotional components of anxiety: Literature review and revised worry-emotionality scale. *Journal of Educational Psychology,* **73**, 541–555.

Paap, K.R. & Ogden, W.G. (1981). Letter encoding is an obligatory but capacity-demanding operation. *Journal of Experimental Psychology: Human Perception and Performance, 7*, 518–528.

Parkinson, L. & Rachman, S.J. (1981, Part II). The nature of intrusive thoughts. *Advances in Behaviour Research and Therapy, 3*, 101–110.

Posner, M.I. & Snyder, C.R.R. (1975). Attention and cognitive control. In R. L. Sobo (Ed.), *Information Processing and Cognition: The Loyola Symposium.* Hillsdale, NJ: Erlbaum.

Rachman, S. (1980). Emotional processing. *Behaviour Research and Therapy, 18*, 51–60.

Rachman, S.J. (1981, Part I). Unwanted intrusive cognitions. *Advances in Behaviour Research and Therapy, 3*, 89–99.

Salkovskis, P.M. (1985). Obsessional-compulsive problems: A cognitive-behavioural analysis. *Behaviour Research and Therapy, 23,* 571–583.

Sarason, I.G. (1984). Stress, anxiety, and cognitive interference: Reactions to tests *Journal of Personality and Social Psychology, 46*, 929–938.

Sarason, I.G., Sarason, B.R., Keefe, D.E., Hayes, B.E. & Shearin, E.N. (1986). Cognitive interference: Situational determinants and traitlike characteristics. *Journal of Personality and Social Psychology, 31*, 215–226.

Sarason, I.G., Sarason, B.R. & Pierce, G.R. (1990). Anxiety, Cognitive interference, and performance. *Journal of Social Behavior and Personality, 5*, 1–18.

Sarason, I.G. & Turk, S. (1983). Coping strategies and group interaction: Their function in improving performance of anxious individuals. Unpublished paper, University of Washington, Seattle, WA.

Schneider, W., Dumais, S.T. & Shiffrin, R.M. (1984). Automatic and control processing and attention. In R. Parasuraman & D.R. Davies (Eds.), *Varieties of Attention.* New York: Academic Press.

Schneider, W. & Shiffrin, R.M. (1977). Controlled and automatic human information processing: I. Detection, search and attention. *Psychological Review, 84*, 1–66.

Shiffrin, R.M. & Schneider, W. (1977). Controlled and automatic human information processing: II. Perceptual learning, automatic attending, and a general theory. *Psychological Review, 84*, 127–190.

Smith, T.W. & Greenberg, J. (1981). Depression and self-focused attention. *Motivation and Emotion, 5*, 323–331.

Tallis, F. & Eysenck, M.W. (1992). Cited in M.W. Eysenck. *Anxiety: The Cognitive Perspective*, pp. 114–120. Hove: Erlbaum.

Tallis, F., Eysenck, M.W. & Mathews, A. (1992). A questionnaire for the measurement of non pathological worry. *Personality and Individual Differences, 13*, 161–168.

Thyer, B.A., Papsdorf, J.D., Himle, D.P., McCann, B.S., Caldwell, S. & Wickert, M. (1981). In vivo distraction—coping in the treatment of test anxiety. *Journal of Clinical Psychology, 37*, 754–764.

Turner, S.M., Beidel, D.C. & Stanley, M.A. (1992). Are obsessional thoughts and worry different cognitive phenomena? *Clinical Psychology Review, 12*, 257–270.

Watts, F.N., Tresize, L. & Sharrock, R. (1986). Processing of phobic stimuli. *British Journal of Clinical Psychology, 25*, 253–261.

Wegner, D.M., Schneider, D.J., Carter, S.R. & White, T.L. (1987). Paradoxical effects of thought suppression. *Journal of Personality and Social Psychology, 5*, 5–13.

Wells, A. (1985). Relationship between private self-consciousness and anxiety scores in threatening situations. *Psychological Reports, 57*, 1063–1066.

Wells, A. (1991). Effects of dispositional self-focus, appraisal and attention instructions on responses to a threatening stimulus. *Anxiety Research*, **3**, 291–301.

Wells, A. (1987). Self-attentional processes in anxiety: An experimental study. Unpublished Ph.D. thesis, Aston University, Birmingham, UK.

Wells, A. (1992a). Cognitive therapy for anxiety and cognitive theories of causation. In G.D. Burrows, M. Roth & R. Noyes (Eds.), *Handbook of Anxiety*, Vol. 5, pp. 233–354. Amsterdam: Elsevier.

Wells, A. (1992b). A multi-dimensional measure of worry: Development and preliminary validation of the Anxious Thoughts Inventory. Paper presented at the World Congress of Cognitive Therapy, Toronto, June, 1992.

Wells, A. & Dattilio, F.M. (1992). Negative outcome in cognitive-behaviour therapy: A case study. *Behavioural Psychotherapy*, **20**, 291–294.

Wells, A. & Hackmann, A. (1993). Imagery and core beliefs in health-anxiety: Content and origins. *Behavioural and Cognitive Psychotherapy*, **21**, 265–273.

Wells, A. & Matthews, G. (in press). *Attention and Emotion: A Clinical Perspective.* Hove: Erlbaum.

Wells, A. & Morrison, A. (in press). Qualitative dimensions of normal worry and intrusive thoughts: A comparative study. *Behaviour Research and Therapy*.

Wenslaff, R.M., Wegner, D.M. & Roper, D.W. (1988). Depression and mental control: The resurgence of unwanted negative thoughts. *Journal of Personality and Social Psychology*, **55**, 882–892.

Williams, J.M.G., Watts, F.N., Macleod, C. & Mathews, A. (1988). *Cognitive Psychology and Emotional Disorders.* Chichester: Wiley.

Wine, J.D. (1971). Test anxiety and the direction of attention. *Psychological Bulletin*, **76**, 92–104.

Wine, J.D. (1982). Evaluation anxiety: A cognitive-attentional construct. In H. W. Krohne & L. Laux (Eds.), *Achievement, Stress and Anxiety*, pp. 207–219. Washington, DC: Hemisphere.

Wise, E.H. & Haynes, S.N. (1983). Cognitive treatment of test anxiety: Rational restructuring versus attentional training. *Cognitive Therapy and Research*, **7**, 69–78.

Wood, J.V., Saltzberg, J.A., Neale, J.M., Stone, A.A. & Rachmiel, T.B. (1990). Self-focused attention, coping responses, and distressed mood in everyday life. *Journal of Personality and Social Psychology*, **58**, 1027–1036.

CHAPTER 5 Worry and explanation-based pessimism

*Andrew K. MacLeod**

There are good reasons for thinking that cognitions about the future play a central role in worry. Worry has been talked about as "a constant preoccupation with things that might go wrong" (Eysenck & Eysenck, 1975), "concern over future events" (Barlow, 1988), and "a persistent awareness of possible future danger" (Mathews, 1990). Empirical findings also reinforce the idea of worry as future-oriented. An early study by Borkovec and his colleagues found that worriers were characterised by concerns over future rather than past or present situations (Borkovec, Robinson, Pruzinsky & DePree, 1983).

Worriers are not only preoccupied with future unpleasant outcomes but show a greater degree of belief in the likelihood of those outcomes. This enhanced belief in the likelihood of future negative outcomes or events will form the focus of this chapter. Belief in the likelihood of events is usually assessed by giving subjects a number of hypothetical future events and asking them to estimate how likely those events are to happen to them. Usually, likelihood is estimated by selecting a number on a scale of probability. For example, MacLeod, Williams & Bekerian (1991) gave chronic worriers a range of future negative outcomes such as "your health will deteriorate" and "you will be unable to express yourself in social situations". Subjects had to estimate how likely each outcome was to happen to them on a 10 point scale anchored by "not at all likely" (1) and "certain" (10). Chronic worriers provided higher subjective probability estimates than matched controls. Similar findings emerge from studies of other groups known to be frequent worriers such as generalised anxiety disorder patients (Butler & Mathews, 1983) and high trait-anxious students (Butler & Mathews, 1987). Depressed subjects have also been

*Royal Holloway, University of London, Egham, UK

Worrying: Perspectives on Theory, Assessment and Treatment. Edited by G.C.L. Davey and F. Tallis.
© 1994 John Wiley & Sons Ltd.

found to show increased subjective probabilities for negative events (Butler & Mathews, 1983), although it is not clear whether this is the result of depressed subjects' accompanying levels of anxiety. Where the probability of future positive events or the probability of non-self-relevant events has been assessed, anxious subjects do not differ from controls (Butler & Mathews, 1983).

There is evidence of a direct relationship between the amount of time spent worrying about an outcome and the belief in the likelihood of that outcome. MacLeod (1989) presented chronic worriers with a range of different possible worries. For each event, subjects had to rate how likely it was to happen to them in the future, how much they had worried about it recently and how long they had worried about it. The particular events which each subject worried most about were those which s/he judged to be most likely to happen. This was especially true for events recently worried about, and the relationship held up even when controlling for other subject variables such as levels of state and trait anxiety.

Worriers give higher subjective probability estimates than controls for negative events. Whether worriers' judgements represent bias or realism is difficult to say. The diagnostic criteria for generalised anxiety disorder specify that the person's worries must be unrealistic. Clearly, this is a difficult judgement to make and assumes a complete knowledge of all the relevant facts as well as an awareness of which facts are relevant and which are not. In the experimental field, the idea of bias as a departure from statistical norms has been extensively questioned (e.g. Dunning & Story, 1991). This point is made forcefully by Tversky & Kahneman (1973) when they note that "each occurrence of an economic recession, a successful medical operation, or a divorce, is essentially unique, and its probability cannot be evaluated by a simple tally of instances" (p. 228). The point is further reinforced by work on "self-fulfilling prophecy" demonstrating that outcomes can be influenced by altering prior expectancies (e.g. Campbell & Fairey, 1985). The only warranted use of bias seems to be in describing a relative difference between worriers and controls.

To summarise, worry seems to be primarily future-directed, is characterised by preoccupation with future aversive events or outcomes, and is associated with a greater degree of belief in the likelihood of those outcomes. The remainder of this chapter will focus on discussing the possible cognitive processes involved in elevated beliefs in the likelihood of future negative events, and the implications for therapy of understanding these cognitive processes. First, some of the theoretical and empirical literature, particularly the work of Tversky & Kahneman, on how we make judgements about the future will be reviewed. The role of explanation-based processes in future judgements will be focused on, with some of the other possible mechanisms involved in future judgements also discussed. Findings from the general judgement literature will then be applied to pessimistic future judgements in worriers and, finally, implications for worry interventions will be drawn out.

COGNITIVE PROCESSES IN SUBJECTIVE PROBABILITY JUDGEMENTS

One way to begin to understand the pessimistic subjective probability judgements of worriers is to see to what extent they can be understood within the frameworks developed to account for general subjective probability judgements. The starting point for this endeavour is the seminal work of Tversky & Kahneman on judgemental heuristics, particularly the *availability heuristic* (Tversky & Kahneman, 1973). A person is using the availability heuristic when s/he estimates frequency or probability by the ease with which instances or associations can be brought to mind. For example, Tversky & Kahneman report an experiment in which subjects were given a particular letter of the alphabet and asked to estimate the number of words either beginning with that letter or having it as the third letter. Despite the fact that all the letters that were used appeared more frequently in the third position, most of the subjects estimated that words having it as the first letter were more frequent. Tversky & Kahneman argue that this is because subjects judge the relative frequencies according to how easily they can construct instances, a task which is easier for words beginning with the letter.

As Tversky & Kahneman point out, such experiments are concerned with frequencies, or probabilities which are readily reduced to frequencies, where there is an objectively correct answer. Of more relevance to the discussion here is where they discuss the application of the availability heuristic to real life situations. They argue that, even although the occurrence of a real life event is unique and has no objective probability of occurrence, the availability heuristic can be used to judge the likelihood of such events. They suggest two mechanisms by which such judgements can be made. When asked to judge how likely an event is, someone may recall similar events from long-term memory, and the ease with which such events are recalled will determine how probable it is judged to be. Alternatively, they may construct scenarios which lead to the event occurring. This involves generating explanations for why the event would come about. The plausibility of such scenarios and explanations, or the ease with which they come to mind, provides a basis for the judgement of likelihood. This second mechanism operates where the event is perceived as unique and past history does not seem relevant to the evaluation of its likelihood. Scenarios which are constructed will not be based on extensive search but rather, only explanations which are relatively simple and most available will be considered and, once generated, they will tend to constrain further thinking.

EXPLANATION-BASED PESSIMISM

This second aspect of the availability heuristic—the construction of scenarios—has been renamed the *simulation heuristic* (Kahneman & Tversky, 1982). The simulation heuristic has been mainly applied to counterfactual thinking about outcomes which have already occurred, that is, how easily an alternative model of reality (something which might have happened) can be constructed and how this might relate to emotions such as regret and frustration. This application of the simulation heuristic is discussed by Kahneman & Miller (1986).

In the case of thinking about future possible outcomes, the simulation heuristic describes the process of constructing a mental model of reality in which the hypothetical event takes place. An important component of the mental model being constructed is a set of causal explanations leading to the event's occurrence. The ease with which causal theories producing the outcome can be generated determines the judged likelihood of the outcome. The emphasis on causal explanations in predictive judgements is consistent with work in a variety of other areas, where there has been much recent interest in the extent to which causal explanations are utilised in cognitive processes such as category judgements (Murphy & Medin, 1984), schema acquisition (Ahn, Brewer & Mooney, 1992) and decision making (Pennington & Hastie, 1988).

There are two features of scenario construction which may be particularly informative for understanding worry. First, people find it easier to think of factors which would bring an event about rather than factors which would prevent it happening (Dunning & Parpal, 1989). Additive information, which facilitates the occurrence of the event, is given more consideration than subtractive information which inhibits the event's occurrence. Second, the particular outcome being considered (the subject of the comparison), is given more weight than another alternative outcome (the referent of the comparison). Applying these principles to worry illustrates why worry may be such a persistent phenomenon. Take the example of someone who is giving a party and is focused on or concerned with the party going well (subject) rather than badly (comparison). The combination of more attention paid to the subject (going well) than to the comparison (going badly) and the tendency to think of facilitative rather than inhibitory factors means that they will mainly think of explanations or reasons why the party will go well. For the worrier who is worried about the party going badly, the subject has changed from the party going well to it going badly and the tendency to think of facilitative reasons now means that what is thought about is reasons why the party will go badly. Furthermore, such reasons may come to mind all too readily, due to the person having worried about similar things on other occasions, and thus, in a sense, having rehearsed such reasons. As Koehler (1991) points out, the reasons may not be strictly causal in a logical sense; the important point is that they have some subjective explanatory value for the outcome. Thus, the worrier may also draw on a pool of negative, self-related information such as "I get very anxious in social situations and make others anxious" or "things always go badly for me". Not only is the search being directed to look for reasons why the party would go badly, such reasons come to mind easily and therefore it will be judged likely to happen.

There is evidence that the accessibility of reasons to explain the occurrence or non-occurrence of negative future-events is related to their judged likelihood. In a study by MacLeod (in preparation), subjects were given self-relevant, future negative events, such as "your health will deteriorate" and "you will have difficulty getting on with friends or family". Subjects were asked to estimate how likely each event was and also to provide reasons why each event would happen (pro reasons) and would not happen (con reasons). They were given one minute to provide each set of reasons for each event. Two measures of accessibility were taken—latency to think of the first reason and number of reasons generated in one minute. The accessibility of pro as opposed to con reasons was strongly correlated with an event's judged probability. Thus, subjects who were able to think of many reasons why an event would happen, and few reasons why it would not, judged that event to be likely. Where few pro reasons relative to con reasons were thought of subjects judged the event to be unlikely. MacLeod et al. (1991), using a similar methodology, found similar effects in a sample of chronic worriers. For both worriers and controls, accessibility of pro and con reasons was highly correlated with the perceived probability of future negative events. In addition, compared with controls, the most anxious worriers showed a greater accessibility of reasons for as opposed to reasons against negative events happening.

The strongest support for the role of explanations in future judgements comes from studies which have manipulated the accessibility of particular types of explanations and observed corresponding effects on judgements.

For example, Levi & Pryor (1987) found that subjects' judgements of who would win a forthcoming presidential debate depended on which candidate they had been asked to explain winning. Estimates of who would win were not affected in subjects simply asked to imagine a particular candidate winning. Thus, it is not simply the ease of bringing to mind a mental picture of the outcome which influences likelihood judgements, but being able to think of explanations for why the outcome would happen.

Asking subjects to think of explanations for why an outcome would occur affects the outcome's perceived likelihood because it makes those explanations more accessible when the person comes to make the likelihood judgement. Of course, showing that asking people to think of explanations can affect judgements does not mean that people naturally use the ease of thinking of explanations as the basis of their judgements. It may be that by asking people to think of explanations, explanations become salient as a source of information and, because of their salience, are used as a basis for the judgement on that occasion. However, where probability judgements have been made before generating reasons (for example, MacLeod, in preparation) the ease of generating subsequent reasons still correlates highly with the subjective probability judgements, suggesting that the ease of explanations was being used in the judgement process, before any mention of explanations was made to subjects.

Explaining why particular outcomes would come about has also been found to affect self-relevant judgements. Subjects asked to explain why they would succeed at a laboratory task predicted they would do well at the task whereas subjects asked to explain why they would do badly predicted that they would do badly (Campbell & Fairey, 1985; Sherman, Skov, Hervitz & Stock, 1981). Hoch (1985) asked final year business students to consider a number of positive personal outcomes (e.g. receiving three job offers on graduation) and give reasons either why those outcomes would happen or why they would not happen. Generating reasons why the outcomes would happen did not affect probability judgements but generating reasons why the outcomes would not happen resulted in lower likelihood estimates. Hoch interpreted the failure to obtain effects in the pro-reason condition as reflecting the tendency of subjects to spontaneously generate pro reasons anyway, at least for positive events. Generating con reasons had an effect on judgements because it made subjects think of possibilities they would not otherwise have considered. This asymmetry of the effects of pro and con reason generation incidentally suggests that effects on judgements of asking subjects to think of explanations are not simply the result of subjects realising they are supposed to change their probability judgements in light of the reasons they have given, as experimental demand should work equally for con reasons and pro reasons. The implications for worry of affecting probabilities through manipulating the availability of explanations will be returned to later. The point being made here is that there is strong evidence of the accessibility of explanations concerning an event's occurrence being causally related to its perceived probability.

OTHER JUDGEMENT PROCESSES IN PESSIMISM

Although there are good theoretical and empirical grounds for believing that the availability of explanations is used in making probability judgements, other information may also be used. As already discussed, Tversky & Kahneman (1973) in their original formulation of the availability heuristic suggest two classes of mental operations that bring things to mind—retrieval of instances and construction of scenarios. It is in fact the retrieval of instances that has received more attention in the literature, despite Tversky & Kahneman's statement that it is of less importance in real-life judgements. However, retrieval of instances from memory may sometimes play a role in likelihood judgements of real-life events. C. MacLeod & Campbell (1992) presented subjects with short descriptions of common pleasant (a welcome invitation) and unpleasant (a painful injury) events. Subjects had to retrieve a specific memory that fitted each event description and rate the probability of experiencing the event description within the next 6 months. Speed of retrieval of an example correlated with probability judgements: items where a previous example was quickly recalled were judged to be likely to happen and items where a particular example was slower to come to mind were judged unlikely.

There are a number of problems with drawing strong conclusions from this study. The average latency of approximately 2.5 seconds, with a cut-off time of 4 seconds, is extremely fast compared with other studies of autobiographical retrieval (e.g. Teasdale & Fogarty, 1979) and especially so when compared with other research which has requested subjects to produce specific memories (e.g. Williams & Scott, 1988). The fast latencies combined with there being no check on whether subjects were actually providing specific memories suggests that subjects may have been operating on the basis of general impressions of whether the events had happened to them in the past rather than retrieving specific examples. Nevertheless, recall of specific examples is a possible mechanism that may on occasion be used to judge the likelihood of a future outcome. How this applies in the case of worry will be returned to later.

A second alternative process to explanation-based future judgement is that when subjects are asked how likely a future event is they simply retrieve an already-formed judgement of its likelihood. That is, they have thought about the outcome before and come to a conclusion about its likelihood. Sherman, Zehner, Johnson & Hirt (1983) asked subjects to read information about two football teams and asked them to explain a hypothetical victory by one of the teams in a forthcoming game, before making a prediction about which team would win. In general, explaining the success of a particular team results in that team being judged to be more likely to win. The exception, however, was when, prior to the explanation task, subjects were encouraged to form their own opinion of which team would win. In this case, the explanation task had no effect on predictions. Sherman et al. (1983) suggest that this was because those subjects, when asked to make a prediction, simply recalled their previous prediction and used that as a basis for their judgement.

A third possibility is that rather than use specific cognitive information—either construction of scenarios, recall of similar past examples, or retrieval of a previous judgement—people may use their mood state as a direct source of information. Schwarz & Clore (1983) report a study which utilised the fact that people's moods are better on sunny days than rainy days. They found that subjects interviewed on a sunny day said they were more satisfied with their lives than those interviewed on a rainy day. The authors interpret this as showing that subjects use their mood state as a direct source of information in making judgements. This interpretation was strengthened by a re-attribution manipulation, where subjects were encouraged to attribute their mood to an external source through the experimenter drawing attention to the weather that day, eliminating differences in life satisfaction ratings. The authors argue that in complex self-relevant judgements people use their mood state as a direct source of information.

It is not clear whether mood state is used as a source of information in judgements about the likelihood of future negative events. The studies by Schwarz and his colleagues (see Schwarz & Clore, 1987 for a review) mainly consist of asking subjects how they feel about their lives. It does not seem particularly surprising that when asking someone a question involving how they feel, they use how they feel as a basis for answering it. The possible use of mood state as a source of information for future judgements by worriers will be discussed in the next section.

JUDGEMENT PROCESSES, PESSIMISM AND WORRY

The application of future judgement processes to understanding pessimism and worry is shown in Figure 5.1. The figure is a schematic represen-

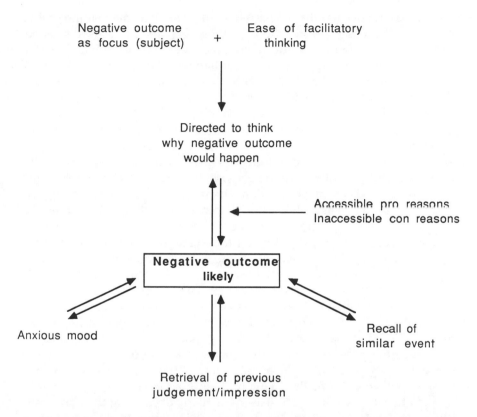

Figure 5.1   A schematic representation of the worry process, outlining the central role of pessimistic future beliefs and the cognitive processes involved in the formalities of those beliefs

tation of the processes and relationships discussed so far. The central feature is the elevated belief in the likelihood of future negative events. There are four suggested routes leading to these pessimistic future judgements.

The first and most important route is through the use of the simulation heuristic. That people give more attention to the subject (focus) of a judgement rather than other possible outcomes (referents), and that facilitative information is easier to think of than subtractive information, has already been discussed. The worrier who is preoccupied with the thought that his/her party might go badly will be directed to think of reasons why it would go badly. What then determines the degree of belief in the outcome is how easily explanations for the outcome come to mind, along with how difficult it is to think of counter reasons for that outcome.

For a worrier, reasons why the party would go badly come to mind easily, because s/he has a greater store of those explanations. As discussed earlier, previous worrying effectively rehearses a set of explanations for why the worried-about outcome would happen. Worry is also associated with a tendency to attend to negative information in the environment (Mathews, 1990), which will also increase the amount of negative information available. Information about the self is a primary source for judgements about future self-relevant outcomes, and worriers will be able to construct on-line explanations derived from negative self-concepts. For example, one worrier asked to think of reasons why she would make the wrong decision about something important gave the following reasons: "I'm bad at decision making; I don't know how to do things right; I'm good at making mistakes; I don't think things through first; I can't see the outcome of what my actions might be". In contrast, explanations against the event occurring are very difficult for worriers to think of, for a number of reasons. First, as already discussed, factors which prevent an event happening are generally more difficult to think of than factors which would bring it about. Second, worriers may have a relatively impoverished store of such information anyway, especially relating to their own abilities. Thirdly, people are known to terminate their search when they find a plausible explanation rather than continue their search to evaluate other possible explanations (Shaklee & Fischoff, 1982). The worrier who has already thought of reasons why the negative event would happen will look no further. Finally, highly accessible pro reasons are thought to actively inhibit con reasons, actually decreasing their accessibility (Tversky & Kahneman, 1973). Hoch (1984) found that subjects were less able to think of either pro or con reasons for a future event if they had first of all been asked to consider the opposite set of reasons.

In fact, the non-worrier may differ from the worrier in two ways. First, for non-worriers the primary focus may be the party going well. This would set them off on a quite different cognitive track of thinking of reasons why it would go well. However, even when the focus is on the party going badly this may not lead to a belief that it will. The non-worrier, when directed to think of why the party will go badly, will not be able to think so easily of reasons why it would go badly, as they do not have a large store of such reasons. The difficulty of thinking of reasons why the party would go badly may lead them to extent their search to why it would not go badly. Drawing on their different pool of knowledge, they may find it easier to think of reasons why it would not go badly. The effect is that the event is not seen as likely. The thought of the party going badly occurred to the non-worrier but it did not persist. The difference between worriers and non-worriers may not be so much in the nature of the thoughts that occur to them but in the relative persistence of such thoughts. The non-worrier may have the same thoughts occurring to him or her as the worrier but is able to dismiss those thoughts because s/he is relatively unable to think of reasons why the negative outcome would happen and is relatively able to think of reasons why the outcome would not happen.

Three other routes to belief in the likelihood of aversive outcomes are shown. One route is through the recall of past relevant experiences. Through the use of the availability heuristic, the ease of recall of past instances will determine the likelihood of the future event. Although it has been argued that the recall of past instances will be less important in pessimistic worry, in cases where a highly salient past instance is available then it may well be used as a basis for the future judgement. Memory for previous instances is more likely to be used for fairly common events or for fairly recent events that could be expected to happen in the near future. Worriers may have more available past instances, either through having had more aversive experiences or having ruminated more on their aversive experiences and thus making them more accessible and salient.

An anxious mood can lead to a belief in the likelihood of aversive outcomes through the utilisation of mood state as a source of information (Schwarz & Clore, 1983). Having to form an impression of the likelihood of a hypothetical future outcome is a complex judgement with a great deal of uncertainty. In the absence of other specific information a person may use their current mood state as a guide to the likelihood of the outcome. This is particularly likely to occur when the person's mood state is very salient, for example, being more anxious than usual, and where there is no obvious source to which the mood can be attributed. One way to make sense of an anxious mood is to attribute it to the likelihood of future aversive events, rather in the manner of "if I feel anxious there must be something bad about to happen".

The third alternative route is simply through the retrieval of a pre-formed judgement. This is perhaps the most obvious way in which worry is self-maintaining. A worrier having already thought about the possibility of an aversive outcome and judged it to be likely (through any of the processes discussed) when thinking again about the outcome will simply retrieve that judgement. The more this routine is gone through the more available this judgement will be and the more entrenched the belief in the likelihood of the negative outcome will become.

The schematic model also illustrates the reciprocal or cyclical nature of beliefs in the likelihood of future negative outcomes and the processes leading to those beliefs. It has been suggested that the function of worry is to alert us to possible danger: "we are rehearsing possible aversive events and outcomes, and at the same time searching for ways of avoiding them" (Mathews, 1990, p. 456). Worry therefore acts as a signal that some possible danger is up ahead and also as a signal that attention should be allocated to it and something done about it. The adaptive response to perceiving a danger as likely or even possible is to allocate attention and resources to the danger to try to prevent it happening. Thus, the automatic and adaptive response to perceiving an aversive outcome is to think about it. Having reached a belief that a negative outcome is likely, the worrier will be inclined to think even more about it. However, when the outcome is thought about what is likely to come to mind is what has been thought about it before—the reasons why it would happen, a strong memory of a previous instance, or the pre-formed belief that it is likely. What comes to mind when attention is allocated to the outcome will be what led to the belief in the likelihood of the outcome in the first place. The belief in the outcome's likelihood will be reinforced, and so a vicious circle is established. This circular quality of pessimism is also the case for the mood-as-information route, but here the reciprocal process is not the allocation of attention to the outcome but the increase in anxious mood which accompanies the perception of the aversive outcome as likely. The perception of likelihood maintains or enhances the anxious mood which, if the mood state is a source of information for the likelihood judgement, maintains or enhances the belief in the likelihood of the outcome.

So far, worry has been talked about in rather a diffuse way. How does "worry" fit into the description just outlined. Worry represents the overall state or activity of the system described. When someone perceives a negative outcome is likely, through, for example, being able to think of reasons why it would happen, and that perception feeds back to produce further rumination on those reasons, thus setting up a cycle, then that person is worrying.

INTERVENTIONS FOR WORRYING

The arguments which have been presented about the formation of pessimistic judgements and the central role of such judgements in worry have numerous implications for intervening in worry. The main therapeutic implication is that if belief in the likelihood of a negative outcome can be reduced, this should lead to less felt need to worry about the outcome. Attention would not be allocated to the negative outcome, thoughts of why the outcome would happen would not come to mind, and so a reduction in worry would take place.

Can pessimistic beliefs be changed? The most obvious place to begin looking for an answer to this question is the work showing that subjective probability judgements can be changed by asking people to think of counterexplanations. As Koehler (1991) points out despite the fact that people do not appear to produce counterexplanations spontaneously, they are capable of doing so and their future judgements are affected when they do produce them. The study by Hoch (1985), showing reductions in optimism about future positive self-relevant outcomes through asking subjects to think of reasons why those outcomes would not happen, is a clear demonstration of the power of counterfactual thinking. There is evidence that counterfactual thinking can also be used to reduce the pessimism of worriers. MacLeod et al. (1991) asked worriers and non worriers to think of reasons either why negative events would happen (pro reasons) or would not happen (con reasons). Whilst non-worriers remained relatively immune to the effects of the explanation task, worriers showed significantly lower subjective probability estimates for the outcomes where they had generated con reasons. Asking worriers to think of reasons why a worried-about event would not happen seems to be a useful strategy for reducing belief in the likelihood of the event. Even though it may be difficult, people are usually able to think of counterfactual reasons and, when they do, it reduces their pessimism. A similar reduction in pessimistic subjective probabilities for negative events through the use of counterexplanations has been found for depressed, suicidal subjects (MacLeod & Tarbuck, in press).

Interestingly, in the MacLeod et al. (1991) study, items where pro reasons were thought of were not judged as more likely to happen than baseline items (where no reasons were asked for). Drawing on Hoch's (1985) argument about spontaneous causal thinking, this would suggest that worriers spontaneously thought of pro reasons for the negative outcomes. Therefore, explicitly asking them to think of pro reasons did not influence their judgements. The fact that worriers do not become more pessimistic when asked to think of pro reasons also has therapeutic implications. When considering the possibility of worried-about events occurring, it is possible to ask someone to think of both pro and con reasons, thus maintaining the therapeutic stance of examining the evidence but also knowing that thinking of pro reasons is unlikely to make the person more pessimistic. Like the findings of Hoch (1985), the asymmetry of effects is also inconsistent with an explanation of the results in terms of experimental demand, as there is no reason to think that demand should work only for worriers in the con reason condition.

The judgement literature has several specific pointers for using a counterexplanation strategy for worry. Asking subjects to explicitly consider counter reasons rather than just consider the issue in an unbiased way seems to be necessary. Lord, Lepper & Preston (1984) presented students, who either favoured or were against capital punishment, with a number of studies and arguments, some for and some against capital punishment. Subjects were asked to evaluate how well done and how convincing the studies were. Subjects who had been given explicit instructions to consider the opposite (whether their evaluations would have been the same if the opposite conclusion had been reached) provided more unbiased (less attitude-congruent) evaluations than those who were given no instructions or those who had been instructed to be as fair and unbiased as possible. The latter two groups did not differ from each other. The authors interpret this finding as demonstrating subjects' tendency to fail to consider alternatives unless explicitly instructed to do so. There is also some evidence that writing an explanation down has a stronger effect on belief than simply thinking of a reason (Anderson, Lepper & Ross, 1980). As would be expected from the material discussed so far, self-generated reasons are more effective in changing beliefs than reasons suggested to the person (Koehler, 1991).

Finally, the judgement literature indicates that gauging the level of difficulty that may be encountered in thinking of counter reasons is important. MacLeod et al. (1991) found that when subjects had great difficulty in thinking of con reasons, or were not able to think of any con reasons, this actually led to a higher subjective probability judgement than where no reasons were asked for. Although the content of what is brought to mind usually influences judgement, for the availability and simulation heuristics it is actually the *process* of recall or construction (how easily the content came to mind) which is utilised in judgement processes. Usually, content and process go hand in hand such that easy to recall content does in fact come to mind whereas difficult to recall content just does not get recalled, as someone is likely to give up trying. Persisting with recall of inaccessible content, even though it may finally be achieved, can be unhelpful because what is used as a basis for the judgement is not whether the content came to mind but *how easily* it came to mind. In a related vein, Schwarz et al. (1991) found that subjects who had to recall 12 examples of being assertive (which was difficult) gave lower assertiveness ratings than subjects who had to recall 6 examples of assertive behaviour (which was easy). Thus, it was the ease of recalling the examples (process) rather than what was recalled (content) which influenced judgements. Clearly, some gradation of the ease or difficulty of counterexplanations for different worries will be useful in employing counterexplanations as a therapeutic tool. In line with standard cognitive–behaviour therapy techniques, one approach would be the construction of a hierarchy of worries, with people achieving success in generating counterexplanations for minor worries before working through the hierarchy and doing the same for more major worries.

Pessimism, and therefore worry, can be changed through increasing counterfactual thinking. Accepting the role of the simulation heuristic also indicates that intervention could target for change the focus or subject of the judgement. Rather than having as the focus why something bad would happen, an intervention could attempt to change the focus to why something good would happen. The natural tendency to engage in facilitatory thinking would then lead to thinking about why the good outcome would happen. This, though, may be a limited strategy. For some worries it just may not be possible. For example, worries about a loved one being involved in a car crash or about oneself suddenly becoming ill do not lend themselves to being rephrased in terms of positive outcomes. In these worries, counterfactual thinking is more appropriate as the good outcome actually represents an absence of the bad outcome; the hoped-for outcomes would be not being involved in a car crash or remaining healthy. In other worries, there may be a more obvious positive focus, such as the party that one is organising being a success. In such cases, it may be easier to change the focus/subject (why the party would be a success) than to change the type of thinking from facilitatory to counterfactual (why the party would not be a failure). Obviously, this strategy would only be successful where the worrier was able to entertain such thoughts. In most cases, even where there is a positive alternative, it is probably easier to begin by thinking about why the worry might not happen, with a second stage perhaps being the replacement of a negative focus with a positive focus. This, of course, depends on the particular person and the particular worry.

Some worries may be particularly linked to the occurrence of a previous event or events and, through the operation of the availability heuristic, similar events are judged as likely to happen in the future. In this situation, the recall of specific details of the event and the examining of the interpretations that may have been built round the event might be the most appropriate strategy for intervention. However, explanation-based processes may also be important here. It has been found that beliefs, including beliefs in the likelihood of future events, persist even after discrediting of the initial information or events upon which those beliefs were based. This "theory perseverance" effect is a consistent finding in the literature. For example, Ross, Lepper, Strack & Steinmetz (1977) gave subjects a number of case histories of individuals and asked them to think of reasons to explain why each person would perform a particular action in the future and also rate the probability that the person would perform the action. Subjects used the case histories as a starting point for explaining why a certain person would perform a particular action. Results showed that explaining an action by a person resulted in it being judged as more likely to happen. Moreover, this effect persisted even after discrediting the initial information upon which the explanations were based (the experimenter telling subjects that the case histories were incorrect). The authors interpret the results as showing that we elaborate upon a particular event, constructing own own causal explanations for the event. These explanations then become autonomous from the evidence upon which they were initially based. The theory perseverance effect can be eliminated through inserting a distraction task between presentation of the initial information and its discrediting, possibly through preventing subjects constructing their own causal explanations in that time (Fleming & Arrowood, 1979).

To apply this argument to worry, take the example of someone who is involved in a car crash. The person may not only be affected directly by the crash, but may also ruminate on the crash, going over thoughts such as "I'm not a safe driver; other people are careless; it's easy to get into a crash; the world is a dangerous place". As we can see, these thoughts may become increasingly abstract and remote from the actual crash, for which there may have been other explanations. The person may also be reinforced in their beliefs by becoming more vigilant at noticing reports of car crashes on television or in newspapers. In one sense, the original event does not really matter anymore. It has started a process which has taken on a life of its own. As well as the original event being worked through, what would need to be restructured would be the elaborated explanations which have been built up subsequently.

The suggestions for intervention techniques in worry are closely related to the practice of cognitive–behaviour therapy particularly techniques such as constructing hierarchies, considering the evidence, and generating alternatives. What has been suggested though are techniques specifically targeting future pessimism in worriers, techniques which have been derived from an analysis and application of the experimental literature on judgement processes. That they turn out to resemble existing techniques provides encouraging support of their validity and applicability.

WORRY AND BEHAVIOUR

So far, worry has been talked about almost exclusively in cognitive terms as a problem "in the head". The relationship between worry and behaviour, especially problem solving, is beyond the scope of this chapter, but will almost certainly prove to be an important ingredient in a full understanding of worry. Worry is certainly seen as a close relative of problem solving (Borkovec et al., 1983; Mathews, 1990) but is clearly different from problem solving in that it does not seem to lead to problem resolution. There have been suggestions that worry and pessimism can have adaptive functions. Janis's concept of "work of worrying" (Janis, 1958) sees worry as functioning to prepare someone for a possible aversive event. Recently, it has been suggested that for some people pessimism can be an adaptive preparatory style, especially useful in the case of achievement-related outcomes (Showers & Ruben, 1990). These "defensive pessimists" are typically successful individuals who nevertheless form pessimistic expectancies about future success. However, the pessimism acts as a spur to increased efforts, and defensive pessimists, unlike mildly depressed subjects, are characterised by effective preparation for situations and non-avoidant ways of coping. Clearly, both work of worrying and defensive pessimism are very different from the worry and pessimism which have been discussed in this chapter. Why is that for worriers, all the attention that is allocated to thinking about future negative outcomes does not lead to some solution to the problem, reduction in the negative outcome's perceived likelihood and reduction in worry?

One answer is that for many events there are no actual problems to be solved or actions that can be taken. In some cases, the threat may not be a real one, that is, the subjective probability is not a realistic appraisal of the event's likelihood so steps cannot be taken to reduce the probability of its occurrence. Problem-solving may also be inhibited because of the type of attention that is given to the possible outcome. It has been argued throughout that worry is associated with a focus on, and ease of thinking of, reasons why a negative event would happen and with a difficulty in thinking of reasons why it would not happen. In fact, reasons why the negative event would not happen may be actively inhibited. The worrier may just not think of anything that s/he can do to reduce the likelihood of the event. Encouraging counterexplanations may not only decrease an unrealistic expectation of the event, it may suggest steps that could be taken to reduce the probability of the event, where that is an appropriate strategy.

SUMMARY AND CONCLUSION

This chapter has taken a deliberately narrow view of worry. The role of pessimistic beliefs about future negative outcomes in worry has been stressed, and the main focus has been on understanding the cognitive processes used in forming those beliefs. Applying theory and findings from the judgement literature has led to the conclusion that explanation-based processes play a central role in pessimism and therefore worry. Implications of explanation-based processes for therapeutic interventions have also been suggested, especially the use of counterfactual thinking. Little has been said about motivational, affective or interpersonal/ systemic aspects of worry. In defence of the emphasis adopted here, worry is, by consensus, essentially a cognitive phenomenon. It seems reasonable, therefore, to try to understand worry by elucidating its underlying cognitive processes. Research is at an early stage and clearly more work needs to be carried out into cognitive processes in worry. In addition to replicating some existing findings, efforts could usefully be directed to examining in more detail the sorts of information that people employ in constructing explanations for future events. The role of personal experiences, either direct (happened to the person themselves) or indirect (heard about it or happened to someone they know) would seem to be an obvious place to look. Also, the use of self-concept information to infer what might happen in the future may also reveal important components of worrying. Perhaps the most fruitful area of research would be evaluating the success of the various therapeutic applications suggested as means of reducing worry, which would also provide the strictest test of the ideas put forward. It is an empirical question how successful the application of theory and findings from the judgement literature will be in understanding and changing worry, or whether there will prove to be important differences in judgement processes in worry. There are good reasons, though, for thinking that future research will produce a good outcome.

REFERENCES

Ahn, W., Brewer, W.F. & Mooney, R.J. (1992). Schema acquisition from a single example. *Journal of Experimental Psychology: Learning, Memory, and Cognition*, **18**, 391–412.

Anderson, C.A., Lepper, M.R. & Ross, L. (1980). Perseverance of social theories: The role of explanations in the persistence of discredited information. *Journal of Personality and Social Psychology*, **39**, 1037–1049.

Barlow, D.H. (1988). *Anxiety and its Disorders*. New York: Guilford.

Borkovec, T.D., Robinson, E., Pruzinsky, T. & DePree, J. (1983). Preliminary exploration of worry: Some characteristics and processes. *Behaviour Research and Therapy*, **21**, 9–16.

Butler, G. & Mathews, A. (1983). Cognitive processes in anxiety. *Advances in Behviour Research and Therapy*, **5**, 51–62.

Butler, G. & Mathews, A. (1987). Anticipatory anxiety and risk perception. *Cognitive Therapy and Research*, **11**, 551–565.

Campbell, J.D. & Fairey, P.J. (1985). Effects on self-esteem, hypothetical explanations and verbalization of expectancies on future performance. *Journal of Personality and Social Psychology*, **48**, 1097–1111.

Dunning, D. & Parpal, M. (1989). Mental addition versus mental subtraction in counterfactual reasoning: On assessing the impact of personal actions and life events. *Journal of Personality and Social Psychology*, **57**, 5–15.

Dunning, D. & Story, A.L. (1991). Depression, realism, and the overconfidence effect: Are the sadder wiser when predicting future actions and events? *Journal of Personality and Social Psychology*, **61**, 521–532.

Eysenck, H.J. & Eysenck, S.G. (1975). *Manual of the Eysenck Personality Questionnaire (Junior and Adult)*. London: Hodder & Stoughton.

Fleming, J. & Arrowood, A.J. (1979). Information processing and the perseverance of discredited self-perceptions. *Personality and Social Psychology Bulletin*, **5**, 201–204.

Hoch, S.J. (1984). Availability and interference in predictive judgement. *Journal of Experimental Psychology: Learning, Memory, and Cognition*, **10**, 649–662.

Hoch, S.J. (1985). Counterfactual reasoning and accuracy in predicting personal events. *Journal of Experimental Psychology, Learning, Memory, and Cognition*, **11**, 719–731.

Janis, I.L. (1958). *Psychological Stress*. New York: Wiley.

Kahneman, D. & Miller, D.T. (1986). Norm Theory: Comparing reality to its alternatives. *Psychological Review*, **93**, 136–153.

Kahneman, D. & Tversky, A. (1982). The simulation heuristic. In D. Kahneman, P. Slovic, & A. Tversky (Eds.), *Judgement Under Uncertainty: Heuristics and Biases*, pp. 201–208. Cambridge: Cambridge University Press.

Koehler, D.J. (1991). Explanation, imagination, and confidence in judgement. *Psychological Bulletin*, **110**, 499–519.

Levi, A.S. & Pryor, J.B. (1987). Use of the availability heuristic in probability estimates of future events: The effects of imagining outcomes vs imagining reasons. *Organizational Behaviour and Human Decision Processes*, **40**, 219–234.

Lord, C.G., Lepper, M.P. & Preston, E. (1984). Considering the opposite: A corrective strategy for social judgement. *Journal of Personality and Social Psychology*, **47**, 1231–1243.

MacLeod, A.K. (1989). Anxiety and judgements of future personal events. Unpublished PhD thesis, University of Cambridge.

MacLeod, A.K. (manuscript in preparation). Pessimism about future personal events is explanation-based.

MacLeod, A.K. & Tarbuck, A. (in press). Explaining why negative events will happen to oneself: Parasuicides are pessimistic because they can't see any reason not to be. *British Journal of Clinical Psychology*.

MacLeod, A.K., Williams, J.M.G. & Bekerian, D.A. (1991). Worry is reasonable: The role of explanations in pessimism about future personal events. *Journal of Abnormal Psychology*, **100**, 478–486.

MacLeod, C. & Campbell, L. (1992). Memory accessibility and probability judgements: An experimental evaluation of the availability heuristic. *Journal of Personality and Social Psychology*, **63**, 890–902.

Mathews, A. (1990). Why worry? The cognitive function of anxiety. *Behaviour Research and Therapy*, **28**, 455–468.

Murphy, G.L. & Medin, D.L. (1984). The role of theories in conceptual coherence. *Psychological Review*, **92**, 289–316.

Pennington, N. & Hastie, R. (1988). Explanation-based decision making: Effects of memory structures on judgements. *Journal of Experimental Psychology: Learning Memory, and Cognition*, **14**, 521–533.

Ross, L., Lepper, M.R., Strack, F. & Steinmetz, J.L. (1977). Social explanation and social expectation: The effects of real and hypothetical explanations on subjective likelihood. *Journal of Personality and Social Psychology*, **35**, 817–829.

Schwarz, N., Bless, H., Strack, F., Klumpp, G., Rittenauer-Schatka, H. & Simons, A. (1991). Ease of retrieval as information: another look at the availability heuristic. *Journal of Personality and Social Psychology*, **61**, 195–202.

Schwarz, N. & Clore, G.L. (1983). Mood, misattribution, and judgements of well-being: Informative and directive functions of affective states. *Journal of Personality and Social Psychology*, **45**, 513– 523.

Schwarz, N. & Clore, G.L. (1987). How do I feel about it?: The informative function of affective states. In K. Fiedler & J. Forgas (Eds.), *Affect, Cognition, and Social Behaviour*. Toronto: Hogrefe International.

Shaklee, H. & Fischoff, B. (1982). Strategies of information search in causal analysis. *Memory and Cognition*, **10**, 520–530.

Sherman, S.J., Skov, R.B., Hervitz, E.F. & Stock, C.B. (1981). The effects of explaining hypothetical future events: From possibility to probability to actuality and beyond. *Journal of Experimental Social Psychology*, **17**, 142–158.

Sherman, S.J., Zehner, K.S., Johnson, J. & Hirt, E.R. (1983). Social explanation: The role of timing, set and recall on subjective likelihood estimates. *Journal of Personality and Social Psychology*, **44**, 1127–1143.

Showers, C. & Ruben, C. (1990). Distinguishing defensive pessimism from depression: negative expectations and positive coping mechanisms. *Cognitive Therapy and Research*, **14**, 385–399.

Teasdale, J.D. & Fogarty, S.J. (1979). Differential effects of induced mood on retrieval of pleasant and unpleasant events from episodic memory. *Journal of Abnormal Psychology*, **88**, 248–257.

Tversky, A. & Kahneman, D. (1973). Availability: A heuristic for judging frequency and probability. *Cognitive Psychology*, **5**, 207–232.

Williams, J.M.G. & Scott, J. (1988). Autobiographical memory in depression. *Psychological Medicine*, **18**, 689–695.

CHAPTER 6 Worry as a component of test anxiety: a multidimensional analysis

Gordon L. Flett* and
Kirk R. Blankstein†

INTRODUCTION

> There is a sizable body of evidence consistent with the idea that proneness to self-preoccupation and, more specifically, worry over evaluation, is a powerful component of what is referred to as test anxiety. (Sarason & Sarason, 1990, p. 485)

Test anxiety is regarded as a construct with two components that reflect worry and emotional arousal. Of course, the focus of this chapter is on the worry component of test anxiety in testing situations. Test taking is ubiquitous in our society and the process of testing applies to students at all levels of the education system. Tests are used to monitor and evaluate the progress of students, to assess problems, to measure intelligence and aptitude, to screen for admission to universities, and to determine whether university students should go on to graduate and professional school (Hembree, 1988). Clearly, much is at stake in these test situations and it should come as no surprise that they assume considerable importance in the lives of the vast majority of students. It is equally evident that anxiety in these evaluative situations is an important personal and social problem. Test anxiety is a distressing and unpleasant experience which plays a critical role in the personal phenomenology of students, and it is assumed to affect their performance and personal development (Sarason & Sarason, 1990). Performance has generally been accepted as the most important criterion variable in test anxiety research (Sud & Sharma, 1990), but from a clinical perspective, we must consider the personal distress and suffering of students who experience extreme test anxiety.

*York University, Canada and †Erindale College, University of Toronto, Canada

Worrying: Perspectives on Theory, Assessment and Treatment. Edited by G.C.L. Davey and F. Tallis.
© 1994 John Wiley & Sons Ltd.

Reports indicate that test anxiety is quite common. Hill & Wigfield (1984) projected the incidence of test-anxious students in the US to be approximately 10 million at precollege levels. A study of 1684 Canadian elementary and high school students (McGuire, Mitic & Neumann, 1987) indicated that in excess of 22% of students were significantly worried about schoolwork and this was the most prevalent stressor by grade 12. Test anxiety is also considered to be pervasive at the university level (see Spielberger, Anton & Bedel, 1976). In our research, we are particularly concerned with test anxiety in college students. We often discuss test anxiety in our classes and request that students raise their hands if they do not experience significant levels of worry associated with test taking. Few hands are ever raised in our upper level classes.

The present chapter addresses several issues pertaining to the nature of worry in test-anxious individuals. The first section addresses the important issue of the association between worry in the form of test anxiety and other forms of worry. We begin with a brief overview of past theory and research on the nature of worry in test anxiety. We review data supporting the view that worry among test-anxious students stems, in part, from negative self-conceptions involving intellectual ability. Next, the results from various studies of trait test anxiety are used to support the argument that dispositional worry among test-anxious students is a pervasive phenomenon that is comparable in many respects to other forms of worry. This extensive analysis of trait worry in test-anxious students is then followed by an examination of numerous issues pertaining to the nature of state worry in evaluative situations. Specifically, we examine the association between state and trait worry, as well as the similarities and differences between state worry and the other dimensions of test anxiety (i.e. test-irrelevant thinking, tension, and bodily symptoms) outlined by Sarason (1984). We conclude with a brief discussion of the treatment implications of research on worry and test anxiety and we suggest some important directions for future research. Before discussing this recent research in detail, we begin with a case study of a student who manifests many of the features associated with worry in evaluative situations. The student described in this account, Winnifred, is a prototypical case of extreme test or evaluation anxiety, according to past research and theory.

Winnifred Orry: A Prisoner of Worry

Winnifred is a 21-year-old fourth year undergraduate student who is working toward a B.Sc. degree in psychology. Winnifred plans to apply to graduate school but doesn't hold out much hope that her application will be successful despite her relatively solid (if somewhat inconsistent) A– average. In her words, she is "probably doomed to failure".

Winnifred acknowledges that she was probably not always anxious in situations in which she is being evaluated or perceives that she is being evaluated. However, she can recall experiences of test anxiety during her early elementary school grades and believes that her anxiety was firmly established by about the fifth grade. She is unable to recall any specific events that could have triggered this anxiety although she does remember being upset when she brought her second grade report card home to show her father and he compared her performance to that of a close cousin and indicated that he expected better results in the future. Winnifred's test anxiety gradually increased throughout high school and university. It is especially severe at this time because, in her appraisal, her future is at stake: "If I screw up now, my whole life is ruined."

Despite her academic record, Winnifred reports that evaluations are difficult and threatening to her and that she sees herself as ineffective and inadequate. In the face of evaluative stressors, she experiences an anxiety reaction that includes cognitive, emotional, behavioral, and physiological components. However, on interview it was clear that for Winnifred the cognitive component was most salient. She seems to be prone to negative self-preoccupation, especially worry, about being evaluated. Even before she sees the questions on a specific test she has a strong expectancy of failure. Her prototypical worry during actual tests is that she will fail. She also questions her intelligence and worries about her ability to perform adequately, she compares herself to the other students and worries that they are doing better than her, she worries about the embarrassment of "failure", she worries about letting her parents down and about being rejected by them, and she worries about the immediate and long-term consequences of not performing at a satisfactory level. As the examination progresses, she becomes increasingly self-critical and her thoughts are even more negatively self-evaluative in content. These intrusive, negative, self-preoccupying thoughts are self-defeating because they divert her attention from the test and interfere with positive, task-related chains of thinking. At times her negative self-focus appears to lead to a virtual immobilization as she "freezes up". She considers fleeing from the test room. Sometimes she becomes so overwhelmed by her negative internal dialogue that she seems to "disengage" from the task, gives up, and loses the motivation to try to answer questions. At these times her mind seems to wander and she daydreams about unrelated events.

In addition to the worry, self-preoccupation and cognitive interference, including mind-wandering, Winnifred complains that prior to and during tests she feels tense, jittery, and uneasy, and experiences distressing physiological changes and symptoms such as increased heart rate, nausea, and headaches. She reported that she is locked in to a vicious circle of escalating anxiety: she is preoccupied with worry, self-doubt, and the consequences of failure, which makes her feel even more tense and jittery and she becomes even more aware of her racing heart, queasy stomach, and throbbing headache.

Although Winnifred has never actually failed an exam, she believes that her performance is adversely affected by her test anxiety and she is never satisifed with the level of her performance. Her response to this "failure" is to dwell on the results, engage in self-blame and worry about future failure. In fact, Winnifred has a tendency to catastrophize and overgeneralize: if she performs relatively poorly on a minor term test, she assumes that she will probably fail the course, perhaps fail all of her courses and be suspended from university.

Although our initial interviews and the measures we administered focused on Winnifred's cognitions during and following a test, it became clear that Winnifred was not worry free at other times. In fact, a great deal of her worry was anticipatory. Although her worries became more active and salient as an examination approached, she claimed that she started to worry at the first meeting of a course when the professor outlined the evaluation format and indicated the due dates for assignments, tests, and examinations. Her worry and self-preoccupation interfered with her studying and preparation for an exam, sometimes weeks before the date of the exam. She claimed that she just could not concentrate on the material. An evaluation of her study skills and strategies identified some minor problem areas; however, we concluded that the primary problem was one of cognitive interference rather than one of deficits in skills. Winnifred often attempted to compensate for her perceived shortcomings by redoubling her efforts and increasing the number of hours spent studying. Despite the increased study time, Winnifred's expectations of success remained low. At other times, her fear of failure caused her to procrastinate and delay studying. The consequence of either strategy was increased worry.

Winnifred's intrusive worries about failure had other consequences. For example, she reported that she often had trouble falling asleep at night. She would lie awake worrying about her prospects for success in her various courses. Sometimes she would awaken early in the morning and the vicious circle of rumination would start all over. She also reported an increasing sense of helplessness as the term progressed and her anxiety was accompanied by mild levels of dysphoria which invariably worsened following her anticipated "failures". Although Winnifred has several close friends she spends less and less time with them as the term progresses and she focuses almost completely on her studies and preparation for examinations. She is also worried about a variety of social-evaluative situations including participating in a class debate, leading a class seminar, attending a necessary social function, and being asked out on a date. Winnifred is distressed, unhappy, and dissatisfied about her current life situation and is worried about her future prospects. In her own words, "The only time I'm not worrying is during summer vacation . . . No, I'm worried then, too!"

MEASURES OF GENERAL WORRY

Research in our laboratory and by other investigators has confirmed that Winnifred's symptoms are not uncommon and represent central aspects of worry in test-anxious students. This research benefits from the extensive literature on worry in test-anxious students. Over the past 35 years, there have been significant advances in the conceptualization and measurement of components of test anxiety. Initially, Mandler & Sarason (1952) examined test anxiety as a unitary phenomenon and demonstrated that test-anxious students had poorer relative-performance in testing situations. Alpert & Haber (1960) then extended this work by making the important conceptual distinction between debilitating test anxiety and facilitating test anxiety. Although the independence of these two dimensions of test anxiety appears questionable (Watson, 1988), Alpert & Haber did draw attention to the possibility that test anxiety is not a unitary concept and that some aspects of anxiety or tension in performance situations may facilitate positive outcomes for some individuals.

Liebert & Morris (1967) furthered the study of test anxiety as a multi-dimensional construct by advancing the notion that test anxiety could be divided into two components representing worry and emotionality. Worry was equated with the cognitive manifestations of test anxiety such as evaluative concerns and negative self-expectations. Emotionality was equated with perceptions of the physiological or arousal component of test anxiety (also see Morris, Davis & Hutchings, 1981). The usefulness of this distinction was demonstrated by various research investigations showing that it is the worry component of test anxiety that is most closely associated with performance (Deffenbacher, 1978, 1980; Seipp, 1991; Tryon, 1980). The stronger association between worry and performance rather than between emotionality and performance can be detected with both trait and state measures of worry (Hembree, 1988; Seipp, 1991).

Measuring the Worry Component of Test Anxiety Research

Past beliefs about the nature of test anxiety are reflected directly in the content of available assessment measures. Historically, items that assess worry have been predominant in measures of test anxiety. Both the final 37 item Test Anxiety Scale (TAS) by Sarason (1978) and earlier versions of the scale included content that reflected worry about the outcome of examinations and the physiological reactions that accompany worry. Typically, the scale has been used as an independent, stratified variable to compare groups of extreme scorers in particular situations or as a dependent variable reflecting the operation of an experimental or clinical treatment. Unfortunately, the TAS does not provide separate scores for worry versus emotionality. Factor analyses indicate that the TAS does have separate factors that correspond to worry and emotionality (Richardson, O'Neill, Whitmore & Judd, 1977), but the validity of the factor structure is questionable (see Spielberger et al., 1978).

In contrast, other common test anxiety measures do enable researchers to clearly distinguish worry and emotionality. Liebert & Morris (1967) provided brief five item measures of worry versus emotionality that focused on these variables at the state level. The subsequent revision of these measures maintained this distinction (see Morris et al., 1981). Similarly, the Test Anxiety Inventory by Spielberger et al. (1978) is a 20 item instrument with separate factors that represent cognitive-worry reactions and physiological reactions.

More recently, Sarason (1984) has further refined the test anxiety concept by examining other dimensions of test anxiety that can be distinguished within the worry and emotionality domains. In a series of four studies, Sarason (1984) developed and refined the Reactions to Tests Scale (RTT). The RTT consists of four 10 item subscales measuring worry (e.g. "The thought 'What happens if I fail this test?' goes through my mind during tests"), test-irrelevant thinking (e.g. "I think about current events during a test"), perceived tension (e.g. "I feel distressed and uneasy before tests"), and bodily symptoms (e.g. "My stomach gets upset before tests"). The worry and test-irrelevant thinking factors reflect the cognitive component of test anxiety, while the tension and bodily symptoms factors reflect the arousal–emotionality component of test anxiety (Sarason, 1984). Several interersting findings have emerged thus far from this research. For instance, analyses with measures of cognitive interference indicated that cognitive interference is associated with all four RTT subscales but the most robust association is between cognitive interference and worry. Sarason observed that cognitive interference is probably due to thoughts of fear of failure and social comparison rather than thoughts that are irrelevant to the situation. On the basis of these findings, Sarason concluded that "The construction of a multifactor instrument may make it possible to define anxiety more sharply and improve the understanding of how it relates to performance" (p. 937).

Test-anxious Worry and Negative Self-conceptions

Research in our laboratory has been based on Sarason's (1984) premise that the test anxiety construct does indeed have at least four components and that it is important to make fine-grained distinctions within the cognitive domain by distinguishing between worry and test-irrelevant thinking. We have used this approach to address several important questions about the nature of worry. We share the predominant view in the literature that worry among test anxious students stems from anticipated failure due to negative self-judgments about ability (see Covington, 1986; Sarason, 1986). This focus on anticipated lack of ability and poor performance is reflected in the content of worry measures. For instance, our state measure of worry in test anxiety has items such as "I worried about failing", "The thought, 'What happens if I fail?' went through my head", "I found myself thinking about how bright the other people are", and "Thoughts of doing poorly interfered with my concentration." The last item is noteworthy because it illustrates the difference between worry and test-irrelevant thinking. Test-irrelevant thinkers experience interference due to thoughts unrelated to the test (e.g. "irrelevant bits of information popped into my head"), while worriers experience cognitive interference due to the uncontrollable and intrusive thoughts they experience about the consequences of failure.

Because our conceptualization and assessment of worry focuses on negative self-perceptions of worry and attendant expectations of failure, most research in our laboratory has focused on test anxious worry and aspects of the self-concept. A consistent finding that has emerged from various thought-listing studies in our laboratory (e.g. Blankstein & Flett, 1991; Blankstein, Flett, Boase & Toner, 1990; Blankstein, Toner & Flett, 1989) is that test anxious students report a preponderance of negative thoughts about the self and a relative absence of positive thoughts about the self, and that this pattern is present with both structured and unstructured thought-listing assessments. A detailed content analysis by Blankstein et al. (1989) revealed few instances where subjects listed thoughts by stating simply "I worried during the task." Rather, subjects were more specific and detailed about their concerns and they incorporated more of an evaluative focus by reporting thoughts such as "I worried about looking stupid" and "I wondered whether I have what it takes to be successful." Thus, analyses of cognitive content emphasize that worry involves negative views and expectations about personal ability.

Unfortunately, the specific link between the worry components and negative self-thoughts was not established in this thought-listing research because the test anxiety measures used in these earlier studies did not enable us to distinguish worry and emotionality. To examine the role of worry versus the other components of test anxiety (i.e. test-irrelevant thinking, tension, and bodily symptoms), we have conducted a program of research that involves administering the trait RTT (Sarason, 1984) and numerous self-concept measures to college students. At present, we have obtained data from over 3000 college students in a variety of studies. Before describing these findings, two important caveats are in order. First, it will be obvious that in many instances the construct under consideration is related to all of the RTT subscales. This is to be expected since the scales are intercorrelated. However, in other instances it will be noted that there are clear differences in the pattern of relations with the various components of test anxiety, thus contributing to the discriminant validity of the different components and substantiating the observation that ". . . the correlations seem low enough to justify comparisons among them concerning their explanatory and predictive value" (Sarason, Sarason & Pierce, 1991, p. 9).

Second, in our analyses, we have not attempted to partial out the effects of any other component (such as tension). Although some investigators choose to hold trait anxiety constant when examining the relation between worry and other constructs (e.g. Davey, 1993; Davey, Hampton, Farrell & Davidson, 1992), and this is a valid statistical strategy, we are not certain that it makes sense conceptually when considering test anxiety. For example, it is rare to find a student who is high on the worry component but low on the tension component. We agree with Pruzinsky & Borkovec (1990) that "worry may not in principle be distinguishable from anxiety (cognitive components are routinely present in complex human anxiety response) except perhaps in brief artificial experimental preparations" (p. 507). Our view is that the RTT is comprised of two cognitive components (worry and test-irrelevant thinking) and two somatic or emotional components (tension and bodily symptoms). Tension appears to be closely linked to worry and bodily symptoms. In fact, Meyer, Miller, Metzger & Borkovec (1990) reported that Penn State Worry Questionnaire (PSWQ) scores were related to both the percentage of the day feeling tension ($r = .44$) and the percentage of the day spent worrying ($r = .64$).

The results of our research on worry and the self-concept are summarized in Table 6.1. This research has examined direct appraisals of the self with self-esteem, self-concept, and self-expectancy measures, as well as related factors involved in the self-regulation process such as self-consciousness and the use of perfectionistic standards. As can be seen in Table 6.1, there is extensive evidence for a link between worry and the negative self-concept per se. For instance, test-anxious worry is related to low scores on the Rosenberg Self-Esteem Scale (Rosenberg, 1965). This finding replicates past indications of a negative correlation between self-esteem and scores on the PSWQ (Meyer et al., 1990). Research with two new measures provides greater specificity in terms of identifying the specific features of the self-concept associated with worry. In one sample, subjects completed the RTT and a new measure entitled the Beck Self-Concept Test (BSC; Beck, Steer, Epstein & Brown, 1990). The BSC measures unfavorable comparisons of the self to others in the areas of intellectual ability, physical appearance, work efficacy, and virtues. Our data indicated that the link with test-anxious worry and the self-concept is specific to unfavorable appraisals of intellectual ability. The RTT measures were not related to other BSC measures. In another study, we examined the link between the RTT and a trait version of the State Self-Esteem Scale (Heatherton & Polivy, 1991). This scale provides separate scores for performance self-esteem, appearance self-esteem, and social self-esteem. As shown in Table 6.1, it was found that test-anxious worry was significantly negatively correlated with all subscales of the Trait Self-Esteem measure. Surprisingly, the strongest effect was for the social subscale, $r = -.65$, $p <$ .01. However, we believe that the worry content of this subscale is confounded with performance.

One interpretation of these data is that test-anxious worriers have a general tendency to be self-punitive. Although past research has focused on self-punitiveness and depression (see Flett, Hewitt & Mittelstaedt, 1991), there are some indications that anxiety is also related to self-punitiveness (Ganellen, 1988). On the basis of past evidence, we feel that test-anxious worriers are particularly prone to find fault with themselves. Carver & Ganellen (1983) distinguished conceptually among three factors that might contribute to the tendency to be self-punitive: the maintenance of high standards for one's self-evaluation, the making of harsh judgments of oneself for failing to make a standard, and integrating a single failure as reflecting upon the totality of one's self-worth. The Attitudes Toward Self Scale (ATS; Carver & Ganellen, 1983) was developed to assess these three components: (1) high standards; (2) self-criticism; and (3) over-generalization. In a subsequent paper, Carver, La Voie, Kuhl & Ganellen (1988) revised the ATS and developed an additional subscale (i.e.

Table 6.1 Correlation between trait reactions to tests and self-concept measures

	RTT dimension			
Measure	Worry	Tension	Thinking	Body
Self-concept measures				
Rosenberg Self-Esteem	−.45**	−.35**	−.21**	−.23**
Trait Self-Esteem Scale				
Performance esteem	−.30**	−.22**	−.25**	−.22**
Appearance esteem	−.40**	−.35**	−.13	−.36**
Social esteem	−.65**	−.49**	−.23**	−.46**
Private self-consciousness	.16*	.21**	.17*	.17*
Public self-consciousness	.27**	.29**	.18*	.07
Social anxiety	.31**	.30**	.05	.17*
Optimism (LOT)	−.50**	−.41**	−.24**	−.35**
Beck Self-Concept				
Intellectual ability	.26**	.17	.09	.00
Attitudes Toward Self (General)				
High standards	.19*	.28**	−.03	.34**
Self-criticism	.32**	.36**	.04	.35**
Overgeneralization	.42**	.41**	.26*	.34**
Attitudes Towards Self (Academic)				
High standards	.18*	.31**	−.05	.29**
Self-criticism	.28**	.36**	−.02	.31**
Overgeneralization	.49**	.43**	.25	.33**
Problem-solving ability				
Academic Problem-Solving Inventory				
Approach–Avoidance	−.18*	−.07	−.30**	−.01
Personal control	−.52**	−.39**	−.48**	−.28**
Confidence	−.42**	−.23**	−.39**	−.22**
Social Problem-Solving Inventory				
Cognitive	−.59**	−.38**	−.52**	−.39**
Emotional	−.63**	−.54**	−.47**	−.46**
Behavioural avoidance	−.44**	−.32**	−.47**	−.23*
Problem definition	−.19*	−.09	−.24**	−.10
Alternative solutions	−.12	−.07	−.23**	−.05
Decision making	−.16*	−.10	−.34**	−.13
Solution implementation	−.14	−.02	−.23**	−.02

** $p < .01$, * $p < .05$.   Sample sizes vary from $n = 123$ to $n = 200$.

perseveration) to assess the tendency to be preoccupied with past failings. Research with the measure has shown that overgeneralization is the factor linked most closely with depression.

We explored the possible relationships between RTT worry and the components of self-punitiveness in two studies. In the first study, we administered the original ATS and a modified version along with the RTT to 202 students. In the modified version, we rewrote the ATS items such that they were specific to academic evaluative situations. In the second study we employed the revised ATS, but the only test anxiety measure in this study was the RTT worry subscale. The results of the first study are summarized in Table 6.1. Consistent with the results for depression, the strongest correlate of test-anxious worry was overgeneralization. Worriers tend to overgeneralize a single failure more broadly to the self-concept, perhaps reflecting a more general tendency to make sweeping inferences and catastrophize (Vasey & Borkovec, 1992). Our first study also confirmed the link between worry and self-criticism and there was a small but significant correlation between worry and high standards, $r = .18$, $p < .05$. In contrast to the results with the worry subscale, the relations between the test-irrelevant thinking component and the ATS suggest that self-criticism is not a factor in test-irrelevant thinking. The second study showed that worry was associated with overgeneralization, $r = .49$, $p < .01$, perseveration, $r = .45$, $p < .01$, and self-criticism, $r = .32$, $p < .05$, but there was virtually no correlation between worry and high standards. The lack of a consistent link between worry and high standards may simply be due to the fact that content of current measures of test-anxious worry focus on concerns about failure *per se*, but the main worry for perfectionists is a fear of not attaining the highest score possible (Hewitt & Flett, 1991). Subsequent research with worry measures that more closely reflect perfectionistic desires should establish a more consistent link between worry and high standards.

A great deal of the work in the test anxiety area has sought to test predictions derived from Carver & Scheier's (1986) self-regulation model. Briefly, this model posits that worry arises from an excessive focus on the self along with a tendency to endorse negative self-expectancies. Carver & Scheier (1986) theorized further that pessimistic students are more likely to withdraw or "disengage" from a task than optimistic students. This pessimism is reflected in psychological distress, off-task thinking and poor academic performance. Rather than being entirely maladaptive, conceptual and empirical analyses indicate that excessive self-focus in the presence of *positive* expectancies may facilitate performance (see Rich & Woolever, 1988).

We have conducted various studies to test predictions derived from this model. In a previous paper (Flett, Blankstein & Boase, 1987) we reported significant associations between the components of the Self-Consciousness Scale (SCS; Fenigstein, Scheier & Buss, 1975) and RTT worry. The SCS comprises three subscales, private self-consciousness (awareness of thoughts, feelings, and attitudes), public self-consciousness (awareness of self as object in social situations), and social anxiety. Although worry was significantly correlated with all subscales of the SCS, the strongest association was between worry and public self-consciousness. These results were replicated in a subsequent study (see Table 6.1), although the effects were not quite as strong. Similar results for general worry have been reported in two studies by Borkovec and his colleagues (Meyer et al., 1990; Pruzinsky & Borkovec, 1990).

Regarding expectancy outcomes, we have already noted the accumulating evidence in support of the link between worry and pessimism about specific life events. Analyses with dispositional measures of optimism–pessimism have confirmed that the link between test anxiety and pessimistic beliefs reflects a more general and enduring personality style. Scheier & Carver (1985) developed the Life Orientation Test (LOT) to measure dispositional optimism (e.g. "In uncertain times, I usually expect the best"). Research by Topman, Kleijn, van der Ploeg & Masset (1992) with the LOT confirmed the presence of a negative relation between optimism and test anxiety. Unfortunately, these researchers did not differentiate among test anxiety components. In our own research, we examined all four RTT components and found a strong negative correlation between RTT worry and scores on the LOT (see Table 6.1) which was replicated in another sample of 158 students, $r = -.48, p < .01$.

Importantly, our research indicates that the link between worry and negative self-expectancies about ability extends to the perceived ability to solve personal problems. Recently, several investigators working in the broader worry domain have suggested that inappropriate or poor problem-solving may play a central role in the maintenance of worry (e.g. Borkovec, 1985; Davey et al., 1992; Mathews, 1990, Tallis, Eysenck & Mathews, 1991) (see Davey, this volume, Chapter 2). As Davey et al. (1992) have suggested, "Worrying may . . . be an *attempt* at problem-solving—but one that fails because of deficiencies in the problem-solving process itself" (p. 134). They suggested that these deficiencies might be due to poor problem-solving confidence or ineffective coping strategies.

Researchers in the test anxiety area have considered the possibility that test anxiety may be associated with poorer problem-solving skills. For example, there is some evidence that high test-anxious subjects possess relatively ineffective test-taking strategies (Bruch, 1981) and are less knowledgeable about appropriate study methods (e.g. Desiderato & Koskinen, 1969). While such studies may be considered as evidence that test-anxious individuals utilize less efficient self-defeating problem-solving strategies, the issue of self-perceived problem-solving strategies and behaviors is equally important. According to Butler & Meichenbaum (1981), self-appraised problem-solving skills (a metacognitive variable) should affect a person's actual problem-solving performance.

We explored worry and perceived problem-solving ability in a previous study (Blankstein, Flett & Batten, 1989) in which we examined the relations between scores on Sarason's (1978) Test Anxiety Scale (TAS) and Heppner & Petersen's (1982) Problem-Solving Inventory (PSI). The PSI was developed to assess individual differences in self-perceived problem-solving ability. It has three subscales measuring perceptions of personal control, problem-solving confidence, and problem approach–avoidance style. We found that the component of the TAS that reflects worry about oneself and one's performance (Richardson et al., 1977) was strongly associated with negative perceptions of personal control, and problem-solving confidence, and a reported tendency to avoid problems.

In a recent study (Blankstein, Flett & Watson, 1992), we examined the relations between the RTT and a modified version of the PSI. We wanted to examine the relations between the worry and other components of the RTT and the subscales of an academic version of the PSI. The Academic Problem-Solving Inventory (APSI) was created by specifying academic problems in the content of each item rather than problems in general (e.g. "when my first efforts to solve an academic problem fail, I become uneasy about my ability to handle the situation"). The results were similar to those reported previously. All of the trait RTT dimensions were correlated significantly with lack of personal control over academic problems, and lack of problem-solving confidence; however, the strongest relations involved the worry component of the RTT.

We recently replicated these findings in a new sample of subjects (see Table 6.1). Worry was associated with lower self-confidence in the ability to solve academic problems and less perceived personal control over academic problems. Comparable relations were found for the test-irrelevant thinking subscale of the RTT. Both worry and test-irrelevant thinking were also correlated with a tendency to avoid academic problems rather than to approach them. This relation was somewhat stronger for test-irrelevant thinking. The results of these studies with the PSI and APSI are comparable to the results reported by Davey et al. (1992) who examined the relations between scores on the Student Worry Scale and the PSI and found that worry was associated with poor problem-solving confidence and poor perceived personal control. When trait anxiety was held constant worry was unrelated to any aspect of self-perceived problem-solving efficacy. However, we believe that extreme worry rarely occurs in the absence of trait anxiety.

In the study summarized in Table 6.1, we also examined the relations between components of the RTT and the subscales of the Social Problem-Solving Inventory (SPSI; D'Zurilla & Nezu, 1990). The SPSI is a new 70 item multidimensional, self-report measure that reflects the prescriptive model of social problem-solving formulated by D'Zurilla and associates. Recently, D'Zurilla & Nezu (1990) summarized this model and noted that it ". . . characterizes social problem-solving as a complex, cognitive–affective–behavioral process that consists of a number of different components, including general motivational variables and a set of specific skills" (p. 156). Consistent with this approach, the SPSI provides a comprehensive assessment of two types of variables: problem orientation and problem-solving skills. The problem orientation subscales assess the generalized cognitive, emotional, and behavioral response sets or evaluative reactions that a person brings to new problem-solving situations. These subscales represent the motivational component of the problem-solving process. In contrast, the problem-solving skills subscales assess four specific goal-directed tasks or facets involved in effective problem-solving: problem definition and formulation; generation of alternative solutions; decision making, and solution implementation and verification (i.e. the ability to effectively implement, monitor, and evaluate solutions or coping responses). The SPSI enables researchers to compare the results obtained with the orientation measures versus the specific measures of problem-solving skills. The importance of conducting separate analyses of problem orientation and problem-solving skills was demonstrated in a recent prospective study by D'Zurilla & Sheedy (1991). These researchers found that undergraduate students' problem orientation was a better predictor of stress than was their problem-solving skills. Whereas problem-solving orientation predicted stress levels, a subsequent study by the same investigators showed that it was the problem-solving skills subscales that were most predictive of objective performance (D'Zurilla & Sheedy, 1992).

Inspection of Table 6.1 reveals that, in one sample of first year undergraduates, the worry component of the RTT was associated with a more maladaptive problem orientation in terms of cognitive, emotional, and behavioral reactions. This negative or inhibitive orientation is more likely to include general tendencies to view a problem as a significant threat to well-being, respond to a problem with strong negative emotions, and avoid or put off dealing with a problem (D'Zurilla & Sheedy, 1991). This negative problem orientation is consistent with the notion that the test-anxious worrier anticipates a more problematic and threatening future. Further inspection of Table 6.1 indicates that the other components of the RTT, and in particular the test-irrelevant thinking subscale, are negatively correlated with all of the subscales of the problem orientation scale.

RTT worry was not strongly associated with the problem-solving skills scale (Table 6.1) although there were small, negative correlations involving the SPSI problem definition and decision-making subscales. The tension and bodily symptoms subscales were unrelated to the problem-solving skills measures. In contrast, the RTT test-irrelevant thinking subscale was correlated negatively with all subscales of the problem-solving skills scale. Each of these skills is assumed to make a distinct contribution to the discovery of adaptive solutions to problems. Thus, while test-anxious worriers and test-irrelevant thinkers both have a negative problem orientation in terms of their reactions to problems, the test-irrelevant thinkers also report deficiencies in the specific skill components required to solve problems.

Test-anxious Worry and More General Domains of Worry

We have seen that worry in test-anxious students has a pervasive link with the negative self-concept in terms of self-appraisals and self-expectancies. In addition to examining how worry differs from other dimensions of test anxiety, it is also important to examine the link between test-anxious worry and other worries. Perhaps the issue of greatest relevance to this volume is the relation between the worry among test-anxious college students and worry in a broader context. In a recent paper, Tallis, Eysenck & Mathews (1992) suggested that "it is debatable whether the worry items included on test anxiety inventories represent anything more than a distant relative of everyday worry" (p. 161). In an earlier critical analysis of theoretical approaches to worry (Talils, Eysenck & Andrews, 1991), they outlined their arguments in support of this conclusion. Their logic relates to issues of form, content, and cues for worry.

Regarding the form of worry, Tallis et al. (1991) argued that the worry items on test-anxious inventories tap "static" thoughts or images whereas the form of everyday worry reflects a "catastrophic narrative". Tallis et al. (1991) suggested further that, "Although the mental events experienced in test situations may reflect some aspects of everyday worry, it seems unlikely that test situations allow sufficient time for rehearsal or narrative development. Presumably the reallocation of attention to task oriented processing would interrupt any narrative development at a very early stage" (p. 100). We agree with Tallis et al. (1991) that test-anxious worry items reflect static thoughts or images but we consider this to be a measurement problem. We believe that our extremely test-anxious students do engage in a catastrophic narrative. In fact, it is precisely because of this narrative that such students have difficulty focusing on the task at hand. Evidence in support of this observation comes from our clinical work with test-anxious students and from the use of various retrospective and concurrent cognitive assessment strategies, such as videotape reconstruction and the think aloud procedure (see Meichenbaum & Butler, 1980b) that tap into the internal dialogue of test-anxious students. Meichenbaum & Butler (1980a) have commented on the fact that the thinking processes of high-anxious people tend "to have a basic orientation that is negative (often 'catastrophizing') rather than positive and coping . . ." (p. 154). However, we believe that the catastrophic thinking of the test-anxious worrier is not limited to test situations.

Regarding thought content in worry, Tallis et al. (1991) examined the content of extant test anxiety measures and concluded that, "Extremely common worries, for example those relating to interpersonal problems, financial difficulties, illness, or political developments, seem only remote relatives of the Liebert and Morris type items" (p. 100). We grant that everyday worry content is much more varied than the worry items on measures of test anxiety which focus on worry about poor performance. However, we have yet to encounter an extremely test-anxious student who worried *only* about performance on tests. Our analyses indicate that most test-anxious students with high levels of worry have at least a moderate level of worry in other life domains and the vast majority of test-anxious students are worried about numerous things, including a number of social evaluation concerns. As Borkovec, Shadick & Hopkins (1991) have observed, "What worries a person in the moment depends on what life events are present or approaching" (p. 47). We expect test-anxious worry to be related to more general measures of worry, especially in a student population, since tests and evaluative concerns are so salient among students. Indeed, Borkovec, Robinson, Pruzinsky & De-Pree (1983) reported that "academic issues" comprised the area of most frequent worries among a predominantly student population. Similarly, Wegner (1989) described research in which students were asked to describe their unwanted intrusive thoughts. Wegner (1989) indicated that the most frequently reported categories in order were problems in relationships, school worries (i.e. failing, not getting things done), general worries about life and the future, death of loved ones, fear of being victimized (i.e. rape, robbery), lack of money, physical appearance, sexual impulses, health, food, and repeating songs. Direct comparisons of college student worriers versus nonworriers indicate that both groups report concerns about academic success as the predominant worry category, but worriers are distinguished by a greater number of statements about physical threats to the self and miscellaneous financial and social threats to the self (Vasey & Borkovec, 1992). Finally, in related research, Craske, Rapee, Jackel & Barlow (1989) found that a control group comprising friends of anxiety center clients reported school/work as their sphere or domain of greatest worry (30.49% of worries based on self-monitoring). This same study examined spheres of worry in generalized anxiety disorder clients. Although they were not the most common worry category, school/work worries were quite common from self-monitoring (13.9%) and a structured interview (16.1%). Although we do not intend to imply that there is any close relation between test-anxious worry and generalized anxiety disorder, we believe that test-anxious worriers are prone to worry in other spheres or domains. We will describe research that supports this view in the section that follows.

Tallis, Eysenck & Andrews (1991) have suggested that worry in testing situations is triggered by external cues that suggest failure or social evaluation whereas everyday worry ". . . is often initiated in the absence of any external cues, for example, before sleep" (p. 101). We believe that test-anxious worry is, indeed, triggered by external evaluative cues; however, we also believe that the worry process is often triggered by internal cues, when students think about future evaluative situations. The latter effect often occurs during attempts to fall asleep. Many test-anxious students complain of difficulty falling asleep or sleep disruption due to worry (see Blankstein, Flett, Watson & Koledin, 1990).

We do not totally disagree with Tallis, Eysenck & Andrews' (1991) conclusion that "the test anxiety literature does not inform a model of worry, or provide answers to important questions relating to function and process" (p. 101). Most test anxiety researchers have accepted the "fact" of test-anxious worry and have attempted to understand the relation between trait or state worry and performance on evaluative tasks. Various theories have been developed in an attempt to explain this relationship. We believe that evaluative concerns are pertinent to many students who suffer from everyday worry and even to clients diagnosed with generalized anxiety disorder and that research on test anxiety will better enable clinicians and researchers to understand everyday worry and abnormal worry in GAD clients (since, presumably, worry could disrupt people's performance on a wide range of tasks). By the same token, general worry research should facilitate the test anxiety researcher's understanding of the target population.

Many insights into the link between test-anxious worry and other types of worry have been obtained from a recent study. In a recent unpublished study, we administered Sarason's (1984) RTT Scale and a battery of worry measures to a large sample of undergraduate students in order to explore the relations between test-anxious worry and everyday worry in students. In addition to the trait measures from the RTT (i.e. worry, test-irrelevant thinking, tension, and bodily symptoms), subjects completed the Student

Worry Scale (SWS; Davey et al., 1992), the Worry Domains Questionnaire WDQ; Tallis et al., 1992), and the Penn State Worry Questionnaire (PSWQ; Meyer et al., 1990). The SWS is a content-based worry questionnaire developed specifically for use with students. The 10 item scale assesses specific worries in 10 major areas of concern (i.e. financial concerns, personal relationships, academic demands, accommodation, health worries, job prospects, world affairs, religious matters, environmental matters, and what people think of me). The SWS provides a single score of worry frequency. The 25 item WDQ was developed for use on nonclinical adult populations. It provides a total score and subscale scores of worry in five domains: relationships (e.g. "That I will lose close friends"), lack of confidence (e.g. "That I might make myself look stupid"), aimless future (e.g. "That I'll never achieve my ambitions"), work incompetence (e.g. "That I make mistakes at work"), and financial worries (e.g. "That my money will run out"). The inclusion of the WDQ enabled us to examine test-anxious worry and worry across several life domains (see Chapter 12, this volume). Finally, the PSWQ is a 16 item questionnaire that provides a single score that reflects the frequency and intensity of pathological worry in general without reference to specific content areas (e.g. "My worries overwhelm me. Once I start worrying, I can't stop") (see Chapter 11, this volume). In a comparison of these worry questionnaires, Davey (1993) argued that the content-based questionnaires seem to capture features of both pathological worrying and task-oriented constructive worrying whereas the PSWQ appears to tap primarily the pathological end of the worrying dimension.

The questionnaires were administered to a sample of 186 college students (Time 1). Three months later, the three general worry measures were readministered to 156 students (Time 2). Our results confirmed that there was a great deal of consistency in worry scores over time. The test–retest reliabilities ranged from $r = .71$ for the SWS to $r = .78$ for the overall scores on the WDQ. In addition, it was established that test-anxious worry is closely related to more general forms of worry.

The intercorrelations between the trait RTT and the three general worry questionnaires are summarized in Table 6.2. It can be seen that the RTT worry scale was positively and moderately correlated with the SWS at initial assessment and at retesting 3 months later. The other RTT components were also correlated significantly with the SWS.

Table 6.2 indicates that there were relatively strong positive correlations between RTT worry and WDQ scores at both Time 1 and Time 2. Consistent with the results for the SWS, all other components of the RTT were also correlated with the WDQ. Separate analyses of the relations between test-anxious worry and the domains of the WDQ indicated that RTT

Table 6.2   Correlations between trait reactions to tests and other adjustment measures

Measure	RTT dimension			
	Worry	Tension	Thinking	Body
Worry measures				
Student Worry Scale				
Time 1	.45**	.38**	.35**	.49**
Time 2	.38**	.39**	.33**	.43**
Worry Domains Questionnaire				
Time 1	.55**	.43**	.43**	.48**
Time 2	.44**	.43**	.36**	.46**
Penn State Worry Questionnaire				
Time 1	.48**	.63**	.08	.52**
Anxiety measures				
Beck Anxiety	.40**	.39**	.21**	.50**
Fear of Negative Evaluation	.43**	.32**	.18	.31**
Fear Survey Schedule-III				
Social fears	.43**	.44**	.14*	.33**
Agoraphobic fears	.33**	.38**	.11	.34**
Bodily injury/death	.23**	.28**	.12	.27**
Sexual/aggressive	.25**	.25**	.06	.26**
Harmless animals	.18**	.30**	−.09	.26**
Affect and somatic measures				
Beck Depression Inventory	.50**	.44**	.41**	.45**
Life Satisfaction	−.29**	−.27**	−.27**	−.27**
PANAS Positive Affect (Trait)	−.40**	−.25**	−.20*	−.17*
PANAS Negative Affect (Trait)	.37**	.38**	.34**	.45**
Hopkins Symptom Checklist-21				
Performance Difficulty	.41**	.42**	.20*	.48**
Somatic Distress	.36**	.33**	.23**	.53**
General Feeling of Distress	.33**	.39**	.25**	.44**
Psychosomatic Symptom Checklist				
Frequency	.33**	.45**	.16**	.33**
Intensity	.30**	.36**	.09	.31**
Stress measures				
Life Experiences–Negative Events	.22**	.14	.16*	.14*
Hassles Persistence				
General	.53**	.44**	.35**	.49**
Academic	.63**	.51**	.41**	.51**
Social	.34**	.26**	.35**	.39**
General Hassles				
Persistence	.21**	.24**	.15*	.20**
Impact	.29**	.26**	.22**	.21**
Coping Ability	.43**	.36**	.33**	.27**
Upset	.38**	.31*	.25**	.24**

$** p < .01, * p < .05$.   Sample sizes vary from $n = 123$ to $n = 200$.

worry was significantly associated with all domains at both assessments, with the exception of the financial domain at Time 2. The strongest associations at Time 1 were with aimless future ($r = .55$), work incompetence ($r = .49$), lack of confidence ($r = .49$), and relationships ($r = .45$). The results of these analyses suggest that test-anxious worriers also worry frequently in other content areas or domains besides evaluative situations.

The relations between the RTT and the PSWQ provide information about the frequency and intensity of pathological worry in test-anxious students. Inspection of Table 6.2 indicates a relatively strong positive relation between test-anxious worry and scores on the PSWQ that is comparable to the associations obtained with the other worry measures. However, several other aspects of the correlations involving the PSWQ warrant comment. First, PSWQ scores were not related to the measure of test-irrelevant thinking. Apparently, students with high scores on test-irrelevant thinking will acknowledge worry in the particular life domains assessed by the SWS and WDQ, but they are less willing to acknowledge the presence of a more pathological, uncontrollable form of worry. The test-irrelevant thinking correlations with the PSWQ also suggest that this component of test anxiety is quite different in meaning from the meaning or significance of the other components. Some salient differences between the two cognitive aspects of test anxiety (i.e. worry and test-irrelevant thinking) will be discussed at length in a subsequent section of the chapter. Second, although the differences are not significant, it should be noted that the PSWQ was more closely linked with the RTT measures of emotionality (i.e. tension and bodily symptoms) than with the RTT worry subscale. These results suggest that there are strong emotional correlates of the general measure of the frequency and intensity of pathological worry. Finally, it should be observed that our results are somewhat at variance with the results reported by Meyer, Miller, Metzger & Borkovec (1990). Meyer et al. reported that all four RTT components were significantly and positively correlated with the PSWQ in a sample of 87 students (rs ranged between .26 and .38). However, in a stepwise multiple regression only the RTT worry subscale predicted PSWQ in the Meyer et al. study.

To further underscore our point that test-anxious worry is related to other specific worries, we used the data from this study to conduct separate analyses involving the specific content areas of the SWS. This revealed that test-anxious worry was significantly correlated with 7 of the 10 content areas at Time 1 and 6 of 10 areas on retest. The strongest relations at Time 1 were with academic demands ($r = .45$), job prospects ($r = .36$), what people think of me ($r = .35$), and personal relationships ($r = .34$). Test-anxious worry was not related to worry about world affairs, environmental matters, and financial concerns.

These findings must be interpreted with caution since they are based on single-item ratings. We decided to proceed with these analyses to test some specific observations made by Wine (1980). Wine observed that the term "test anxiety" is misleading because students who score high on measures of test anxiety tend to interpret a wide range of situations as evaluative and react with cognitive concerns and performance deficits that generalize across a number of settings and target areas. In fact, she argued that a more general term like "evaluation apprehension" may be more suitable. Wine's observations appear to be supported by the data. In our study, students worried about academic failure, but they also worried about job prospects and important interpersonal relationships. The social-evaluative concerns of test-anxious worriers are also illustrated by another study of college students ($n - 158$) in which we found that scores on the RTT worry subscale were correlated positively with scores on the Social Avoidance and Distress Scale (Watson & Friend, 1989), $r = .27$, $p < .01$, the Social Reticence Scale (Jones, Briggs & Smith, 1986), $r = .35$, $p < .01$, and the UCLA Loneliness Scale (Russell, Peplau & Cutrona, 1980), $r = .25$, $p < .01$. Collectively, these results with various measures of anxiety and dispositional self-focus suggest that test-anxious worry can be more generally considered as a manifestation of general evaluative anxiety that encompasses broad concern with issues involving social disapproval and the public self.

Overall, these results support our hypothesis that test-anxious worry is strongly associated with worry in other content areas or domains and with the frequency and intensity of general worry. It would be of interest to have test-anxious worriers self-monitor their general worrying on a daily basis to determine the extent of worrying in related spheres or domains. Presumably, the test-anxious worrier encounters many social-evaluative cues that trigger worrisome activity in a number of interrelated domains, in addition to test situations. This conclusion is consistent with observations by Borkovec and his colleagues (Borkovec et al., 1991; Roemer & Borkovec, 1993) who suggested that there may be strong links among different worry spheres. They cited unpublished research by Metzger which demonstrates that worry acts as a superordinate category such that accessing one worry area primes other content-unrelated spheres of worry. Thoughts of other worrisome topics presumably lead the person back to the original concern, and thus maintain a self-perpetuating cycle of worry.

Test-anxious Worry and Other Personality Characteristics

Our results consistently indicate that worry in the form of test anxiety is related to many of the same measures that have been associated positively with the PSWQ, SWS, and WDQ. We have numerous pieces of additional evidence to support out contention that test-anxious worry is not altogether different from a more general form of worry. For instance, Pruzinsky & Borkovec (1990) administered the Imaginal Processes Inventory (IPI) to high versus low worriers. The IPI is a trait measure of the more negative cognitive intrusions experienced during attentional tasks. Analyses of IPI subscales indicated that worriers reported poorer attentional control and a tendency to engage in negative daydreaming. Likewise, we administered the abbreviated IPI (Huba, Singer, Aneshensel & Antrobus, 1982) and the RTT to a sample of students and found that worry was associated with poor attentional control and a form of daydreaming involving themes of guilt and fear of failure. Similarly, Meyer et al. (1990) reported results indicating that high scorers on the PSWQ are characterized by maladaptive coping styles that involve self-blame, wishful thinking, and problem avoidance. Our research also indicates that worriers tend to respond to stress with negative forms of emotion-focused and avoidant coping styles, in part due to negative appraisals and expectancies about their ability to solve problems (Blankstein, Flett & Batten, 1989; Blankstein et al., 1992). In short, many of the findings from test anxiety research replicate findings obtained with other worry measures, and the test anxiety research extends this literature by addressing some issues that have not been the focus of other research.

Given that worry in test anxiety situations is related empirically to worry in other domains, it follows that many findings from research on worry and test anxiety should apply to more general forms of worry. At the same time, it must be acknowledged that there are certain critical aspects of the testing situation that may contribute to some important differences between test-anxious worry and other forms of worry. Rather than invalidating the study of worry in evaluative situations, our position is that exposure to testing situations represents an important contextual factor that informs us greatly about the nature of worry. What are some features that may distinguish test-anxious worry from other types of worry in other domains? Whereas worry in most domains occurs in an attempt to avoid the negative outcome from occurring, there is little doubt that the test-anxious individual must encounter the situation and this poses special challenges (see Carver & Scheier, 1986, for a related discussion). The negative outcome itself can still be avoided (i.e. failure), but the worrying, test-anxious individual will have fewer options available in terms of avoidance, and the number of options will decrease as the test grows closer. Thus, the stimulus that elicits worry is inevitable and must be confronted. This is sometimes but not always the case with worry in other life domains.

It is also likely that test-anxious worry differs from other forms of worry in a variety of respects that involve the testing of academic ability. As people mature, they become increasingly aware of the fact that ability is a relatively stable entity that reflects a person's character and it is distinct from luck and effort (see Nicholls, Jagacinski & Miller, 1986; Ruble & Flett, 1988). The negative outcome in test anxiety (failure) is extremely threatening when maximum effort is exerted because of the longstanding negative implications that go along with a demonstrated lack of ability. At the same time, achievement-related outcomes include an element of perceived personal control that may be lacking in certain other worry domains, such as relationship outcomes or financial problems. That is, students who are worried about failure can exert greater effort by studying harder or by availing themselves of various sources of help offered by their educational institution, but it is difficult to prevent other possible outcomes that involve less personal control, such as the death of a loved one or an economic recession. Although it remains to be tested, we would predict that test-anxious worry is more ego-involving than other types of worry because of the realization that a negative outcome reflects an enduring aspect of the self. If so, then worry in the test anxiety domain, relative to worry in other domains, should be accompanied by a wider variety of defensive strategies designed to protect the self such as self-handicapping and the withdrawal of effort.

Finally, there is a particular dilemma that is more problematic for test-anxious worriers compared to other kinds of worriers. It is generally accepted that worriers attribute their worries to an inability to engage in cognitive self-distraction (Borkovec et al., 1983; Rachman & de Silva, 1978; Wegner & Schneider, 1989). A key goal for the general worrier is to distract oneself by focusing attention on environmental events (see Borkovec et al., 1983). Unfortunately, in terms of test anxiety, many of the environmental cues available to worriers in a testing situation only serve as a further reminder of the possibility of failure. Such cues include available social comparison feedback in the form of other students' performance and temporal cues that indicate that time is dwindling. The only form of distraction that is adaptive for test-anxious individuals is to focus on the test itself and attempt to provide the correct answers. For the test-anxious individual, cognitive disengagement in the form of mind wandering and distraction are deleterious responses that only serve to exacerbate the problem. Our point, then, is that an adaptive response for one type of worry is not necessarily an adaptive response for other types of worry.

These differences notwithstanding, it is important to recognize that there are many aspects of worry that are similar in test anxiety and other domains. Clearly, there is an urgent need for additional research on the similarities and differences between test-anxious worry and worry in other domains. Such research will serve as a useful guide for understanding the nature of worry in various contexts.

Worry and Measures of Adjustment

We have obtained other useful insights into the nature of worry by examining how the RTT scores relate to other measures of adjustment. The study on the various domains of worry was but one in a series of studies examining the link between scores on the RTT worry scale and other concurrent measures of anxiety and fear responses. Given the close link between worry and fear (see Borkovec, Metzger & Pruzinsky, 1986), it is not at all surprising that RTT worry scores are strongly correlated with other indices of anxiety. As indicated in Table 6.2, RTT worry is significantly correlated with anxiety symptoms as measured by the Beck Anxiety Scale (BAI; Beck, Brown, Epstein & Steer, 1988) in various samples. There is also a relatively strong relation between the RTT bodily symptoms subscale and the BAI that is probably due to the emphasis on physical symptoms on the BAI.

Borkovec et al. (1991) have argued that worry is associated with social-evaluative fear and our own findings with the RTT worry component are consistent with their conclusion. Hembree (1988) reported that fear of negative evaluation is a reliable correlate of test anxiety. In a previous study (summarized in Table 6.2), Flett et al. (1987) reported a correlation of $r = .43$, $p < .01$, between RTT worry and a measure of fear of negative evaluation. In a replication with 158 subjects the correlation was $r = .43$, $p < .01$. This finding suggests that test-anxious worriers are disposed to experience anxiety in diverse situations involving social evaluation. Our findings with the Fear Survey Schedule (FSS-III; Wolfe & Lang, 1964) are also consistent with this interpretation. Factor analyses (e.g. Arrindell, Emmelkamp & van der Ende, 1984) have shown that the instrument consists of five factors (see Table 6.2). Test-anxious worry was most highly correlated with the social-fears factor (e.g. feeling rejected by others) followed by agoraphobic fears (e.g. being in a strange place). Item-by-item analyses indicated that worry was significantly associated with 59 items on the 80 item scale (two additional fears were added because of their relevance to students). Some of the strongest associations were with fears of examinations in school ($r = .53$), adopting to college life ($r = .45$), failure ($r = .42$), feeling disapproved of ($r = .37$), being watched working ($r = .37$), making mistakes ($r = .36$), losing control ($r = .33$), feeling rejected by others ($r = .32$), and being criticized ($r =$

.31). These results are consistent with results using a different fear survey schedule reported by Borkovec et al. (1983), and support the conclusion that among FSS-III items, social-evaluative situations are of considerable concern to the test-anxious worrier.

Related research has examined the broader relationship between trait levels of worry as assessed by the RTT and more general indices of negative affectivity or psychopathology. It is generally acknowledged that anxiety and depression are highly correlated in various populations (see Kendall & Watson, 1989; Vredenburg, Flett & Krames, 1993), and measures of anxiety are associated with a host of measures that reflect psychological and somatic symptoms (see Clark & Watson, 1991; Gotlib, 1984). Other research on worry with the PSWQ has confirmed a link between worry and depression in college students (Meyer et al., 1990). Thus, it is not surprising to see a strong link between worry and depression as assessed by the Beck Depression inventory (BDI; Beck, Rush, Shaw & Emery, 1979). We have replicated these findings with the BDI in various samples (see Table 6.2). These findings with trait worry and depression are consistent with outcomes involving general measures of worry (e.g. Borkovec et al., 1983; MacLeod, Williams & Bekerian, 1991). Whereas anxiety stems typically from concerns about future threats that may or may not occur, depression usually results from perceived losses in the past (Beck & Emory, 1985; Sarason, 1986). One interpretation of the current findings then is that although test-anxious worriers may constantly ruminate about negative outcomes for future events (e.g. failure on an upcoming test), they may also dwell on perceived past failures, or treat future "failures" as already having happened (Beck et al., 1987).

In terms of associations with other measures of general psychopathology, inspection of Table 6.2 reveals moderately strong relations between the subscales of the 21 item version of the Hopkins Symptom Checklist (HSC-21; Green, Walkey, McCormick & Taylor, 1988) and the RTT worry component. Worry was most strongly correlated, as would be expected, with the performance difficulty subscale. Additional evidence supported the discriminant validity of the RTT components; for example, test-irrelevant thinking was only weakly correlated with all subscales of the HSC, suggesting that students who score high on this scale are not especially distressed. Also, the RTT bodily symptoms subscale was strongly associated with the somatic distress subscale of the HSC. However, related research with the SUNYA revision of the Psychosomatic Symptom Checklist (Attanasio, Andrasik, Blanchard & Arena, 1984) indicates that most of the test anxiety components are associated positively with the frequency and intensity of psychosomatic symptoms (see Table 6.2).

Taken together, these data indicate the presence of a consistent association between test anxiety and poor personal adjustment in the form of negative affect and general indices of psychopathology. Because recent findings have indicated that negative affect and positive affect may be orthogonal (Clark & Watson, 1991), it is also important to examine the link between components of test anxiety and measures of positive affect. This issue was addressed by administering the RTT along with the Satisfaction With Life Scale (SWLS; Diener, Emmons, Larsen & Griffin, 1985) and the Positive and Negative Affect Schedule (PANAS; Watson, Clark & Tellegen, 1988) to college students. The SWLS is a measure of a person's own judgment of satisfaction with life as a whole, while the version of the PANAS used in this research provides separate indices of trait positive and negative affect. Table 6.2 indicates that there is a pervasive negative association between life satisfaction and test anxiety that generalizes across all four trait RTT dimensions. These same RTT dimensions are associated with the absence of positive affect, but it should be observed that the link between test anxiety and the absence of positive affect is particularly strong for the RTT worry dimension. Finally, further inspection of Table 6.2 indicates that all four RTT dimensions were associated with negative affect. These data suggest that test-anxious worriers experience a variety of aversive mood states, such as anger, contempt, disgust, guilt, fear and nervousness.

Worry and Negative Life Events, Hassles, and Uplifts

There are a variety of ways to define levels of adjustment. In addition to directly examining negative and positive affect and related symptoms, it is also possible to examine the association between worry and actual or perceived life stress. One interpretation of worry is that it is a cognitive phenomenon that is elicited by proximal or distal life events (Borkovec et al., 1986). Intrusive thoughts arise, in part, from the perceived experience of traumatic events. If so, then it should be the case that there is a positive relationship between test-anxious worry and stressful life events. We have examined the relationships between worry and the daily minor stressors that people experience and between worry and life changes of more major significance to the student in a series of three studies. Our findings provide support for the hypothesis that test-anxious worriers are characterized by elevated levels of stress.

In the first study, we examined the relations between the RTT and responses to the Life Experiences Survey (LES; Sarason, Johnson & Siegel, 1978). The LES measures the impact of negative life events and positive life events. The student version describes 55 life experiences. The measures of positive and negative life stress represent the intensity of the events during the past year, as determined by the subject's subjective rating of experienced events.

Inspection of Table 6.2 indicates that there was a small but significant positive correlation between test-anxious worry and the perceived negative impact of life events. Worry was unrelated to positive life events. Overall, the positive link between worry and negative life events stress contrasts with the results of a recent study by Russell & Davey (1993) who failed to detect a relation between scores on the Student Worry Scale and the LES. However, it must be acknowledged that the significant link in our study was less than robust.

In light of this observation, we decided to test the possibility that perhaps test-anxious worry is more related to appraisals of daily life stressors. An important recent development in stress research is the proliferation of studies on daily life "hassles" and adaptational outcomes. Kanner and associates (Kanner, Coyne, Schaefer & Lazarus, 1981, p. 3) developed the Hassles Scale to measure "The irritating, frustrating, distressing demands that to some degree characterize everyday transactions with the environment." The original Hassles Scale consisted of 117 minor stressors that occur on a frequent basis, including such minor occurrences as losing things, financial concerns and even getting a traffic ticket. There is now extensive evidence of a significant relation between self-reported hassles and poor psychological and physical adjustment (e.g. Blankstein & Flett, 1992; Blankstein, Flett & Koledin, 1991; DeLongis et al., 1982; Kanner et al., 1981). In fact, some studies have demonstrated that daily hassles are more predictive of adaptational outcomes than are traditional measures of major life event (e.g. DeLongis et al., 1982; Kanner et al., 1981).

In our own work with students we have employed three new multidimensional measures of hassles that we have developed to provide a comprehensive assessment of daily stress in college students (Blankstein & Flett, 1993). The three measures are the General Hassles Inventory, the Academic Hassles Inventory and the Social Hassles Inventory. In each case respondents rate 28 frequent hassles in the specified domain in terms of four characteristics: (1) persistence of the daily stressor; (2) impact of the daily stressor; (3) perceived ability to cope with the daily stressor; and (4) degree of upset associated with the daily stressor. These new scales were created because there are many advantages associated with the use of hassles scales that are designed specifically for the college student population (see Blankstein et al., 1991) and because it is generally accepted that there is a need for measures that provide a more comprehensive assessment of the various dimensions of stress (see Lazarus, 1990).

In one study, we examined the link between RTT worry and the three new multidimensional measures of hassles. The students in this particular study responded only to the persistence rating scale. The results from this sample indicated that there is a strong association between test-anxious worry and the hassles measures (see Table 6.2). As would be predicted, the strongest relation was between test-anxious worry and the Academic Hassles Inventory. It should be noted that the other components of the RTT were all significantly correlated with the persistence of hassles, but the strongest association was with the worry subscale. The RTT measures were unrelated to a measure of positive daily events.

In a subsequent study, we examined the relations between RTT worry and the full General Hassles Scale that included measures of persistence, impact, coping ability, and upset (see Table 6.2). Although the effect for persistence was not as strong as in our previous study, the results from this sample indicate that there is an extensive assocation between test-anxious worry (and the other RTT components) and general hassles. Test-anxious worry was associated with all four hassles indices; worriers not only indicated that their hassles were more persistent, they also reported that the hassles had a greater impact, that they had a relatively lower ability to cope with these hassles, and that they experienced a greater degree of upset. The finding that worriers report diminished ability to cope with daily stressors is consistent with the earlier findings of a link between worry and negative appraisals of a problem-solving ability.

In general, our results are consistent with the findings reported by Russell & Davey (1993) using the SWS and the original Kanner et al. (1981) hassles and uplifts scales. Russell & Davey (1993) hypothesized that there may be a circular relationship between daily hassles and measures such as worry; viz. hassles (in the case of students we believe that academic hassles are most relevant) influence worry, and worry in turn influences the perception of daily events as problematic.

Clearly, several issues related to worry and stress remain to be investigated. One important direction for future research in this area is the possible link between worry and the anticipation of stressful events. No analysis of worry and stress would be complete without consideration of the notion of anticipatory stress. It has been noted repeatedly (e.g. Borkovec et al., 1986) that worry tends to relate to future concerns and the anticipation of future events (see also Tallis, Davey & Capuzzo, this volume, Chapter 3). Thus, it should be the case that worriers not only perceive current daily events as stressful, they also anticipate the experience of similar events in the future. A key aspect of the stress appraisal process is the expectation that aversive experiences are about to be experienced

(Girodo & Roehl, 1978; Girodo & Stein, 1978; Shipley, Butt & Horwitz, 1979; Spacapan & Cohen, 1983). In many respects, worry can be equated with the anticipation of encountering stressful situations. This can be maladaptive because a consistent focus on anticipated stress should serve to ensure that chronic worriers are always engaged in the process of either confronting an actual stressor or generating stress for themselves due to the anticipated experience of future stressors. This would account for the link between worry and somatic symptoms and this prolonged exposure to stress over time could lead to some fairly dramatic health consequences.

Indeed, various studies have provided empirical evidence of a link between worry and the esitmated probability of future life events (see Butler & Mathews, 1983, 1988; MacLeod et al., 1991), but test-anxious worry has not been the focus of this research. Indirect evidence in our laboratory of the link between test-anxious worry and anticipated difficulties was provided in a study that examined the extent to which the trait RTT and other measures of negative affectivity were associated with expectations about future life problems and pleasures (Flett, 1988). Secondary analyses of data from 195 students indicated that worry is associated with the belief that the future will involve numerous and consistently present life problems that involve various life domains (i.e. academic, social, financial, and emotional problems). However, worry was unrelated to expectations about future life pleasures.

Taken together, the results indicate that trait worry in test-anxious students is associated broadly with other measures of anxiety and related indices of negative affectivity. Test-anxious worriers also suffer from a relative absence of positive affect. Test-anxious worriers also report being troubled by the perceived presence of daily stressors in a variety of domains and the anticipation of future life problems. One factor that may underscore the tendency to worry is a negative self-concept. Worriers, as assessed by the trait RTT, report lower self-esteem, a more negative self-concept for intellectual tasks, a sense of personal pessimism, and excessive self-focused attention.

Test Anxiety and the Nature of State Worry in Evaluative Situations

In an earlier section of this chapter, we outlined various factors that distinguish worry in test anxious students from worry in other life domains. Another consideration involves the notion of worry from a state perspective. To our knowledge, researchers examining worry in other life domains have made no attempt thus far to examine trait versus state worry in a systematic fashion. In fact, it can be argued that more general research in the anxiety literature has not directly contrasted the roles of state worry and trait worry. For instance, the Endler Multidimensional Anxiety Scales (EMAS) by Endler, Edwards, Vitelli & Parker (1989) has a state measure of worry but the trait measures assess dispositional concerns in the areas of social evaluation, physical danger, daily routines, and novel situations. The EMAS does not yield a trait measure of worry. On a similar note, the Spielberger State Trait Anxiety Scale (Spielberger, Gorsuch & Lushene, 1970) permits comparisons of state versus trait anxiety, but it cannot be assumed that this measure is informative about the specific role of state versus trait worry; unfortunately, the Spielberger has been treated as a unidimensional measure and the scale content is confounded with symptoms that more closely resemble depression than anxiety (for related discussions see Endler, Cox, Parker & Bagby, 1992; Vredenburg et al., 1993).

We have been able to test various issues about state versus trait worry by creating a state version of Sarason's RTT. The availability of this measure enabled us to compare state versus trait worry in terms of their relative ability to predict performance and to establish the relative ability of state worry versus the other test anxiety dimensions to predict other measures involving cognition, affect, and performance. Conceptually, there should be some important qualitative differences between worry and test-irrelevant thinking, for example, and these differences should be reflected in terms of their respective associations with cognitive reactions, affective reactions, and behavioral performance measures in salient situational contexts.

We have been developing the resultant measure, the State Reactions to Tests Scale (SRTT), for the past decade. The final version of the SRTT has four six-item subscales measuring worry, tension, test-irrelevant thinking, and bodily symptoms. Space limitations preclude describing the development and validation of this measure in this chapter. However, our analyses indicate that the measure has acceptable psychometric properties for research purposes. Moreover, a factor analysis of data from 180 students confirmed the multidmensional nature of the scale.

Currently, we are using this measure in ongoing cross-sectional and longitudinal research to address several important issues. These issues include: (1) the relation between components of state test anxiety and indices of trait test anxiety and performance; (2) the relative ability of state and trait measures to predict unique variance in performance and related cognitive measures; and (3) the stability of levels of state test anxiety over time. In a prototypical study, a sample of students who had already completed the trait RTT would complete the SRTT with reference to an actual class test on one or more occasions. Other measures would also be obtained, including indices of performance, cognitive interference, and self-judgments in the form of unstructured or structured responses. However, some studies have been conducted with the use of analog testing situations.

The main findings of this research may be summarized as follows. First, as expected, there is a close relationship between trait and state measures of the components. That is, individuals who report elevated levels of trait worry also report elevated levels of state worry. Evidence to support this point was provided in a study that examined the association between trait anxiety and state anxiety experienced during a study session and a test session. This study was based on our belief that worry and self-preoccupation increase in test-anxious studies as an examination approaches. Further, we hypothesized that this negative self-preoccupation will occur during study periods, while students attempt to prepare for an upcoming test. Meichenbaum & Butler (1980a) suggested the need for assessment of test-anxious students during study periods. In this study, we examined the components of state anxiety both during a study session in anticipation of a subsequent test and during the actual test itself. In order to have strict control over the time and duration of the study period, we assessed subjects who differed in test anxiety during an analog study and test session. We sought to determine the relationship between the components of trait test anxiety and the concordant components of state test anxiety, the relationship between state anxiety during a study period and anxiety during a test, the changes in components of state anxiety from study periods to test period, and the relationship, if any, between anxiety while studying and performance during the subsequent test. We believe that anxiety, in particular worry, while studying interferes with the encoding and retention of the material being studied.

The subjects were 134 students (73 females, 61 males) enrolled in an introductory psychology course. The study session was carried out in a classroom setting and subjects were run in groups ranging from 6 to 12 participants. Subjects were presented with study instructions which informed them that they would have 30 minutes to read and study a brief (1075 words) scientific article. They were also informed that they could use any combination of study methods (e.g. making notes, underlining sections of the article, etc.) that they would normally use in studying for a test, but that at the conclusion of the study period, all study material, including the article, had to be handed in to the experimenter. Immediately after the 30-

minute study period subjects completed the SRTT, with instructions modified to assess subjects' specific reactions during the study period. Subjects were reminded that they would have to write a test in 3 days on the article's topic. Subjects were tested in the same classroom as that of the study session, under similar circumstances, except the session was structured such that it was as comparable to an actual academic examination as possible. The duration of the test was 10 minutes. It consisted of 10 multiple choice questions, and a short answer and essay question. The proctor announced the time remaining at 5 minutes, 2 minutes, and 1 minute. Following the test, subjects completed an SRTT. They were instructed to rate their reactions during the test period. Subjects subsequently completed the trait RTT embedded among other measures.

We first examined the relations between the components of trait anxiety and state anxiety during the study period and state anxiety during the actual test. The correlations are summarized in Table 6.3. Inspection reveals that congruent RTT and SRTT components were significantly correlated during both study and test periods, and, with one exception, congruent correlations were stronger than non-congruent correlations. For example, trait worry was correlated at $r = .69$, $p < .01$ with worry during the study period, and $r = .71$, $p < .01$, during the test session. The correlations between trait worry and the remaining components, although all significant, ranged between $r = .23$ and $.50$. The one exception was for the trait and state tension correlations. RTT tension was more strongly associated with state worry than with state tension both during studying and while taking the test.

Table 6.3 Correlations between trait RTT and SRTT measures during study and test sessions and mean SRTT scores

	Trait dimension					
	Worry	Tension	Thinking	Body	Mean	SD[†]
SRTT—study session						
Worry	.69**	.55**	.35**	.44**	9.5	3.8
Tension	.47**	.47**	.38**	.43**	9.8	3.4
Thinking	.23**	.13	.51**	.09	11.3	3.8
Body	.39**	.37**	.21*	.53**		
SRTT—test session						
Worry	.71**	.62**	.28**	.43**	10.3	3.8
Tension	.50**	.55**	.21*	.53**	10.8	3.6
Thinking	.28**	.22**	.52**	.15	8.3	2.9
Body	.28**	.28**	.17	.47**	7.1	1.6

* $p < .05$, ** $p < .01$, † Standard Deviation.

Additional correlation analyses confirmed that state anxiety during studying was associated significantly with state anxiety during the test. For example, the congruent worry measures correlated at $r = .68, p < .01$. The corresponding correlations for the tension, test-irrelevant thinking, and bodily symptoms subscales, were $r = .65, .45$, and $.46$, respectively (all significant at $p < .01$). Thus, students who reacted with worry during the study period were also inclined to worry during the actual test.

Second, although state and trait anxiety are closely related, there are numerous indications that measures of trait and state test anxiety are not redundant with each other. A consistent finding from our research is that the state measures account for a significant proportion of unique variance in outcome measures, over and above the variance accounted for by trait measures. In our analyses, we have found repeatedly that state levels of worry continue to be robust predictors of performance, with the usual pattern of worry being associated with poor performance.

Third, there is a degree of stability in state test anxiety scores if subjects are tested repeatedly in naturalistic situations. In one longitudinal study, we assessed levels of state test anxiety following a class test on five separate occasions in a sample of college students. The intercorrelations among the state worry measures at the five timepoints ranged from $r = .33$ to $r = .66$, thus indicating that there is a consistent level of worry that is exhibited when situations are repeatedly encountered. These results are consistent with other indications (e.g. Usala & Hertzog, 1991) that state anxiety may be somewhat stable. However, this should not be interpreted as evidence for the view that state worry is invariant. This study also found that there were significant decreases in mean levels of test anxiety over time that were present for all of the RTT components except bodily symptoms. As the term progressed, the students in this study reported less anxiety in each test situation. Moreover, significant differences were detected in the study that compared levels of state anxiety in the study session with the more threatening test session. The means and standard deviations for the SRTT components during the study and test periods for the group as a whole are found in Table 6.3. A series of one-way analyses of variance with type of session as a within-subject factor tested whether there were significant changes from the study session to the test session. State worry increased significantly from the study to the test sessions, $F(1, 133) = 8.66, p < .01$). There was also a significant increase in tension from the study period to the test session, $F(1, 133) = 16.84, p < .001$. However, reports of test-irrelevant thoughts *decreased* from the study period to the test, $F(1, 133) = 94.81, p < .001$. This result suggests that subjects were more task focused during the actual test, relative to the study period.

This study is but one of several studies that have yielded some critical differences between the worry component and the test-irrelevant thinking component. Other evidence comes from our hierarchical regression analyses which show that state worry but not state test-irrelevant thinking accounts for unique variance in performance scores.

Perhaps the most compelling evidence of the distinction between the two cognitive factors was obtained in the first study that was conducted to develop the SRTT. A total of 70 subjects completed the SRTT along with a series of single-item, 7 point ratings of specific test reactions such as feelings of helplessness, upset, self-control, etc. These ratings were included to further our understanding of the similarities and differences between the test anxiety dimensions. The results of these analyses must be accepted with caution since they are based on single-item ratings of unknown reliability and validity. Nevertheless, these results provide important information about the meaning of the worry subscale relative to the test-irrelevant thinking subscale.

SRTT worry during the test was correlated with the expected mark rating prior to the test ($r = -.35$) and with the similar rating after the test ($r = -.58$). Worry was unrelated to ratings of motivation to perform well, and to the extent of preparation for the test taken prior to the test. However, worry was significantly related to a number of affective reactions during the test, including sense of helplessness ($r = .81$), frustration ($r = .77$), downhearted ($r = .69$), feelings of inadequacy ($r = .68$) anger/hostility ($r = .66$), and anticipation of punishment ($r = .57$), loss of status and esteem ($r = .55$), satisfaction ($r = -.53$), anxiety ($r = .44$), and desire to terminate the test session. Although worry was significantly negatively related to perceived control over positive, facilitating thoughts during the test ($r = -.54$), it was unrelated to control over negative, interfering thoughts. Worry was related to perceived difficulty remembering the material in the test ($r = .60$). Worry was also unrelated to perceived deficiencies in study habits and skills; however, it was related to perceived deficiencies in test-taking strategies and skills ($r = -.40$).

A different pattern of results emerged when the correlations between test-irrelevant thinking during the test and the individual ratings were examined. In contrast to the pattern involving worry, test-irrelevant thinking was related to pre-test ratings of motivation ($r = -.54$), and preparation ($r = -.49$) and to perceived control over the outcome ($r = -.37$). It was also related to the estimate of time spent writing the test ($r = -.37$): test-irrelevant thinkers hand their test papers in early. Although test-irrelevant thinking was related to many of the same affects and behaviors during the test as worry, the magnitude of the correlations was much smaller. These were two important exceptions: test-irrelevant thinking was highly related to boredom ($r = .51$) and it was unrelated to anxiety ($r = .03$). As was the case with worry, test-irrelevant thinking was related to desire to terminate the test session ($r = .52$). Perhaps worriers want to terminate the session because of their pervasive, negative, self-preoccupation, whereas test-irrelevant thinkers want to leave because they are bored and lack sufficient motivation.

As was the case with worry, test-irrelevant thinking was related to difficulty remembering the material ($r = .48$). Perhaps worried students have difficulty remembering the material due to the interference as a consequence of negative intrusive thoughts, whereas high test-irrelevant thinking students have difficulty because they are bored and their minds are wandering. Alternatively, the correlation may reflect an encoding problem since test-irrelevant thinking was related to perceived adequacy of study habits and skills ($r = -.35$), but it was unrelated to perceived test-taking skills and strategies. These findings are interesting because they accord with other observations about differences between test-irrelevant thinking and worry. Kalechstein, Hocevar, Zimmer & Kalechstein (1989) examined the trait RTT and a measure of procrastination over test preparation in 70 students. Their results suggested a link between procrastination about studying and test-irrelevant thinking. Analyses with the RTT found that test-irrelevant thinking was the dimension with the strongest correlation ($r = .39$). The authors concluded that test-irrelevant thinkers have a general tendency to avoid tasks and delay preparation, suggesting a lack of appropriate motivation. Similarly, Birenbaum (1990) examined levels of test anxiety and test-related measures in a sample of 172 undergraduate and graduate students. The test anxiety measure was the trait RTT. The RTT measure of test-irrelevant thinking was the dimension linked most closely with self-reported deficits in test-taking preparation. Regarding the essence of test-irrelevant thinking, Klinger (1984) suggested that some test-anxious individuals may engage in test-irrelevant thinking not because of cognitive interference but because the test-relevant thoughts are simply not present at the outset. The lack of relevant thoughts can be traced back to lack of preparation or ineffective preparation. In contrast, worry is a cognitive dimension that is distinguished by a focus on possible failure and an orientation toward avoiding negative outcomes in the future, rather than past or current deficits in motivation or cognition.

To summarize, several findings have emerged from research on state test anxiety with our new multidimensional measure. Specifically, the findings are the following: (1) state and trait test anxiety are closely related; (2) elements of state test anxiety account for unique variance in test-taking outcome measures despite the overlap between state and trait measures; (3) there is a degree of temporal stability to state measures assessed over time in test situations, but changes in situational factors (i.e. repeated exposure to similar testing conditions over time, being in a study session as opposed to a test situation) are associated with changes in levels of state test anxiety; and (4) a growing body of evidence indicates that there are some subtle but important differences between the two cognitive test anxiety dimensions (i.e. worry and test-irrelevant thinking) that may be due, in part, to deficits in motivation that underscore test-irrelevant thinking. We regard these results as evidence for the need to examine worry from a state–trait perspective.

Therapeutic Implications

There is little doubt that the research on trait and state test anxiety has important implications for the treatment of students with problematic levels of anxiety. An extensive analysis of past treatment programs for test anxiety is beyond the scope of this chapter. We will provide a brief review of past approaches along with an integration of our findings to emphasize the practical implications of our work.

Over the past 20 years, a variety of interventions have been used to treat test anxiety. Numerous intervention approaches have been found to be effective. The picture that tends to emerge is that various treatments have been successful in isolation, but combinations of treatment approaches are especially useful.

Treatment research focused on the individual has been conducted in the form of treatments directed toward either or both the cognitive-worry and emotionality components of test anxiety, and study skills and test-taking strategies (see reviews by Allen, Elias & Zlotow, 1980; Denney, 1980; Hembree, 1988; Tryon, 1980). Frequently used interventions include self-controlled relaxation, systematic desensitization, participant modeling, biofeedback training, study skills training, cognitive–behavioral treatments, rational–emotive therapy, and cognitive therapy. Early interventions were primarily behavioral in nature and emphasized relaxation training and desensitization. The past decade has witnessed an increased emphasis on cognitive treatments of test anxiety, perhaps in recognition of the important role that worry plays in the test anxiety–performance relationship (e.g. Crowley, Crowley & Clodfelter, 1986; Naveh-Benjamin, 1991; Zeidner, Klingman & Papko, 1988).

Hembree's (1988) meta-analytic review of 137 test anxiety treatment studies is most informative. A total of 36 of these studies focused on the worry–emotionality distinction. Hembree equated behavioral treatments with an attempt to treat the emotionality component and cognitive treatments with an attempt to treat the worry component. Cognitive–behavioral treatments focused on worry but also included elements to reduce emotionality. On the basis of his review, Hembree (1988) concluded that behavioral treatments and cognitive–behavioral treatments were equally effective in reducing the emotionality and worry components. Moreover, he concluded that study skills treatments were not effective in reducing test anxiety unless combined with behavioral or cognitive–behavioral treatments. Hembree concluded further that purely cognitive interventions are ineffective.

Unfortunately, the meta-analytic review did not include a number of cognitive intervention studies that indicate otherwise. On the basis of these more recent studies, several authors (e.g. Sarason & Sarason, 1990; Spielberger & Vagg, 1987) have concluded that purely cognitive treatments are effective. Although cognitive therapies directed toward reducing the worry component have been successful in reducing worry and emotionality, these therapies have not been consistently successful in improving performance (Dendato & Diener, 1986). Consequently, other researchers have incorporated a dual focus on cognitive interventions to reduce distress and study skills programs designed to improve levels of performance. For instance, Dendato & Diener (1986) compared a combination of relaxation/cognitive therapy (designed to treat both the emotionality and worry components of test anxiety) along with study skills training (designed to teach efficient study habits and test-taking strategies) versus the two treatment components in isolation. Consistent with past findings, they found that study skills training alone was not effective in reducing anxiety or improving test performance. Whereas a purely cognitive approach reduced anxiety but did not improve performance, the combined intervention produced anxiety reductions and significant improvements in performance. Dendato & Diener (1986) concluded that "The student who is unprepared or who lacks effective test-taking skills may benefit little from attempts to reduce worry directly" (p. 134) and they discussed at length the importance of substituting effective on-task behavior for worry cognitions and other off-task behavior. In appraising this study, Sarason & Sarason (1990) noted that the superiority of the combined therapy "suggests the value of having interventions sufficiently complex to deal with the major facts of the test-anxiety experience" (p. 490).

The use of a combination of procedures accords with the findings of a recent study by Smith, Arnkoff & Wright (1990). Smith et al. conducted a comprehensive assessment of the nature of test anxiety. They included measures that represented three theoretical orientations (i.e. cognitive–

attentional theories, cognitive skills, and social learning models of test anxiety). A state measure of worry was included to represent the cognitive–attentional approach. The authors found that variables representing all three orientations accounted for unique variance in test anxiety, with variables representing the cognitive–attentional approach having the most predictive power. Given that variables from each of the various approaches were significant predictors of unexplained variance, the authors concluded that multimodal counseling that includes all three orientations would be best.

Thus, a growing body of literature suggests that several procedures may be used in conjunction to treat test anxiety successfully. Unfortunately, because extant research has not used measures such as the RTT and SRTT and their attendant distinction between worry and test-irrelevant thinking, there are no data on the relative ability to ameliorate worries about failure versus irrelevant thoughts of a more general nature, either at the trait or state level. Future research in our laboratory will directly examine this issue.

An important question is how does the treatment of test-anxious worry relate to treatment of worry in generalized anxiety disorder (GAD) patients? Although the GAD client may not be as worried about evaluation as the test-anxious student, we believe that the treatment of GAD is relevant to test anxiety treatment and vice versa. A recent review of the cognitive–behavioral treatment of GAD (Craske, Rapee & Barlow, 1992) emphasized treatments that were similar to those used to treat test anxiety—namely, relaxation techniques and cognitive restructuring. For example, Blowers, Cobb & Mathews (1987) found that relaxation alone was not as effective as relaxation plus cognitive restructuring. Borkovec and his colleagues have undertaken the most comprehensive treatment research program for GAD. In their initial published study, Borkovec et al. (1987) reported that relaxation plus nondirective therapy was not as effective as relaxation plus cognitive restructuring. However, Borkovec & Mathews (1988) found no differences between relaxation plus nondirective therapy, relaxation plus cognitive therapy, and relaxation plus coping desensitization. The results of Borkovec's current treatment program are described in Roemer & Borkovec (1993). The description of this major attempt at intervention provides many specific suggestions for what can be incorporated into the development of treatment intervention packages for test-anxious students.

Directions For Future Research

Ironically, even though test anxiety research has a long history, many questions remain to be answered before a more complete understanding of test-anxious worry is possible. Several directions for future research have been alluded to throughout this chapter. We will conclude by outlining some additional issues in the hope that it will stimulate research in this area.

First, it is essential that researchers examine worry in evaluative situations from a developmental perspective. Research on test anxiety in children and adolescents has confirmed many of the findings obtained with adult college students (e.g. Zatz & Chassin, 1983, 1985). Unfortunately, this research must be interpreted with caution due to some psychometric and interpretative difficulties inherent in test anxiety measures for children (see Wigfield & Eccles, 1989, for a summary). Insight into the nature and roots of worry versus other dimensions of test anxiety awaits the development of multidimensional trait and state measures that are suitable for administration to children.

Second, it is important that subsequent research in this area examines possible gender differences. There has been a remarkable tendency in the general worry literature thus far to ignore possible differences between males and females, despite numerous indications from the test anxiety literature that results may vary by gender (e.g. Sarason, 1978; Spielberger et al., 1978). Indeed, our own research is limited by the fact that our subject sample is usually drawn from a population that is characterized by a preponderance of women. When we have been able to obtain a sufficient number of men in the study, gender differences have been detected. For instance, in one study, we established that women, relative to men, reported higher levels of state tension and bodily symptoms, but they did not differ significantly in worry and test-irrelevant thinking. The pattern of correlational findings was similar for men and women, but one important difference did emerge; worry was associated negatively with performance among women but not among men. Because the factors that contribute to these differences may be particularly revealing about the nature of worry, researchers should endeavor to conduct analyses for gender differences whenever possible.

Finally, the advent of a state worry measure means that it is feasible to examine the extent to which worry is influenced by situational or task characteristics. Investigators in this area could and should follow the lead of other researchers (e.g. Endler & Magnusson, 1976) by applying a trait by situation interaction approach to the study of worry.

SUMMARY

In summary, our analysis has provided extensive evidence that is consistent with the view that test-anxious worry does indeed reflect evaluative concerns about anticipated failure that stem, in large part, from a negative view of the self. Our analysis indicated that characterological levels of worry, as assessed by test anxiety inventories, are related not only to more general forms of worry, they are also associated broadly with measures of stress and maladjustment. As would be expected, our research with the SRTT indicated that state and trait worry are closely linked, but that the state measure accounts for variance in test-related outcomes that is not accounted for by a trait measure. We concluded by discussing the relatively effective means that exist for treating test anxiety and by outlining some critical directions for future investigation.

It is our hope that this chapter will serve as an impetus for further research on test-anxious worry and related phenomena. The results of the research conducted thus far suggests that additional research on worry and other cognitive aspects of test anxiety is indeed warranted and it promises to provide us with greater insight into the nature, development, and treatment of such students as our case example, Winnifred.

REFERENCES

Allen, G., Elias, M. & Zlotow, S. (1980). Behavioral interventions for alleviating test anxiety: A methodological overview of current therapeutic practices. In I.G. Sarason (Ed.), *Test Anxiety: Theory, Research, and Applications*, pp. 155–185. Hillsdale, NJ: Erlbaum.

Alpert, R. & Haber, R.N. (1960). Anxiety in academic achievement situations. *Journal of Abnormal and Social Psychology*, **61**, 207–215.

Arrindell, W.A., Emmelkamp, P.M.G. & van der Ende, J. (1984). Phobic dimensions: I. Reliability and generalizability across samples, genders, and nations. The Fear Survey Schedule (FSS-III) and Fear Questionnaire (FQ). *Advances in Behaviour Research and Therapy*, **9**, 207–245.

Attanasio, V., Andrasik, F., Blanchard, E.B. & Arena, J.G. (1984). Psychometric properties of the SUNYA revision of the Psychosomatic Symptom Checklist. *Journal of Behavioral Medicine*, **7**, 247–257.

Beck, A.T., Brown, G., Epstein, N. & Steer, R.A. (1988). An inventory for measuring clinical anxiety: Psychometric properties. *Journal of Consulting and Clinical Psychology*, **56**, 893–897.

Beck, A.T., Brown, G., Steer, R.A., Eidelson, J.I. & Riskind, J.H. (1987). Differentiating anxiety and depression: A test of the cognitive content-specificity hypothesis. *Journal of Abnormal Psychology*, **96**, 179–183.

Beck, A.T. & Emory, G. (1985). *Anxiety Disorders and Phobias*. New York: Basic Books.

Beck, A.T., Rush, A.J., Shaw, B.F. & Emery, G. (1979). *Cognitive Therapy for Depression: A Treatment Manual*. New York: Guilford.

Beck, A.T., Steer, R.A., Epstein, N. & Brown, G. (1990). Beck Self-Concept Test. *Psychological Assessment: A Journal of Consulting and Clinical Psychology*, **2**, 191–197.

Birenbaum, M. (1990). Test anxiety components: Comparison of different measures. *Anxiety Research, 3,* 149–159.

Blankstein, K.R. & Flett, G.L. (1991). Cognitive components of test anxiety: A comparison of assessment and scoring methods. In M. Booth-Butterfield (Ed.), *Communication, Cognition, and Anxiety,* pp. 187–202. (Special issue of the Journal of Social Behavior and Personality). London: Sage.

Blankstein, K.R. & Flett, G.L. (1992). Specificity in the assessment of daily hassles: Life stress, locus of control and adjustment in college students. *Canadian Journal of Behavioural Science, 24,* 382–398.

Blankstein, K.R. & Flett, G.L. (1993). Development of general, social, and academic measures of daily life stressors in students. Manuscript in preparation.

Blankstein, K.R., Flett, G.L. & Batten, I. (1989). Test anxiety and problem-solving self-appraisals of college students. *Journal of Social Behavior and Personality, 4,* 531–540.

Blankstein, K.R., Flett, G.L., Boase, P. & Toner, B.B. (1990). Thought listing and endorsement measures of self-referential thinking in test anxiety. *Anxiety Research, 2,* 103–111.

Blankstein, K.R., Flett, G.L. & Koledin, S. (1991). The Brief College Students Hassles Scale: Development, validation, and relation with pessimism. *Journal of College Student Development, 32,* 258–264.

Blankstein, K.R., Flett, G.L. & Watson, M. (1992). Test anxiety, coping, and academic problem-solving ability. *Journal of Clinical Psychology, 48,* 37–46.

Blankstein, K.R., Flett, G.L., Watson, M.S. & Koledin, S. (1990). Test anxiety, self-evaluative worry, and sleep disturbance in college students. *Anxiety Research, 3,* 193–204.

Blankstein, K.R., Toner, B.B. & Flett, G.L. (1989). Test anxiety and the contents of consciousness: Thought listing and endorsement measures. *Journal of Research in Personality, 23,* 269–286.

Blowers, C., Cobb, J. & Mathews, A. (1987). Generalized anxiety: A controlled treatment study. *Behaviour Research and Therapy, 25,* 493–502.

Borkovec, T.D. (1985). Worry: A potentially valuable concept. *Behaviour Research and Therapy, 23,* 481–482.

Borkovec, T.D. & Mathews, A.M. (1988). Treatment of nonphobic anxiety disorders: A comparison of nondirective, cognitive, and coping desensitization therapy. *Journal of Consulting and Clinical Psychology, 56,* 877–884.

Borkovec, T.D., Mathews, A.M., Chambers, A., Ebrahimi, S., Lytle, R. & Nelson, R. (1987). The effects of relaxation training with cognitive restructuring or nondirective therapy and the role of relaxation-induced anxiety in the treatment of generalized anxiety. *Journal of Consulting and Clinical Psychology, 55,* 883–888.

Borkovec, T.D., Metzger, R.L. & Pruzinsky, T. (1986). Anxiety, worry, and the self. In L.M. Hartman & K.R. Blankstein (Eds.), *Perception of Self in Emotional Disorder and Psychotherapy,* pp. 219–260. New York: Plenum.

Borkovec, T.D., Robinson, E., Pruzinsky, T. & DePree, J.A. (1983). Preliminary exploration of worry: Some characteristics and processes. *Behaviour Research and Therapy, 21,* 9–16.

Borkovec, T.D., Shadick, R.N. & Hopkins, M. (1991). The nature of normal and pathological worry. In R. Rupee & D.H. Barlow (Eds.). *Chronic Anxiety: Generalized Anxiety Disorder and Mixed Anxiety–Depression,* pp. 29–51. New York: Guilford Press.

Bruch, M.A. (1981). Relationship of test-taking strategies to test anxiety and performance: Toward a task analysis of examination behaviour. *Cognitive Therapy and Research*, **5**, 41–56.

Butler, G. & Mathews, A. (1983). Cognitive processes in anxiety. *Advances in Behaviour Research and Therapy*, **5**, 51–62.

Butler, G. & Mathews, A. (1988). Anticipatory anxiety and risk perception. *Cognitive Therapy and Research*, **11**, 551–565.

Butler, L. & Meichenbaum, D. (1981). The assessment of interpersonal problem-solving skills. In P.C. Kendall & S.D. Hollon (Eds.), *Assessment Strategies for Cognitive-Behavioral Intervention*, pp. 197–226. New York: Academic Press.

Carver, C.S. & Ganellen, R.J. (1983). Depression and components of self-punitiveness: High standards, self-criticism, and overgeneralization. *Journal of Abnormal Psychology*, **92**, 722–728.

Carver, C.D., La Voie, L., Kuhl, J. & Ganellen, R.J. (1988). Cognitive concomitants of depression: A further examination of the roles of generalization, high standards, and self-criticism. *Journal of Social and Clinical Psychology*, **7**, 350–365.

Carver, C.D. & Scheier, M.F. (1986). Functional and dysfunctional responses to anxiety: The interaction between expectancies and self-focused attention. In R. Schwarzer (Ed.), *Self-related Cognitions in Anxiety and Motivation*, pp. 111–141. Hillsdale, NJ: Erlbaum.

Clark, L.A. & Watson, D. (1991). Tripartite model of anxiety and depression: Psychometric evidence and taxonomic implications. *Journal of Abnormal Psychology*, **100**, 316–336.

Covington, M.V. (1986). Anatomy of failure-induced anxiety: The role of cognitive mediators. In R. Schwarzer (Ed.), *Self-related Cognitions in Anxiety and Motivation*, pp. 247–263. Hillsdale, NJ: Erlbaum.

Craske, M.G., Rapee, R.M. & Barlow, D.H. (1992). Cognitive-behavioral treatment of panic disorder, agoraphobia, and generalized anxiety disorder. In S.M. Turner, K.S. Calhoun & H.E. Adams (Eds.), *Handbook of Clinical Behavior Therapy*, 2nd edn, pp. 39–66. New York: Wiley.

Craske, M.G., Rapee, R.M., Jackel, L. & Barlow, D.H. (1989). Qualitative dimensions of worry in DSM-II-R generalized anxiety disorder subjects and nonanxious controls. *Behaviour Research and Therapy*, **27**, 397–402.

Crowley, Crowley & Clodfelter (1986). Effects of a self-coping cognitive treatment for test anxiety. *Journal of Counseling Psychology*, **33**, 84–86.

Davey, G.C.L. (1993). A comparison of three worry questionnaires. *Behaviour Research and Therapy*, **31**, 51–56.

Davey, G.C.L., Hampton, J., Farrell, J. & Davidson, S. (1992). Some characteristics of worrying: Evidence for worrying and anxiety as separate constructs. *Personality and Individual Differences*, **13**, 133–147.

Deffenbacher, J.L. (1978). Worry, emotionality, and task-generated interference in test anxiety: An empirical test of attentional theory. *Journal of Educational Psychology*, **70**, 248–254.

Deffenbacher, J.L. (1980). Worry and emotionality in test anxiety. In I.G. Sarason (Ed.), *Test Anxiety: Theory, Research, and Applications*, pp. 111–128. Hillsdale, NJ: Erlbaum.

DeLongis, A., Coyne, J.C., Dakof, G., Folkman, S. & Lazarus, R.S. (1982). Relationship of daily hassles, uplifts, and major life events to health status. *Health Psychology*, **1**, 119–136.

Dendato, K.M. & Diener, D. (1986). Effectiveness of cognitive/relaxation therapy and study-skills training in reducing self-reported anxiety and improving the academic performance of test anxious students. *Journal of Counseling Psychology*, **33**, 131–135.

Denney, D. (1980). Self-control approaches to the treatment of test anxiety. In I.G. Sarason (Ed.), *Test Anxiety: Theory, Research, and Applications*, pp. 209–243. Hillsdale, NJ: Erlbaum.

Desiderato, O. & Koskinen, P. (1969). Anxiety, study habits and acadmic achievement. *Journal of Consulting Psychology*, **16**, 162–165.

Diener, E., Emmons, R.A., Larsen, R.J. & Griffin, S. (1985). The Satisfaction With Life Scale. *Journal of Personality Assessment*, **49**, 71–75.

D'Zurilla, T.J. & Nezu, A.M. (1990). Development and preliminary evaluation of the Social Problem-Solving Inventory. *Psychological Assessment: A Journal of Consulting and Clinical Psychology*, **2**, 156–163.

D'Zurilla, T.J. & Sheedy, C.F. (1991). Relation between social problem-solving ability and subsequent level of psychological stress in college students. *Journal of Personality and Social Psychology*, **61**, 841–846.

D'Zurilla, T.J. & Sheedy, C.F. (1992). The relation between social problem-solving ability and subsequent level of academic competence in college students. *Cognitive Therapy and Research*, **16**, 589–599.

Endler, N.S., Cox, B.J., Parker, J.D.A. & Bagby, M.R. (1992). Self-reports of depression and state-trait anxiety: Evidence for differential assessment. *Journal of Personality and Social Psychology*, **63**, 832–838.

Endler, N.S., Edwards, J.M., Vitelli, R. & Parker, J.D.A. (1989). Assessment of state and trait anxiety: Endler Multidimensional Anxiety Scales. *Anxiety Research*, **2**, 1–14.

Endler, N.S. & Magnusson, D. (1976). Toward an interactional psychology of personality. *Psychological Bulletin*, **83**, 956–974.

Fenigstein, A., Scheier, M. & Buss, A. (1975). Public and private self-consciousness: Assessment and theory. *Journal of Consulting and Clinical Psychology*, **43**, 522–527.

Flett, G.L. (1988). Depression and preattributions for life problems and pleasures: A test of Kelley's model. Unpublished doctoral dissertation, University of Toronto.

Flett, G.L., Blankstein, K.R. & Boase, P. (1987). Self-focused attention in test anxiety and depression. *Journal of Social Behaviour and Personality*, **2**, 259–266.

Flett, G.L., Hewitt, P.L. & Mittelstaedt, W. (1991). Dysphoria and components of self-punitiveness: A re-analysis. *Cognitive Therapy and Research*, **15**, 201–219.

Ganellen, R.J. (1988). Specificity of attributions and overgeneralization in depression and anxiety. *Journal of Abnormal Psychology*, **97**, 83–86.

Girodo, M. & Roehl, J. (1978). Cognitive preparation and coping self-talk: Anxiety management during the stress of flying. *Journal of Consulting and Clinical Psychology*, **46**, 978–989.

Girodo, M. & Stein, S.J. (1978). Self-talk and the work of worrying in confronting a stressor. *Cognitive Therapy and Research*, **2**, 305–307.

Gotlib, I.H. (1984). Depression and general psychopathology in university students. *Journal of Abnormal Psychology*, **93**, 19–30.

Green, D.E., Walkey, F.H., McCormick, I.A. & Taylor, J.W. (1988). Development and evaluation of a 21-item version of the Hopkins Symptom Checklist with New Zealand and United States respondents. *Australian Journal of Psychology*, **40**, 61–70.

Heatherton, T.F. & Polivy, J. (1991). Development and validation of a scale for measuring state self-esteem. *Journal of Personality and Social Psychology*, **60**, 895–910.

Hembree, R. (1988). Correlates, causes, effects, and treatment of test anxiety. *Review of Educational Research*, **58**, 47–77.

Heppner, P.P. & Petersen, C.H. (1982). The development and implications of a personal problem solving inventory. *Journal of Counseling Psychology*, **29**, 66–75.

Hewitt, P.L. & Flett, G.L. (1991). Perfectionism in self and social contexts: Conceptualization, assessment, and association with psychopathology. *Journal of Personality and Social Psychology*, **60**, 456–470.

Hill, K. & Wigfield, A. (1984). Test anxiety: A major educational problem and what can be done about it. *Elementary School Journal*, **85**, 105–126.

Huba, G.J., Singer, J.L., Aneshensel, C.S. & Antrobus, J.S. (1982). *Short Imaginal Processes Inventory: Manual*. Port Huron, MI: Research Psychologists Press.

Jones, W.H., Briggs, S.R. & Smith, T.G. (1986). Shyness: Conceptualization and measurement. *Journal of Personality and Social Psychology*, **51**, 629–639.

Kalechstein, P., Hocevar, D., Zimmer, J.W. & Kalechstein, M. (1989). Procrastination over test preparation and test anxiety. In R. Schwarzer, H.M. van der Ploeg, & C.D. Spielberger (Eds.), *Advances in Test Anxiety Research*, Vol. 6, pp. 63–75. Lisse, The Netherlands: Swets & Zeitlinger.

Kanner, A.D., Coyne, J.C., Schaefer, C. & Lazarus, R.S. (1981). Comparison of two modes of stress measurement: Daily hassles and uplifts versus major life events. *Journal of Behavioural Medicine*, **4**, 1–39.

Kendall, P.C. & Watson, D. (1989). *Anxiety and Depression: Distinctive and Overlapping Features*. New York: Academic Press.

Klinger, E. (1984). A consciousness-sampling analysis of test anxiety and performance. *Journal of Personality and Social Psychology*, **47**, 1376–1390.

Lazarus, R.S. (1990). Theory-based stress measurement. *Psychological Inquiry*, **1**, 3–13.

Liebert, R.M. & Morris, L.W. (1967). Cognitive and emotional components of test anxiety: A distinction and some initial data. *Psychological Reports*, **20**, 975–978.

MacLeod, A.K., Williams, J.M.G. & Bekerian, D.A. (1991). Worry is reasonable: The role of explanations in pessimism about future personal events. *Journal of Abnormal Psychology*, **100**, 478–486.

Mandler, G. & Sarason, S.B. (1952). A study of anxiety and learning. *Journal of Abnormal and Social Psychology*, **47**, 166–173.

Mathews, A. (1990). Why worry? The cognitive function of anxiety. *Behaviour Research and Therapy*, **28**, 455–468.

McGuire, D.P., Mitic, W. & Neumann, B. (1987). Perceived stress in adolescents: What normal teenagers worry about. *Canada's Mental Health*, June, 2–5.

Meichenbaum, D. & Butler, L. (1980a). Cognitive ethology: Assessing the streams of cognition and emotion. In K.R. Blankstein, P. Pliner & J. Polivy (Eds.), *Assessment and Modification of Emotional Behaviour*, Vol. 6, pp. 139–163. New York: Plenum.

Meichenbaum, D. & Butler, L. (1980b). Toward a conceptual model for the treatment of test anxiety: Implications for research and treatment. In I.G. Sarason (Ed.), *Test Anxiety: Theory, Research and Applications*, pp. 187–208. Hillsdale, NJ: Erlbaum.

Meyer, T.J., Miller, M.L., Metzger, R.L. & Borkovec, T.D. (1990). Development and validation of the Penn State Worry Questionnaire. *Behaviour Research and Therapy*, **28**, 487–495.

Morris, L.W., Davis, M.A. & Hutchings, C.H. (1981). Cognitive and emotional components of anxiety: Literature review and a revised worry-emotionality scale. *Journal of Educational Psychology*, **73**, 541–555.

Naveh-Benjamin, M. (1991). A comparison of training programs intended for different types of test-anxious students: Further support for an information-processing model. *Journal of Educational Psychology*, **83**, 134–139.

Nicholls, J.G., Jagacinski, C.M. & Miller, A.T. (1986). Conceptions of ability in children and adults. In R. Schwarzer (Ed.), *Self-related Cognition in Anxiety and Motivation*, pp. 265–284. Hillsdale, NJ: Erlbaum.

Pruzinsky, T. & Borkovec, T.D. (1990). Cognitive and personality characteristics of worriers. *Behaviour Research and Therapy*, **36**, 507–512.

Rachman, S. & de Silva, P. (1978). Abnormal and normal obsessions. *Behaviour Research and Therapy*, **16**, 233–248.

Rich, A.R. & Woolever, D.K. (1988). Expectancy and self-focused attention: Experimental support for the self-regulation model of test anxiety. *Journal of Social and Clinical Psychology*, **7**, 246–259.

Richardson, F.C., O'Neill, H.F., Jr., Whitmore, S. & Judd, W.A. (1977). Factor analysis of the Test Anxiety Scale and evidence concerning the components of test anxiety. *Journal of Consulting and Clinical Psychology*, **45**, 704–705.

Roemer, L. & Borkovec, T.D. (1993). Worry: Unwanted cognitive activity that controls unwanted somatic experience. In D.M. Wegner & J. Pennebaker (Eds.), *Handbook of Mental Control*. New York: Guilford.

Rosenberg, M. (1965). *Society and the Adolescent Self-image*. Princeton, NJ: Princeton University Press.

Ruble, D.N. & Flett, G.L. (1988). Conflicting goals in self-evaluative information-seeking: Developmental and ability level analyses. *Child Development*, **59**, 97–106.

Russell, D., Peplau, L.A. & Cutrona, C.E. (1980). The revised UCLA Loneliness Scale: Concurrent and discriminant validity evidence. *Journal of Personality and Social Psychology*, **39**, 472–480.

Russell, M. & Davey, G.C.L. (1993). The relationship between life event measures and anxiety and its cognitive correlates. *Personality and Individual Differences*, **14**, 317–322.

Sarason, I.G. (1978). The Test Anxiety Scale: Concept and research. In C.D. Spielberger & I.G. Sarason (Eds.), *Stress and Anxiety*, Vol. 5, pp. 193–216. Washington, DC: Hemisphere.

Sarason, I.G. (1984). Stress, anxiety, and cognitive interference: Reactions to tests. *Journal of Personality and Social Psychology*, **46**, 929–938.

Sarason, I.G. (1986). Test anxiety, worry, and cognitive interference. In R. Schwarzer (Ed.), *Self-related Cognitions in Anxiety and Motivation*, pp. 19–33. Hillsdale, NJ: Erlbaum.

Sarason, I.G., Johnson, J.H. & Siegel, J.M. (1978). Assessing the impact of life changes: Development of the Life Experience Survey. *Journal of Consulting and Clinical Psychology*, **46**, 932–946.

Sarason, I.G. & Sarason, B.R. (1990). Test anxiety. In H. Leitenberg (Ed.), *Handbook of Social and Evaluation Anxiety*, pp. 475–495. New York and London: Plenum.

Sarason, I.G., Sarason, B.R. & Pierce, G.R. (1991). Anxiety, cognitive interference, and performance. In M. Booth-Butterfield (Ed.), *Communication, Cognition, and Anxiety*, pp. 1–18. (Special issue of the Journal of Social Behavior and Personality). London: Sage.

Scheier, M.F. & Carver, C.S. (1985). Optimism, coping, and health: Assessment and implications of generalized outcome expectancies. *Health Psychology*, **4**, 219–247.

Seipp, B. (1991). Anxiety and academic performance: a meta-analysis of findings. *Anxiety Research*, **4**, 27–41.

Shipley, R.H., Butt, J.H. & Horwitz, E.A. (1979). Preparation to reexperience a stressful medical examination: Effect of repetitious videotape exposure and coping style. *Journal of Consulting and Clinical Psychology*, **47**, 485–492.

Smith, R.J., Arnkoff, D.B. & Wright, T.L. (1990). Test anxiety and academic competence: A comparison of alternative models. *Journal of Counseling Psychology*, **37**, 313–321.

Spacapan, S. & Cohen, S. (1983). Effects and aftereffects of stressor expectations. *Journal of Personality and Social Psychology*, **45**, 1243–1254.

Spielberger, C.D., Anton, W. & Bedel, J. (1976). The nature and treatment of test anxiety. In M. Zuckerman & C.D. Spielberger (Eds.), *Emotion and Anxiety: New Concepts, Methods, and Applications*, pp. 317–345. Hillsdale, NJ: Erlbaum.

Spielberger, C.D., Gonzales, H.P., Taylor, C.J., Algaze, B. & Anton, W.D. (1978). Examination stress and test anxiety. In C.D. Spielberger & I.G. Sarason (Eds.), *Stress and Anxiety*, Vol. 5, pp. 167–191. New York: Hemisphere/Wiley.

Spielberger, C.D., Gorsuch, R.L. & Lushene, R.E. (1970). *Manual for the State-Trait Anxiety Inventory*. Palo Alto, CA: Consulting Psychologists Press.

Spielberger, C.D. & Vagg, P.R. (1987). The treatment of test anxiety: A transactional process model. In R. Schwarzer, H.M. van der Ploeg, & C.D. Spielberger (Eds.), *Advances in Test Anxiety Research*, Vol. 5, pp. 179–186. Lisse, The Netherlands: Swets & Zeitlinger.

Sud, A. & Sharma, S. (1990). Two short-term, cognitive interventions for the reduction of test anxiety. *Anxiety Research*, **3**, 131–147.

Tallis, F., Eysenck, M.W. & Andrews, A. (1991). Worry: A critical analysis of some theoretical approaches. *Anxiety Research*, **4**, 97–108.

Tallis, F., Eysenck, M. & Mathews, A. (1992). A questionnaire for the measurement of nonpathological worry. *Personality and Individual Differences*, **13**, 161–168.

Tallis, F., Eysenck, M. & Mathews, A.M. (1991). Elevated evidence requirements and worry. *Personality and Individual Differences*, **12**, 21–27.

Topman, R.M., Kleijn, W.C., van der Ploeg, H.M. & Masset, E.A. (1992). Test anxiety, cognitions, study habits and academic performance: A prospective study. In K.A. Hagtvet & T.B. Johnson (Eds.), *Advances in Test Anxiety Research*, Vol. 7, pp. 239–258. Lisse, The Netherlands: Swets & Zeitlinger.

Tryon, G.S. (1980). The measurement and treatment of test anxiety. *Review of Educational Research*, **50**, 343–372.

Usala, P.D. & Hertzog, C. (1991). Evidence of differential stability of state and trait anxiety in adults. *Journal of Personality and Social Psychology*, **60**, 471–479.

Vasey, W.W. & Borkovec, T.D. (1992). A catastrophizing assessment of worrisome thoughts. *Cognitive Therapy and Research*, **16**, 505–520.

Vredenburg, K., Flett, G.L. & Krames, L. (1993). Analogue versus clinical depression: A critical re-appaisal. *Psychological Bulletin*, **113**, 327–344.

Watson, D., Clark, L.A. & Tellegen, A. (1988). Development and validation of brief measures of positive and negative affect: The PANAS Scales. *Journal of Personality and Social Psychology*, **54**, 1063–1070.

Watson, D. & Friend, R. (1969). Measurement of social-evaluative anxiety. *Journal of Consulting and Clinical Psychology*, **33**, 448–457.

Watson, J.M. (1988). Achievement anxiety test: Dimensionality and utility. *Journal of Educational Psychology*, **80**, 585–591.

Wegner, D.M. (1989). *White Bears and other Unwanted Thoughts: Suppression, Obsession, and the Psychology of Mental Control*. New York: Viking.

Wegner, D.M. & Schneider, D.J. (1989). Mental ghosts: The war of the ghosts in the machine. In J.S. Uleman & J.A. Bargh (Eds.), *Unintended Thought*, pp. 287–305. New York: Guilford.

Wigfield, A. & Eccles, J.S. (1989). Test anxiety in elementary and secondary school students. *Educational Psychologist*, **24**, 159–183.

Wine, J.D. (1980). Cognitive–attentional theory of test anxiety. In I.G. Sarason (Ed.), *Test Anxiety: Theory, Research, and Applications*, pp. 349–385. Hillsdale, NJ: Erlbaum.

Wolpe, J. & Lang, P.J. (1964). Fear Survey Schedule for use in behaviour therapy. *Behaviour Research and Therapy*, **9**, 401–410.

Zatz, S. & Chassin, L. (1983). Cognitions of test anxious children. *Journal of Consulting and Clinical Psychology*, **51**, 526–534.

Zatz, S. & Chassin, L. (1985). Cognitions of test-anxious children under naturalistic test-taking conditions. *Journal of Consulting and Clinical Psychology*, **53**, 393–401.

Zeidner, M., Klingman, A. & Papko, O. (1988). Enhancing students' test coping skills: Report of a psychological education program. *Journal of Educational Psychology*, **80**, 95–101.

SECTION II   Worry in selected population groups

INTRODUCTION

Worry affects individuals at all stages in life. In the following section, worry is considered as a phenomenon relevant to childhood, adulthood and old age. Moreover, worry is not exclusive to generalized anxiety disorder (GAD). Worry is a problem for individuals suffering from most, if not all, of the anxiety disorders. Recent evidence suggests that worry may be particularly important with respect to obsessive–compulsive disorder (OCD). For this reason, a chapter is included that provides guidelines for differentiating obsessions in OCD from extreme worry in GAD.

Vasey & Daleiden (Chapter 7) argue that if the concept of worry is to be understood in children, then it must be placed within a developmental framework. They show that the content of children's worries reflects their developing understanding of themselves, others, and the world around them. Moreover, the manner in which children worry will be strongly influenced by the changing cognitive structures and operations that are a normal part of the maturational process. These ideas will necessarily inform the debate as to whether childhood anxiety should be understood in terms of a developmental delay or a developmental deviation. In the final section of their contribution, Vasey & Daleiden outline assessment and treatment methods relevant to worry in childhood.

In Chapter 8, Butler concentrates on the treatment of worry in the context of generalised anxiety disorder. A conceptual scheme is provided within which therapists can target (1) the process of worry, (2) maintaining factors, (3) cognitions, and (4) feelings. However, the long-term consequences of GAD are also given due consideration, in particular, "demoralisation", a complex state characterised by hopelessness, fatigue, reduced activity, and reduced self-esteem. Although specific interventions are suggested, the fact that the focus of worry shifts repeatedly means that patients must understand general principles if therapy is to be successful. The essential points relating to practice are substantiated with case material.

Brown, Dowdall, Côté & Barlow (Chapter 9) review the diagnostic criteria for GAD and OCD and detail current definitions of worry and obsessions. These definitions are placed in context with respect to theoretical models devised to explain the aetiology and maintenance of both GAD and OCD. Despite a number of areas of overlap, the authors conclude that worry and obsessions have several unique features which validate the distinction made between GAD and OCD. A case example serves to elucidate key points, and recommendations for future research are made.

Wisocki (Chapter 10) presents epidemiological data on worry and anxiety in elderly populations; however, she instructively informs the reader of the numerous problems associated with assessing the elderly. The development of a self-report measure, the Worry Scale, is described, and an account of its relationship with other measures is provided. A central section explores the phenomenology of worry in the elderly; reference is made to content areas of particular relevance to the elderly (for example health worries) and several qualitative parameters. Wisocki suggests that the worry research would be enriched, if the construct were studied across the life span. Moreover, sensitivity to the changing content and meaning of worry for the ageing individual promises to inform clinical practice.

CHAPTER 7   Worry in children

Michael W. Vasey and
*Eric L. Daleiden**

While the theoretical and empirical literature concerning worry has grown large in the past decade, surprisingly little of it concerns worry among children and adolescents. Only recently have researchers begun to consider clearly the role played by worry and other cognitions in the anxiety of young people (Francis, 1988; Kendall & Chansky, 1991; Vasey, 1993). The separate study of worry in children is essential since the dramatic changes in children's cognitive, social, and emotional capacities as they develop are likely to have important implications for understanding the role of worry in childhood anxiety (Vasey, 1993). Toward that end, this chapter begins by considering a conceptualization of worry in childhood against the backdrop of current adult conceptualizations and the implications of development. Second, we discuss the nature and role of worry in normal and pathological childhood anxiety. Third, we consider issues relevant to the assessment of worry in young people and provide a review of available measures and assessment techniques. Finally, we discuss the treatment of worry in childhood. Throughout the chapter we emphasize discussion of our own and others' recent research and attempt to identify important directions for future research.

CONCEPTUALIZATIONS OF WORRY IN CHILDHOOD

Historically, mediating cognitive processes in childhood anxiety and fear have been largely neglected (Graziano, DeGiovanni & Garcia, 1979; King, Hamilton & Ollendick, 1988). The recent advances in the adult worry literature have depended largely on the adoption of clear conceptualizations of the worry process (Borkovec, Robinson, Pruzinsky & DePree, 1983; Mathews, 1990). Unfortunately, until recently, much of the research on worry in childhood has been hindered by the lack of a clearly

*The Ohio State University, Columbus, USA

Worrying: Perspectives on Theory, Assessment and Treatment. Edited by G.C.L. Davey and F. Tallis.
© 1994 John Wiley & Sons Ltd.

specified, developmentally-informed conceptualization (Vasey, 1993). In many cases, studies have provided no formal definition of worry, or have treated it as synonymous with fear (e.g. Orton, 1982).

Given its apparent pervasiveness among adults (Borkovec et al., 1983), it is not surprising that worry also appears to be a common phenomenon among children. For example, Orton (1982) found that over 70% of fifth and sixth graders reported ten or more things about which they worry. Brown, O'Keefe, Sanders & Baker (1986) have shown that anxious antic-ipation and ruminative thoughts during stress are prevalent from middle childhood through late adolescence. Bell-Dolan, Last & Strauss (1990) evaluated the prevalence of worry in a sample of never-psychiatrically-ill children 5–18 years of age and found that over 30% endorsed symptoms of excessive worry. Finally, in DSM-III-R, worry in more severe forms is also a defining feature of the childhood anxiety disorder category of overanxious disorder (OAD) (American Psychiatric Association, 1987).

The absence of a definition of worry in past research has prevented the formulation of meaningful hypotheses regarding its development or rela-tionship to childhood anxiety. In an attempt to stimulate and focus future research, we have recently offered a working model of worry in child-hood (Vasey, 1993). The adoption of this model allows consideration of what aspects of development may be most relevant for our understand-ing of worry and leads to specific testable predictions for future research. The efforts of several researchers in the adult anxiety literature have provided the basis for this model. For example, Mathews (1990) has de-fined worry as "awareness of possible future danger, which is repeatedly rehearsed without being resolved" (p. 456). Similarly, Borkovec et al. (1983) have defined worry as a chain of thoughts and images surrounding "an issue whose outcome is uncertain but contains the possibility of one or more negative outcomes" (p. 10). In general, worry is an anticipatory process involving repetitive, unwanted, and intrusive thoughts whose content pertains to potentially threatening possibilities and their implica-tions (Borkovec, Shadick & Hopkins, 1991).

In our model we assume that the defining features of worry in childhood are largely consistent with current adult definitions. While caution is necessary when applying adult-based models to children (Garber, 1984), their careful use can provide an important heuristic for initial research efforts. As research progresses, we expected that a more developmentally appropriate model of worry in childhood will emerge. With these caveats, we have defined worry in childhood as primarily an anticipatory cogni-tive process involving repetitive, primarily verbal thoughts (Romer & Borkovec, 1993) related to possible threatening outcomes and their potential consequences. Furthermore, worry typically involves more than the anticipation of a single threatening event. Instead, the worrier also verbally elaborates an event's potential negative consequences. We further assume that child worriers, like their adult counterparts, will demonstrate an attentional bias toward threat cues (Mathews, 1990), exaggerate the likelihood and magnitude of threatening possibilties (Beck & Emery, 1985; MacLeod, Williams & Bekerian, 1991), and selectively interpret ambiguous stimuli as threatening (Mathews, 1990).

Since the anticipation of possible threats to one's well-being is an important human activity, worry must be differentiated from the normal adaptive process of anticipating and preparing for possible negative events. Parkhurst & Asher (1985) suggest that a certain level of "negative concern" on a child's part is necessary to motivate consideration of possible shortcomings of their plans or obstacles that may interfere with their implementation. The anticipation of future threats normally produces mild anxiety that appears to serve as a cue for adaptive efforts directed at preparing for or preventing such possibilities. While the role played by such "concerns" in children's problem-solving efforts is of interest, such thoughts do not constitute worry. Instead, worrisome thoughts are defined as difficult to control, often repetitively intrusive, and not leading to effective problem-solving (Borkovec et al., 1991). Parkhurst & Asher (1985) describe worry as a state in which children become overly concerned about negative outcomes and overestimate their likelihood. Instead of constructively devising strategies for surmounting or preventing problems, when worried, children shift to strategies geared toward avoiding negative outcomes seen as unrealistically likely. In keeping with current adult theories (e.g. Mathews, 1990), we argue that worry is primarily an attempt to anticipate and avoid all possible negative outcomes. Thus, worry is a distortion of normally adaptive attempts at anticipation and preparation. It rarely leads to effective solutions because problem-solving attempts are disrupted by further anticipations of problems or cognitive avoidance (Borkovec et al., 1991).

Adopting this definition of worry allows for clearer consideration of the implications of development for the role of worry in childhood anxiety. Below, we offer a brief discussion of the impact of developmental factors on worry in childhood. The reader is referred to Vasey (1993) for a more thorough discussion.

THE IMPLICATIONS OF DEVELOPMENT

To clarify the normal development of worry, we will separately discuss two main aspects. The first, which has historically received the most attention, concerns differences in the frequency and content of children's worries. These characteristics of worry have typically been examined in relation to demographic variables such as age, gender, and ethnicity but few studies attempt to explain the reasons for such demographic differences. The second aspect, which has historically received far less consideration, concerns the process of worry. This domain includes largely neglected questions about the role and development of various cognitive operations and structures (see Kendall & Ingram, 1987) in childhood worry.

Frequency of Children's Worries

Studies of the frequency of children's worries reveal a fairly consistent pattern of demographic differences. For example, younger children tend to report more frequent worry than older children. Morris, Finkelstein & Fisher (1976) found that worry scores decreased with increasing age in a sample of third to eighth grade children. Similarly, Hoffner & Cantor (1991) found that when shown a threatening film sequence, 5–7-year-olds reported more worry than 9–11-year-old children.

Gender differences also appear in studies of worry frequency. In general, girls score higher on measures of anxiety than boys and this appears to hold true for specific measures of worry frequency. For example, Wasserstein, La Greca & Silverman (1992) found that females describe more categories of worries than males. Morris et al. (1976) found that females scored higher than males on their worry scale and Gjesme (1983) found that females scored higher than males on the worry scale of the Test Anxiety Scale for Children (TASC; Sarason et al., 1960).

Ethnic differences also appear for worry frequency. However, they appear to vary depending on children's age and gender. For example, Wasserstein et al. (1992) report that African-American boys worry more than Caucasian and Hispanic boys, but found no similar effect for girls. They also found that younger African-American children worry more than younger Caucasian and Hispanic children, but that there were no differences for older children.

In summary, the frequency of worry in childhood and adolescence appears to vary with age, gender and race. However, these patterns do not always appear and one reason for occasional contradictory findings is that children of different ages, genders, and races may not worry about the same things. Thus, any measure of worry frequency may or may not tap the appropriate domains for any given group. In order to understand such differences more fully, we must consider the content of children's worries.

Content of Children's Worries

Over the past 50 years a large body of normative research on the content of children's worries and fears has been collected (see Graziano et al., 1979, and Gittelman, 1986, for reviews). While many of these studies suffer from methodological and conceptual problems (Graziano et al., 1979), as a group they provide a remarkably consistent picture. In general, children show a decline in fear of animals, the dark, and imaginary creatures or monsters as they approach middle childhood (e.g. Bauer, 1976), while fear of psychological distress (e.g. Miller, Barrett, Hampe & Noble, 1972) and school and social fears (e.g. LaPouse & Monk, 1959) increase as children become preadolescents.

There are also gender differences in worry content. For example, Orton (1982) found that females report more worries than males about family, personal adequacy, personal health or well-being, and imaginary or unreasonable concerns. Similarly, Simon & Ward (1982) found that 12–13-year-old females report more worries than males in the domains of family, social relationships and situations, school, and imaginary concerns. Kaufman et al. (1993) reported a variety of gender differences in the content of adolescents' worries. Boys reported more worry than females about topics like "having too much free time", "trouble with the law", and "popularity with friends and classmates". In contrast, females reported more worry about such topics as "my periods", "getting bad grades", and "death or illness of a family member".

Finally, children's worries appear to vary depending on ethnicity. For example, Kaufman et al. (1993) found that the content of worries endorsed by African-American adolescents differed considerably from those endorsed by Caucasians. African-American adolescents reported more worry about topics such as "getting bad grades", "feeling that I'm a bad person", and "people being afraid of me". Caucasian adolescents reported more worry concerning topics like "going to a new home", "going out on a date", and "going to a new school".

The fact that the content of children's and adolescents' worries vary depending on such factors is not surprising since their concerns must necessarily be an expression of their cognitive developmental level and the environments in which they live (Campbell, 1986; Vasey, 1993). For example, it would not be surprising to find differences between inner city

and suburban children given that the possible threats in their lives probably differ tremendously. Similarly, young children's understanding of the
world is vastly different from older children's or adolescents'. In general,
it appears that the content of children's worries reflects their developing
understanding of themselves, others, and the world in general (Campbell,
1986; Vasey, 1993).

Since worry in adulthood is predominantly self-referent (Borkovec,
Metzger & Pruzinsky, 1986) in our own research, we hypothesized that
the content of worry in childhood will also be focused primarily upon
threats to one's own well-being. Our research findings support this hypothesis. Vasey, Crnic and Carter (in press) reported a study which evaluated the proportion of children's worries which focused on threats to
oneself versus those involving threats to others (typically caregivers) in a
sample of children aged 5–6, 8–9, and 11–12 years. Consistent with
Borkovec et al.'s (1986) findings for adults, self-referent threats clearly
predominated for all three age groups.

Since worry in childhood is predominantly self-referent, its content
should be integrally tied to the development of children's self-definitions
(Vasey, 1993). Self-concept development is a reflection of growth in a
wide range of social and cognitive domains such as the ability to take
another person's perspective and engage in social comparison (Damon &
Hart, 1990). The content of children's worrisome thoughts should reflect
developmental changes in their emerging perceptions of themselves and
their relationship to their physical and social environments. Several relevant age-related changes in children's self-understanding have been documented (see Damon & Hart, 1990, for a review). Prior to about 8 years of
age, children tend to conceive of themselves mainly in "physicalistic"
terms having to do with characteristics of their bodies and possessions.
Subsequently, characteristics related to behavioral competence become
more important as children enter preadolescence, and psychological traits
play an increasingly important role. Also at about 8 years of age, children
begin to be capable of engaging in social-comparison in forming their self-
definitions and become increasingly aware that others may be evaluating
them. This awareness becomes even more heightened as they enter
adolescence.

There is evidence that the content of children's worries follows this progression from physicalistic to psychological and abstract threats. Magnusson (1985) reported this pattern for 12-, 15-, and 18-year-olds who were
asked about what made them anxious and why. Reports focusing on
physical properties of the situation and external bodily consequences
decreased in frequency with age while reports referring to anticipated

psychological consequences such as shame or guilt increase with age. In our own research we have evaluated the relationship between 5–6-, 8–9-, and 11–12-year-old children's level of self-concept development and worry content (Vasey et al., in press). Consistent with expectations, children whose self-concepts were less advanced produced greater proportions of worry content related to their physical well-being. In contrast, children whose self-concepts reflected more advanced development produced greater proportions of worrisome possibilities related to social evaluation and psychological well-being.

In summary, the content of children's anxiety-related cognitions is a reflection of their level of cognitive and social development. This suggests that it may be useful to compare the developmental level of the content of anxious and non-anxious children's worrisome thoughts. It may be that some anxious children's worries reflect developmental delays or deviations. Another relevant aspect of development is the illogical or "magical" thinking inherent in the reasoning of very young children (Flavell, 1977). This is often reflected in an inabilty to distinguish the real from the imaginary. Worries and fears concerning imaginary or supernatural threats are prevalent among children prior to about 7 or 8 years of age, but decline in middle childhood (Bauer, 1976). Anxious children may also demonstrate developmental delays in the form of fears that reflect pre-operational thought (e.g. magical thinking). If so, it may be that interventions can be tailored to promote more logical thinking in relation to anxiety-provoking topics.

The Process of Worry

We believe that the occurrence of worry in childhood requires a specific set of cognitive structures and operations and that the manner in which children worry will change as these requisite operations and structures develop. In general, cognitive development brings increased capacity to respond adaptively to one's concerns about future events, but it also brings the potential to conceive of a multitude of threats and elaborate them in infinite ways. In general, children probably become far more capable of mediating severe, generalized anxiety through worry as their cognitive abilities develop (Vasey, 1993). Paradoxically, it may be that under certain circumstances, which are discussed in the next section, the acquisition of advanced cognitive abilities may bring increased risk for worry (Gallagher, 1990).

The ability to mentally represent the future is a necessary starting point for the worry process. This requires the ability to go beyond what is observable and consider what is merely possible. In essence, worry is conceptualized as a process characterized by the anticipation and elaboration of catastrophic possibilities. This ability appears to follow a predictable developmental course (Horobin & Acredolo, 1989). Prior to 7–8 years of age, children appear to possess only a vague ability to consider the future. This gradually becomes more extended and complex through middle childhood and becomes completely abstract and highly elaborated in adolescence with the achievement of formal reasoning skills (Vasey, 1993). However, the ability to anticipate even one threatening possibility may be sufficient for worry to occur. For example, a child might remember a threatening event and consider its possible recurrence in the near future. From this perspective, even toddlers may be capable of worrying about events such as separation from their caregivers (Littenberg, Tulkin & Kagan, 1971). The ability to anticipate negative outcomes is even more clearly observable in the preschool period. Morris, Brown & Halbert (1977) demonstrated that behaviors assumed to reflect the worry component of test anxiety can be reliably observed in children 4–5 years of age. These findings suggest that anticipatory thoughts of threat play an active role in anxiety experiences even among preschoolers.

One question that warrants future attention is whether such anticipatory anxiety in very young children fits our definition of worry. One difference may be that young children may not represent future events in the same way as older children or adults. Kosslyn (1980) has suggested that young children tend to rely much more upon visual images in their representation of information than older children or adults. Since young children lack well-developed verbal language, it is thought that visual images as well as motor schemes (Piaget, 1970) play a significantly greater role in their representations of the world. If so, when young children call up threatening event representations, such images may more readily activate the physiological and behavioral responses associated with anxiety than primarily verbally-based representations (Lang, 1985). This may be important since there is some evidence that worry is primarily verbal in nature (Borkovec & Inz, 1990) and interferes with activation of such fear responses (Borkovec & Hu, 1990). Romer & Borkovec (1993) argue that this interference with physiological arousal serves to maintain worry via negative reinforcement. Thus, if young children's representations of future threats are predominantly imagery-based, they may not serve the same function as the verbal representations characteristic of worry.

Related to future representations is the ability to elaborate the implications of future events. Since children's ability to reason about future possibilities improves dramatically as they mature (Horobin & Acredolo,

1989), the ability to consider multiple threatening outcomes and to elaborate their potential negative consequences should also increase (Vasey, 1993). Prior to early adolescence, children's ability to reason about consequences is limited to possibilities that are directly observable by the child or that have previously been experienced (Piaget, 1987). Determining the level of such reasoning necessary for worry is difficult. Our own research has shown that even 5–6-year-olds mention anticipatory thoughts (e.g. "I thought the other kids might be mean to me") in their descriptions of worry, fear and nervousness (Vasey et al., in press). However, while such evidence indicates that even young children anticipate threats, the development of abstract reasoning skills is likely to dramatically increase children's ability to worry. For example, catastrophic thinking is likely to become significantly more elaborate as children become capable of considering the consequences of anticipated threats. Our research has shown that 8–9- and 11–12-year-olds are significantly more able than 5–6-year-olds to elaborate potential catastrophic consequences of worrisome events (Vasey et al., in press).

The implications of such developmental differences for children's anxiety remain to be determined. However, increased ability to conceptualize elaborate sequences of negative consequences is likely to increase the potential severity and generality of worry. Thus, this perspective predicts that generalized anxiety disorders should become increasingly prevalent and the role of worry in mediating anxiety should increase as children develop. A thorough test of these hypotheses awaits future longitudinal studies of the developmental course of childhood anxiety disorders.

In summary, developmental factors have important implications for the frequency, content, and process of worry in childhood. It remains unclear at what age children become capable of engaging in the process described by the current model of worry. However, at the very least, it is clear that children's capacity to elaborate and broaden their worries increases dramatically as they develop. The impact of such changes on normal and pathological anxiety in children should be explored in the future.

NORMAL AND PATHOLOGICAL WORRY IN CHILDHOOD

Despite its common occurrence, little is known about worry in normal childhood anxiety or how it may differ from that in various anxiety disorders. From the perspective of developmental psychopathology, the role of worry in childhood anxiety disorders can only be understood in the context of normal development (Cicchetti, 1984). Recently researchers have begun to examine non-pathological forms of worry in adulthood (Tallis, Eysenck & Mathews, 1992) and similar studies with children are necessary in order to understand the development of pathological forms of worry. A recent study of symptoms of anxiety disorders in normal children by Bell-Dolan et al. (1990) provides an excellent starting point for future studies.

From a cognitive–behavioral perspective, only those children who possess anxiety-promoting cognitive deficits and distortions should be at-risk to develop problematic worry and anxiety (Kendall, 1985). Skills related to the regulation of emotion, specifically anxiety, comprise one domain in which overly anxious children seem likely to be deficient. Emotional self-regulation is defined as the automatic or deliberate use of behavioral, physiological, and/or cognitive responses to alter one's emotional responses (Dodge, 1989; Thompson, 1990). By definition, excessive worry is an example of emotional dysregulation. Earlier we suggested that worry rarely leads to effective problem solutions. One simple explanation for this may be that worriers utilize anxiety management strategies, such as cognitive avoidance and distraction, which interfere with problem-solving and prevent the prolonged exposure necessary for habituation of the anxiety associated with the worrisome thought.

A variety of research suggests that anxious children may indeed cope differently with anxiety than non-anxious children. For example, Olah et al. (1989) found a significant positive relationship between a measure of trait anxiety and escape coping for both boys ($r = .29, p < .01$) and girls ($r = .44, p < .01$). In contrast, they found a significant negative relationship between trait anxiety and constructive coping (e.g. direct problem-solving efforts) for both boys ($r = -.43, p < .01$) and girls ($r = -.27, p < .01$). While such results support the existence of coping differences based on anxiety levels, the basis of this effect remains unclear. Anxious children may lack adequate knowledge of effective strategies such as problem-solving. Alternatively, they may possess such skills but be unable to use them effectively due to interference from other responses designed to give immediate relief from anxiety.

In our research we have begun to examine these possibilities. Our preliminary results suggest that children with clinical levels of worry do not differ from matched normal controls in the types of strategies they suggest for regulating worry when they are asked how other children manage their worries (Vasey, Daleiden & Williams, 1992). However, when asked how they cope with their own worrisome thoughts, child worriers report greater reliance than controls on emotion-focused strategies such as distraction and cognitive avoidance. In contrast, normal controls rely more heavily on problem-focused strategies such as problem-solving thoughts and actions. Thus, our preliminary findings suggest that child worriers are not deficient in their knowledge of strategies for managing worry. Instead, the problem appears to be related to performance. They tend to rely on strategies that offer immediate relief from anxiety but which directly interfere with strategies that offer more hope of reducing anxiety over the longer term. Such a pattern is consistent with a two-factor theory of worry in which worrisome thoughts are associated with increased negative arousal, and responses such as distraction, which provide immediate relief, are negatively reinforced.

Our results are consistent with several similar studies examining the coping patterns of anxious and non-anxious adults. For example, Davey, Burgess & Rashes (1992) have found that scores on the Fear Survey Schedule were positively correlated with the frequency of endorsement of avoidance coping strategies and were negatively correlated with at least one problem-focused strategy, i.e. threat devaluation. They found similar effects for both panic disorder and simple phobic patients compared to normal controls. Similarly, Genest, Bowen, Dudley & Keegan (1990) reported significant positive correlations between state and trait anxiety levels and escape–avoidance strategies and distracting cognitions. They reported significant negative correlations between anxiety and more problem-focused strategies (e.g. facing the situation).

To understand these differences more fully, they must be interpreted in the context of the normal development of such skills. It may be that these differences represent a developmental delay, i.e. that children who worry excessively are similar to younger children in attempting to cope with worrisome thoughts. Alternatively, these differences may represent a developmental deviation, i.e. the coping strategies of children who worry excessively may be different from those of all normal children regardless of age. Unfortunately, little is currently known about the normal development of children's attempts to cope with worrisome thoughts. We are currently conducting a study of normal children aged 7–14 years in order to better understand the ways they attempt to regulate the anxiety associated with worrisome thought intrusions.

If a child's tendency to experience uncontrollable worry is related to maladaptive coping strategies, then an examination of the origins and growth of such responses may provide insights into the etiology and maintenance of worry. In general, young children rely heavily upon others to regulate their emotional states, particularly through the responses modeled and taught by their parents (Vasey, 1993). Ideally, parents and other adults would enable children to learn effective skills for managing anxiety and other emotions by providing a cognitive scaffold appropriate for the child's existing skills and the demands of the situation (Thompson, 1990). However, it is also likely that parents inadvertently teach many things about anxiety-management strategies through their own behavior. Since such skills are thought to have their basis in the regulating efforts of parents, it is possible that the parents of anxious children may have failed to teach their children effective skills.

Part of our research program has focused on parents' knowledge of effective strategies that children can use to manage worry. Preliminary results suggest that parents of children who worry excessively differ from parents of normal controls in the type of strategies they think that children should use to help themselves stop worrying (Vasey, Hilliker, Williams & Daleiden, 1993). Avoidance and distraction strategies appear to make up a larger proportion of the responses of parents of chronic worriers.

We have also examined the possibility that parents of worriers emphasize different strategies when they attempt to help their own children cope with worry. For example, there may be differences between parents of worriers and non-worriers in their preference for helping their children distract themselves from their worries. From the perspective of Foa & Kozak's (1986) theory of emotional processing, an effective way for parents to help their children overcome their worries would be to help them focus on the worry and help them correct any misconceptions that may be contributing to it. From this perspective, it is possible that parents of anxious children teach their children to rely excessively on avoidance and distraction responses that then contribute to the maintenance of their fears.

Our preliminary results do not support this hypothesis. In general, parents of worriers and parents of controls appear to emphasize attempts to help their children actively focus on the worrisome possibility and assist the child in problem-solving or cognitive restructuring. Thus, it does not appear that anxious children choose distraction and avoidance strategies because their parents encourage them to do so. However, there are many other ways that parents might influence their children's selection of worry management strategies. For example, in order to provide appropriate scaffolding, they must be able to recognize when their child needs assistance and then to intervene before the child's arousal becomes too great. Since parents of worriers appear to have different beliefs than parents of normal controls about the extent to which children should use distraction and avoidance in coping with their worries, they may be less likely to intervene if their child seems to be distracting him/herself effectively. Future research should examine more closely parents' beliefs about when children need assistance and how well they are able to recognize such instances when they occur.

Parents must also provide an appropriate level of support for the child's level of development. Unfortunately, we currently know little about developmental changes in patterns of support given by parents of normal children. Until such normal patterns of parenting are understood, we can say little about whether or not the practices of parents of child worriers are developmentally appropriate. However, one interesting hypothesis which warrants research attention is the possibility that parents of anxious children hold developmentally inappropriate expectations for their children.

At least some mechanisms of self-regulation relevant to worry may occur outside of awareness, early in the information processing sequence. Considerable research has shown that anxious adults show an attentional bias in favor of threat-related stimuli (Mathews, 1990). In one well-researched paradigm, anxious subjects have been shown to react more rapidly to probes on a computer screen when they have been preceded by threat-related rather than neutral words (e.g. MacLeod, Mathews & Tata, 1986). In contrast, normal controls have sometimes been shown to direct their attention away from such stimuli. Thus, anxious adults appear to be deficient in their ability to inhibit the processing of threat stimuli. According to Thompson (1990) and Dodge (1989), use of selective attention is an important affective self-regulatory skill.

Because such attentional biases have the potential to play an important role in the maintenance of anxiety, research in our laboratory has begun to focus upon the question of their occurrence in childhood anxiety. We have recently completed two studies using a developmentally appropriate modification of the task used by MacLeod et al. (1986). The first study compared anxiety-disordered children and normal controls (Vasey & El-Hag, 1993) while the second compared high versus low test-anxious children (Vasey et al., 1993). Results from both studies indicate that anxious children show an attentional bias toward threat cues. It also appears that low anxious children exhibit the same tendency to direct attention away from threat cues as their adult counterparts (Vasey et al., 1993). Thus, our results show that high and low anxious children in effect perceive the world in very different ways. However, many questions remain unanswered. For example, does such an attentional bias serve as a risk factor for later anxiety disorders?

Children who worry excessively should also show other information-processing biases. For example, adult research suggests that individuals who worry excessively tend to select more threatening interpretations of ambiguous cues than normal controls (Mathews, 1990). Since many of the cues that potentially signal threat in children's everyday lives are likely to be ambiguous, it is important that these research efforts be extended to include child populations. Bell-Dolan (1992) has used the social information-processing task of Dodge (1985) to examine the possibility that anxious children are biased in their interpretation of social cues. She found no differences between anxious and normal fourth and fifth graders in identifying hostile intentions in hostile and ambiguous situations. However, anxious children were more likely to misinterpret non-hostile situations as hostile. She also found differences in children's proposed responses to hostile situations. Anxious children proposed more appeals to authority and less adaptive strategies than expected by chance. Nonanxious children proposed more adaptive and aggressive strategies, and fewer appeals to authority. This is the first demonstration in children of the type of biased processing of environmental cues shown in anxious adults (Mathews, 1990). Specific links between such biased social information-processing and worry should be examined in future research.

ASSESSMENT OF WORRY IN CHILDHOOD

The assessment of a cognitive phenomenon like worry presents many problems even in adulthood. However, because young children may lack adequate verbal and metacognitive skills to report reliably or validly on their thoughts, these problems are especially serious when attempting to assess worry in childhood. In particular, there are many potential complications brought by the wide developmental differences in children's understanding of relevant concepts and ability to provide reliable and valid self-reports. For a more thorough discussion of such issues, the reader is referred to an excellent chapter by Beidel & Stanley (1993).

One problem emphasized by Beidel & Stanley (1993) concerns the likelihood that young children may not adequately understand terms like worry or nervousness or the distinctions between them. Therefore, their responses to such questions may not be meaningful. In our research program we have examined the ability of 5–6-, 8–9-, and 11–12-year-olds to understand the concepts of worry, fear and nervousness (Vasey, 1991). Our results support the concern of Beidel & Stanley. While 11–12-year-olds appeared to understand and differentiate all three terms adequately, the younger children did not. While 8–9-year-olds did differentiate fear from the other two concepts, they had difficulty distinguishing between worry and nervousness. Unlike the 11–12-year-olds, they did not understand that worry refers to thoughts of future threat possibilities while nervousness is more associated with physiological symptoms of anxiety. Thus, we must question whether the responses of 8–9-year-old children to questions about worry versus nervousness are meaningfully different. This is potentially significant since some measures of test anxiety, such as the *School Anxiety Questionnaire* (SAQ; Morris et al., 1976), yield separate worry and emotionality scores which rely on the assumption that children differentiate these two terms. Finally, our sample of 5–6-year-olds failed to distinguish the three concepts and viewed worry and nervousness as synonymous with fear. Future research must attend to such limitations in children's understanding.

Below, we provide a review of a variety of measures and techniques that may be useful for studying worry in childhood. For a more thorough review of cognitive assessment techniques for childhood anxiety the reader is referred to Kendall & Chansky (1991). The first group of measures is focused on the content and frequency of children's worries. We have omitted some widely used measures of fear content such as the Fear Survey Schedule for Children—Revised (Ollendick, 1983) since they do not specifically assess worry. The *Worry Inventory for Children* (WIC; Wasserstein, La Greca & Silverman, 1992) is a structured interview targeted at children's worries in 13 areas such as school, friends, personal harm, and performance. The interviewer asks the child to list worries in each content area and then obtains ratings with respect to the severity, frequency, and perceived reality of each worry. The one week test–retest reliability of category rankings was .87, and the test–retest correlations for the total number of worries and total number of categories was .74 and .78, respectively. Test–retest correlations range from .66 to .87 depending on children's age. The Worries Inventory (WI; Orton, 1982) is a self-report questionnaire that asks children to rate the frequency of 62 worries on a 3 point scale. The eight categories of worry represented by the items are school, family, personal health and well-being, social adequacy, imaginary or unreasonable, personal adequacy, economic, and ornamental. Unfortunately, no psychometric data have been provided for the WI. The Worry List Questionnaire (WLQ; Simon & Ward, 1974) contains 100 items representing eight categories of worry: family, school, economic, social, personal adequacy, personal health, animal, and imagination. The WLQ requires children to endorse items that worry them often as well as items that worry them deeply or upset them badly. In 12–14-year-olds, correlations between teacher rankings of students and student responses ranged from .85 to .90.

A second group of measures have focused on providing more general indices of a child's tendency to worry. The most widely used of these is the Revised Children's Manifest Anxiety Scale (RCMAS; Reynolds & Richmond, 1978). The RCMAS is a 37 item self-report instrument which has been standardized on a sample of 4972 children between the ages of 6 and 19 years (Reynolds & Richmond, 1985). Internal consistency estimates for the 12 age groups of the standardization sample ranged from alpha coefficients of .79 to .85. The 9 month test–retest stability coefficients were .68 for the Total Anxiety score and .58 for the Lie Scale. Factor analysis of the RCMAS has yielded three factors, of which the worry/oversensitivity scale is relevant to our discussion.

Another large group of measures has focused on school-related anxiety. Most of these provide measures of the dimensions of worry and emotionality which are commonly found in test anxiety. For example, the *Math Anxiety Questionnaire* (MAQ; Wigfield & Meece, 1988) is an 11 item questionnaire that requires subjects to rate each item on a 7 point scale. Factor anaysis of the MAQ in a sample of 5th–12th grade students produced two negatively correlated factors ($r = -.40$). The first factor is described as negative affective reactions (emotionality) and the second as worry. These scales appear to have adequate internal consistency (.82 and .76 respectively). The School Anxiety Questionnaire (SAQ) developed by Morris et al. (1976) divides items with respect to the dimensions of worry and emotionality. The SAQ is a 105 item questionnaire that asks subjects to rate each item on a 5 point scale of frequency. Every item on the SAW contains either the word "worry", "nervous", or "bother". The "worry" items are assumed to assess cognitive concern and therefore the worry component, whereas the "nervous" items are assumed to assess the physiological arousal, i.e. emotionality, component of anxiety. No psychometric data are provided.

Many other measures have focused specifically on thoughts associated with test or performance anxiety. Many of the categories assessed overlap with worry, especially: (1) catastrophizing or magnification of threat; (2) selective attention to negative features of an event; (3) overgeneralization of negative outcomes; (4) inappropriate self-blame for negative events. Examples of such techniques include the *Cognitive Behavior Questionnaire* (CBQ; Houston, Fox & Forbes, 1984) which is a 7 item self-report questionnaire that asks subject to rate on a 5 point scale the extent to which each item reflected what they were thinking and feeling during a specified time period. These items reflect seven categories of thoughts: analytic attitude, derogation of other, justification of positive attitude, performance denigration, performance reassurance, preoccupation, and situation-irrelevant thoughts. The *Children's Cognitive Assessment Questionnaire* (CCAQ; Zatz & Chassin, 1985) is a 50 item yes–no self-report measure of categories of thoughts experienced while taking a test. These categories include positive and negative evaluations, on- and off-task thoughts, and coping self-statements. Psychometric data for samples of fifth and sixth graders appear adequate. Internal consistencies for these scales range from .68 to .88. Six week test–retest correlations for the scales range from .63 to .71.

There are a variety of other techniques which show considerable promise. For example the Cognitive Questionnaire (CQ) of Brown et al. (1986) has been used to assess the occurrence of coping and catastrophizing cognitions in a sample of 8–18-year-olds. The CQ is a self-report questionnaire that elicits cognitions in three stressful situations (e.g. presenting a class report). After reading a brief description asking the subject to imagine being in each situation, subjects are asked to write down all of the things that are going through their mind, what they are saying to themselves, and what they are thinking. Interrater agreement ranged from 77% to 100% among the three situations for the coping and catastrophizing categories. Examples of catastrophizing included focusing on or exaggerating negative aspects of the situation, making denigrating self-statements, or thinking of escape or avoidance. Catastrophizing thoughts were considerably more prevalent than coping thoughts in all age groups and most frequently took the form of focusing on negative affect, anxious anticipation, or rumination. This type of thought sampling warrants further attention in studies of worry in childhood.

Behavioral observations may also be used to study worry in childhood. Morris et al. (1977) presented kindergarten children with a test situation. Before the task was begun, subjects were asked if the task looked easy or hard and if they thought they could do it successfully. After a 5 minute trial of the task, subjects were asked what they were thinking, how well they did, if they thought the task was easy or hard, and if they were nervous. Verbal and behavioral expressions of worry were coded. Verbal expressions indicative of worry were defined as negative expectancy, negative self- and task-evaluations, and off-task responses. Behavioral indications of worry were frowning, shaking of the head, referencing the experimenter for feedback, and looking at task-irrelevant stimuli. These authors also showed that such indications of worry can be manipulated independently of indications of physiological arousal. This suggests that despite the inability of young children to understand concepts such as worry and nervousness, they may be assessed in other ways.

The Experience Sampling Method (ESM) has been developed by Larson & Lampman-Petraitis (1989) in order to study emotional experiences among preadolescents. It requires subjects to carry electronic pagers and a booklet of self-report forms for one week. Each day is divided into seven 2-hour time blocks from 7:30 a.m. to 9:30 p.m. One signal is sent to the pagers at a random time within each block. Subjects are instructed to complete one self-report form immediately upon receiving each signal. While this technique has not been used to study worry directly, the method is amenable to use with any self-report assessment device. In a sample of fifth to ninth grade children, Larson et al. report subject compliance to 84% of the signals that were sent. Such an approach may provide considerable insight into the role of worry in children's daily experience.

TREATMENT OF WORRY IN CHILDHOOD

To date, the best researched treatment program for children who worry excessively is that of Kendall and his colleagues at Temple University. Initially, Kane & Kendall (1989) reported positive outcome for four children diagnosed with overanxious disorder (OAD) treated with a comprehensive package of cognitive–behavioral tecniques. Recently, Kendall (in press) has completed a randomized clinical trial of the effectiveness of this treatment package with a substantial sample of children who were predominantly diagnosed with OAD. Using multiple measures of outcome, this study demonstrates that this treatment package is significantly more effective than no treatment (wait-list control). This program, described by Kendall, Kane, Howard & Siqueland (1990), is of particular interest because worry is one of its main targets. The belief that anxious children tend to be ill-equipped to cope effectively with their anxiety and cope instead in maladaptive ways is a fundamental premise of the program. Specifically, Kendall et al. (1990) teach children to recognize when they are worrying and to combat such thoughts with more realistic and adaptive self-talk, including problem-solving and cognitive restructuring, and actions such as relaxation or direct attempts to change the situation. These goals are consistent with our demonstration of maladaptive patterns of coping among anxiety-disordered children.

We have made use of Kendall's program in treating a number of OAD cases. John, an unusually bright 9-year-old, reported many bouts of worry and was capable of clearly verbalizing his worries. Like many children who present with OAD, John's parents reported that he would ask many "what if?" questions prior to even mildly stressful events and exaggerate his worries out of proportion to the actual danger. During treatment, John learned to recognize when he was worrying and began to substitute adaptive alternative responses. For example, one of his worries concerned the possibility that a cricket would bite him if he played in his basement. He was assigned the homework task of learning more about crickets in order to test whether he was exaggerating the danger of being bitten. He returned the next week and excitedly reported that "crickets don't even have the right kind of mouth parts to bite people!" This discovery allowed him to counter his worrisome thoughts while he played in his basement.

Eisen & Silverman (in press) have suggested that treatments for OAD will be most effective if they are matched to the child's predominant type of anxiety response. Specifically, by treating four OAD children, they evaluated the effectiveness of an exposure treatment combined either with relaxation training, cognitive therapy, or the combination of the two. They concluded that all treatment combinations were effective, but the greatest improvement was shown when treatment matched response style. Thus, for children who can clearly verbalize worries, cognitive therapy in combination with exposure appears more effective. In contrast, for children whose anxiety is expressed somatically (e.g. excessive muscle tension or stomach aches), the combination of exposure and relaxation is more effective. It is important to note that this study examined only four children and results are merely suggestive. However, Eisen (1992) has recently reported a replication of this study in which he obtained the same effects.

SUMMARY AND CONCLUSIONS

Research on worry in children is in its infancy. We have offered a heuristic model of childhood worry in the hope that it will stimulate others to offer alternatives and provide an enriched environment for future research. Clearly cognitive, social, and emotional development have important implications for worry in childhood that must be explored further. It is especially important for future research to expand our understanding of developmental changes in the process of worry. Increased understanding of the normal development of worry and its role in normal childhood anxiety is also important. Only in such a context can we fully understand pathological forms of childhood worry. Further research like our own on the roles of emotional regulation strategies and biases or errors in social information-processing (e.g. Bell-Dolan, 1992) appears particularly important as it offers the hope of improved treatment methods as we begin to understand the role of worry in childhood anxiety disorders.

REFERENCES

American Psychiatric Association (1987). *Diagnostic and Statistical Manual of Mental Disorders*, 3rd edn—rev. Washington, DC: American Psychiatric Association.

Bauer, D.H. (1976). An exploratory study of developmental changes in children's fears. *Journal of Child Psychology and Psychiatry*, **17**, 69–74.

Beck, A.T. & Emery, G. (1985). *Anxiety Disorders and Phobias: A Cognitive Perspective*. New York: Basic Books.

Beidel, D.C. & Stanley, M.A. (1993). Developmental issues in measurement of anxiety. In C.G. Last (Ed.), *Anxiety Across the Lifespan: A Developmental Perspective*. New York: Springer.

Bell-Dolan, D.J. (1992, April). Social cue interpretation in anxious children. Presentation at the thirteenth annual meeting of the Anxiety Disorders Association of America, Houston.

Bell-Dolan, D.J., Last, C.G. & Strauss, C.C. (1990). Symptoms of anxiety disorders in normal children. *Journal of the American Academy of Child and Adolescent Psychiatry*, **29**, 759–765.

Borkovec, T.D. & Hu, S. (1990). The effect of worry on cardiovascular responses to phobic imagery. *Behaviour Research and Therapy*, **28**, 69–73.

Borkovec, T.D. & Inz, J. (1990). The nature of worry in generalized anxiety disorder: A predominance of thought activity. *Behaviour Research and Therapy*, **28**, 153–158.

Borkovec, T.D., Metzger, R. & Pruzinsky, T. (1986). Anxiety, worry, and the self. In L. Hartman & K.R. Blankstein (Eds.), *Perceptions of Self in Emotional Disorders and Psychopathology*, pp. 219–260. New York: Plenum Press.

Borkovec, T.D., Robinson, E., Pruzinsky, T. & DePree, J.A. (1983). Preliminary exploration of worry: Some characteristics and processes. *Behaviour Research and Therapy*, **21**, 9–16.

Borkovec, T.D., Shadick, R. & Hopkins, M. (1991). The nature of normal worry and pathological worry. In R.M. Rapee & D.H. Barlow (Eds.), *Chronic Anxiety: Generalized Anxiety Disorder and Mixed Anxiety–Depression*, pp. 29–51. New York: Guilford Press.

Brown, J.M., O'Keefe, J., Sanders, S.H. & Baker, B. (1986). Developmental changes in children's cognition to stressful and painful situations. *Journal of Pediatric Psychology*, **11**(3), 343–357.

Campbell, S.B. (1986). Developmental issues in childhood anxiety. In R. Gittelman (Ed.), *Anxiety Disorders of Childhood*, pp. 24–57. New York: Guilford Press.

Cicchetti, D. (1984). The emergence of developmental psychopathology. *Child Development*, **55**, 1–7.

Damon, W. & Hart, D. (1990). *Self-understanding in Childhood and Adolescence*. Cambridge: Cambridge University Press.

Davey, G.C.L., Burgess, I. & Rashes, R. (1992). Coping strategies and phobias: The relationship between fears, phobias, and methods of coping with stressors. Unpublished manuscript, the City University, London.

Dodge, K.A. (1985). Attributional bias in aggressive children. In P.C. Kendall (Ed.), *Advances in Cognitive–Behavioral Research and Therapy*, Vol. 4, pp. 73–110. New York: Academic Press.

Dodge, K.A. (1989). Coordinating responses to aversive stimuli: Introduction to a special section on the development of emotion regulation. *Developmental Psychology*, **25**, 339–342.

Eisen, A.R. (1992, November). Matched and mismatched cognitive-behavioral treatments for overanxious disorder. In A.M. Albano (Chair). *Recent Advances in Cognitive–Behavioral Treatments of Childhood Anxiety Disorders*. Symposium conducted at the twenty-sixth annual meeting of the Association for the Advancement of Behavior Therapy, Boston.

Eisen, A.R. & Silverman, W.K. (in press). Should I relax or change my thoughts? A preliminary examination of cognitive therapy, relaxation training and their combination with overanxious children. *Journal of Cognitive Psychotherapy: An International Quarterly*.

Flavell, J.H. (1977). *Cognitive Development*. Englewood Cliffs, New Jersey: Prentice Hall.

Foa, E.B. & Kozak, M. (1986). Emotional processing of fear: Exposure to corrective information. *Psychological Bulletin*, 99, 20–35.

Francis, G. (1988). Assessing cognitions in anxious children. *Behavior Modification*, 12, 267–280.

Gallagher, J J (1990). Editorial: The public and professional perception of the emotional status of gifted children. *Journal for the Education of the Gifted*, 13, 202–211.

Garber, J.A. (1984). Classification of childhood psychopathology: A developmental perspective. *Child Development*, 55, 30–48.

Genest, M., Brown, R.C., Dudley, J. & Keegan, D. (1990). Assessment of strategies for coping with anxiety: Preliminary investigations. *Journal of Anxiety Disorders*, 4, 1–14.

Gittelman, R. (1986). *Anxiety Disorders of Childhood*. New York: Guilford.

Gjesme, T. (1983). Worry and emotionality components of test anxiety in relation to situational and personality determinants. *Psychological Reports*, 52, 267–280.

Graziano, A.M., DeGiovanni, I.S. & Garcia, K.A. (1979). Behavioral treatment of children's fears: A review. *Psychological Bulletin*, 86, 804–830.

Hoffner, C. & Cantor, J. (1991). Factors affecting children's enjoyment of a frightening film sequence. *Communication Monographs*, 58, 41–62.

Horobin, K. & Acredolo, C. (1989). The impact of probability judgements on reasoning about multiple possibilities. *Child Development*, 60, 183–200.

Houston, B.K., Fox, J.E. & Forbes, L. (1984). Trait anxiety and children's state anxiety, cognitive behaviors and performance under stress. *Cognitive Therapy and Research*, 8, 631–641.

Kane, M.T. & Kendall, P.C. (1989). Anxiety disorders in children: A multiple-baseline evaluation of a cognitive-behavioral treatment. *Behavior Therapy*, 20, 499–508.

Kaufman, K.L., Brown, R.T., Graves, K., Henderson, P. & Revolinski, M. (1993). What, me worry? A survey of adolescents' concerns. *Clinical Pediatrics*, 6, 8–14.

Kendall, P.C. (1985). Toward a cognitive-behavioral model of child psychopathology and a critique of related interventions. *Journal of Abnormal Child Psychology*, 13, 357–372.

Kendall, P.C. (in press). Treating anxiety disorders in youth: Results of a randomized clinical trial. *Journal of Consulting and Clinical Psychology*.

Kendall, P.C. & Chansky, T.E. (1991). Considering cognition in anxiety-disordered children. *Journal of Anxiety Disorders*, 5, 167–185.

Kendall, P.C. & Ingram, R. (1987). The future for the cognitive assessment of anxiety: Let's get specific. In L. Michaelson & L.M. Asher (Eds.), *Anxiety and Stress Disorders: Cognitive–behavioral Assessment and Treatment*, pp. 89–104. New York: Guilford Press.

Kendall, P.C., Kane, M., Howard, B. & Siqueland, L. (1990). *Cognitive–Behavioral Therapy for Anxious Children: Treatment Manual*. Temple University, Philadelphia, PA.

King, N.J., Hamilton, D.I. & Ollendick, T.H. (1988). *Children's Phobias: A Behavioral Perspective*. New York: Wiley.

Kosslyn, S.M. (1980). *Image in Mind*. Cambridge, MA: Harvard University Press.

Lang, P.J. (1985). The cognitive psychophysiology of emotion: fear and anxiety. In A.H. Tuma & J.D. Maser (Eds.), *Anxiety and the Anxiety Disorders*, pp. 131–170. Hillsdale, New Jersey: Erlbaum.

Lapouse, R. & Monk, M.A. (1959). Fears and worries in a representative sample of children. *American Journal of Orthopsychiatry*, **29**, 803–818.

Larson, R. & Lampman-Petraitis, C. (1989). Daily emotional states as reported by children and adolescents. *Child Development*, **60**, 1250–1260.

Littenberg, R., Tulkin, S. & Kagan, J. (1971). Cognitive components of separation anxiety. *Developmental Psychology*, **4**, 387–388.

MacLeod, A.K., Williams, J.M.G. & Bekerian, D.A. (1991). Worry is reasonable: The role of explanations in pessimism about future personal events. *Journal of Abnormal Psychology*, **100**, 478–486.

MacLeod, C., Mathews, A. & Tata, P. (1986). Attentional bias in emotional disorders. *Journal of Abnormal Psychology*, **95**, 15–20.

Magnusson, D. (1985). Situational factors in research in stress and anxiety: Sex and age differences. In C.D. Spielberger, J.G. Sarason & P.B. Defares (Eds.), *Stress and Anxiety*, Vol. 9, pp. 69–78. Washington, DC: Hemisphere.

Mathews, A. (1990). Why worry? The cognitive function of anxiety. *Behaviour Research and Therapy*, **28**, 455–468.

Miller, L.C., Barrett, C.L., Hampe, E. & Noble, H. (1972). Factor structure of childhood fears. *Journal of Consulting and Clinical Psychology*, **39**, 264–268.

Morris, L.W., Brown, N.R. & Halbert, B.L. (1977). Effects of symbolic modeling on the arousal of cognitive and affective components of anxiety in preschool children. In C.D. Spielberger & I.G. Sarason (Eds.), *Stress and Anxiety*, Vol. 4. New York: Wiley.

Morris, L.W., Finkelstein, C.S. & Fisher, W.R. (1976). Components of school anxiety: Developmental trends and sex differences. *Journal of Genetic Psychology*, **128**, 49–57.

Olah, A., Torestad, B. & Magnusson, D. (1989). Coping behaviors in relation to frequency and intensity of anxiety-provoking situations. *Perceptual and Motor Skills*, **69**, 935–943.

Ollendick, T.H. (1983). Reliability and validity of the Revised Fear Survey Schedule for Children (FSSC-R). *Behaviour Research and Therapy*, **21**, 685–692.

Orton, G.L. (1982). A comparative study of children's worries. *Journal of Psychology*, **110**, 153–162.

Parkhurst, J.T. & Asher, S.R. (1985). Goals and concerns: Implications for the study of children's social competence. In B.B. Lahey & A.E. Kazdin (Eds.), *Advances in Clinical Child Psychology*. Vol. 8, pp. 199–228. New York: Plenum Press.

Piaget, J. (1970). Piaget's theory. In P.H. Mussen (Ed.), *Carmichael's Manual of Child Psychology*, Vol. 1, pp. 703–732. New York: John Wiley.

Piaget, J. (1987). *Possibiliy and Necessity, Vol. 1. The Role of Possibility in Cognitive Development*. Minneapolis: University of Minnesota Press.

Reynolds, C.R. & Richmond, B.O. (1978). What I think and feel: A revised measure of children's manifest anxiety. *Journal of Abnormal Child Psychology*, **6**, 271–280.

Reynolds, C.R. & Richmond, B.O. (1985). *Manual for the Revised Children's Manifest Anxiety Scale*. Los Angeles: Western Psychological Services.

Romer, L. & Borkovec, T.D. (1993). Worry: unwanted cognitive activity that controls unwanted somatic experience. In D.M. Wegner & J.W. Pennebaker (Eds.), *Handbook of Mental Control*, pp. 220–238. Englewood Cliffs, NJ: Prentice Hall.

Sarason, S.B., Davidson, K.S., Lighthall, F.F., Waite, R.R. & Ruebush, B.K. (1960). *Anxiety in Elementary School Children*. New York: John Wiley & Sons.

Simon, A. & Ward, L.O. (1974). Variables influencing the sources, frequency, and intensity of worry in secondary school pupils. *British Journal of Social and Clinical Psychology*, **13**, 391–396.

Simon, A. & Ward, L.O. (1982). Sex-related patterns of worry in secondary school pupils. *British Journal of Clinical Psychology*, **21**, 63–64.

Tallis, F., Eysenck, M. & Mathews, A. (1992). A questionnaire for the measurement of nonpathological worry. *Personality and Individual Differences*, **13**, 161–168.

Thompson, R. (1990). Emotion and self-regulation. In R.A. Thompson (Ed.), *Nebraska Symposium on Motivation 1988: Vol. 36. Socioemotional development*, pp. 367–467. Lincoln, NE: University of Nebraska Press.

Vasey, M.W. (1993). Development and cognition in childhood anxiety: The example of worry. In T.H. Ollendick & J.R. Prinz (Eds.), *Advances in Clinical Child Psychology*, Vol. 15, pp. 1–39). New York: Plenum Press.

Vasey, M.W., Crnic, K.A. & Carter, W.G. (in press). Worry in childhood: A developmental perspective. *Cognitive Therapy and Research*.

Vasey, M.W., Daleiden, E. & Williams, L.L. (1992, November). Coping with worrisome thoughts: Strategies of anxiety-disordered and normal children. Poster presented at the twenty-sixth annual meeting of the Association for the Advancement of Behavior Therapy, Boston.

Vasey, M.W., Daleiden, E.L., Williams, L.L. & Brown, L.M. (1993, November). Attentional biases in childhood anxiety disorders. Poster presented at the twenty-seventh annual meeting of the Association for the Advancement of Behaviour Therapy, Atlanta.

Vasey, M.W. & El-Hag, N. (1993, November). Attentional bias in high versus low test-anxious children. Poster presented at the twenty-seventh annual meeting of the Association for the Advancement of Behaviour Therapy, Atlanta.

Vasey, M.W., Hilliker, D., Williams, L.L., & Daleiden, E.L. (1993, March). The regulation of worrisome thoughts in anxiety-disordered and normal children: Parental perspectives. Poster presented at the biennial meeting of the Society for Research in Child Development, New Orleans.

Wasserstein, S.B., La Greca, A.M. & Silverman, W.K. (1992, November). Developmental Assessment of Children's Worries. Paper presented at the twenty-sixth annual meeting of the Association for the Advancement of Behavior Therapy, Boston.

Wigfield, A. & Meece, J.L. (1988). Math anxiety in elementary and secondary school students. *Journal of Educational Psychology*, **80**, 210–216.

Zatz, S. & Chassin, L. (1985). Cognitions in test-anxious children under naturalistic test-taking conditions. *Journal of Consulting and Clinical Psychology*, **53**, 393–401.

CHAPTER 8 Treatment of worry in generalised anxiety disorder

*Gillian Butler**

Thinking about treatment of worry immediately raises a paradox. Therapists and their patients can talk about the problem with very little difficulty. They understand each other relatively easily, and both parties to the interaction can be sure that they have first hand experience of the phenomenon they are talking about (even if one of them doubts that this is true). But at the same time worry does not have a clear and accepted definition, and we still know little about exactly what it is or what it does. Current research on worry has been stimulated by interest in cognitive aspects of fear and anxiety, and has been most interesting and productive, but it is still at the stage when it fails the therapist at a number of crucial points.

First, patients use words that do not entirely fit with current academic thinking about worry. They say "I felt really worried", or "even though I know nothing terrible is going to happen, I still feel worried". Of course they also say "I worry about not being able to cope", or "So many worries were racing through my head that I couldn't sleep", but their language, and ours too, reflects a common assumption that worry is a feeling as well as a thought. This language also reflects the possibility that feeling worried is different from feeling anxious, fearful or frightened. The feeling of being worried, as well as the cognitive activity, may indeed be amongst the main subjective complaints of patients who suffer from generalised anxiety disorder (GAD).

Second, patients seem to be more convinced than many research psychologists that worry can be useful. Of course this may be their mistake. They may be making cognitive errors, and need only to be guided onto more logical and fruitful tracks. But this phenomenon too is well supported by

*Warneford Hospital, Oxford, UK

Worrying: Perspectives on Theory, Assessment and Treatment. Edited by G.C.L. Davey and F. Tallis.
© 1994 John Wiley & Sons Ltd.

our ordinary language: "I worried away at these ideas until they started to fall into place". Worrying away at something is different from thinking it through. The activity has a different shade of meaning, possibly coloured by the feelings that accompany it, that reflects a commendable and productive kind of persistence, quite unlike the counterproductive, more ruminative activity that can be so distressing in the middle of the night.

Third, patients use very economical forms of language. In very few words they can refer to a complex and confusing phenomenon. "That worries me" can mean that it makes me feel bad in a specific kind of way, that it sets off an intrusive train of cognitive activity that is hard to control and unproductive, and that this train of thoughts conceals predictions or underlying beliefs such as: "I shan't be able to cope", 'I'll do something wrong" or "others will see how anxious I am". It can thus reflect an individual's sense of personal vulnerability with its own idiosyncratic shades of meaning.

The main implication of these points is that it is helpful for therapists to be aware of the paradox: that we both know and do not know what we are talking about when talking about worry. It is important to bear our ignorance in mind while using the ordinary language in which therapy takes place so as to develop hypotheses about what a particular statement is telling us. Despite the illusion of communicating clearly with someone who is talking about their worry it is also easy to misunderstand them. They may be referring to cognitive processes, to affective states, to underlying beliefs or to combinations of these things. They may be talking about an activity that they believe is useful and about which they are fundamentally ambivalent, or about one that they perceive as wholly negative—a bad habit that interferes with ongoing activities, reveals their weaknesses and which they "should" be able to stop. In whichever way they are talking many patients with GAD seem to be aware of the self-maintaining aspect of worry. Before starting treatment, therefore, the potential cost of giving it up, or the disadvantages that doing so brings, may have to be acknowledged and discussed.

Thinking about treatment of worry also raises a dilemma. Current literature tells us little about which treatment methods are demonstrably effective, but many potentially useful ideas and strategies are available. Focusing exclusively on what we know would impoverish the discussion and, I think, be less useful to practising clinicians. Broadening the focus runs all the risks of speculation. In this chapter I have tried to solve this problem in two ways. First, I have started with a discussion of the nature of GAD, trying to elaborate the bones of the definition provided in DSM-III-R (American Psychiatric Association, 1987) so as to provide a sense of what it feels like to be a worrier of this kind, and second I have structured the discussion of treatment methods as if they can be targeted specifically at some of the different aspects of worry that have been highlighted in recent research. This makes logical sense, provided the therapist remembers that we know even less about mechanisms of change where worry is concerned than we do about the nature and functions of worry. The way in which a particular treatment strategy works, or the way in which it is used, may or may not accord with the researcher's theory or with the therapist's intention. The experimental literature provides us with many potentially useful ideas about worry but specific treatment methods that demonstrably succeed in targeting its different features have yet to be validated.

WORRY IN GAD

In DSM-III-R the main defining feature of GAD is "apprehensive expectation" or worry, about two or more life circumstances. Future revisions to the criteria are likely to suggest that the worry need not be unrealistic but should be excessive, and is likely to have been present more days than not during the past 6 months; that the worry is not fixed on one particular concern, is hard to control, and interferes with attention to the tasks in hand (Barlow & Di Nardo, 1991).

This cognitive definition of GAD, by focusing on worry as the main defining feature, has contributed greatly to the field and helped to stimulate relevant experimental and clinical research. However, as all definitions made for use in diagnosis, its purpose is rather to differentiate one form of anxiety from another than to provide a flavour of what it feels like to suffer from GAD. Various aspects of the definition need expanding if the therapist is to achieve a thorough understanding of these patients' problems. Three sources of additional information are drawn on here: clinical observations made when treating relatively large groups of patients suffering from GAD (Butler et al., 1987; Butler, Fennell, Robson & Gelder, 1991); recent research findings (for reviews see Mathews, 1990; Borkovec, Shadick & Hopkins, 1991; Edelmann, 1992; as well as this volume); and an illustrative case history. The case will subsequently be used as a basis for discussion of the application of some of the treatment methods described in the later part of this chapter.

Clinical Observations

Clinical observation reveals that the focus of worry shifts repeatedly, giving rise at times to concerns more typical of patients with other kinds

of anxiety disorder such as social phobia, agoraphobia or hypon-
chondriasis. Therapists can easily be misled. If they, for instance, start
treating agoraphobic aspects of the problem using graded exposure, the
problem may well "improve". The improvement, however, is likely to be
illusory if it coincides with a shift in the focus of worry. The shifting focus
contributes to making patients feel vulnerable and confused, as they are
unable to predict when or where they will be safe from their symptoms.
At the same time therapists can repeatedly be misled into using standard
methods of treatment for transitory aspects of the problem, greeting each
new focus of worry with another treatment technique. If the source of the
problem is the worry, rather than the content of a particular bout of
worry, this approach may confuse the therapist as well as the patient. The
speed of these shifts, however, appears to be immensely variable. Some
people can run through a whole gamut of worries at a single sitting.
Others appear to latch on to one at a time, and may be troubled by, for
instance, concerns about their functioning at work, or their health for a
relatively long period.

About two-thirds of the patients in the research trial described in Butler et
al., 1991, said that they had "always been worriers". Not surprisingly,
longstanding problems give rise to secondary problems as well, such as
social anxiety and depression. GAD tends in the end to "get people
down", to make them feel less good than others and more at risk of
negative evaluation by them. A third long-term consequence of GAD,
demoralisation, is perhaps the most common of all. I understand demoralisation to refer to a non-depressed kind of hopelessness which includes fatigue, withdrawal from activities which demand an effort but
which may have been a source of pleasure or reward, and loss of confidence or self-esteem. Demoralisation makes it hard for GAD sufferers to
believe in the possibility of change and easy for them to feel that their
lives are more burdensome than pleasurable.

Although consistent phobic avoidance is absent in GAD (by definition),
avoidance also plays an important part in the disorder. For example at
times when they are feeling more vulnerable patients may avoid anything
that might make their symptoms worse. Or they may avoid thinking their
worries through. Worry itself may be a way of avoiding distressing imagery or the affect associated with it (Borkovec et al., 1991). There are many
subtle types of avoidance open to people with complex problems such as
GAD (prevaricating, not talking about feelings, not accepting challenges,
keeping a low profile and so on). Avoidance of all kinds, subtle as well as
specific, will maintain anxiety if left untreated. So people with GAD are
not only worriers. They are often confused, sometimes depressed, frequently demoralised, and so on the lookout for ways of avoiding that

may make them, temporarily, feel better. As the whole constellation of problems is confusing (without help few people for example are able to distinguish primary from secondary aspects of the problem), they also worry about worrying (see Wells, this volume, Chapter 4) and about the consequences of worrying, whether real (being unable to sleep or to concentrate) or imagined (losing their minds or going mad).

Findings from Recent Research Studies

With the aid of recent research findings our understanding of what worry is, and what it does, is now growing fast. Only some of the main points available at the time of writing will be alluded to here. Worry as opposed to emotionality correlates negatively both with performance and with performance expectations (Deffenbacher, 1980). The process is predominantly verbal (cognitive or conceptual) rather than visual (Borkovec & Inz, 1990), and has been associated with a lower level of emotional arousal than imagery (Borkovec & Hu, 1990). Worry also disrupts attentional processes and decision making, and increases hypervigilance and self-focused attention (Wells, 1991, 1992). However, Borkovec et al. (1991) argue that its most salient feature is its uncontrollability (see also Craske, Rapee, Jackel & Barlow, 1989; Barlow, 1988). Worry can be distinguished from other types of cognitive activity also associated with anxiety such as intrusive thoughts (Gross & Eifert, 1990), and may be triggered by the tendency to direct attention (preattentively as well as consciously) towards environmental threat cues (Mathews & MacLeod, 1987). It is correlated with the tendency to overestimate the risk of unpleasant events occurring to the self (Butler, 1990), and worriers with GAD tend to interpret ambiguous information as threatening (Butler & Mathews, 1983; Russell & Davey, 1993). The strength of this tendency may even contribute to the prediction of response to psychological treatment (Butler, 1993).

Sanderson & Barlow (1990) report that the most frequent worries of GAD patients concern family issues, finances, work and personal illness. Russell & Davey (1993) have found that worry is more strongly related to "daily hassles" than to life events or world events, and Butler (1990) has found that more patients with GAD than control subjects (worriers and non-worriers) worry about the feared consequences of anxiety such as being unable to cope, losing control or breaking down.

Borkovec suggests that chronic worriers "worry in order to anticipate and avoid future catastrophes" (Borkovec et al., 1991, p. 43). On this hypothesis worry functions as a cognitive type of avoidance response which is maintained by reduced experience of distressing affect. Distressing thoughts or images, and other triggers of automatic arousal, are avoided by worrying, and consequently are incompletely processed. Consistent with this view, Butler, Wells & Dewick (1994) have found that, compared with imagery, worry after exposure to a distressing stimulus is associated with an immediate, short-term reduction in anxiety, but this is followed by a higher frequency of subsequent intrusions. These findings are consistent with the view that worry suppresses emotional activation, interferes with emotional processing and contributes to the maintenance of anxiety. If worry is not made a target of treatment for GAD change may be less likely. More specific implications of these findings for treatment will be discussed below.

An Example of GAD

Lesley readily admitted that she was a "born worrier". She had seen a school counsellor at the age of 15 when anxious about examinations, but had not previously received psychological treatment when she was referred for help at the age of 28. Her main complaint at assessment concerned severe headaches, with pain behind her eyes. She was worrying about the possibility that the headaches might never go, and that the pain would interfere with her performance at work. She held a temporary, and junior, post in a small publisher, and in her spare time helped to teach on the introductory copy-editing course that she herself had recently completed. In quick succession she spoke about the potential she believed she had and her fear that she would never be able to realise it. Her ability to do the job well was jeopardised by poor concentration, indecisiveness and tiredness following nights of disturbed sleep. She was frustrated and angry with herself, as well as anxious about how her work was being appraised. She spent many evenings preparing for her teaching commitments, and no longer had time to go to her exercise class or see her friends.

Lesley's partner Andrew worked for a local estate agent and she relied on him to listen whenever she was bothered about something. She commented that he did not help her in the right way and no longer seemed to take her worries seriously. They enjoyed the same kinds of music, visiting new places and cooking for their friends, when they had time to do it—and when Lesley's worries permitted. During the past year Lesley had had a series of chest infections and a recurrence of childhood allergies as well as the headaches that precipitated her referral. Her doctor remarked that his reassurances no longer seemed to be helpful to her, and mentioned that recently she had shown signs of becoming depressed.

ASSESSMENT OF WORRY IN GAD

Assessment starts with observation. The first time we met Lesley talked incessantly, with an apparent inability to focus on anything properly. Whatever the topic discussed she had fears or worries about it, and one thing led to another. Talking about work she ranged quickly over fears that she would lose her job, would have severe financial problems, would ("as usual") be criticised by her parents for not managing better, compared unfavourably with her sisters, and so on. Talking about her headaches provoked a train of thoughts about all the aches and pains she had recently suffered, until she strayed into worries about the demands she was placing on her relationship with Andrew by talking about them. Bringing her back again to her headaches produced a train of thoughts that led in a different direction, skirting round and dismissing the possibility that she had a serious illness, she mentioned how helpful her doctor was, and how difficult it would be for her to manage if she should have to move away from the area. Her distress was evident, and she had a semi-humorous, self-deprecating way of relating that was quite engaging. However, the process was also frustrating. Her inability to stick to the point made it hard to understand exactly what she was worrying about, to draw up a problem list or to find out much about her problem-solving skills and internal resources. The obvious hypothesis at this stage was that she was readily able to externalise an internal process, and that this process, while focusing specifically on a range of unwelcome possibilities, was also inherently unfocused. We need to know more about what is going on.

A number of questionnaires are now available to amplify these observations. Measuring both trait and state anxiety (e.g. using the STAI; Spielberger et al., 1983), and the trait of worry itself with the Penn State Worry Questionnaire (PSWQ; Meyer, Miller, Metzger & Borkovec, 1990), indicates to what degree observations such as these reflect an enduring characteristic as opposed to a transient state, and the level of associated anxiety. Depression can be measured using the Beck Depression Inventory (BDI; Beck et al., 1961) and interpretation of scores should be amplified, using information about the course of onset so as to check out whether associated depression is primary or secondary. This cannot be ascertained on the basis of BDI scores alone. The average BDI score of the 57 patients with GAD as their primary diagnosis in the Butler et al., 1991 study was 19.3 (range 1–45). Assessment of self-evaluation can also be helpful, e.g. using the Fear of Negative Evaluation scale (Watson & Friend, 1969) and meausres of self-esteem such as Rosenberg (1965).

For work with specific groups of worriers a few other measures are available: the Test Anxiety Questionnaire (Liebert & Morris, 1967) and the Student Worry Questionnaire (Davey, Hampton, Farrell & Davidson, 1992) are useful with student populations, and the Worry Domains Questionnaire (Tallis, Eysenck & Mathews, 1992; see Tallis et al, this volume, Chapter 12) for measurement of non-pathological worry. Specific measures are available for assessing worry in the elderly (Wisocki, Handen & Morse, 1986; see Wisocki, this volume, Chapter 10) and in children (Simon & Ward, 1982; see Vasey & Daleiden, this volume, Chapter 7). In practical terms assessment of the content of worry is less useful for clinical than for research purposes, given the shifting and spreading nature of the activity, though work is continuing on the development of an instrument of specific diagnostic value (Davey, 1993).

In clinical practice perhaps the most useful, ongoing, means of assessment is self-monitoring. Borkovec, in his research, has categorised worriers by the percentage of the day that they spend worrying and this measure was used in the outcome study reported by Barlow, Rapee & Brown (1992). However, Lesley reported that she was unable to make this estimate, and in routine clinical practice I have found this to be a common problem. Other aspects of worry that it may be informative to monitor include the number of "daily hassles" (see Russell & Davey, 1993), the degree of distress associated with worry, and the level of interference with daily life through ratings of concentration, decision making, sleep, relaxation, enjoyment and so on as relevant in each particular case.

Another aspect of assessment that the therapist needs to bear in mind concerns hypotheses about the way in which to conceptualise the case. For a conceptualisation to have useful implications for treatment it should include hypotheses about maintenance cycles: was Lesley avoiding thinking about possible sources of her headaches? Had she learned to reduce her anxiety predominantly by seeking reassurance? And about underlying themes: does Lesley believe she is at risk of losing control? And if so, what would she mean by that? Or does she believe that she needs other people to support her in order to be able to cope? It might also include ideas about the origin of the problem: had Lesley been frequently criticised by her parents for her inability to cope? One of the tasks of therapy will be to distinguish between the various hypotheses using a number of different sources of information, including homework assignments. Interpretation of the results of these will help to resolve uncertainties that cannot easily be resolved in other ways and will ensure that assessment remains one of the ongoing processes of treatment.

TREATMENT OF WORRY IN GAD

Most ideas about methods of treating worry, and about their effectiveness, come from work on the treatment of GAD rather than of worry. I only know of one study in which a specific strategy for dealing with worry has been evaluated: that of Borkovec, Wilkinson, Folensbee & Lerman, which was published 10 years ago, in 1983. So hopes that the specificity of the definition would lead to more specific treatments have not yet been realised. Perhaps this is partly because the more we learn about worry the more complex an activity it appears to be, and partly because there are already many strategies available which can be adapted for dealing with worry and combined in many different ways. Most of the treatments for GAD are package treatments, and the effectiveness and specificity of their separate elements for dealing with worry have not been disentangled. On the assumption that strategies are targeted at different aspects of worry, the discussion below is structured by focusing in turn on these different targets.

General aims shared by treatments for GAD are to increase the patients' sense of control and to reduce their sense of confusion. Control can presumably be enhanced by redressing the coping balance so that perceived threats no longer outweigh perceived coping resources. For worriers both sides of the equation usually need to be addressed. However, confusion can easily be increased rather than reduced if the package offered is too large, or presented without a coherent rationale. Given the shifting focus of worry, a strategy that only applies to a specific concern will only have limited use. The principle behind it will have wider application, so the same strategy explained so as to make explicit the underlying theory and related rationale can more easily be generalised. The challenge to the therapist is thus to help people understand general principles as well as to learn specific strategies so that they can apply them in differing situations.

Patients will often have reservations about the methods suggested which many are reluctant to discuss. To start with Lesley found it hard to focus on anything other than the content of specific concerns that were troubling her at that particular time. She explained that unless we were talking about a particular worry she felt increasingly out of control during the session, worrying that she would have to go away without having sorted it out. She had come to believe that she was incapable of learning ways of dealing with the process of worry that could be applied generally, because she was a "worrying type". In her case we had to adopt a "try and see" method, devoting part of the time to specific concerns and part to discussion of more general points, the purpose of which was to identify strategies that were helpful and to phrase them in terms general enough to apply to other concerns also. The process was intended both to increase control and to reduce confusion. Bearing these aims in mind appears to facilitate treatment for worry in GAD.

Targeting the Process

Borkovec et al.'s (1983) suggestions for their "stimulus control" treatment have obvious face validity. It is designed to interrupt the process as soon as possible after it has begun, and to replace the worry with other more productive activity. Patients first set aside a daily half hour worry period. They learn to monitor and identify episodes of worry, and then postpone the activity until the designated time. In order to make this easier they focus instead on "present moment experience". When it comes to the half hour worry period they are both told to worry and engage in problem-solving relevant to their particular concerns. After minimal training (a single group training session lasting one hour) student subjects were able significantly to reduce their worry using this method.

The intrusiveness of worry is higher in patients than in normal subjects, and it is therefore not quite so easy to control. Lesley started off by using a related method that involved working through a decision tree. This is intended to facilitate the decision not to worry (a somewhat mysterious process that some non-pathological worriers describe as if it were perfectly simple and straightforward). She asked herself a series of questions, the answer to each of which determined the next step. First she named the worry. She tried to put into words what she was worrying about. This is not always a simple process and some of the difficulties with it are discussed further below. Then she asked "Is there anything I can do about this?" If the answer was "Yes", the next questions helped her decide what she could do (for example collect some information or talk to someone) and when she could do it. If something could be done straight away, then she should do it immediately. If not she should plan when to do it, and then use distraction as a means of controlling further (useless) worry. Whenever she reached the decision that there was nothing to be done right away she should switch into distraction instead. The purpose of the previous steps is to make it easier to decide to let the worry drop—to decide that the activity is not useful now, and not likely to become any more useful if it is prolonged.

There are many ways of postponing the activity: writing the worries down to get them out of the head and onto the paper, saying something to yourself like "worrying only upsets you. It's not useful", or "this is not the time"; imaginal methods like putting the worries away in a worry box and closing the lid, or hanging them on a tree and allowing the wind to blow them away, and so on.

However, it is crucial to remember that distraction is certainly an ambiguous activity, and not without its pitfalls. If patients are able to focus on "present moment experience" all is well and good. Often they are not able to do this, or in doing so they unwittingly make the problem worse by focusing on their internal present moment experience (self-focused attention is especially likely in worriers) as opposed to external (presumably non-threatening) present moment experience. Even an external focus can be risky. People with high trait anxiety, which we know correlates with the tendency to worry, attend selectively to threat-relevant stimuli in their environments, and are often unaware that they do this. They also interpret ambiguous information as threatening. The aim of engaging the person in the kind of activity that will leave little attention over for worrying is therefore fraught with difficulty, and it is not surprising to find in clinical practice that the kinds of distraction that work are immensely variable. At first Lesley found she could use distraction when her present moment activity was sufficiently engaging: when preparing teaching material or talking to someone, but not when she was insufficiently engaged or tired: on the bus to work, or watching television in the evening. Once she understood the principle: in her terms, "to occupy my mind with something non-troublesome rather than just turning away from troubles", she became much better at using this method. It was hard for me, her therapist, to know what would next trigger off worry for Lesley, but relatively easy for her to know which were safe and which were unsafe tracks to direct her attention towards.

Her ability to use distraction increased, but then she complained that it was tiring, not to say exhausting, constantly to have to redirect her thoughts. She did not want to spend the rest of her life working hard at not thinking about things that seemed to her to be important. This reservation is common and understandable. It also fits with the observation that, while distraction is a useful short-term strategy, it can be counterproductive in the long-term if used as a kind of avoidance. The suggestion made by Borkovec et al. that worry should be postponed, rather than "prohibited", is therefore most interesting.

The question is, what do patients do, and what should they be encouraged to do, at the times when they focus on, rather than away from, their worries. Sometimes, of course the instruction to worry has a paradoxical effect. Trying to worry can inhibit or interfere with the activity. Trying to go to sleep, or to walk along a straight line, has a similar (but in these cases more rather than less worrying) effect. There may be advantages to be gained from making the automatic process intentional in the case of worry. More often though, patients with GAD report little difficulty in initiating the worry process, and it remains important to discuss ways of changing the activity itself.

The most obvious suggestion is to turn it into problem-solving. Worry may well be partially reinforced by occasionally reaching solutions, though more often the process gives rise to a spreading series of negative possibilities. If on rare occasions a useful solution to a problem is found by worrying the activity will be greatly strengthened (an instance of the partial reinforcement effect). Lesley was quite a good problem-solver, but she was unable to use the method to reduce her worry about some of the more nebulous concerns (her headaches, the implications of her behaviour for her relationship with Andrew). However, while the "perceived threat" side of the coping balance was not amenable to problem-solving the "perceived resources" side of the balance was. Lesley's use of distraction played an important part in her treatment, even though she was well aware that at times it shaded into avoidance. It showed her that she had the potential to learn how to control the worrying. At this stage she needed above all encouragement that if she could learn one method, then she could probably learn others also.

Targeting Maintaining Factors

This section focuses on dealing with three of the ways in which worry in GAD may be maintained: avoidance, the belief that worry is useful, and reassurance seeking.

The message about avoidance is by now a familiar and straightforward one: avoidance keeps a problem going, and avoidance can be reduced using graded exposure. The hypothesis suggested by Borkovec is that worry is a kind of cognitive avoidance. When worriers engage the conceptual, cognitive system they succeed in avoiding arousing greater degrees of distressing affect by, for example, provoking distressing images. The process may go completely unawares. It is more comfortable to worry about someone who is late arriving home than to think carefully about, or dwell on, images of what might have happened to them (presuming of course that the negative frame of mind has been engaged in the first place). Therapists should not be misled into supposing that because worry is the main defining feature of GAD it is therefore the focus of all distress. In practice it often seems to be the better of two evils. Patients may hang on to it "for fear of finding something worse", and repeated exposure to the "something worse", provided it can be identified, may therefore be a particularly useful method of treatment.

Discussing with Lesley the ways in which she was using distraction led with no prompting to the admission that it could be a kind of avoidance. During the second phase of treatment she therefore started to limit her use of distraction and to think about what she might be avoiding. Typically for a chronic worrier, her avoidance was cognitive and she found this stage of treatment extremely distressing—just as distressing as it would be for a phobic to approach a situation high up on the hierarchy. She disclosed by degrees fears that she was seriously ill, worries about not being able to cope with illness, and worries about being constitutionally unable to cope on her own in general. These worries were eventually tackled using standard cognitive methods which will be discussed further in the next section. However, with repeated prompting, and sensitive listening, she became gradually able to talk about a range of fears and to "take them out one by one and look at them", instead of hiding them away by worrying and then controlling the worry using distraction. This process itself could be likened to cognitive exposure, and often appears to be beneficial in its own right. One can only speculate about which processes are necessary for change to occur. Just a few of the possibilities include habituation; making accessible new information so that cognitive restructuring, or emotional processing, occurs "spontaneously" and the guided discovery encouraged by cognitive therapy; identifying, re-examining and testing out the validity or usefulness of negative cognitive activity, including images and worry as well as thoughts.

It is often difficult to progress beyond this stage of treatment without confronting the belief that worry is useful. This belief can take many forms. Worry can feel like problem solving, and as already mentioned, occasionally it does produce solutions to problems; it can be superstitious: "if I don't worry, bad things will be more likely to happen", or anticipatory: "if I worry I'll cope better when things go wrong", or protective: "if I keep on my toes I'll be able to avert a possible disaster", and probably serve other functions as well. Therapists can be faced with a dilemma at this point: should they think about the possible adaptive functions of worry (alarm, prompt and preparation according to Tallis, Eysenck & Mathews, 1992; Borkovec, this volume, Chapter 1) or about the dysfunctional nature of the activity for their patient with GAD? The difficulty is that, although hypotheses about the function of worry are plausible, we do not know how much worry is adaptive—or how much you have to worry in order for it to become maladaptive.

The appeal to ordinary language can be helpful at this point. Patients with GAD, especially those like Lesley who describe themselves as "born worriers", are well aware of its counterproductive and distressing aspects. Keeping the word "worry" for the problematic side of the activity, and finding out exactly what this means in each particular case, allows one to label its adaptive aspects with different words, and to find different ways of achieving its supposed advantages. Taking sensible precautions, learning how to judge risks, thinking or planning ahead, or rehearsing and imagining ways of coping can be offered as ways of achieving ends such as "alarm, prompt and preparation". The assumption here is that it will become less confusing if the supposed advantages of worry can be achieved in other ways and called by different names. An all out attack on worry can then be mounted to achieve some of the other aims of treatments such as greater control.

Reassurance seeking is the third maintaining factor to be discussed here. This is often considered to be more of a problem for patients suffering from hypochondriasis or obsessive–compulsive disorder than from GAD, but it is sufficiently common in GAD to warrant a mention here also. Whenever she had a new or particularly upsetting worry Lesley talked it over with her partner Andrew. If he was unable to help, she telephoned her sister, and when it became too much to handle she went to see her general practitioner. For a brief period after each "fix" of reassurance her mind was set at rest. However, as the GP had said in his referral letter, the efficacy of the reassurances appeared to be wearing off. This is a common pattern, and one that is easily repeated during treatment. Lesley admitted that she had mentioned a number of new worries in one of our early sessions, about a sudden skin rash and about the possibility that chronic worrying would permanently impair her ability to think straight, to test out my reaction. This would tell her whether or not they should be taken seriously. My failure to be alarmed was, unintentionally, reassuring.

Lesley found it extremely difficult, and very anxiety provoking, to break the habit of asking for reassurance. The most useful strategy we found for her involved identifying the question she wanted to ask of others, and answering it herself, or identifying what she wanted them to say (the answer she wanted to hear), and looking herself for the evidence for this message. The intention was to help her rely on herself rather than others, and the rationale for this apparent cruelty (her word for it) was discussed both with Andrew and with her doctor.

Targeting Cognitions

This is not the place for an introduction to cognitive methods of treatment. The assumption here will be that worry is a cognitive activity, and as such cognitive methods for dealing with it have *prima facie* validity. It is also assumed that the cognitive methods used to facilitate guided discovery such as developing a collaborative relationship, using a structured approach, being open and explicit about the model and one's own way of understanding the patient's problem, or the conceptualisation, are appropriate and helpful. Instead this section will focus selectively on some of the cognitive processes that are frequently observed in worriers with GAD.

First, their worry is future oriented. Although people say "I'm worried about what I might have said", or "I'm bothered about having lost my passport" I think that they are worrying about the future effects of past events. If I have said something offensive they *will* reject/dislike/criticise me. If I have lost my passport I *will have* to go through a lot of hassle to get another. If the worry did not refer to some "unfinished business" in this way I suggest that the matter would either be forgotten or be a cause for feelings associated with the past such as regret or sadness rather than the future such as worry.

If this is correct, then worry conceals hidden predictions: for example about the likelihood of unpleasant events, about one's own inability to cope with them or both. It is therefore useful to identify and to re-evaluate the predictions being made, which are often of a catastrophic nature. Lesley worried about getting through all the preparatory work for her teaching commitments. She made two specific, easily testable predictions: she would not get it all done in time, and she would not be able to occupy the class for the whole of the lesson. The first prediction was confirmed (she could not do all that she wished to in time), but revealed a more important one: that if she did not do sufficient preparation she would be unable to cope. The second one was disconfirmed: she had to think on her feet and managed successfully to occupy the whole lesson. Careful discussion of this event, and of her tendency to discount it as a chance occurrence, enabled her seriously to consider it as evidence that she could cope (or learn to cope) better than she had supposed, and thus provided information upon which she could start to build her confidence.

Unfortunately, cognitive work with worriers is often less straightforward than this. Predominantly worriers express their fears in vague terms or as questions: "what did they think of me?" "what if I get in a muddle?" "supposing something goes wrong . . ."; "something dreadful might happen—or have happened" and so on. Reflecting the question or uncertainty back can help patients think about the assumptions they might be making or their own supposed answers to these questions. Then conventional cognitive work can focus on a relevant issue. However, sometimes no clarification is immediately forthcoming. At this point it is always worth asking whether any images come to mind, if necessary asking the patient to repeat the question or the uncertainty. My hypothesis as a therapist is that these uncertain, questioning and worrying cognitions signal the type of cognitive avoidance achieved by worrying. There is something behind them that is too alarming to face. The "what if . . .?" approach allows worriers to remain in doubt and saves them from facing the potential alarm. Asking questions and expressing vaguely doom-laden uncertainties may themselves be cognitive strategies that illustrate the theory that worry enables people to avoid distressing imagery and high degrees of unpleasant affect. When Lesley thought more carefully about what would happen if her demands on Andrew really did undermine their relationship she imagined herself as a child, crying and helpless.

Often worries are hard to specify, avoidance is not the only reason for this. Sometimes the meanings or beliefs underlying the worries seem to be equally pertinent (and are themselves avoided). The meaning to Lesley of this image of herself seemed to suggest that she felt helpless. She believed she was at risk, or vulnerable, as she was "no good at managing by herself". The origin of this belief appeared to be, at least partly, a consequence of the message she had absorbed as a child, that she could never manage as well as her sisters. Cognitive and behavioural methods can be combined when working with beliefs and assumptions such as this. The assumption behind this way of working is that the meaning of an event interacts with the emotional response to that event, and that meanings may be represented by automatic thoughts, or by underlying beliefs, and reflected in the whole range of cognitive activity including images, attitudes, memories, intrusive thoughts and, of course, worry. This line of thinking is often productive in clinical practice, even though it ignores the possibility that feelings can themselves be a source of information (see e.g. Safran & Segal, 1992). Lesley insisted that *feeling* worried told her something important. She felt that it was information that she could not, indeed dare not, ignore.

Targeting Feelings

Worry is not the only mental activity that appears to be both cognitive and affective. We also talk about "feeling" curious, sceptical or interested and so on. The problem is well recognised: investigations into worry have proceeded by inducing a "worrisome state" and comparing the effects of this with induction of a "neutral mood state" (York, Borkovec, Vasey &

Stern, 1987). The issue is raised here because often when treating worriers, attempts to direct specific strategies at separate targets, for instance
the process, the maintaining factors or the various aspects of cognition,
are not wholly successful. The bad feelings may remain.

One way of targeting feelings, if they are a source of information, is by
targeting their meanings, using for instance the cognitive strategies already
referred to: "worry means I'm not as capable as others"; "if you're a
worrier you will never be able to enjoy yourself and relax"; However, there
are other ways in which people have tried to change feelings, directly or
indirectly. Three strategies that patients with GAD spontaneously mentioned as helpful (Butler et al., 1991; Butler and Booth, 1991) are relaxation,
taking exercise and keeping warm (sitting by the fire, having a hot drink or
taking a bath). Why such methods may be helpful to worriers we can only
speculate. They may have specific effects or less specific ones derived from
doing something to try to help, or looking after oneself. Another possibility
is that they may lower the level of (affective) arousal and reduce anxiety,
which may itself lower the probability of feeling worried.

Strategies to reduce the demoralisation that is so often a secondary characteristic of GAD may also, though indirectly, change feelings. The most
commonly used strategies are planning pleasurable and rewarding activities, reducing the tendency to withdraw that seems to result from the
fatigue associated with chronic worry (and poor sleep), taking up hob-
bies, keeping in touch with friends and building up a repertoire of relaxing, recreational activities. Lesley had stopped reading thrillers, and she
and Andrew no longer cooked together for their friends. Having been
persuaded to try these things once more she said that she felt better about
herself, but, perhaps more importantly, also more in control of her life
than previously, when she had felt at the mercy of an endless series of
worries.

Other potentially useful strategies, used by worriers in the general public
but not yet incorporated into standard clinical practice or evaluated in the
course of research, have been described by Gendlin in his book on *Focusing* (1989), and by Kabat-Zinn (1990) in his book on the "Mindfulness"
method of meditation. The present moment focus of these more con-
templative methods, which may help to integrate different levels of
meaning represented for example by thoughts and feelings, would directly counteract the future oriented concern of worriers. They also introduce methods for allowing concerns both to come to mind in their natural
way and for allowing them to flow on, so that they do not monopolise
attentional processes in a way that interferes with on-going activities and
seems to be so counterproductive for worriers.

CONCLUDING COMMENTS

One of the difficulties in thinking about treatment for worry in GAD is the enormous number of potentially useful strategies available. The difficulty for a therapist is to select between them. One way of doing this is to think carefully about which aspect of the problem is to be targeted first, and the more we know about worry the better able we shall be to target relevant processes, bearing in mind that two of the main aims are likely to involve increasing the sense of control and reducing the degree of confusion.

An overall guiding strategy given the present state of our knowledge might go through the following steps. If someone is able to specify what they are presently worried about, then use a specific strategy targeted at a specific aspect of the problem, for example attentional control, cognitive methods, the decision tree or problem-solving. As the focus of worry will shift, whichever method is used will need to be phrased and explained in general terms to increase its breadth of application. If someone is worried but they are unable to specify what about, then it may be more useful initially to use distraction, provided that this is backed up by further exploration, thinking especially about avoidance and asking about images. If someone is worried and finds it hard even to articulate what this is about, it could be helpful to identify themes, meanings and beliefs. If all of these steps have been tried and the person still feels worried then it could be helpful to learn more holistic or integretive methods, and to introduce strategies for managing feelings. Finally informal questioning of non-pathological worriers carried out in the course of pilot work for research into the processes involved in worry suggest that the three most common strategies these people use to control worry are distraction, problem-solving and "deciding not to worry". Perhaps if we found out more about how they do these things we would become better able to help our worried patients.

REFERENCES

American Psychiatric Association (1987). *Diagnostic and Statistical Manual of mental disorders*, 3rd edn—Rev. Washington, DC.

Barlow, D.H. (1988). *Anxiety and its Disorders: the Nature and Treatment of Anxiety and Panic*. New York: Guilford Press.

Barlow, D.H. & Di Nardo, P.A. (1991). The diagnosis of Generalized Anxiety Disorder: development, current status, and future directions. In R.M. Rapee & D.H. Barlow (Eds.), *Chronic Anxiety and Mixed Anxiety–Depression*. New York, Guilford Press.

Barlow, D.H., Rapee, R.M. & Brown, T.A. (1992). Behavioural treatment of generalized anxiety disorder. *Behavior Therapy*, **15**, 431–449.

Beck, A.T., Ward, C.H., Mendelson, M., Mock, J. & Erbaugh, J. (1961). An inventory for measuring depression. *Archives of General Psychiatry*, **4**, 561–571.

Borkovec, T.D. & Hu, S. (1990). The effect of worry on cardiovascular response to phobic imagery. *Behaviour Research and Therapy*, **28**, 69–73.

Borkovec, T.D. & Inz, J. (1990). The nature of worry in generalized anxiety disorder: a predominance of thought activity. *Behaviour Research and Therapy*, **28**, 153–158.

Borkovec, T.D., Shadick, R. & Hopkins, M. (1991). The nature of normal and pathological worry. In R. Rapee & D.H. Barlow (Eds.), *Chronic Anxiety and Mixed Anxiety–Depression*. New York: Guilford Press.

Borkovec, T.D., Wilkinson, L., Folensbee, R. & Lerman, C. (1983). Stimulus control applications to the treatment of worry. *Behaviour Research and Therapy*, **21**, 247–251.

Butler, G. (1990). Anxiety and subjective risk. Unpublished doctoral thesis. Open University, UK

Butler, G. (1993). Predicting outcome after treatment for GAD. *Behaviour Research and Therapy*, **31**, 211–213.

Butler, G., Fennell, M., Robson, P. & Gelder, M. (1991). A comparison of behavior therapy and cognitive behavior therapy in the treatment of generalised anxiety disorder. *Journal of Consulting and Clinical Psychology*, **59**, 67–175.

Butler, G. & Booth, R. (1991). Developing psychological treatments for generalized anxiety disorder. In R.M. Rapee & D.H. Barlow (Eds.), *Chronic Anxiety and Mixed Anxiety-Depression*. New York: Guilford Press.

Butler, G., Cullington, A., Hibbert, G., Klimes, I. & Gelder, M. (1987). Anxiety management for persistent generalised anxiety. *British Journal of Psychiatry*, **151**, 535–542.

Butler, G. & Mathews, A. (1983). Cognitive processes in anxiety. *Advances in Behaviour Research and Therapy*, **5**, 51–62.

Butler, G., Wells, A. & Dewick, H. (1994). Differential effects of worry and imagery after exposure to a stressful stimulus. *Behavioural Psychotherapy*, in press.

Craske, M.G., Rapee, R.M., Jackel, L. & Barlow, D.H. (1989). Qualitative dimensions of worry in DSM-III-R generalized anxiety disorder subjects and nonanxious controls. *Behaviour Research and Therapy*, **27**, 397–402.

Davey, G.C.L. (1993). A comparison of three worry questionnaires. *Behaviour Research and Therapy*, **31**, 51–56.

Davey, G.C.L., Hampton, J., Farrell, J. & Davidson, S. (1992). Some characteristics of worrying: evidence for worrying and anxiety as separate constructs. *Personality and Individual Differences*, **13**, 133–147.

Deffenbacher, J.L. (1980). Worry and emotionality. In I.G. Sarason (Ed.), *Test Anxiety: Theory Research and Applications*. Hillsdale, NJ: Erlbaum.

Edelmann, R. (1992). *Anxiety: Theory, Research and Intervention in Clinical and Health Psychology*. Chichester: Wiley.

Gendlin, E.T. (1981). *Focusing*. New York: Bantam.

Gross, P.R. & Eifert, G.H. (1990). Components of generalized anxiety: the role of intrusive thoughts vs worry. *Behaviour Research and Therapy*, **28**, 421–428.

Kabat-Zinn, J. (1990). *Full Catastrophe Living*. New York: Delta.

Liebert, R.M. & Morris, L.W. (1967). Cognitive and emotional components of test anxiety: a distinction and some initial data. *Psychological Reports*, **20**, 975–978.

Mathews, A.M. (1990). Why worry? The cognitive function of anxiety. *Behaviour Research and Therapy*, **28**, 455–468.

Mathews, A. & MacLeod, C. (1987). An information processing approach to anxiety. *Journal of Cognitive Psychotherapy*, **1**, 24–30.

Meyer, T.J., Miller, M.L., Metzger, R.L. & Borkovec, T.D. (1990). Development and validation of the Penn State Worry Questionnaire. *Behaviour Research and Therapy*, **28**, 487–495.

Rosenberg, M. (1965). *Society and the Adolescent Self Image*. Princeton: Princeton University Press.

Russell, M. & Davey, G.C.L. (1993). The relationship between life event measures and anxiety and its cognitive correlates. *Personality and Individual Differences*, **14**, 317–322.

Safran, J.D. & Segal, Z.V. (1990). *Interpersonal Process in Cognitive Therapy*. New York: Basic Books.

Sanderson, W.C. & Barlow, D.H. (1990). A description of patients diagnosed with DSM-III revised generalized anxiety disorder. *Journal of Nervous and Mental Disease*, **178**, 588–591.

Simon, A. & Ward, L.O. (1982). Sex-related patterns of worry in secondary school pupils. *British Journal of Clinical Psychology*, **21**, 63–64.

Spielberger, C.D., Gorsuch, R.L., Lushene, R., Vagg, P.R. & Jacobs, G.A. (1983). *Manual for the State-Trait Anxiety Inventory*. Palo Alto, Calif.: Consulting Psychologists Press.

Tallis, F., Eysenck, M. & Mathews, A. (1992). A questionnaire for the measurement of nonpathological worry. *Personality and Individual Differences*, **13**, 161–168.

Watson, J.P. & Friend, R. (1969). Measurement of social-evaluative anxiety. *Journal of Consulting and Clinical Psychology*, **33**, 448–457.

Wells, A. (1991). Effects of dispositional self-focus, appraisal and attention instructions on responses to a threatening stimulus. *Anxiety Research*, **3**, 291–301.

Wells, A. (1992). The mulitple factor structure of worry: development and validation of the anxious thoughts inventory. Paper presented at the World Congress of Cognitive Therapy, Toronto, June 1992.

Wisocki, P.A., Handen, B. & Morse, C.K. (1986). The worry scale as a measure of anxiety among homebound and community elderly. *Behaviour Therapist*, **5**, 91–95.

York, D., Borkovec, T.D., Vasey, M. & Stern, R. (1987). Effects of worry and somatic anxiety induction on thought intrusions, subjective emotion, and physiological activity. *Behaviour Research and Therapy*, **25**, 523–526.

CHAPTER 9

Worry and obsessions: the distinction between generalized anxiety disorder and obsessive–compulsive disorder

Timothy A. Brown,
Deborah J. Dowdall, Guylaine Côté
*and David H. Barlow**

An examination of the diagnostic criteria for the various anxiety disorders from DSM-III (American Psychiatric Association, 1980) to DSM-IV (American Psychiatric Association, in press) reveals that no diagnosis has undergone more change than has generalized anxiety disorder (GAD). In DSM-III, GAD was a residual category reflecting the presence of gener- alized, persistent anxiety as evidenced by symptoms from at least three of four categories: (1) motor tension; (2) autonomic hyperactivity; (2) ap- prehensive expectation; and (4) vigilance and scanning. Accordingly, due to its residual status and lack of key diagnostic feature, GAD could not be assigned as a diagnosis if clients met criteria for another mental disorder. However, the status and criteria for GAD were changed considerably in DSM-III-R (American Psychiatric Association, 1987). Specifically, the ap- prehensive expectation cluster contained in the DSM-III criteria was re- structured such that GAD had its own key symptom: excessive and/or unrealistic worry in two or more areas that are unrelated to another Axis I disorder. DSM-III-R criteria for GAD also specified that the worry occur more days than not for a period of 6 months or more (partly as a means of clarifying the boundary between GAD and transient reactions to life stress). The three remaining clusters from the DSM-III criteria were re- tained, with modification, to form the associated symptom criterion for DSM-III-R GAD; namely, that at least 6 of the 18 symptoms comprising

---

*University at Albany, State University of New York, USA

Worrying: Perspectives on Theory, Assessment and Treatment. Edited by G.C.L. Davey and F. Tallis.
© 1994 John Wiley & Sons Ltd.

these clusters are often present when anxious. The emphasis on cognitive processes (i.e. excessive and uncontrollable worry) as the defining feature of GAD is even more evident in the DSM-IV diagnostic criteria for GAD.

Despite these rather substantial revisions to the diagnostic criteria for GAD, studies examining the reliability of anxiety disorders have consistently noted that GAD is among the disorders with the lowest diagnostic agreement (e.g. Di Nardo et al., 1983, 1993; Mannuzza et al., 1989). Thus, although its residual status was considered to be a factor contributing to the lower reliability of DSM-III GAD (Barlow, 1988; Barlow et al., 1986a, 1986b), diagnostic agreement rates have not improved for DSM-III-R GAD (e.g. kappas = .57 for both DSM-III and DSM-III-R GAD; cf. Di Nardo et al., 1983, 1993). This is despite evidence indicating that the content and presence of GAD-related spheres of worry can be identified reliably (e.g., Barlow & Di Nardo, 1991; Borkovec, Shadick & Hopkins, 1991; Craske, Rapee, Jackel & Barlow, 1989; Sanderson & Barlow, 1990).

In attempting to reconcile findings pertaining to the "fair" diagnostic reliability of GAD, it is important to consider recent conceptualizations of the disorder which refer to GAD as the "basic" anxiety disorder because its defining features (i.e. worry or "anxious expectation") reflect fundamental processes of anxiety (Barlow, 1988, 1991; Rapee, 1991). As we have articulated elsewhere (e.g. Brown, in press; Brown, Barlow & Liebowitz, 1993), if these conceptual models of GAD are valid, then one would expect that the distinctiveness of GAD would be mitigated by the fact that its "key" diagnostic features are present to some extent in all of the emotional disorders.

The possibility that worry is a ubiquitous feature to all emotional disorders, rather than a distinguishing feature of GAD, is particularly evident when the diagnostic criteria for obsessive–compulsive disorder (OCD) are considered. Unlike GAD, the diagnostic definitions of OCD have changed very little since DSM-III. With the modifications in the diagnostic criteria for GAD introduced in DSM-III-R, GAD joined OCD in representing the only anxiety disorder in which an excessive cognitive process comprised a core criterion of the diagnosis (i.e. excessive worry in GAD; obsessions in OCD). Indeed, during the process of evaluating and revsing the extant diagnostic criteria of anxiety disorders for DSM-IV, researchers recognized the resemblance and possible overlap between worry and obsessions; namely, that both represent excessive and/or uncontrollable cognitive processes associated with negative affect. Subsequent reviews of the literature have concluded that little research exists on the relationship and distinction between worry and obsessions (cf. Turner, Beidel & Stanley, 1992). Turner et al. (1992) have cogently described this unresolved issue to be whether worry and obsessions represent "uniquely different cognitive phenomena or whether they simply refer to the same mental process, perhaps reflecting different degrees of intensity" (p. 257).

In this chapter, we will review the extant literature pertaining to research on the definitions and nature of worry and obsessions. Following this review, we will point to areas of convergence and distinctiveness of these two domains and present some of the literature bearing on this area, primarily that of clinical comparisons of patients with GAD and patients with OCD.

DIAGNOSTIC DISTINGUISHABILITY OF GAD AND OCD

Despite the paucity of data directly comparing the characteristics of worry and obsessions in clinical and nonclinical samples, a recently completed study from our clinic examined the extent to which GAD and OCD could be distinguished diagnostically (Brown, Moras, Zinbarg & Barlow, 1993). Subjects were 46 patients with a principal DSM-III-R diagnosis of GAD and 31 patients with a principal diagnosis of OCD. Diagnoses were established using the Anxiety Disorders Interview Schedule-Revised (ADIS-R; Di Nardo & Barlow, 1988). Roughly 53% of the patients were administered two independent ADIS-R interviews for the purpose of assessing interrater reliability.

Of the 24 cases where two interviews were administered to patients who ultimately received a consensus diagnosis of GAD, 8 cases (33%) were associated with diagnostic disagreements (i.e. discrepancies between the principal diagnoses assigned by the two independent interviewers). Four (24%) disagreements occurred for OCD, out of 17 double diagnostic interviews. Interestingly, of the 41 patients who received two ADIS-R interviews, in no case did one interviewer assign a principal diagnosis of GAD and the other, OCD. Thus, whereas diagnostic disagreements did occur for both diagnoses, these discrepancies did not appear to be due to difficulties in distinguishing between GAD and OCD. Or, taken in the context of the prior discussion regarding the reliability of GAD, the findings from this study suggest that the lower diagnostic agreement rates for GAD are not due to a boundary problem with OCD.

If there is considerable overlap between worry and obsessions, one might expect to observe a high rate of comorbidity between GAD and OCD. However, consistent with the findings of larger-scale comorbidity studies (cf. Brown & Barlow, 1992; Sanderson, Di Nardo, Rapee & Barlow, 1990),

Brown, Moras et al. (1993) found a low rate of co-occurrence of GAD and OCD. Indeed, only one patient with a principal diagnosis of GAD received an additional diagnosis of OCD; two patients with OCD were assigned with an additional diagnosis of GAD. Although these data could be interpreted as indirectly supporting the distinguishability of GAD and OCD and their associated processes, Brown, Moras et al. (1993) raised the possibility that the ADIS-R interviewers *did* observe features of both GAD and OCD in the patient, but subsumed the features of one of the diagnoses under the diagnosis that was assigned as principal (e.g. subsuming excessive worry under the OCD diagnosis in patient evidencing clear compulsions). Nevertheless, this interpretation was considered unlikely in light of the findings indicating no diagnostic disagreements involving GAD vs. OCD as well as the fact that the two diagnostic groups could be differentiated on the basis of self-report measures of the key features of GAD and OCD (these findings are discussed below).

The findings indicating that GAD and OCD may not be difficult for diagnosticians to distinguish are noteworthy in light of the presence of at least two other parameters that might obfuscate these diagnoses' boundaries. For instance, despite the prior assertion that obsessions and OCD may have the strongest association with depression relative to other anxiety disorders and anxiety disorder processes (e,.g. Rachman & Hodgson, 1980), recent evidence indicates that patients with GAD and patients with OCD do not differ appreciably in levels of depressive symptomatology as indicated by self-report inventories, clinician rating scales, and patterns of diagnostic comorbidity (e.g. Brown, Moras et al., 1993).

Secondly, whereas it would seem that OCD could be differentiated from GAD by the fact that roughly 75% of patients with OCD evidence clear compulsions (e.g. Barlow, 1988; Brown, Moras et al., 1993; Rachman & Hodgson, 1980), a recent study (Craske et al., 1989) indicated that over half (52.6%) of patients with GAD report engaging in some form of behavioral act in response to their worry (e.g. checking on the safety of a loved one). Thus, in addition to the question regarding the distinguishability of worry and obsessions, diagnosticians may also need to differentiate compulsions from "worry behavior" (although the latter has never comprised a diagnostic criterion in any DSM definition of GAD).

DEFINITIONS OF WORRY AND OBSESSIONS

Although the findings of Brown, Moras et al. (1993) suggest that diagnosticians are able to distinguish between GAD and OCD, they provide little information as to the decision rules used by clinicians to differentiate worry and obsessions. In this section, definitions of worry and obsessions will be considered as well as data pertaining to their distinguishability.

Definitions of Worry

Borkovec and his colleagues (e.g. Borkovec, Robinson, Pruzinsky & De-Pree, 1983) have defined worry as "a chain of thoughts and images, negatively affect laden and relatively uncontrollable. The process of worry represents an attempt to engage in mental problem-solving on an issue whose outcome is uncertain but contains the possibility of one or more negative outcomes" (p. 10). On the basis of recent findings from studies examining the nature of worry in clinical and nonclinical samples, Borkovec and colleagues (Borkovec, Shadick & Hopkins, 1991; Roemer & Borkovec, 1993) have further stated that worry is primarily a conceptual activity that is initiated as an attempt to control negative experiences including future negative events and immediate somatic arousal that is elicited in response to perceived threat. Accordingly, worry has been conceptualized as a negative reinforcer that serves to dampen physiological reactivity accompanying extensive processing of more disturbing images and thoughts (Borkovec & Hu, 1990; Roemer & Borkovec, 1993).

Paradoxically, although worry is conceptualized as a strategy attempting to control unwanted internal and external experiences, worry itself becomes an aversive experience due to its uncontrollable and self-perpetuating nature. Indeed, it is these parameters (i.e. perceived uncontrollability, pervasive nature) that have been found to best delineate clinical and normal worry (e.g. Borkovec et al., 1991; Craske et al., 1989; Roemer & Borkovec, 1993; Sanderson & Barlow, 1990; See Davey, Chapter 2, this volume). For example, comparisons of GAD and nonclinical samples have indicated that the two groups do not differ substantially in the content of worry (cf. Borkovec et al., 1991). Although no clear patterns have emerged across studies regarding the identification of predominating worry content areas, these investigations have produced converging evidence indicating that topics of worry reported by patients with GAD are usually connected to normal life circumstances (e.g. work, family, health, finances; cf. Borkovec et al., 1991; Eysenck, 1992; Tallis, Eysenck & Mathews, 1992). However, whereas normal and clinical worry does not seem to differ appreciably with regard to worry content, research has shown that considerable differentiation exists on indices reflecting the parameters of uncontrollability, excessiveness, and pervasiveness of the worry process (eg. percentage of the day worried, frequency of unprecipitated worry, number of worry topics, worry about minor matters, self-perceptions of uncontrollability, realism, and dismissibility of worry; cf. Borkovec, 1992; Borkovec et al., 1991; Craske et al., 1989; Di Nardo, 1991). In addition, chronic worry/anxiety has been demonstrated to be differentiated reliably by a variety of information-processing parameters including attentional bias of threat cues, heightened distractibility and visual scanning, and heightened estimations of the likelihood of negative events (see Eysenck, 1992, for a review).

To summarize, in addition to the aforementioned parameters, recent conceptualizations specify that pathological worry: (a) consists of a predominance of thought activity that is initiated in part to suppress imagery of feared consequences and its associated somatic activation (e.g. Borkovec & Inz, 1990); (b) is initially reinforcing as a method of reducing the perceived likelihood of a future negative event (e.g. Mathews, 1990); and (c) becomes an unwanted experience itself due to its uncontrollable and self-perpetuating nature (resulting from repeated attempts to suppress or distract from the worry process; cf. Roemer & Borkovec, 1993).

Definitions of Obsessions

Obsessions are defined in DSM-III-R as "persistent ideas, thoughts, impulses, or images that are experienced, at least initially, as intrusive and senseless . . ." and in which "the person attempts to ignore, suppress, or neutralize with some other thought or action" (p. 245, American Psychiatric Association, 1987; cf. Rachman & Hodgson, 1980). In addition to these parameters (i.e. repetitive and distressing nature, precipitate attempts to neutralize or resist), DSM-III-R requires that the individual recognize that the obsessions are internally generated (rather than being imposed from without as would be more characteristic of a delusional disorder).

A variety of systems have been proposed to classify the form (e.g. doubt, image, impulse) and content (e.g. contamination, religion, aggression) of obsessions. A review of the extant literature has indicated that, in general, the most common form and content of obsessions are obsessional doubting and contamination, respectively (cf. Turner et al., 1992). As is the case with studies on worry, a substantial literature indicates that some form of obsessional phenomenon is commonly found in nonclinical samples (e.g. Niler & Beck, 1989; Parkinson & Rachman, 1981; Rachman, 1978; Rachman & de Silva, 1978; Salkovskis, 1989a). Another similarity to the literature on worry is the finding that the feature of uncontrollability and its associated parameters (e.g. dismissibility, unacceptability) helps form the threshold between pathological and nonclinical obsessions (cf. Barlow,

1988). For example, Rachman & de Silva (1978) concluded that although similar in form and content, pathological obsessions can be differentiated from nonpathological obsessions by their greater duration, frequency, intensity, and extent with which they result in resistance. Salkovskis & Harrison (1984) replicated and extended these findings by noting that discomfort ratings were more strongly correlated to the degree of difficulty in dismissing the obsession than to the frequency or type of obsession.

Researchers have often asserted that difficulties in controlling or dismissing obsessions are related to the extent to which an individual finds the obsessions distressing or unacceptable (e.g. Clark & de Silva, 1985; Parkinson & Rachman, 1981; although see England & Dickerson, 1988). Relating to this point, Salkovskis (1985, 1989a) has proposed a cognitive model of obsessions. This model states that it is the occurrence of negative automatic thoughts, avoidant behavior, and neutralizing behavior that is responsible for the maintenance of obsessions and the distinction from normal intrusive thoughts. Thus, individual differences regarding the cognitive appraisal of normal intrusions is viewed as an important factor determining whether these events develop into a clinical disorder. Salkovskis (1989a, 1989b) has asserted that these negative automatic thoughts may take the form of exaggerated assumptions about whether actual harm can result from the intrusive thoughts themselves (e.g. thinking about an action may lead to committing that action) and about the extent of responsibility for preventing harm to oneself or others (e.g failing to prevent harm relating to the thought is the same as having caused the harm directly). Mood disturbance, a byproduct of obsessive symptomatology and mediated by negative automatic thoughts, is viewed as increasing the frequency and intensity of these negative attributions and discomfort, whereas anxiety is viewed as eliciting more frequent intrusions.

The distress elicited by obsessional phenomena frequently precipitates additional symptoms at the behavioral level. Neutralization refers to any behavioral response that is effortfully and intentionally performed in response to cognitive intrusions in order to prevent the processing of these intrusions by means of engaging in other incompatible tasks (Freeston, Ladouceur, Thibodeau & Gagnon, 1991; Salkovskis, 1989c). Neutralization behaviors in the form of compulsions are a predominant feature of OCD. They involve behavioral (overt) or cognitive (covert) strategies emitted in response to obsessional ideation that elicit anxiety in order to terminate (escape/avoid) contact with these stimuli as a means of decreasing distress. Salkovskis (1985, 1989a) has argued that neutralization occurs primarily in the context of negative automatic thoughts pertaining to strong feelings of responsibility or guilt. He maintained that the probability of performing compulsions is greater in patients with OCD who hold strong beliefs in their individual responsibility for the potential consequences of their unwanted thoughts.

Although they may result in short-term relief of negative affect, attempts to neutralize are conceptualized as maintaining the obsessional pattern in several ways (e.g. prevents disconfirmation of fears of harm, increases acceptance of worries about responsibility). Moreover, in light of recent claims that neutralization behaviors occur to disrupt processing of intrusions and that processing resources are insufficiently distributed to neutralization efforts, they are considered maladaptive responses to pathological intrusions (Edwards & Dickerson, 1987; Freeston, Ladouceur, Thibodeau & Gagnon, 1992). Misdistribution of these processing resources leads to stereotyped, ineffectual, and seemingly senseless compulsive behaviors and may perpetuate the obsessive–compulsive cycle (see Jakes, 1989a, 1989b, and Salkovskis, 1989a, for a critical discussion of the model).

WORRY AND OBSESSIONS: SIMILARITIES AND DIFFERENCES

The prior discussion on the nature of worry and obsessions offers a basis for delineating their sources of overlap discriminability. As has been noted previously (e.g. Brown, Moras et al., 1993; Turner et al., 1992), this discussion must be principally at the level of speculation as there is a paucity of empirical investigations directly comparing the nature of these cognitive phenomena.

In their earlier review of this literature, Turner et al. (1992) concluded that pathological worry and obsessions have the following similarities: (1) both are present in nonclinical and clinical populations; (2) they possess a similar form and content; (3) for both phenomena, heightened frequency and perceptions of uncontrollability help distinguish clinical and nonclinical samples; and (4) both are mediated by negative affect, which in turn is mediated by attentional biases and negative misattributions. Despite these similarities, Turner et al. (1992) concluded that worry and obsessions can be differentiated on a number of important dimensions. Areas of divergence include: (1) worry is more likely to be self-initiated and/or precipitated by common circumstances of daily living; (2) the content worry is apt to be related to common circumstances of daily living (e.g. finances, family, work) whereas the content of obsessions is likely to be more bizarre or outside the range of the individual's typical experience (e.g. religion, contamination, sex); (3) worry represents a predominance of thought activity whereas obsessions may take a variety of forms (e.g. images, impulses, thoughts); and (4) although both clinical worry and clinical obsessions may be perceived as uncontrollable, obsessions may be associated with a greater degree of resistance and perceptions of unacceptability.

Much of the research reviewed earlier in this chapter provides indirect support for the distinctions established by Turner et al. (1992) with regard to precipitants (cf. Craske et al., 1989; Rachman & da Silva, 1978), content (cf. Borkovec et al., 1991; Eysenck, 1992; Rachman & Hodgson, 1980), form (cf. Borkovec & Inz, 1990; Rachman & Hodgson, 1980; Roemer & Borkovec, 1993), and acceptabilty (cf. Rachman & Hodgson, 1980; Roemer & Borkovec, 1993). Moreover, whereas both worry and obsessions are often followed by behavioral acts that are initiated to reduce negative affect (cf. Brown, Moras et al., 1993; Craske et al., 1989; Rachman & Hodgson, 1980), it could be asserted that the behavioral sequelae to worry may be less time-consuming, repetitive, and bizarre/superstitious in nature (see Tallis, Davey & Capizzo, Chapter 3, this volume). However, as is the case with worry and obsessions, no research has been conducted to date that has directly compared the nature of worry behavior and compulsions.

Distinguishability of GAD and OCD on Measures of Worry and Obsessions

Although detailed, direct comparisons between worry and obsessions have not been conducted, we have recently examined the extent to which measures of worry and obsessions/compulsions differentiate patients with GAD from patients with OCD (e.g. Brown, Antony, & Barlow, 1992; Brown, Moras et al., 1993; Zinbarg & Barlow, 1992). In a study evaluating the psychometric properties of the Penn State Worry Questionnaire (PSWQ; Meyer, Miller, Metzger & Borkovec, 1990) in large clinical sample, patients with a principal diagnosis of GAD ($n = 50$) obtained significantly higher scores on this measure of worry than patients with other anxiety disorders, including a group of 24 patients with OCD (Brown et al., 1992; see Molina & Borkovec, Chapter 11, this volume).

In a more direct comparison of GAD and OCD (Brown, Moras et al., 1993), the PSWQ was again found to differentiate patients with GAD ($n = 46$) from patients with OCD ($n = 31$). In this study, the two groups were also compared using total and subscale scores from the Maudsley Obsessive Compulsive Inventory (MOCI; Hodgson & Rachman, 1977). Results indicated that patients with OCD obtained significantly higher scores on the MOCI Total scale as well as on the subscales of Checking, Washing, and Repetition; the difference on the Doubting subscale was not significant (cf. Steketee, Grayson, & Foa, 1987).

In addition, Brown, Moras et al. (1993) compared the two groups on their responses to ADIS-R screening items for GAD and OCD. Consistent with prior findings (e.g. Di Nardo,1991; Sanderson & Barlow, 1990), responses to the item, "Do you worry about minor matters?", differentiated GAD from OCD. Indeed, 97% of patients with GAD responded affirmatively to this item, compared with 41% of patients with OCD. Moreover, patients with GAD could be discriminated from patients with OCD on the ADIS-R items, "bothered by worries more days than not over the past 6 months" (100% vs. 55%), and the "percentage of the day over the past month feeling tense or worried" (Means = 55.43 and 32.00, respectively).

Conversely, ADIS-R screening items for obsessions and compulsions differentiated patients with OCD from patients with GAD. Whereas 75% of patients with OCD responded affirmatively to the ADIS-R screening item for obsessions, this item was endorsed by only 15% of patients with GAD. Furthermore, the groups differed in the percentage who responded affirmatively to the compulsions screening item (75% and 15% of patients with OCD and GAD, respectively).

Although the two groups could be differentiated on measures evaluating the key features of GAD and OCD, Brown, Moras et al. (1993) concluded that these findings could be interpreted to suggest that indices of worry evidenced the lowest degree of discriminability as indicated by: (a) though statistically significant, effect sizes involving between-group comparisons on the PSWQ were among the lowest; (b) a large percentage of patients with OCD endorsed ADIS-R items of worry whereas a much smaller percentage of patients with GAD cross-endorsed the ADIS-R item on obsessions. Though requiring further study, this pattern of findings was interpreted as providing some support for current conceptualizations (e.g. Barlow, 1988) delineating worry as a characteristic inherent to all anxiety disorders. This conclusion could also be viewed as concordant with the conceptualization discussed earlier (i.e. Salkovskis, 1989a) stating that negative appraisals (worry) over obsessional phenomena may start the progression toward a clinical disorder as well as represent a parameter contributing to the boundary between nonclinical and pathological obsessive–compulsive symptomatology.

Bearing on the issue of the construct and discriminant validity of the anxiety disorders, Zinbarg & Barlow (1992) factor analyzed the scores from 23 measures assessing the key features of anxiety and related affects (e.g.

anxiety sensitivity, obsessions, compulsions, worry, social anxiety). Subjects were 432 patients presenting to our clinic and 32 normal controls. The following factors were derived: Panic, Agoraphobia, Social Anxiety, Obsessions and Compulsions, Generalized Anxiety, Simple Fears, as well as higher-order factor, Negative Affect. Following the calculation of factor-score estimates for each of the above dimensions, the authors used discriminant function analysis (DFA) to examine the extent to which the DSM-III-R principal diagnostic groups (determined by the ADIS-R) displayed characteristic factor-score profiles. Relevant to the present chapter, the DFA yielded six statistically significant functions; the fifth function, defined primarily by the Obsessions and Compulsions factor, discriminated patients with OCD from the other diagnostic groups. On the other hand, patients with GAD, while having higher factor scores than normal controls on all of the factors, were not differentiated from the other anxiety disorder groups on any one factor. Nevertheless, profile analyses indicated that patients with GAD had a characteristic factor-score profile relative to the other groups.

Thus, in the context of the present discussion, Zinbarg & Barlow's (1992) results indicate that, in addition to providing support for the construct validity of the DSM-III-R classification of anxiety disorders, symptomatology associated with the diagnosis of OCD forms a factor that is distinct from other dimensions of anxiety. Moreover, this factor distinguishes patients with OCD from patients with other anxiety disorders (as evidenced by the fifth function of the DFA). Whereas a factor labelled "Generalized Anxiety" emerged from the initial factor analyses, patients with GAD could not be differentiated from other anxiety disorder groups on this or any other single dimension, although their profile of factor scores was distinctive. This pattern of findings may also attest to the proposition that, whereas the key feature (worry) is ubiquitous across the emotional disorders, GAD nonetheless possesses a unique presentation that is discernible from "neighboring" disorders (cf. Brown, Barlow & Liebowitz, 1993).

Correlational Evaluations

In addition to recent correlational and factor analyses indicating that worry and trait anxiety are separate constructs (e.g. Meyer et al., 1990; Davey, 1993; Davey, Hampton, Farrell & Davidson, 1992), similar analyses have produced evidence that worry and obsessions represent distinct constructs. For example, using a large sample of patients with a variety of anxiety and mood disorders ($n = 533$), Brown, Moras et al. (1993) evaluated the pattern of correlations between the Penn State Worry Questionnaire (PSWQ) and the Maudsley Obsessive Compulsive

Inventory (MOCI). Tests of the relative strength of correlations revealed that the PSWQ and the MOCI Doubting and Checking subscales were significantly larger than those between the PSWQ and the MOCI compulsion subscales (i.e. Washing, Repetition). Moreover, the correlation between the MOCI Doubting and Checking subscales (r = .58) was significantly larger than those between each of these subscales and the PSWQ (rs = .45 and .43, respectively). The authors concluded that whereas there is reliable overlap between the constructs of worry and obsessions, considerable differentiation existed as well (the MOCI Doubting and Checking subscales shared roughly 34% of their variance which was significantly larger than what either subscale shared with the PSWQ (19%)).

Similar results have been obtained in studies of nonclinical samples (e.g. Gross & Eifert, 1990; Moore & Davey,1992; Tallis & de Silva, 1992). For example, Gross & Eifert (1990) performed a factor analysis of a variety of measures of anxiety obtained from 162 college students. Results of this analysis indicated that worry and intrusive thought items loaded onto separate factors, which the authors interpreted as supporting the hypothesis that worry and intrusive thoughts could be differentiated.

Tallis & de Silva (1992) administered the Worry Domains Questionnaire (WDQ; Tallis et al., 1992) and the MOCI to 235 nonclinical subjects. Results indicated that the WDQ was correlated with the Checking and Doubting subscales (rs = .17 and .18), but not the Washing or Repetition subscales (rs = .09 and .07). Whereas the authors concluded that these findings might suggest that worry and checking are functionally similar (e.g. both are oriented towards a future threat), these data provide further evidence of considerable differentiation between measures of worry and obsessions.

Using 100 college students, Moore & Davey (1992) also found a modest correlation between worry and intrusive thoughts (as measured by the Student Worry Scale and an intrusive thought/impulse checklist). In addition, regression analyses revealed that the measure of worry continued to account for a modest but significant amount of variance in the intrusive thoughts measure after measures of depression and trait anxiety had been partialled out. The authors concluded that the oft-observed relationship between worry and negative cognitions is not entirely mediated by worry-induced states of negative affect.

Case Example

Having reviewed the empirical and clinical evidence regarding the distinguishability of worry and obsessions and their corresponding disorders, the following clinical case example is offered as a means of elucidating these distinctions.

In K.C. is a 34-year-old, married homemaker and the mother of a preschool-aged boy. She presented to the clinic after experiencing an unexpected panic attack while working as a hospital nurse. After this panic attack, she grew increasingly concerned about committing serious errors at work such as giving the wrong medication to a patient, failing to give a patient medication, or accidentally poisoning a patient with food, drinks, medications, or ointments. As the result of these concerns, K.C. reported retrieving medication labels from the garbage to repeatedly check that the proper medication had been administered. Her distress over the possibility of committing such an error became so great that she ultimately resigned her position at the hospital.

Nevertheless, K.C.'s concerns generalized beyond the hospital setting. She became increasingly concerned that she would poison herself and her family through the process of cooking meals or other care-taking (e.g. giving vitamins to her son). She stated that these concerns would often be accompanied by a panic attack and could be elicited by an off-hand comment from one of her family (e.g. her husband's inquiry as to whether she was using a new brand of apple sauce). Consequently, she would repeatedly check medications when administering them to her family as well as the spices and other ingredients in the food she prepared. She would often ask her husband for reassurance as to the correctness of her actions or would avoid these activities altogether unless he was present.

When her husband was out of town and she needed to take her medication (she was taking a small dosage of alprazolam), she would become increasingly anxious regarding the possibility that she might poison herself. However, she feared that if she did not take her medication, she would be unable to get the proper amount of sleep. Her anxiety was further exacerbated by her concern that deprivation from sleep would cause her to become ill or be unable to care for her son sufficiently.

Although the experience of an "unexpected" panic attack had prompted her presentation to the clinic, the ADIS-R interview revealed that all of K.C.'s panics were elicited by the aforementioned cognitions. Thus, K.C. was assigned a principal diagnosis of OCD. Nevertheless, this case illustrates the potential overlap that can be observed occasionally between presentations of GAD and OCD. Clearly, evidence of GAD-like worry can be seen in the above example (e.g. concern about becoming ill following sleep loss). However, K.C. was not assigned an additional diagnosis of GAD given that all of her "worries" were deemed to be related to another Axis I disorder (OCD). Unlike dimensions that have been posited as distinguishing worry and obsessions, the phenomena ultimately labeled as "obsessions" in this case example could be viewed as primarily taking the form of thought (excessive doubting); their content could be viewed as corresponding to events associated with normal, daily activity (e.g. cooking, taking medications). Nevertheless, important areas of departure from prototypical GAD worry included the degree of unacceptability/ resistance associated with these concerns as well as the fact that the concerns would precipitate repetitive, time-consuming behaviors initiated in an effort to reassure that a grave error had not been committed. Thus, this cognitive activity could be conceptualized not so much as an attempt to problem-solve or prepare for a possible future negative event, but as an intrusive doubt that could not be dismissed by some form of behavior aimed at ensuring that the feared consequence had not occurred.

RECOMMENDATIONS FOR FUTURE RESEARCH

Repeatedly throughout this chapter, we have noted the paucity of data derived from the direct comparisons of worry and obsessions and their associated parameters (e.g. behavioral sequelae, mood states). The most direct comparisons of this nature to date have involved studies examining the extent to which GAD and OCD can be distinguished at the diagnostic and symptom level (e.g. Brown et al., 1992; Brown, Moras et al., 1993). Whereas these studies indicate that the two disorders can be differentiated reliably by clinicians, they say little about the parameters used to make these distinctions. Moreover, given that the majority of patients with OCD used in these studies evidenced overt compulsions, these data do not address the extent to which GAD can be differentiated from presentations of OCD that involve obsessions alone.

Given that the treatment of GAD has been reviewed extensively elsewhere in this volume (see Butler, Chapter 8, this volume), we have not opted to discuss treatment strategies in the present chapter. However, it is interesting to note that new treatments for GAD have been developed to directly target the key features of the disorder (cf. Brown, O'Leary & Barlow, 1993; Craske, Barlow & O'Leary, 1992). Interestingly, these new treatments have begun to share several similarities to longstanding treatments for OCD (e.g. imaginal exposure to the content of worry; prevention of behavioral responses typically initiated in response to the worry). However, despite these similarities, these new treatments for GAD contain many unique elements that have evolved from leading conceputalizations of worry (e.g. Barlow, 1988; Borkovec & Hu, 1990). Another interesting direction for future research would be to examine the extent to which patients with OCD respond to these new treatments that have been designed to specifically target worry. Differential response to these treatments may also point to important distinctions between worry and obsessions.

REFERENCES

American Psychiatric Association (1980). *Diagnostic and Statistical Manual of Mental Disorders*, 3rd edn. Washington, DC: American Psychiatric Association.

American Psychiatric Association (1987). *Diagnostic and Statistical Manual of Mental Disorders*, 3rd edn.—Rev. Washington, DC: American Psychiatric Association.

American Psychiatric Association (in press) *Diagnostic and Statistical Manual of Mental Disorders*, 4th edn. Washington, DC: American Psychiatric Association.

Barlow, D.H. (1988). *Anxiety and its Disorders: The Nature and Treatment of Anxiety and Panic*. New York: Guilford Press.

Barlow, D.H. (1991). The nature of anxiety: Anxiety, depression, and emotional disorders. In R.M. Rapee & D.H. Barlow (eds.), *Chronic Anxiety: Generalized Anxiety Disorder, and Mixed Anxiety Depression*, pp. 1–28. New York: Guilford Press.

Barlow, D.H., Blanchard, E.B., Vermilyea, J.A., Verimlyea, B.B. & Di Nardo, P. A. (1986a). Generalized anxiety and generalized anxiety disorder: Description and reconceptualization. *American Journal of Psychiatry*, **143**, 40–44.

Barlow, D.H. & Di Nardo, P.A. (1991). The diagnosis of generalized anxiety disorder: Development, current status, and future directions. In R.M. Rapee & D.H. Barlow (Eds.), *Chronic Anxiety: Generalized Anxiety Disorder, and Mixed Anxiety Depression*, pp. 95–118. New York: Guilford Press.

Barlow, D.H., Di Nardo, P.A., Vermilyea, B.B., Vermilyea, J.A. & Blanchard, E.B. (1986b). Comorbidity and depression among the anxiety disorders: Issues in diagnosis and classification. *Journal of Nervous and Mental Disease*, **174**, 63–72.

Borkovec, T.D. (1992, December). Recent empirical information relevant to the definition of generalized anxiety disorder. Paper presented at the meeting of the American College of Neuropsychopharmacology, San Juan, Puerto Rico.

Borkovec, T.D. & Hu, S. (1990). The effect of worry on cardiovascular response to phobic imagery. *Behaviour Research and Therapy*, **28**, 69–73.

Borkovec, T.D. & Inz, J. (1990). The nature of worry in generalized anxiety disorder: A predominance of thought activity. *Behaviour Research and Therapy*, **28**, 153–158.

Borkovec, T.D., Robinson, E., Pruzinsky, T. & DePree, J.A. (1983). Preliminary exploration of worry: Some characteristics and processes. *Behaviour Research and Therapy*, **21**, 9–16.

Borkovec, T.D., Shadick, R. & Hopkins, M. (1991). The nature of normal and pathological worry. In R.M. Rapee & D.H. Barlow (Eds.), *Chronic Anxiety: Generalized Anxiety Disorder, and Mixed Anxiety Depression*, pp. 29–51. New York: Guilford Press.

Brown, T.A. (in press). Validity of the DSM-III-R and DSM-IV classification systems for anxiety disorders. In R.M. Rapee (Ed.), *Current Controversies in the Anxiety Disorders*. New York: Guilford Press.

Brown, T.A., Antony, M.M. & Barlow, D.H. (1992). Psychometric properties of the Penn State Worry Questionnaire in a clinical anxiety disorders sample. *Behaviour Research and Therapy*, **30**, 33–37.

Brown, T.A. & Barlow, D.H. (1992). Comorbidity among anxiety disorders: Implications for treatment and DSM-IV. *Journal of Consulting and Clinical Psychology*, **60**, 835–844.

Brown, T.A., Barlow, D.H. & Liebowitz, M.R. (1993). *The empirical basis of generalized anxiety disorder*. Manuscript submitted for publication.

Brown, T.A., Moras, K., Zinbarg, R.E. & Barlow, D.H. (1993). Diagnostic and symptom distinguishability of generalized anxiety disorder and obsessive-compulsive disorder. *Behavior Therapy*, **24**, 227–240.

Brown, T.A., O'Leary, T.A. & Barlow, D.H. (1993). Generalized anxiety disorder. In D.H. Barlow (Ed.), *Clinical Handbook of Psychological Disorders: A Step-by-step Treatment Manual*, 2nd edn, pp. 137–188. New York: Guilford Press.

Clark, D.A. & de Silva, P. (1985). The nature of depressive and anxious intrusive thoughts: Distinct or uniform phenomena? *Behaviour Research and Therapy*, **23**, 383–393.

Craske, M.G., Barlow, D.H. & O'Leary, T.A. (1992). *Mastery of your Anxiety and Worry*. Albany, NY: Graywind Publications.

Craske, M.G., Rapee, R.M., Jackel, L. & Barlow, D.H. (1989). Qualitative dimensions of worry in DSM-III-R generalized anxiety disorder subjects and nonanxious controls. *Behaviour Research and Therapy*, **27**, 189–198.

Davey, G.C.L. (1993). Worrying and trait anxiety as predictors of scores on the Fear Survey Schedule. Manuscript submitted for publication.

Davey, G.C.L., Hampton, J., Farrell, J. & Davidson, S. (1992). Some characteristics of worrying: Evidence for worrying and anxiety as separate constructs. *Personality and Individual Differences*, **13**, 133–147.

Di Nardo, P.A. (1991). MacArthur reanalysis of generalized anxiety disorder. Unpublished manuscript.

Di Nardo, P.A. & Barlow, D.H. (1988). *Anxiety Disorders Interview Schedule-Revised (ADIS-R)*. Albany, NY: Graywind Publications.

Di Nardo, P.A., Moras, K., Barlow, D.H., Rapee, R.M. & Brown, T.A. (1993). Reliability of the DSM-III-R anxiety disorder categories using the Anxiety Disorders Interview Schedule—Revised. *Archives of General Psychiatry*, **50**, 251–256.

Di Nardo, P.A., O'Brien, G.T., Barlow, D.H., Waddell, M.T. & Blanchard, E.B. (1983). Reliability of DSM-III anxiety disorder categories using a new structured interview. *Archives of General Psychiatry*, **40**, 1070–1074.

Edwards, S. & Dickerson, M. (1987). On the similarity of positive and negative intrusions. *Behaviour Research and Therapy*, **25**, 207–211.

England, S.L. & Dickerson, M. (1988). Intrusive thoughts: Unpleasantness not the major cause of uncontrollability. *Behaviour Research and Therapy*, **26**, 279–282.

Eysenck, M.W. (1992). *Anxiety: The Cognitive Perspective*. Hillsdale, NJ: Erlbaum and Associates.

Freeston, M.H., Ladouceur, R., Thibodeau, N. & Gagnon, F. (1991). Cognitive intrusions in a nonclinical population: I. Response style, subjective experience, and appraisal. *Behaviour Research and Therapy*, **29**, 585–597.

Freeston, M.H., Ladouceur, R., Thibodeau, N. & Gagnon, F. (1992). Cognitive intrusions in a nonclinical population: II. Associations with depressive, anxious, and compulsive symptoms. *Behaviour Research and Therapy*, **30**, 263–271.

Gross, P.R. & Eifert, G.H. (1990). Components of generalized anxiety: The role of intrusive thoughts vs. worry. *Behaviour Research and Therapy*, **28**, 421–428.

Hodgson, R.J., & Rachman, S. (1977). Obsessional-compulsive complaints. *Behaviour Research and Therapy*, **15**, 389–395.

Jakes, I. (1989a). Salkovskis on obsessional-compulsive neurosis: A critique. *Behaviour Research and Therapy*, **27**, 673–675.

Jakes, I. (1989b). Salkovskis on obsessional-compulsive neurosis: A rejoinder. *Behaviour Research and Therapy*, **27**, 683–684.

Mannuzza, S., Fyer, A. J., Martin, M.S., Gallops, M.S., Endicott, J., Gorman, J.M., Liebowitz, M.R. & Klein, D.F. (1989). Reliability of anxiety assessment: I. Diagnostic agreement. *Archives of General Psychiatry*, **46**, 1093–1101.

Mathews, A. (1990). Why worry?: The cognitive function of anxiety. *Behaviour Research and Therapy*, **28**, 455–468.

Meyer, T.J., Miller, M.I., Metzger, R.L. & Borkovec, T.D. (1990). Development and validation of the Penn State Worry Questionnaire. *Behaviour Research and Therapy*, **28**, 487–495.

Moore, S., Davey, G.C. (1992). *Intrusive thoughts, negative automatic thoughts, and worrying*. Manuscript submitted for publication.

Niler, E.R. & Beck, S.J. (1989). The relationship among guilt, dysphoria, anxiety, and obsessions in a normal population. *Behaviour Research and Therapy*, **27**, 213–220.

Parkinson, L. & Rachman, S. (1981). The nature of intrusive thoughts. *Advances in Behaviour Research and Therapy*, **3**, 101–110.

Rachman, S.J. (1978). An anatomy of obsessions. *Behaviour Analysis and Modification*, **2**, 253–278.

Rachman, S. & de Silva, P. (1978). Abnormal and normal obsessions. *Behaviour Research and Therapy*, **16**, 233–248.

Rachman, S.J. & Hodgson, R.J. (1980). *Obsessions and Compulsions*. Englewood Cliffs, NJ: Prentice Hall.

Rapee, R.M. (1991). Generalized anxiety disorder: A review of clinical features and theoretical concepts. *Clinical Psychology Review*, **11**, 419–440.

Roemer, L. & Borkovec, T.D. (1993). Worry: Unwanted cognitive activity that controls unwanted somatic experience. In D.M. Wegner & J.W. Pennebaker (Eds.), *Handbook of Mental Control*, pp. 220–238. Englewood Cliffs, NJ: Prentice Hall.

Salkovskis, P.M. (1985). Obsessional-compulsive problems: A cognitive-behavioural analysis. *Behaviour Research and Therapy*, **23**, 571–583.

Salkovskis, P.M. (1989a). Obsessive and intrusive thoughts: Clinical and nonclinical aspects. In P.M.G. Emmelkamp, F. Kraaimaat, I. Florin & I.M. Marks (Eds.), *Fresh Perspectives on Anxiety Disorders* (pp. 197–213). Berwyn, PA: Swets North America, Inc.

Salkovskis, P.M. (1989b). Cognitive-behavioural factors and the persistence of intrusive thoughts in obsessional problems. *Behaviour Research and Therapy*, **27**, 677–682.

Salkovskis, P.M. (1989c). Obsessions and compulsions. In J. Scott, J.M.G. Williams & A.T. Beck (Eds.), *Cognitive Therapy: A Clinical Casebook*. London: Croom Helm.

Salkovskis, P.M. & Harrison, J. (1984). Abnormal and normal obsessions: A replication. *Behaviour Research and Therapy*, **22**, 549–552.

Sanderson, W.C. & Barlow, D.H. (1990). A description of patients diagnosed with DSM-III-R generalized anxiety disorder. *Journal of Nervous and Mental Disease*, **178**, 588–591.

Sanderson, W.C., Di Nardo, P.A., Rapee, R.M. & Barlow, D.H. (1990). Syndrome comorbidity in patients diagnosed with DSM-III-R anxiety disorder. *Journal of Abnormal Psychology*, **99**, 308–312.

Steketee, G., Grayson, J.B. & Foa, E.B. (1987). A comparison of characteristics of obsessive-compulsive disorder and other anxiety disorders. *Journal of Anxiety Disorders*, **1**, 325–335.

Tallis, F. & de Silva, P. (1992). Worry and obsessional symptoms: A correlational analysis. *Behaviour Research and Therapy*, **30**, 103–105.

Tallis, F., Eysenck, M.W. & Mathews, A. (1992). A questionnaire for the measurement of nonpathological worry. *Personality and Individual Differences*, **13**, 161–168.

Turner, S.M., Beidel, D.C. & Stanley, M.A. (1992). Are obsessional thoughts and worry different cognitive phenomena? *Clinical Psychology Review*, **12**, 257–270.

Zinbarg, R.E. & Barlow, D.H. (1992, November). The construct validity of the DSM-III-R anxiety disorders: Empirical evidence. Paper presented at the meeting of the Association for Advancement of Behaviour Therapy, Boston, MA.

CHAPTER 10 The experience of worry among the elderly

*Patricia A. Wisocki**

It seems logical to assume a relationship between worry and old age. Old age is often characterized by many real objective problems, such as physical decline, loss of significant others, and financial concerns, all of which present legitimate sources for worry. Concentration difficulties, behavioral slowing, and lower activity levels, frequently experienced by many elderly people, may also provide circumstances which prompt the occurrence of worry (Borkovec, 1984). Worry appears to influence the maintenance of insomnia (Borkovec, 1979), anxiety, and depression (Borkovec, Wilkinson, Folensbee & Lerman, 1983), problems common to older adults. Many of the diseases which occur in old age, such as coronary heart disease, hypertension, hypoglycemia, and hypertriglyceridemia, may be significantly worsened by high levels of anxiety and stress (Hersen & Van Hasselt, 1992).

The exploration of the experience of anxiety and worry among the older adult population would, therefore, seem to be a worthwhile endeavor. This chapter is directed to that end.

The chapter is divided into four parts. In the first part the epidemiological and comparative data relevant to the occurrence of anxiety in older adults are presented. The second part contains a description of the development of a Worrry Scale for older adults. The third part presents the findings from a number of research studies conducted in the United States and Canada using that scale. In the final part the research findings with elderly worriers are compared with the findings from the research with younger populations and conclusions about worry across the life-span are drawn.

*University of Massachusetts, Amherst, USA

Worrying: Perspectives on Theory, Assessment and Treatment. Edited by G.C.L. Davey and F. Tallis.
© 1994 John Wiley & Sons Ltd.

THE INCIDENCE OF ANXIETY AMONG THE ELDERLY

A number of epidemiological surveys conducted over the past few years suggest that anxiety occurs in high rates among elderly people. Himmelfarb & Murrell (1984) found that 17% of the elderly men and 21.5% of the elderly women in a community sample in Kentucky had enough high intensity anxiety symptoms to require therapeutic intervention. Leighton et al. (1963) reported that roughly 10% of a sample of 1010 Canadian elderly were anxious. Lindsay, Briggs & Murphy (1989) identified prevalence rates of 3.7% for generalized anxiety disorder and 10% for phobic disorders in an elderly British population. Even institutionalized elderly seem to experience significant amounts of anxiety. Haley (1983) found, for instance, that anxiety was the second most frequent problem requiring intervention for this population.

It is important to note, however, that while prevalence rates for anxiety-related problems are high for the elderly, they are generally lower than those for other age groups (Myers et al., 1984; Oxman, Barrett, Barrett & Gerber, 1987; Robins et al., 1984). In an extensive study conducted at Duke University Medical Center by Blazer, George & Hughes (1991), 900 elderly men and women were interviewed for 2 hours about their experience of symptoms of panic disorder, phobia, obsessive–compulsive disorder, psychotropic drug use, and generalized anxiety. Their responses were compared with those of 3500 younger participants in the age categories of 18–24, 25–44, 45–65 who were also interviewed. For each of the anxiety disorders investigated, those participants in the 45–64 year range consistently expressed higher prevalence rates than the elderly age group. Lifetime prevalence rates of anxiety symptoms were also lower for the group over 65 years of age.

In examining the data by race, gender, and age Blazer et al. (1991) reported that elderly Black females experienced more generalized anxiety than all the other subgroups (i.e. Caucasian males and females and Black males). They also found that only 3% of the elderly participants reported that their anxiety symptoms manifested themselves for the first time in old age, and that the average duration of anxiety disorders was greater for older adults than for middle-aged adults, suggesting that the disorders have a long experiential history.

The most common anxiety disorders among the elderly are phobias, including agoraphobia, social phobia, and simple phobia, followed by generalized anxiety syndrome (Blazer et al., 1991; Myers et al., 1984). Obsessive–compulsive disorder and panic disorder are relatively rare occurrences for the elderly (McCarthy, Katz & Foa, 1991).

Our confidence about these findings must be tempered by a number of concerns typical of work with elderly populations and reflective of the sparsity of research in this area. First, it is commonly believed that the elderly tend to underreport their symptoms. Second, accurate recall of past emotional experience is difficult at any age, making suspect any retrospective information provided by older people who naturally have a longer history. Third, the language used to describe or define anxiety is often unclear. For example, the terms anxiety, agitation, and nervousness, are often used interchangeably. Fourth, there is no agreement about the diagnostic criteria for anxiety in the elderly, differentiating them from younger populations and from subgroups within their own broad age classification (e.g. do people over 75 or 85 or 95 differ from people between 65 and 75 years of age?). Fifth, diagnoses of anxiety are frequently confounded by diagnoses of other psychological problems, such as depression, schizophrenia, restlessness, dementia, or delirium, or medical conditions, such as hypertension and cardiovascular disease, which can imitate or initiate anxiety symptoms. Sixth, as a group the elderly take a number of medications simultaneously, the interactions of which may cause or exacerbate anxiety. Seventh, it is difficult to compare anxiety syndromes from patients in different age groups because there are considerable variations in the brain substrates of aging individuals. As Sunderland, Lawlor, Martinez & Molchan (1991) point out, there is little correspondence between what is known about anxiety in younger patients and older ones. In comparing the biological markers of anxious patients with elderly subjects, these authors report that some of the biological changes which occur normally as people age are similar to the characteristics associated with anxiety disorders. And while it is possible that aging persons are more susceptible to anxiety (Raskind et al., 1988), definitive research in support of this point is not yet available. Eighth, the assessment instruments used in surveys have not generally been normed on older adults and are often not relevant for them. In fact, in a review of studies on anxiety in the elderly, Hersen & Van Hasselt (1992) report that studies "have not clearly differentiated anxiety as a symptomatic manifestation and anxiety as a disorder" (p. 621).

THE DEVELOPMENT OF A WORRY SCALE FOR OLDER ADULTS

The original Worry Scale, described first in Wisocki, Handen & Morse (1986), is a 35 item questionnaire that covers three areas of concern:

finances, health, and social conditions. The items were specifically selected from fears and concerns commonly associated with aging. For example, the category of finances includes such items as loss of home, inability to support oneself, inability to help one's children, etc. The category of health concerns contains items pertaining to loss of specific physical functions and sensorium, the experience of illness by oneself or one's spouse, necessity of care by others, loss of independence, etc. In the social category are items relating to physical appearance, problems in interactions with others, psychological problems, concerns about crime, etc.

Respondents score each item on a five point Likert scale, ranging from "never worried" to "worried much of the time". The Worry Scale is scored from zero to +4 in ascending order along a five point scale. The maximum possible score is 140.

Initial work on the Worry Scale with 98 and 94 subjects respectively by Wisocki, Handen & Morse (1986) and Wisocki (1988) demonstrated significant correlations between all subscales and between individual items and the subscale totals. These authors found that the Worry Scale correlated significantly with two other measures of anxiety: the Symptom Checklist-90 (SCL-90) and the Multiple Affect Adjective Checklist. There were significant positive correlations between the health worry subscale and the various health measures. Scores on the financial worry subscale correlated significantly in a negative direction with income levels when social-economic status was held constant. There were also significant negative correlations between the social worry subscale and the respondents' perceptions of social support. Worry did not correlate with age (except in one sample of homebound elderly), gender, or depression measures.

Additional support for the scale was provided by three Canadian investigators. Cappeliez (1988) found positive correlations between scores on the health and social conditions subscales of the Worry Scale and scores on state and trait anxiety measures, taken by 25 community active elderly and 25 elderly nursing home residents. Cappeliez found no correlations between the financial worry subscale and state and trait anxiety scores. Skarborn & Nicki (1992) reported a significant positive correlation between the Worry Scale and a 3 day diary of worry completed by 30 homebound and 70 community active elderly and between the Worry Scale and the anxiety, depression, and obsession subscales of the SCL-90 and the MUNSH Happiness/Depression Scale.

In a recent study by Wisocki, Hunt & Souza (1993) a small group of 28 elderly who identified themselves as chronic worriers completed the Worry Scale along with the Geriatric Depression Scale, the SCL-90R, the

Rosenberg Self-Esteem Scale, and the Inventory of Socially Supportive Behaviors. Correlational data from these questionnaires indicate a significantly positive relationship between the total Worry Scale scores and nine of the ten SCL-90R subscales (i.e. somatization, obsessive–compulsiveness, interpersonal sensitivity, depression, anxiety, hostility, phobic anxiety, psychoticism); only the subscale dealing with paranoid ideation did not correlate with the Worry Scale scores. The Worry Scale was also significantly positively correlated with the Geriatric Depression Scale and it was significantly negatively correlated with the Rosenberg Self-Esteem Scale. There was no relationship between the Worry Scale scores and the social support measure. Nor did worry correlate with age or gender in this study.

Wisocki, Hunt & Souza also found that the Worry Scale scores correlated significantly positively with other measures of worry, including perceived troublesomeness of the worries, difficulty in stopping the worry process, and the number of physical and psychological conditions subjects reported experiencing which they related to worry (such as backaches, headaches, insomnia, irritability, etc.). There was no correlation between the frequency of worry during a given day and the Worry Scale scores.

While these correlations indicate good construct validity for the Worry Scale, all of the measures used in these studies were based on self-report and thus, there is concern about the problems occurring from shared method variance. Concurrent validity is enhanced by the diary data collected by Skarborn & Nicki (1992) and by Wisocki, Hunt & Souza (1993) who supplemented Worry Scale measures with structured interview data from focus groups.

Indeed, the information obtained from the focus group study has resulted in a revision of the Worry Scale. The number of items was expanded to 88 in order to include the specific worries elicited from the elderly subjects themselves. Additional sections were added as well. The scale now contains questions about the amount of time spent worrying; the age at which worrying began and was most common; significant life events associated with worry; feelings and physical conditions which may accompany worry; methods used to control worry; the degree of troublesomeness associated with worry; the amount of difficulty experienced in controlling worry; the relationship of worry to time; various functions of worry, and items about social relationships, religious beliefs, and financial concerns.

A study comparing the responses of a national group of elderly subjects to the Revised Worry Scale, the original Worry Scale and the Penn State Worry Questionnaire is now underway.

Additional normative data are required to enhance the suitability of the Worry Scale for a variety of elderly populations. The data reported here were derived from samples of elderly, who were primarily Caucasian, middle class, female, fairly healthy and in fair to good financial conditions. While we are currently analyzing information from a small number of African-American elderly who participated in the focus group study, much more work is required with elderly of different races, health status, and socio-economic conditions in order to achieve a more balanced picture of worry among the elderly population.

Hersen & Van Hasselt (1992) point out that the Worry Scale should also be administered to groups of elderly who can be reliably differentiated on pathology, and "contrasted with psychologically normal and healthy elderly and with psychologically normal and unhealthy elderly . . . (in order to) permit evaluation of the discriminant power of the scale" (p. 626).

RESEARCH FINDINGS

There have been six studies on worry with subjects drawn from the general elderly population (Wisocki, Handen & Morse, 1986; Cappeliez, 1988; Wisocki, 1988; Powers, Wisocki & Whitbourne, 1992; Skarborn & Nicki, 1992; Wisocki, 1993) and one study in which the participants identified themselves as worriers (Wisocki, Hunt & Souza, 1993). In Table 10.1 the mean Worry Scale scores are listed for each population sample. These data indicate that worrying, as measured by this particular scale, is a low frequency event for these elderly men and women. Of a total possible score of 140, the average score from the general population of American elderly was 21; for the two sets of Canadian samples the average score of 10 is much lower than the scores of the American subjects. It is interesting to note that the mean Worry Scale score doubled for those American elderly who identified themselves as worried, as compared with scores from the other studies in which subjects were drawn from the general population of senior adults. In two of the three studies which compared community active elderly with chronically ill elderly, the elderly in the latter category tended to experience more worry. The one study which included younger subjects (Powers et al., 1992) found a higher mean score for the college students than that achieved by the general population of elderly, but not as high as that achieved by the elderly worriers.

In the study reported by Wisocki (1988) a subgroup of elderly worriers (15% of the population sample) who scored high on the Worry Scale were compared with the low scoring elderly on the indicators of anxiety and

Table 10.1   A comparison of mean Worry Scale scores from seven studies involving elderly subjects

Investigators	Population	Mean worry score
Wisocki et al., 1986	54 community active, from 10 senior centers in US mean age = 70	15.0
	44 homebound, from meals on wheels programs in US mean age = 77	23.7
Cappeliez, 1988[a]	25 community active, from Canadian social clubs mean age = 71	6.3
	25 Canadian nursing home residents mean age = 71	6.1
Wisocki, 1988	94 community active, from 11 US senior centers mean age = 72	17.0
Powers et al., 1992	89 community active, from 4 senior centers in US mean age = 78	24.3
	74 college students mean age = 20	32.6
Skarborn & Nicki, 1992	70 community active, from Canadian senior centers mean age = 72	10.4
	30 homebound, from Canadian home-care service organizations mean age = 83	17.3
Wisocki, 1993[b]	149 respondents to a national magazine survey in US mean age = 65	26.2
Wisocki, Hunt & Souza, 1993[b]	28 community active, from 3 US senior centers; self-identified as worriers mean age = 78	44.7

[a] These data form the basis for this study, but appear only in an unpublished version of the study.

[b] These studies have not been published as of the date of this chapter writing.

health. Worried elderly were found to be significantly more anxious and in poorer health than the nonworried group. They were also less vigorous, less contented, and tended to have more chronic illnesses. With these elderly there was no relationship between worry and depression. These findings have been supported by the work of Skarborn & Nicki (1992) with a population of Canadian seniors.

In examining the differences between a group of healthy and chronically ill elderly who were homebound, Wisocki et al. (1986) determined that while the homebound elderly expressed few worries overall, they did express significantly more worry than the healthy elderly on three specific health items: the ability to get around by oneself, the illness of a close family member or spouse, and the inability to care for one's spouse. With this group there was also an inverse correlation between age and the total worry scale scores and the financial and social worry scale scores.

Powers et al. (1992) compared a group of elderly with a group of college students, and found that the younger subjects worried more than the elderly subjects about finances and social relations and had equal concerns about health. The elderly were more focused on the past and present and less oriented toward the future. They also had more favorable attitudes about the past and present than the young, who were in turn more positive about the future. When compared on locus of control scales, the elderly were more external than the young and they had a more positive outlook about life in general.

For both elderly and young people, worry was related to external locus of control. That is, the feeling that one is controlled by luck, fate, chance, is associated with a greater degree of worrying. In both groups, those who worried more were also more negative about life in general. We also found that the young who worried were preoccupied with the present while the worried old were concerned with the future, which they saw as negative.

We have not found significant gender differences in worrying in any of our studies, but any confidence in that conclusion is tempered by the fact that 80% of the subjects in these studies were female. A study by Croake, Myers & Singh (1988) about the fears expressed by 23 elderly men and 43 elderly women did report a gender difference, however. Older women expressed more fearfulness than older men. These authors also found that college females expressed more fearfulness than their male counterparts.

Cappeliez (1988) asked 50 elderly adults from Canadian social clubs and nursing homes about the strategies they used to cope with their worries, as measured by the Worry Scale. He found that distancing, the adoption of a detached attitude, and positive reappraisal, creating a positive outlook and meaning for the event, were the most frequently used coping methods. Confrontive coping, escape–avoidance and seeking social support were reported as the least frequently used strategies. Cappeliez also found that the coping strategy called self-controlling, which includes efforts to regulate feelings and actions by delaying action and keeping feelings inward, was positively correlated with a significantly higher level of state anxiety among those elderly who were living independently.

Wisocki, Hunt & Souza (1993) screened 300 elderly adults to obtain a sample of chronic worriers. Fifty-eight worriers were identified, using criteria of self-designation and the percentage of days spent worrying in one week. Individuals from this group were invited to attend one of five three hour focus groups conducted over the course of one year. Twenty-eight people were able to be scheduled. The mean size of each group was five. Two hours were devoted to a discussion of the following topics: what is difficult about being older these days; how is worry defined; what does it mean to worry; what are the effects of worry; how does worry differ from/relate to anxiety and depression; how is worry controlled; what kinds of things does one worry about; are these worries typical of older people; has worry changed over the life span. The questions were not presented in any particular order, but were included in each group discussion at some point. The third hour was spent in completing the various questionnaires described earlier in this chapter which were used to determine possible correlations with worry variables.

This group of subjects described "getting old" in mainly negative terms: loneliness, being alone, and living quietly; dependence on others for even minor problems; greater chance of physical illness for oneself and one's friends and relatives, difficulty in figuring out what is wrong, more people to take care of; inaccessibility to friends; being confined and unable to do things. Some people pointed out that aging is a matter of attitude and a process of learning to accept the changes that accompany old age. Several positive aspects of being old were indicated: time to do enjoyable or productive things; lack of responsibilities; no one to tell them what to do or where to be. A few people announced that getting old is a sudden discovery, emphasizing the speed at which time seems to move: "You're 50 one minute and 80 the next."

The definition of worry derived from the discussions within these groups is as follows: worry is an involuntary, undesirable process of negatively-charged cognitions about a future event which cannot be resolved, but which occupies a central place in one's mental state. It creates anxiety and depression, but is not as serious as either one. It is a useless, unnecessary process which may be triggered by a small event or it may deal with something large and important.

The effects of worry were catalogued in the following ways: first, it prohibits action, either by preventing one from doing constructive things, by immobilizing one altogether, or by interfering with efficiency; second, it affects cognitive processes in that one makes more errors and has more difficulty making decisions; third, it creates physical effects, such as fatigue and wrinkles and it decreases or increases appetite; fourth, it leads to health problems, such as increased blood pressure, heart and gastrointestinal difficulties; fifth, it produces the psychological effects of insecurity, depression, anxiety, sadness, loneliness, insomnia or other sleep problems, and a sense of morbidity; sixth, it affects social relationships in that a person may become isolated or withdrawn from others or may become more irritated with people in general.

The subjects had a great deal of difficulty in distinguishing worry from anxiety. They felt that anxiety was more severe than worry, required medical treatment, could not be controlled, and is focused on the present, while worry is focused on the future.

It was easier for them to explain the differences between worry and depression. Depression was considered the result of worrying (anxiety was considered the cause of worry), and was seen as much more debilitating.

These elderly subjects believed that the worry process is affected by significant life events and the obligations imposed by life events, like marriage, having children and grandchildren; the stage of life one is in, along with one's age; being alone and the amount of time on one's hands; social problems; health conditions of oneself or one's spouse; and financial conditions. There was no clear agreement about gender effects in the discussion. The groups (composed primarily of women) alternately said that men shrug off worry, while women carry it within themselves and hold on to it, or they said that men keep it inside and do not talk about it, while women tend to be more expressive of worry.

The subjects suggested a large number of ways to stop or control worry. They proposed: talking and reasoning with oneself; forgetting about the worry; doing something for someone else; being active and associating with friendly, positive people; visiting family; developing a positive attitude; distracting oneself and keeping one's mind occupied; thinking young; meditating; writing down worries; taking a drink; going to bed late; sleeping; and eating.

The subjects were divided on the question of whether or not the worry process has changed for them over time. A small group of people felt that one is born with a predisposition to worry and it is a lifelong process. The majority, however, felt that worries are deeper, more morbid, and stronger in the later years. They believed that when an older person worries, it is about something very serious or sad; when a younger person worries, it is usually about something trivial.

From these discussions, Wisocki, Hunt & Souza (1993) determined that there were three levels of worry, based on frequency of occurrence. On the first level, subjects reported worry over *family*, particularly the quality of life possible for children and grandchildren, along with specific concerns about their health, education, and troubling behaviors; *health*, which encompassed their own physical decline, an ability to maintain independence, and death concerns (i.e. needing help to die and the loss of others); *finances*, which included concerns about insufficient funds, the need to continue support for children, and the inter-relationship of money and health (i.e. one needs money to stay healthy).

The second level of worries included being alone and lonely; loss of independence; the possibility of criminal acts committed against them; the desirability of leaving things in order after death; being able to make decisions; problems in driving.

The third level of worries, occurring very infrequently, focused on environmental and political issues (e.g. the existence of nuclear power plants, loss of the ozone layer, the economic direction of the country, AIDS, etc.); social-evaluative judgments made by others (e.g. do people like me; what will people think; will there be someone at my funeral); and single occurrence miscellaneous worries (e.g. keeping busy, meeting deadlines, spending money on self).

AN INTEGRATION OF WORRY FINDINGS AMONG YOUNG AND OLD ADULTS

There are a number of consistent findings from this series of research studies. It is clear that worrying occurs among older adults and is troubling for them, but neither the prevalence rates nor the frequency rates are as high for the elderly as they are for younger populations. At best in these studies, 15% of any elderly sample might reliably be considered worriers. This percentage, incidentally, corresponds closely to the prevalence rates determined for anxiety problems experienced by elderly adults.

Gender effects were not evident in these elderly subjects. Other investigators studying younger subjects, however, have reported significant gender effects for particular worries. Borkovec, Robinson, Pruzinsky & DePree (1983) found that male worriers were more often concerned with interpersonal issues than were male nonworriers, while female worriers were more concerned with financial and academic issues than female nonworriers.

Borkovec and his colleagues (1991) point out that "worry reflects the evolution of a conceptual avoidance response to perceived threat and contributes significantly to the maintenance of anxiety disorders" (p. 42). Cappeliez (1988) provides evidence that this statement is pertinent to elderly people as well. He found a significantly positive relationship between high levels of state anxiety and the use of an avoidance coping strategy.

With the elderly, as with other age groups, worry is closely interconnected with anxiety. Worry scores consistently correlated with measures of anxiety and various types of pathology. Worry scores did not typically correlate with measures of depression, unlike the research evidence from younger subjects. In only one study (Wisocki, Hunt & Souza, 1993), where the subjects were chronic worriers, was there a relationship between worry and depression. In that same study there were also positive correlations between depression and anxiety measures and the experience of worry as being troublesome and difficult to stop. The uncontrollability of worry is regarded as "its prime pathological feature" (Borkovec et al., 1991, p. 41) for both normal and pathological worriers (see Tallis, Davey & Capuzzo, this volume, Chapter 3; Borkovec, this volume, Chapter 1).

Worry for the elderly seems to lack the problem-solving component included by Borkovec, Robinson, Pruzinsky & DePree (1983) in their definition of worry. They state: ". . . The worry process represents an attempt to engage in mental problem-solving on an issue whose outcome is uncertain but contains the possibility of one or more negative outcomes . . ." (p. 10). When asked to define worry, the elderly subjects in the focus group study of Wisocki, Hunt & Souza (1993) made no mention of this feature; instead they stressed the fact that no resolution of the worry was possible. This point is merely suggestive since it was not derived from a controlled experiment, but it is probably worthy of future exploration.

There are many similarities in the topics of worry reported by older and younger adults. Elderly participants worried primarily about health concerns, family, and finances. College students worried about health issues as much as their elderly counterparts and worried more about finances than the elderly (Powers et al., 1992). Sanderson & Barlow (1990) found that health/illness/injury concerns predominated among clients diagnosed with generalized anxiety disorder, while controls classified work/ school items as evoking the greatest worry.

There are considerable differences, however, between the age groups over the area of social concerns. Borkovec, Shadick & Hopkins (1991) have pointed out that with younger adults, degree of worry correlates most highly with social evaluative fears, such as fears of criticism, making mistakes, and meeting someone for the first time. With the elderly, there were very few social-evaluative concerns noted in their descriptions of worrisome items.

Such social fears have been suggested as the basis for the original etiology of chronic worry. Borkovec et al. (1991) have stated that "chronic worriers may have a history of aversive events associated with other people, especially events having to do with emotional expression, the potential loss of love or approval, and the use of internal and external language to try to cope with these" (p 47)

This theoretical speculation is challenged somewhat by the data obtained from elderly subjects who seem to lack these social concerns, even though there is an identifiable group of elderly worriers. It is possible, of course, that the original worries of these worried elderly were of a social nature and, with time, worrying became an independent, non-specific process and then in older age, worries focused primarily on the immediately relevant things common to an aging individual, such as health and finances. Most of the elderly subjects who participated in the focus group study (Wisocki, Hunt & Souza, 1993), however, believed that worry intensified over their life spans. Several of them acknowledged that worry in their younger years pertained to social events, but they now regard those concerns as "trivial". They also strongly emphasized the relationship between worry and significant life events when they were engaged in the activities of marrying, raising children, maintaining a job, etc. Now that those activities are complete and one is not as likely to make a mistake, worrying may take on a different face. Additional research on the development of this facet of worry across the lifespan and the process by which people cope with worry as they age will be enlightening and interesting.

REFERENCES

Blazer, D., George, L. & Hughes, D. (1991). The epidemiology of anxiety disorders: an age comparison. In C. Salzman & B. Lebowitz (Eds.), *Anxiety in the Elderly: Treatment and Research*, pp. 17–30. New York: Springer.

Borkovec, T. (1979). Pseudo-(experimental) insomnia and idiopathic (objective) insomnia: theoretical and therapeutic issues. *Advances in Behaviour Research and Therapy*, **2**, 27–55.

Borkovec, T. (1984). Worry: physiological and cognitive processes. Paper presented at the 14th meeting of the European Association of Behaviour Therapy, Brussels.

Borkovec, T., Robinson, E., Pruzinsky, T. & DePree, A. (1983). Preliminary exploration of worry: some characteristics and processes. *Behaviour Research and Therapy*, **21**, 9–16.

Borkovec, T., Shadick, R. & Hopkins, M. (1991). The nature of normal and pathological worry. In R. Rape & D. Barlow (Eds.), *Chronic Anxiety*, pp. 29–51. New York: Guilford Press.

Borkovec, T., Wilkinson, L., Folensbee, R. & Lerman, C. (1983). Stimulus control applications to the treatment of worry. *Behaviour Research and Therapy*, **21**, 247–251.

Cappeliez, P. (1988). Daily worries and coping strategies: implications for therapists. *Clinical Gerontologist*, **8**, 70–72.

Croake, J., Myers, K. & Singh, A. (1988). The fears expressed by elderly men and women: a lifespan approach. *International Journal of Aging and Human Development*, **26**, 139–146.

Haley, W. (1983). A family-behavioral approach to the treatment of the cognitively impaired elderly. *Gerontologist*, **23**, 18–20.

Hersen, M. & Van Hasselt, V. (1992). Behavioral assessment and treatment of anxiety in the elderly. *Clinical Psychology Review*, **12**, 619–640.

Himmelfarb, S. & Murrell, S. (1984). The prevalence and correlation of anxiety symptoms in older adults. *Journal of Psychiatry*, **116**, 159–167.

Leighton, D., Harding, J., Macklin, D., MacMillan, A. & Leighton, A. (1963). *The Character of Danger: Psychiatric Symptoms in Selected Communities, III*. New York: Basic Books.

Lindsay, J., Briggs, K. & Murphy, E. (1989). The Guys/Age Concern Survey: prevalence rates of cognitive impairment, depression, and anxiety in an urban elderly community. *British Journal of Psychiatry*, **155**, 317–329.

McCarthy, P., Katz, I. & Foa, E. (1991). Cognitive-behavioral treatment of anxiety in the elderly: a proposed model. In C. Salzman & B. Lebowitz (Eds.), *Anxiety in the Elderly: Treatment and Research*, pp. 197–214. New York: Springer.

Myers, J.K., Weisman, M.M., Tischler, G.L., Holzer, C.E., Leaf, P., Orvaschel, H., Anthony, J., Boyd, J., Burke, J., Kramer, M. & Stoltzman, R. (1984). Six-month prevalence of psychiatric disorders in three communities. *Archives of General Psychiatry*, **41**, 959–967.

Oxman, T., Barrett, J.E., Barrett, J. & Gerber, P. (1987). Psychiatric symptoms in the elderly in a primary care practice. *General Hospital Psychiatry*, **9**, 167–173.

Powers, C., Wisocki, P. & Whitbourne, S. (1992). Age differences and correlates of worrying in young and elderly adults. *Gerontologist*, **32**, 82–88.

Raskind, M., Peskind, E., Veith, R., Beard, J., Gumbrecht, G. & Halter, J. (1988). Increased plasma and cerebrospinal fluid norepinephrine in older men: differential suppression by clonidine. *Journal of Clinical Endocrinology and Metabolism*, **66**, 438–443.

Robins, L.N., Helzer, J., Weissman, M., Orvaschel, H., Gruenberg, E., Burke, J. et al. (1984). Lifetime prevalence of specific psychiatric disorders in three sites. *Archives of General Psychiatry*, **38**, 381–389.

Sanderson, W. & Barlow, D. (1990). A description of patients diagnosed with DSM III Revised generalized anxiety disorder. *Journal of Nervous and Mental Disease*, **178**, 588–591.

Skarborn, M. & Nicki, R. (1992). Worry among Canadian seniors. Paper presented at the 21st Annual Scientific and Educational Meeting of the Canadian Association on Gerontology, Edmonton, Alberta.

Sunderland, T., Lawlor, B., Martinez, R. & Molchan, S. (1991). Anxiety in the elderly: neurobiological and clinical interface. In C. Salzman & B. Lebowitz (Eds.), *Anxiety in the Elderly: Treatment and Research*, pp. 105–129. New York: Springer.

Wisocki, P.A. (1988). Worry as a phenomenon relevant to the elderly. *Behavior Therapy*, **19**, 369–379.

Wisocki, P.A. (1993). The results of a national survey on the worries of older adults. Manuscript in preparation, University of Massachusetts, Amherst, Massachusetts.

Wisocki, P.A., Handen, B. & Morse, C. (1986). The Worry Scale as a measure of anxiety among home bound and community active elderly. *Behavior Therapist*, **9**, 91–95.

Wisocki, P.A., Hunt, J. & Souza, S. (1993). An in-depth analysis of worry and its correlates among elderly chronic worriers. Manuscript in preparation, University of Massachusetts, Amherst, Massachusetts.

SECTION III   The assessment of worry

INTRODUCTION

Worry is essentially a cognitive phenomenon. It has been frequently suggested that the private nature of worry has deterred academic interest in the past. This was especially true in the period just prior to the ascendence and expansion of contemporary cognitive–behavioural clinical psychology. The success of cognitive therapy, in which self-monitoring is a cornerstone feature, appears to have inspired new confidence in the validity of self-report and associated measures.

In the following section two self-report measures of worry are described, the first of which, the Penn State Worry Questionnaire (PSWQ), is recommended for use on clinical populations. The second, the Worry Domains Questionnaire (WDQ), is especially recommended for use on non-clinical populations.

Molina & Borkovec (Chapter 11) describe the development and characteristics of the PSWQ, an instrument designed to provide a trait assessment of pathological worry. Its 16 items capture some of the most important features of clinically relevant worry, namely the (1) generality of worry over time and situations, the (2) intensity/excessiveness of worry, and the (3) uncontrollability of worry. A comprehensive account of the instrument's psychometric properties is included, and normative data are provided for several populations. These include both clinical and non-clinical groups. Finally, a very thorough account of the relationship between the PSWQ and other self-report measures is presented.

Tallis, Davey & Bond (Chapter 12), describe the development of the WDQ; a 25 item measure of worry content, the construction of which was guided by modular theories of information storage in long-term memory. The WDQ yields a total score, which is the sum of scores on five subscales titled (1) Relationships, (2) Lack of Confidence, (3) Aimless Future, (4) Work and (5) Financial. Scores on the WDQ are systematically associated with performance on cognitive tests. Normative data are reported for non-clinical and clinical groups and the relationship between WDQ scores and a number of other self-report measures is briefly described. The WDQ is unique, insofar as scores will reflect aspects of constructive and adaptive worry, as well as the more distressing aspects of worry.

The reader should note that the assessment of worry is considered elsewhere in this volume in more specific contexts. Vasey & Daleiden (Chapter 7) review a range of instruments and methods applicable to children. These include structured interview, self-report measures, and "experience sampling". Examples are given of each. At the other extreme of the developmental continuum, Wisocki (Chapter 10), describes the characteristics of the Worry Scale, a self-report measure for use on older adults. Normative data, in the form of means, are provided. Flett & Blankstein (Chapter 6), discuss the relationship between test-anxious worry and measures of general worry, and also describe a range of instruments for measuring the worry component of test anxiety. In a slightly different vein, Butler (Chapter 8), emphasises the role of clinical observation with respect to individuals suffering from generalised anxiety disorder (GAD). Traditional cognitive therapy techniques such as self-monitoring are recommended, in addition to several other self-report measures relevant to this clinical group.

CHAPTER 11

The Penn State Worry Questionnaire: psychometric properties and associated characteristics

Silvia Molina and T. D. Borkovec*

The need for a clinically relevant trait measure of the construct of worry became apparent toward the end of the 1980s. During the prior 10 years, interest in the experimental elucidation of the phenomenon was emerging and was reinforced by the introduction of DSM-III-R's (American Psychiatric Association, 1987) definition of generalized anxiety disorder (GAD) as centrally a problem of chronic worry. The present chapter describes an instrument designed to provide a trait assessment of pathological worry and summarizes existing data on its properties.

If a trait measure of worry were to be created, it would be important for such an instrument to evaluate (a) the *typical* tendency of the individual to worry, (b) the *excessiveness* or intensity of worry experience, and (c) the tendency to worry *in general* without restricting the topic to one or a small number of situations. These requirements also had relevance to three of the diagnostic criteria for GAD: the worry had to be chronic (6 month minimum), excessive, and generalized (not just focused on a single area of concern). Basic research on GAD over the past few years has indicated just how chronic and diffuse the worrying is in this disorder. Average duration of severe GAD in extant therapy outcome investigations is 5.5 years (Borkovec & Whisman, in press); one of the most distinguishing features of GAD relative to the other anxiety disorders is an affirmative response to the question, "Do you worry about minor things?" (Borkovec, Shadick & Hopkins, 1991); and content classification studies

*Penn State University, University Park, USA

Worrying: Perspectives on Theory, Assessment and Treatment. Edited by G.C.L. Davey and F. Tallis.
© 1994 John Wiley & Sons Ltd.

indicate that GAD worry topics are so wide-ranging that a quarter of them cannot be easily categorized, whereas virtually all of the worry topics of nonanxious people fit neatly into a small number (four) of areas (Borkovec et al., 1991).

Until 1990, two primary methods of worry assessment had been used in experimental investigations, and each had significant limitations that precluded their use as general measures of the trait of worry for either clinical or experimental research purposes. One method came from the test anxiety literature. Research in this area had empirically established the partial separateness of worry and emotionality components in anxiety. This had been accomplished by the creation of self-report questionnaires (e..g the Test Anxiety Inventory, Spielberger et al., 1980) whose items assessed both of these domains and by demonstrations of their differing relationships with other variables such as examination performance (cf. Deffenbacher, 1980) (see Flett & Blankstein, this volume, Chapter 6). As useful as these questionnaires were for their particular area, the items referred exclusively to examination situations and were not broadly developed to assess a general, pathological predisposition to worry.

The second method did attempt to measure a general tendency to worry without regard to topical areas, but it did so with merely a single question, "What percent of the day do you typically worry?" (e.g., Borkovec, Robinson, Pruzinsky & DePree, 1983). This question was sometimes supplemented by the additional query, "Do you consider worry to be a problem for you?", in order to identify people for whom worrying was distressing and whose research outcomes would have potentially greater clinical relevance. Again, although interesting information about worry emerged from the study of individuals so selected, there were disadvantages to this approach. A single item instrument is unlikely to have favorable psychometric characteristics, the amount of time spent worrying does not necessarily reflect excessiveness or high intensity of the worrying, and, as stated, the question fails to assess the diffuseness of worry because one could worry much of the day about only a single area of concern.

Tom Meyer's (1988) purpose for his master's thesis project was to develop a trait measure of worry which focused on clinically significant and pathological aspects of the process. The Penn State Worry Questionnaire (PSWQ) that he created ultimately met the previously mentioned requirements and was found to possess high degrees of reliability and validity, as will be described in this chapter. Because the PSWQ has existed in published form for only 2 years at the time of this writing, the amount of publicly available research information on its properties and uses is limited. We will review extant data based on the five published articles (Borkovec & Costello, 1993; Brown, Antony & Barlow, 1992; Brown, Moras, Zinbarg & Barlow, 1993; Davey, 1993; Meyer, Miller, Metzger & Borkovec, 1990), four conference presentations (Keortze & Burns, 1992; Ladouceur et al., 1992; Roemer, M. Borkovec, Posa & Lyonfields, 1991a; Roemer, Posa & Borkovec, 1991b) and three unpublished manuscripts (Davey, 1992; Freeston et al., 1992; Hodgson, Tallis & Davey, 1992) that we were able to locate, as well as recently collected data from our current GAD therapy outcome investigation at the Penn State project.

DEVELOPMENT OF THE PSWQ

Meyer (1988) generated 161 initial items related to worry, drawing from clinical and research experience with GAD clients and worriers, daily diaries from GAD clients, a prior cognitive–somatic anxiety inventory, and theoretical views of worry. The resulting questionnaire which asked subjects to rate each item on a five-point scale ("not at all typical" to "very typical") was administered to 337 college students and submitted to a factor analysis with oblique rotation. Seven factors emerged. Factor 1 reflected a general worry factor and accounted for the most (22.6%) variance (see Meyer et al. (1990) for item loadings). Factor 2 (4.2%) loaded on items related to physical safety and health concerns, Factor 3 (3.1%) to social evaluation, Factor 4 (2.6%) to the use of worry as a positive coping response, Factor 5 (2.1%) to depression, Factor 6 (1.7%) to concerns about future success in relationships, and Factor 7 (1.6%) to method (i.e. reverse-scored items). Because the goal was to create a trait measure of the general tendency to worry without regard to the content of specific topics, subsequent attention was focused on the first factor. It included 58 items loading .40 or greater (.30 or greater for reverse-scored items) and possessed high internal consistency (coefficient alpha = .97). A repeated process of deleting lowest loading, ambiguous or redundant items and recalculation of internal consistency resulted in the final 16 item version of the PSWQ with alpha = .93, five reverse-scored items, and a possible range of scores = 16 to 80. Table 11.1 provides the PSWQ as it is currently given at our clinical research setting. Inspection of its content indicates that the 16 items variously relate to the previously mentioned requirements for a trait measure of worry and also to crucial aspects of clinically significant worry: the generality of worry over time and situations, the intensity/excessiveness of the experience, and the uncontrollability of the process. The latter aspect has recently acquired increased clinical importance. The revised definition of GAD proposed for DSM-IV (American Psychiatric Association, 1993) now includes uncontrollability as an

Table 11.1   The Penn State Worry Questionnaire

Enter the number that best describes how typical or characteristic each item is of you, putting the number next to each item.

1	2	3	4	5
Not all typical		Somewhat typical		Very typical

—— 1. If I don't have enough time to do everything, I don't worry about it. (R)

—— 2. My worries overwhelm me.

—— 3. I don't tend to worry about things. (R)

—— 4. Many situations make me worry.

—— 5. I know I shouldn't worry about things, but I just can't help it.

—— 6. When I'm under pressure, I worry a lot.

—— 7. I am always worrying about something.

—— 8. I find it easy to dismiss worrisome thoughts. (R)

—— 9. As soon as I finish one task, I start to worry about everyghing else I have to do.

—— 10. I never worry about anything. (R)

—— 11. When there is nothing more I can do about a concern, I don't worry about it anymore. (R)

—— 12. I've been a worrier all my life.

—— 13. I notice that I have been worrying about things.

—— 14. Once I start worrying, I can't stop.

—— 15. I worry all the time.

—— 16. I worry about projects until they are all done.

(R) indicates a reverse-scored item.

additional criterion, because review of empirical research indicated that this feature may be the most distinguishing characteristic of pathological worry, especially for GAD clients (cf. Borkovec et al., 1991).

FACTOR STRUCTURE

Two investigations have factor analyzed the PSWQ and found only a single, general factor. In the Ladouceur et al. (1992) study with 196 college students, the factor accounted for 85% of the total variance. In the Brown et al. (1992) study with 396 anxiety disorder clients, it accounted for 51.1% of the variance.

RELIABILITY

Internal Consistency

The 16 item PSWQ has routinely been found to possess high internal consistency in both college samples (coefficient alphas = .92 in Davey, 1993; .91, .88, .91, and .91 in Ladouceur et al., 1992, Studies 1, 2, and 3; .94, .95, and .91 in Meyer et al., 1990, Studies 4, 5, and 6) and in a large sample of mixed anxiety disorders (alpha = .93) and GAD clients (alpha = .86) (Brown et al., 1992).

Stability

Test–retest assessments have also shown that the PSWQ is stable over time, as would be expected for a trait measure of a psychological variable, although this information has been derived solely from unselected college samples. Ladouceur et al. (1992) used a 4 week interval with a reported $r = .86$. Meyer et al. (1990) in their series of studies found varying but relatively high correlations over several time intervals: 2 week $r = .75$ (Study 4), 4 week $rs = .74$ and .93 (Studies 4 and 5), and 8–10 week $r = .92$ (Study 3).

PSWQ MEANS, STANDARD DEVIATIONS, AND CRITERION GROUP VALIDITY

Table 11.2 presents PSWQ means and standard deviations compiled from all existing data sets and categorized by particularly relevant criterion samples of individuals who have completed the questionnaire. The purpose in providing this information in this way is to (a) establish the criterion validity of the PSWQ and (b) facilitate decisions about possible cut-off scores for use in selecting worriers and nonworriers for experimental investigation and in operationally defining "clinically significant change" (cf. Jacobson & Traux, 1991) in therapy outcome investigations. A description of the characteristics of each sample is provided below.

General Samples

The General Sample category includes (a) Unselected Groups of individuals who were not chosen on the basis of any criteria (Ladouceur et al., 1992; Meyer et al., 1990) and (b) Nonanxious Selected Groups who were chosen because of a demonstrated absence of anxiety or worry.

Table 11.2 Means and standard deviations on the Penn State Worry Questionnaire by criterion groups

	n	Number of data sets	Mean	Standard deviation
General Samples				
Unselected groups	1323	9	47.65	12.99
Nonanxious selected groups	2130	9	43.81	11.32
GAD-Q screen	2056	6	44.27	11.44
ADIS-R screen	74	3	30.98	8.13
Analog Clinical Samples				
GAD by ADIS-R screen	21	2	65.77	9.60
GAD by GAD-Q screen	324	7	63.24	9.33
PTSD by questionnaire	11	1	57.40	7.30
OCD by questionnaire	12	1	54.80	12.20
Partial-GAD by GAD-Q screen	503	5	52.88	11.25
Clinical Samples				
GAD by ADIS-R screen	174	4	67.66	8.86
OCD by ADIS-R screen	50	2	60.79	14.42
Panic disorder/agoraphobia	64	1	58.30	13.65
Social phobia	54	1	53.99	15.05
Panic disorder	97	1	53.80	14.76
Simple phobia	21	1	46.98	16.99

GAD-Q: Generalized Anxiety Disorder Questionnaire; ADIS-R: Anxiety Disorder Interview Schedule—Revised; PTSD: post-traumatic stress disorder; OCD: obsessive compulsive disorder.

Although the Unselected Groups provide an estimate of worry in a general population, the vast majority of its subjects were college students; thus the data possess limited generalizability beyond that particular group. It is noteworthy that the mean for this group nearly matches the actual middle score (48) of the PSWQ.

Two methods for identifying Nonanxious Selected Groups have been used, and PSWQ data are separately presented for the groups as a whole and for each of these two subgroups. The more liberal approach (Keortze & Burns, 1992; Roemer et al., 1991a, 1991b; Meyer et al., 1990) has employed the Generalized Anxiety Disorder Questionnaire (GAD-Q), a self-report instrument whose questions cover the DSM-III-R criteria for GAD (whether worry is excessive, unrealistic, or uncontrollable; whether the worrying has been bothersome more days than not in the past 6 months; whether the worry involves more than a single topic; and whether the person often experiences at least six of 18 predominantly somatic anxiety symptoms when feeling anxious). Data collected from subjects so selected have also involved only college student samples. Research has shown that no subject failing to meet diagnostic criteria on the GAD-Q will be found diagnosable by experienced clinical assessors using the Anxiety Disorders Interview Schedule—Revised (ADIS-R; DiNardo & Barlow, 1988), whereas 74–80% of people who meet GAD criteria on this questionnaire will be diagnosed GAD by the interview (Roemer et al., 1991b). Although subjects cleared of the presence of GAD by GAD-Q are thus unlikely to have extensive problems with worry, they nonetheless could have other diagnosable anxiety disorders not covered by the questionnaire; 13.3% of such subjects in the Roemer et al. (1991b) study did in fact have other anxiety disorders diagnosed in interview. This fact places some restriction on the "nonanxious" characterization of this control group.

Full diagnostic interviewing by experienced assessors using the ADIS-R has been the more conservative approach, insuring that control subjects not only fail to meet GAD criteria but also do not have any other diagnosable anxiety or mood disorder. Thus, this particular Nonanxious Selected Group would be the least likely to have significant worry or anxiety problems and would represent the best defined "nonanxious" comparison condition. All 74 nonanxious subjects in the ADIS-Screened group came from therapy outcome investigations of GAD clients (Borkovec & Inz, 1990; Brown et al., 1992; Penn State current project), and these control subjects were matched to the clients on a variety of demographic variables. Thus, they also represent the best available general community sample.

Given the above observations about the General Samples, it is not surprising that the mean for the Unselected Groups is significantly higher than that of the Nonanxious Selected Groups, $t(3451) = 14.77$, $p < .001$, and within the latter groups, the mean for subjects selected by questionnaire is significantly higher than that of the ADIS-screened subjects, $t(2129) = 9.90$, $p < .001$.

Analog Clinical Samples

The Analog Clinical Sample category provides data on subjects (all college students) who have met full or partial criteria for GAD (Meyer et al., 1990; Roemer et al., 1991a, 1991b; Keortze & Burns, 1992). The partial-GAD groups are of interest because they represent conservative comparison conditions wherein anxiety is present but not all requirements for GAD diagnosis are met. For further comparison purposes, we also provide data from two papers (Keortze & Burns, 1992; Meyer et al., 1990, Study 7) in which subjects meeting criteria for other anxiety disorders (post traumatic stress disorder (PTSD) and obsessive compulsive disorder (OCD)) had been included. Although the majority of subjects were selected for these various diagnostic groups by questionnaire methods, a subgroup of 21 subjects did receive GAD diagnoses on the basis of ADIS-R interview (Roemer et al., 1991b), and their data are separately presented. The highest PSWQ mean is found for this latter, conservatively defined GAD group, followed closely and nonsignificantly by GAD subjects selected by questionnaire. The PTSD, OCD, and partial-GAD groups had means significantly lower than both GAD groups, $ts \geq 2.05$ and $d.f. \geq 31$, and did not differ significantly from each other. On the basis of these analog samples, then, the PSWQ has clear criterion validity.

Clinical Samples

Finally, Table 11.2 presents data from actual clinical samples involving clients who were seeking treatment for their anxiety problems, all of whom were diagnosed by ADIS-R interviews (Borkovec & Costello, 1993; Brown et al., 1992, 1993; Penn State current project). GAD and OCD data are based on composites from multiple studies, whereas the scores for the remaining disorders are taken from a single study (Brown et al., 1992). The composite GAD groups had the highest PSWQ mean, and they differed significantly from the composite OCD groups which had the next highest mean, $t(224) = 4.14$, $p < .001$. The Brown et al. (1992) study had already reported the significantly greater PSWQ scores of their GAD sample compared to all of the other anxiety disorder groups participating in their investigation. These data provide even stronger support for the criterion validity of the PSWQ, given the wide range of carefully diagnosed clinical anxiety disorder groups employed.

GENDER DIFFERENCES

Investigators have not routinely tested for gender effects on the PSWQ. When they have done so, in unselected samples women sometimes scored significantly higher than men (Meyer et al., 1990, Studies 2 and 4) and sometimes not (Meyer et al., 1990, Studies 5 and 6). In samples selected for the diagnosed presence of GAD, however, no gender difference has been found, neither among analog GAD subjects (Meyer et al., 1990, Study 7) nor among GAD clients (Borkovec & Inz, 1990; Brown et al., 1992; Meyer et al., 1990, Study 8). It is interesting to note that women tend to be represented more frequently in therapy outcome studies of clinical GAD (65%, Borkovec & Whisman, in press). Thus, while worry, especially severe and chronic worry, may be somewhat more prevalent among women, all clients who meet criteria for GAD show the same degree of worry as assessed by the PSWQ, irrespective of gender.

RELATIONSHIP TO OTHER WORRY MEASURES

Among unselected student samples, the PSWQ has been found to correlate significantly with the single item question about the percentage of the day spent worrying ($rs = .64$, Meyer et al., 1990; .65 and .70, Ladouceur et al., 1992), with Davey's (1992) measure of the frequency of worrying about a past traumatic event, and with the amount of worry over tests, the number of worrisome topics listed, and the frequency of worrying about topics of current concern (Meyer et al., 1990). In a clinical GAD sample, however, the PSWQ was unrelated to reported percentage of the day spent worrying (Brown et al., 1992).

The PSWQ has also been found to correlate significantly with two recently developed, alternative questionnaires for assessing worry. Both were deliberately created to measure worry in specific content domains. The Student Worry Scale (SWS; Davey, Hampton, Farrell & Davidson, 1992) was based on listings of personal worrisome topics provided by 52 college students. Inspection of the listing by the authors led to the use of 10 content items (e.g. health worries, personal relationships, academic demands) that were to be rated on a scale representing how much the respondent worried about that topic. The Worry Domains Questionnaire (WDQ; Tallis, Eysenck & Mathews, 1992) was specifically designed to measure nonpathological worry and was initially based on listings of 155 worrisome topics provided by 71 general community respondents. Ninety-five further respondents rated each item on scales reflecting frequency of worrying about each topic and how upsetting each topic was for them. A cluster analysis approach on collapsed ratings followed by coherence ratings of clusters by judges led to the selection of five items for each of six clusters of semantic content (e.g. relationships, lack of confidence, aimless future), to be rated for how much the subject worries about each item. (See Tallis et al., this volume, Chapter 12.)

Because the PSWQ was designed as a trait measure of the general predisposition to engage in pathological worry irrespective of worry content whereas the other two questionnaires were created to tap into normal worry based on specific content areas, significant though only moderately high correlations would be expected. Indeed, in an unselected college sample, the correlation between the PSWQ and the SWS was $r = .59$, and that between the PSWQ and the WDQ was $r = .67$ ($n = 136$, Davey, 1992).

RELATIONSHIP TO ANXIETY AND DEPRESSION

In unselected, predominantly student samples, the highest correlations between the PSWQ and measures of psychological experience other than worry have been found with instruments assessing anxiety (range of rs = .40 to .74). These have included the trait version (and with smaller correlation, the state version) of Spielberger et al.'s (1983) State–Trait Anxiety Inventory (STAI) (Meyer et al., 1990; Davey, 1992), Beck, Epstein, Brown & Steer's (1988) Beck Anxiety Inventory (Ladouceur et al., 1992), Schwartz, Davidson & Goleman's (1978) Cognitive Somatic Anxiety Questionnaire (CSAQ, total score as well as cognitive and somatic subscales) (Meyer et al., 1990), and the worry and emotionality subscales of Spielberger et al.'s (1980) Test Anxiety Inventory (TAI) (Meyer et al., 1990). Because worry is hypothetically a cognitive aspect of anxiety, significant but moderate correlations with such measures would be expected. Indeed, the cognitive subscale of the CSAQ was significantly more related to the PSWQ than the somatic subscale, providing further discriminant and convergent validity. This was not the case with the worry and emotionality subscales of the TAI, although the absence of predicted relationships was due to problems inherent in the TAI (cf. Meyer et al., 1990). It is also important to note that even the highest correlations of the PSWQ with other anxiety measures (.74 with STAI–Trait) indicates only 50% shared variance, suggesting that worry is tapping a somewhat separate construct.

Only one study has reported the relationship between PSWQ and depression in a student group (Meyer et al., 1990): The Beck Depression Inventory (BDI; Beck et al., 1961) showed a lower correlation with the PSWQ (r = .36) than has been typical of PSWQ's relationships to the anxiety measures.

The empirical picture is quite different when looking at interrelationships among PSWQ, anxiety, and depression in client samples. Worry is clearly a separate construct when clinically severe anxiety, especially GAD, is present. In the clinical GAD sample of 13 clients in Meyer et al. (1990) Study 8, PSWQ did not correlate significantly with any of five commonly used measures (STAI-Trait, Zung (1975) Self-Rating for Anxiety, Hamilton (1959) Anxiety Rating Scale, BDI, and Hamilton (1960) Rating Scale for Depression), even though eight of the 10 possible correlations among the latter measures were significant. For the purpose of this chapter, we reanalyzed these data with the inclusion of the entire sample of 55 clients. Only the STAI was even moderately associated (r = .44) with the PSWQ, whereas seven of the 10 interrelationships among the other measures were significant. Within an entire sample of 436 mixed anxiety disorder clients in the Brown et al. (1992) study, the PSWQ correlated significantly with Lovibond's (1983) Self-Analysis Questionnaire subscales of Tension (.54), Anxiety (.35), and Depression (.39) as well as with the number of additional anxiety disorder diagnoses received beyond the principal diagnosis. However, within the subsample of 47 GAD clients alone, only the relationship to the Tension measure was significant (.36), the correlation with the number of additional diagnoses was marginally significant, and the PSWQ did not correlate with either the Hamilton Anxiety or Depression Scales.

RELATIONSHIP TO OBSESSIVE THINKING

The possibility that worry is present to some extent in all anxiety disorders (Barlow, 1988) is particularly salient when examining obsessive compulsive disorder. OCD is characterized by persistent, intrusive, unpleasant thoughts, images, or urges, and/or ritualistic compulsions that are subjectively distressing and interfere with the individual's daily functioning (American Psychiatric Association, 1987). Thus, excessive, uncontrollable cognitive process is not only evident in GAD but in OCD as well (cf. Turner, Beidel & Stanley, 1992).

Despite the possible overlap between worry and obsessional thinking, Turner et al. (1992) reported in their review of relevant literature that the content of these two processes is distinct. GAD clients typically report concerns with normal life experiences (Sanderson & Barlow, 1986) and their cognitive activity is predominantly conceptual as opposed to imaginal (Borkovec et al., 1991). OCD clients, on the other hand, typically report intrusive, abhorrent thoughts or images and aggressive impulses (Turner et al., 1992).

Although descriptive literature exists for worry and obsessions, only two empirical investigations have directly compared worry as measured by the PSWQ and obsessions as measured by the Maudsley Obsessive Compulsive Inventory (MOCI; Hodgson & Rachman, 1977), a 30 item questionnaire designed to assess the frequency of OCD symptoms, or the Padua Inventory (Sanavio, 1988), a 60 item self-report instrument which measures obsessions and compulsions. Brown et al. (1993) correlated the PSWQ and the four subscales of the MOCI among 423 anxiety disorder clients and 32 nonanxious subjects. The PSWQ was significantly more related to Doubting and Checking than it was to Repetition or Washing, suggesting some overlap between trait worry and the obsessional features of OCD. However, the Doubting and Checking subscales were significantly more associated with each other than with the PSWQ, indicating reliable discrimination between obsessional cognitive process and trait worry. Somewhat similar results emerged from Freeston et al.'s (1992) study of 145 hospital waiting-room subjects who showed a significantly greater correlation of the PSWQ with the Mental Control subscale (e.g. having intrusive thoughts, inventing doubts and problems) of the Padua Inventory than with its Checking, Impulses, and Contamination subscales. (See Brown, Dowdell, Côté & Barlow, this volume, Chapter 9).

RELATIONSHIP TO EMOTIONAL CONTROL AND COPING STRATEGIES

A few investigations have examined the sense of emotional control and the types of coping strategies associated with varying degrees of trait worry as measured by the PSWQ.

Emotional Control

The PSWQ predicted at a low but significant level the frequency of worrying about past traumas among college students, and it also predicted at a moderate level how much anxiety was experienced when worrying about the event; the more content-specific and less clinically relevant WDQ did not (Davey, 1992). No relationship existed between either the PSWQ or the WDQ and feeling more in control or thinking that worrying about the event helped to solve problems. Rather, the degree to which effective problem-solving was felt to occur during worry was a function of the degree of subjective and objective potential controllability of the event.

Within mixed clinical anxiety disorder groups, the PSWQ was moderately associated with a lower sense of emotional control on the Rapee, Craske & Barlow (1989) Emotional Control Questionnaire (Brown et al., 1992). Indeed, analog GAD groups have also been found to score significantly lower (less control) on this questionnaire than have either partial-GAD or non-GAD groups (Roemer et al., 1991a).

Coping Strategies

Among unselected college students, regression analyses revealed that the PSWQ predicted the degree of negative mood experienced after receiving an examination grade. It also predicted the use of the coping styles of self-blame, wishful thinking and dread, and problem avoidance in response to this feedback, as assessed by 12 factor-analytically derived scales (Miller & Thayer, 1991) from Lazarus & Folkman's (1984) Ways of Coping Scale. These relationships emerged independently of actual examination score (Meyer et al., 1990, Study 5). Worry was unrelated to the other nine, mostly problem focused, constructive, and adaptive styles (action planning, looking for the positive, reflection, feeling expression, information seeking and analysis, externalizing to others, ignoring, and tension reduction). Perhaps the most illuminating data on worry and coping has come from Davey's (1993) earlier mentioned comparisons of the PSWQ, SWS, and WDQ. By simple correlation, the PSWQ was found to relate at low but significant levels to avoidance coping and emotional discharge from the Health and Daily Living Form (Moos, Cronkite, Billings & Finney, 1986) and monitoring and the monitoring/blunting difference from Miller's (1987) Behavioral Style Scale. The other two content-specific, "normal worry" questionnaires similarly correlated with the same scales except monitoring/blunting difference. More importantly, when the contribution of trait anxiety was removed by partial correlation, PSWQ scores were no longer associated with any coping style, whereas SWS (with active behavioral coping) and WDQ (with active coping and avoidance coping) continued to predict the use of some adaptive strategies. Davey (1993) argued that because the PSWQ was designed to assess pathological worry and is thus less independent of anxiety, worry so measured is less likely to relate to constructive, problem-focused strategies. The nonpathological worry instruments, on the other hand, would more likely be predictive of the use of such methods.

RELATIONSHIP TO SELF AND SELF-EVALUATIVE CHARACTERISTICS

There appears to be a very strong and intimate link between trait worry and social evaluation. Social phobia is the most frequent additional diagnosis among principal GAD clients; worry correlates most highly with social and social evaluative items of the fear survey schedule; and worry is mostly inner speech, and speech is fundamentally a social communication device (see Chapter 1, by Borkovec, this volume). It would be expected, then, that a trait measure of worry would relate to aspects of self-perception and to social evaluative concerns. This has been the case. In the Meyer et al. (1990) studies of college student samples, high scores on the PSWQ have been found to be associated with (a) high degrees of social anxiety and public and private self-consciousness on the Fenigstein, Scheier & Buss (1975) Self-Consciousness Scale (a replicated effect in the Ladouceur et al., 1992) study, (b) high perfectionism (Burns, 1980), (c) elevated scores on the Self-Handicapping Scale (i.e. claims that some uncontrollable internal factor interferes with performance; Jones & Rhodewalt, 1982), and in separate samples (d) low scores on Harris & Snyder's (1986) Self-Esteem Certainty Index and Rosenberg's (1979) Self-Esteem Inventory. Also in two separate samples in the Meyer et al. (1990) investigation, Locus of Control (Rotter, 1966) bore no relationship to the PSWQ. Significantly for psychometric properties, the PSWQ did not correlate with the Marlowe–Crowne Social Desirability Scale ($r(163) = -.09$; Crowne & Marlowe, 1964). This is somewhat remarkable, given that worriers show evidence of considerable fear of other people's opinions, yet they do not try to present a favorable impression when reporting on their worrying.

The PSWQ has not been associated with two other measures relevant to the self and social situations (Meyer et al., 1990). High worriers are not characterized by a lack of personal or social identity (Hogan & Cheek, 1983), nor do they report a lessened ability to adapt their behavior to changing interpersonal situations on Paulhus & Martin's (1988) Battery of Interpersonal Capabilities.

RELATIONSHIP TO OTHER PSYCHOLOGICAL CHARACTERISTICS

The Meyer et al. (1990) investigation also examined the relationship of the PSWQ to a variety of other features reflective of the psychological experience of worriers, some of which are less obviously deducible from current theoretical views of worry. On Zuckerman's (1979) Sensation Seeking Scale (Form V), low but significant associations were found that characterized the high worrier as one who is a low thrill seeker and has a high degree of boredom susceptibility, although general experience seeking and disinhibition were not discriminating. Worriers are also excessively time urgent with high nervous energy (Landy, Rastegary, Thayer & Colvin's (1991) Time Urgency Scale). They are not characterized by a preference for, or enjoyment of, cognitive tasks (Cacioppo, Petty & Kao's (1984) Need for Cognition), a tendency to make decisions based on rational information (Burns' (1986) Objectivism Scale), or motivation to be in control of important daily events (Burger & Cooper's (1979) Desire for Control Scale). Ladouceur et al. (1992), however, did find the PSWQ to be significantly associated with irrational beliefs (Malouff & Schutte's (1986) Beliefs Scale).

It also appears that worry is related to both concurrent and future (4 week) psychological and physical health status. Hodgson et al. (1992)

found both the PSWQ and the WDQ to correlate significantly with each construct (the General Health Questionnaire for psychological complaint (Goldberg, 1972) and the Common Health Problems Questionnaire devised by the authors to assess frequency of occurrence of common illnesses) and at both time periods. A series of hierarchical multiple regressions, however, found that the relationships involving the PSWQ were largely due to the contribution of trait anxiety. (See Tallis et al., this volume, Chapter 12.)

RESPONSIVENESS TO THERAPY

Only one therapy outcome investigation (Borkovec & Costello, 1993) has assessed the impact of treatment on the PSWQ. Cognitive behavioural therapy produced significantly greater PSWQ improvement from pretherapy to post-therapy relative to a nondirective therapy condition; applied relaxation fell close to the former condition but was nonsignificantly different from either of the other two groups. At one-year follow-up, further gains were seen in the cognitive behavioral group, no further change occurred for applied relaxation, and the change from pre-therapy to follow-up was nonsignificant for the nondirective condition.

SUMMARY AND CONCLUSIONS

The Penn State Worry questionnaire appears to be an excellent self-report instrument for the trait assessment of clinically significant, pathological worry. Its 16 items provide a measurement of the tendency of an individual to engage in excessive, generalized, and uncontrollable worry and are not influenced by social desirability. Reliability has been shown to be high in terms of both internal consistency and test–retest stability. The PSWQ significantly distinguishes people meeting criteria for GAD from nonanxious controls and each of the other anxiety disorders; this is true with both analog and clinical samples. Gender differences favor higher PSWQ scores and greater frequency of GAD diagnosis among women, although in clinical GAD samples no gender effect is observed in PSWQ scores. The instrument bears a moderate relationship to nonpathological and content-specific worry questionnaires. Anxiety measures correlate most highly with the PSWQ among a variety of evaluated psychological inventories in general samples, college student groups, and mixed anxiety disorders, but in GAD it shows a general independence from commonly used measures of anxiety and depression. Poor emotional control and emotion focused coping are characteristics of high scorers on the PSWQ, possibly due to their commonly high levels of trait anxiety. Low self-esteem, per-fectionism, time urgency, concern with social evaluation, and poor psy-chological and physical health, among other features, typify the worrier. Among GAD clients, cognitive behavioral therapy appears to be specifi-cally effective for reducing chronic worry as measured by the PSWQ.

Much has been learned about worry in the past decade. The present volume is a testament to that fact. Worry is a very important phenomenon in both its normal and pathological forms, and it is hoped that the recent availability of valid and reliable instruments for its assessment, like the PSWQ, will facilitate future research as a selection device and as an out-come measure of relevance to GAD as well as all of the other anxiety disorders.

ACKNOWLEDGEMENT

Preparation of this chapter was supported in part by Grant MH-39172 to the second author from the National Institute of Mental Health.

REFERENCES

American Psychiatric Association. (1987). *Diagnostic and Statistical Manual of Mental Disorders*, 3rd edn—Rev. Washington, DC: American Psychiatric Association.

American Psychiatric Association. (1993). *DSM-IV Draft Criteria*. Washington, DC.

Barlow, D.H. (1988). *Anxiety and its Disorders: The Nature and Treatment of Anxiety and Panic*. New York: Guilford Press.

Beck, A.T., Epstein, N., Brown, G. & Steer, R.A. (1988). An inventory for measur-ing clinical anxiety: Psychometric properties. *Journal of Consulting and Clinical Psychology*, **56**, 893–897.

Beck, A.T., Ward, C.H., Mendelson, M., Mock, J. & Erbaugh, J. (1961). An invent-ory for measuring depression. *Archives of General Psychiatry*, **4**, 561–571.

Borkovec, T.D. & Costello, E. (1993). Efficacy of applied relaxation and cognitive behavioral therapy in the treatment of generalized anxiety disorder. *Journal of Consulting and Clinical Psychology*, **61**, 611–619.

Borkovec, T.D. & Inz, J. (1990). The nature of worry in generalized anxiety disor-der. A predominance of thought activity. *Behaviour Research and Therapy*, **28**, 153–158.

Borkovec, T.D., Robinson, E., Pruzinsky, T. & DePree, J.A. (1983). Preliminary exploration of worry: Some characteristics and processes. *Behaviour Research and Therapy*, **21**, 9–16.

Borkovec, T.D., Shadick, R. & Hopkins, M. (1991). The nature of normal versus pathological worry. In R. Rapee & D.H. Barlow (Eds.), *Chronic Anxiety and Generalized Anxiety Disorder*. New York: Guilford Press.

Borkovec, T.D. & Whisman, M.A. (in press). Psychosocial treatment for gener-alized anxiety disorder. In M. Mavissakalian & R. Prien (Eds.), *Anxiety Disor-*

ders: Psychological and Pharmacological Treatments. Washington, DC: American Psychiatric Association.

Brown, T.A., Antony, M.M. & Barlow, D.H. (1992). Psychometric properties of the Penn State Worry Questionnaire in a clinical anxiety disorders sample. *Behaviour Research and Therapy*, **30**, 33–37.

Brown, T.A., Moras, K., Zinbarg, R.E. & Barlow, D.H. (1993). Diagnostic and symptom distinguishability of obsessive–compulsive disorder and generalized anxiety disorder. *Behavior Therapy*, **24**, 227–240.

Burger, J.M. & Cooper, H.M. (1979). The desirability of control. *Motivation and Emotion*, **3**, 381–393.

Burns, D.D. (1980). The perfectionist's script for self-defeat. *Psychology Today*, **14**, 34–52.

Cacioppo, J.T., Petty, R.E. & Kao, C.F. (1984). The efficient assessment of need for cognition. *Journal of Personality Assessment*, **48**, 306–307.

Crowne, D.P. & Marlowe, D. (1964). *The Approval Motive: Studies in Evaluative Dependence.* New York: Wiley.

Davey, G.C.L. (1992). Trait and situational factors predicting worrying about significant life stressors. Unpublished manuscript.

Davey, G.C.L. (1993). A comparison of three worry questionnaires. *Behaviour Research and Therapy*, **31**, 51–56.

Davey, G.C.L., Hampton, J., Farrell, J. & Davidson, S. (1992). Some characteristics of worrying: Evidence for worrying and anxiety as separate constructs. *Personality and Individual Differences*, **13**, 133–147.

Deffenbacher, J.L. (1980). Worry and emotionality in test anxiety. In I.G. Sarason (Ed.), *Test Anxiety: Theory, Research, and Applications*, pp. 111–128. Hillsdale, NJ: Erlbaum.

DiNardo, P.A. & Barlow, D.H. (1988). *Anxiety Disorders Interview Schedule—Revised (ADIS-R).* Albany: Center for Stress and Anxiety Disorders.

Fenigstein, A., Scheier, M.F. & Buss, A.H. (1975). Public and private self-consciousness: Assessment and theory. *Journal of Consulting and Clinical Psychology*, **43**, 522–527.

Freeston, M.H., Ladouceur, R., Rheaume, J., Letarte, H., Gagnon, F. & Thibodeau, N. (1992, November). Self-report of obsessions and worry. Paper presented at the Annual Convention of the Association for the Advancement of Behavior Therapy, Boston, Massachusetts.

Goldberg, D.P. (1972). *The Detection of Psychiatric Illness by Questionnaire.* Oxford University Press: New York.

Hamilton, M. (1959). The assessment of anxiety states by rating. *British Journal of Medical Psychology*, **32**, 50–55.

Hamilton, M. (1960). A rating scale for depression. *Journal of Neurology, Neurosurgery and Psychiatry*, **23**, 56–62.

Harris, R.N. & Snyder, C.R. (1986). The role of uncertain self-esteem in self-handicapping. *Journal of Personality and Social Psychology*, **51**, 451–458.

Hodgson, R.J. & Rachman, S. (1977). Obsessive–compulsive complaints. *Behaviour Research and Therapy*, **15**, 389–395.

Hodgson, S., Tallis, F. & Davey, G.C.L. (1992). Worried sick: The relationship between worrying and psychological and physical health status. Unpublished manuscript.

Hogan, R. & Cheek, J.M. (1983). Identity, authenticity, and maturity. In T.R. Sarbin & K.E. Scheibe (Eds.), *Studies in Social Identity*, pp. 339–357. New York: Praeger.

Jacobson, N.S. & Traux, P. (1991). Clinical significance approach to defining meaningful change in psychotherapy. *Journal of Consulting and Clinical Psychology*, **59**, 12–19.

Jones, E.E. & Rhodewalt, F. (1982). Self-handicapping scale. Unpublished manuscript. Princeton University.

Keortze, S.G. & Burns, G.L. (1992, November). The relation between worry, generalized anxiety disorder, and obsessive compulsive disorder. Paper presented at the Annual Convention of the Association for Advancement of Behavior Therapy, Boston, Massachusetts.

Ladouceur, R., Freeston, M.H., Dumont, J., Letarte, H., Rheaume, J., Thibodeau, N. & Gagnon, F. (1992, June). The Penn State Worry Questionnaire: Psychometric properties of a French Translation. Paper presented at the Annual Convention of the Canadian Psychological Association, Quebec City, Canada.

Landy, F.J., Rastegary, H., Thayer, J. & Colvin, C. (1991). Time urgency: The construct and its measurement. *Journal of Applied Psychology*, **76**, 644–657.

Lazarus, R.S. & Folkman, S. (1984). *Stress, Appraisal and Coping*, New York: Springer.

Lovibond, S.H. (1983, May). The nature and measurement of anxiety, stress, and depression. Paper presented at the Annual Convention of the Australian Psychological Society, University of Western Australia.

Malouff, J.M. & Schutte, N.S. (1986). Development and validation of a measure of irrational belief. *Journal of Consulting and Clinical Psychology*, **54**, 860–862.

Meyer, T.J. (1988). Development of a screening questionnaire to identify levels of chronic worry. Unpublished master's thesis, Penn State University, University Park, PA.

Meyer, T.J., Miller, M.L., Metzger, R.L. & Borkovec, T.D. (1990). Development and validation of the Penn State Worry Questionnaire. *Behaviour Research and Therapy*, **28**, 487–495.

Miller, M.L. & Thayer, J.F. (1991). Referent cognitions theory, coping theory, and affective reactions to success and failure: Toward synthesis. Manuscript under review.

Miller, S.M. (1987). Monitoring and blunting: Validation of a questionnaire to assess styles of information-seeking under threat. *Journal of Personality and Social Psychology*, **52**, 345–353.

Moos, L.H., Cronkite, R.C., Billings, A. & Finney, J.W. (1986). *Health and Daily Living Form*. Social Ecology Laboratory, Veterans Administration of Stanford University Medical Centers.

Paulhus, D.L. & Martin, C.L. (1988). Functional flexibility: A new conception of interpersonal flexibility. *Journal of Personality and Social Psychology*, **55**, 88–101.

Rapee, R.M., Craske, M.G. & Barlow, D.H. (1989, November). The Emotional Control Questionnaire. Paper presented at the Annual Convention of the Association for Advancement of Behavior Therapy, Washington, D.C.

Roemer, L., Borkovec, M., Posa, S., & Lyonfields, J. (1991a, November). Generalized anxiety disorder in an analogue population: The role of past trauma. Paper presented at the Annual Convention of the Association for the Advancement of Behavior Therapy, New York.

Roemer, L., Posa, S. & Borkovec, T.D. (1991b, November). A self-report measure of generalized anxiety disorder. Paper presented at the Annual Convention of the Association for the Advancement of Behavior Therapy, New York, New York.

Rosenberg, M. (1979). *Conceiving the Self*. New York: Basic Books.

Rotter, J.B. (1966). Generalized expectancies for internal versus external control of reinforcement. *Psychological Monographs, 80*, 1.

Sanavio, E. (1988). Obsessions and compulsions: The Padua Inventory. *Behaviour Research and Therapy, 26*, 169–177.

Sanderson, W.C. & Barlow, D.H. (1986, November). Domains of worry within the proposed DSM-III Revised generalized anxiety disorder category: Reliability and description. Paper presented at the Annual Convention of the Association for the Advancement of Behavior Therapy, Chicago.

Schwartz, G.E., Davidson, R.J. & Goleman, D.J. (1978). Patterning of cognitive and somatic processes in the self-regulation of anxiety: Effects of meditation versus exercise. *Psychosomatic Medicine, 40*, 321–328.

Spielberger, C.D., Gonzalez, H.P., Taylor, C.J., Anton, W.D., Algaze, B., Ross, G.R. & Westberry, L.G. (1980). *Preliminary Professional Manual for the Test Anxiety Inventory ("Test Attitude Inventory"): TAI.* Palo Alto, Calif.: Consulting Psychologists Press.

Spielberger, C.D., Gorsuch, R.L., Lushene, R., Vagg, P.R. & Jacobs, G.A. (1983). *Manual for the State-Trait Anxiety Inventory (Form Y) ("Self-Evaluation Questionnaire").* Palo Alto, Calif.: Consulting Psychological Press.

Tallis, F., Eysenck, M. & Mathews, A. (1991). Elevated evidence requirements and worry. *Personality and Individual Differences, 12*, 21–27.

Turner, S.M., Beidel, D.C. & Stanley, M.A. (1992). Are obsessional thoughts and worry different cognitive phenomena? *Clinical Psychology Review, 12*, 257–270.

Zuckerman, M. (1979). *Sensation Seeking: Beyond the Optimal Level of Arousal.* Hillsdale, NJ: Erlbaum.

Zung, W.W.K. (1975). A rating instrument for anxiety disorders. *Psychosomatics, 12*, 371–379.

CHAPTER 12   The Worry Domains Questionnaire

Frank Tallis, Graham C. L. Davey†
and Alyson Bond‡*

CONTENT BASED MEASURES OF WORRY

Worry is a construct with several parameters. For example, intensity, duration and intrusivity are all legitimate targets for a self-report measure;
however, two indices in particular appear to have been favoured above
others to date. These are frequency, that is, how often an individual
engages in worry, and content, namely, what the individual worries about.
The Penn State Worry Questionnaire (PSWQ; Meyer, Miller, Metzger &
Borkovec, 1990; see Molina & Borkovec, Chapter 11, this volume) is principally an example of the former; the Worry Domains Questionnaire
(WDQ; Tallis, Eysenck & Mathews, 1992), on the other hand, is principally
an example of the latter. Although a crude distinction can be made between
frequency and content measures it should be noted that there is a considerable degree of overlap, in that most content measures request respondents
to endorse items with respect to how often they are experienced.

The investigation of worry content has a long tradition. Indeed, initial
investigations preceded the modern worry literature (e.g. Borkovec,
Robinson, Pruzinsky & DePree, 1983), the test anxiety literature (Liebert
& Morris, 1967), and the historically important work of Janis (1958). As
early as 1939, Pinter & Lev had produced a children's "Worry Inventory"
which was essentially content based. It contains a comprehensive range
of items, from the pedestrian ("losing your fountain pen") to the exotic
("witches"). The authors imposed an arbitrary classification scheme on
their data (Pinter & Lev, 1940) and items were grouped under several
headings. Most, if not all, are as relevant today as they were in the 1930s,
e.g. "School", "Family", "Economic", "Personal health and well being",
"Social adequacy".

*Charter Nightingale Hospital, London. †The City University, London. ‡Institute of Psychiatry, London,
UK

Worrying: Perspectives on Theory, Assessment and Treatment. Edited by G.C.L. Davey and F. Tallis.
© 1994 John Wiley & Sons Ltd.

The division of content questionnaires into spheres or domains is a central feature of this kind of measurement. For example, Simon & Ward (1976) developed a questionnaire which is designed to ascertain the frequency and intensity of children's worries and items are grouped under headings such as "School" or "Imagination and animals". More recently, Wisocki (1988; see Wisocki, Chapter 10, this volume), has developed a "Worry Scale" for use on elderly populations which has three clear domains: "Finances", "Health", and "Social conditions". It is interesting to note that some of the concerns expressed by Pinter & Lev's fifth and sixth grade children in the 1930s resonate with the concerns expressed by Wisocki's senior citizens in the 1980s, suggesting remarkable stability with respect to the focus of some worry domains.

Although worry items are readily grouped together into semantically cohesive domains, this cohesion may have more than just aesthetic significance. Eysenck (1984) postulated the existence of organized clusters of worry related information in long-term memory (LTM). He suggested that the important determinant of how often and for how long an individual experiences worry is the number and structure of worry clusters. The clustering of information in LTM is supported by numerous theoretical accounts acknowledging the importance of modular storage (e.g. Collins & Loftus, 1975; Bower, 1981). Moreover, the related concept of schemas, (essentially organised information in LTM) has had a profound influence on theoretical models of psychopathology and subsequently clinical practice (Beck, 1976; Kovacs & Beck, 1978).

The WDQ is perhaps different from other content measures in that the procedures employed during its development were strongly influenced by a particular cognitive theory of worry, namely the storage characteristics theory proposed by Eysenck (1984). However, it should be noted that the WDQ can be used as a face valid measure of worry independent of theoretical orientation. In the following, the development of the questionnaire will be described, and normative data reported. Information on the relationship between the WDQ and other measures is also provided.

THE DEVELOPMENT OF THE WDQ

A community sample were requested to volunteer their worries. These worry items were incorporated into a 155 item General Worry Questionnaire (GWQ) on which members of a further community sample were requested to rate items on 0–8 point scales with respect to their frequency of occurrence and unpleasantness. Frequency and intensity (unpleasantness) ratings were then subject to separate cluster analyses. The distance measure command selected to cluster cases was squared euclidean, while the method command specifying the type of cluster linkage was average linkage between groups. Although factor analysis might have been employed to group data, cluster analysis was selected for theoretical reasons. The worry structures proposed by Eysenck are reflected more closely in the products of cluster analysis, where a more direct correspondence between mathematical clusters and modular storage is achieved.

Cluster selection was determined according to a set of arbitrary mathematical rules and the degree to which independent judges rated resulting clusters as semantically cohesive. The reader is referred to Tallis et al. (1992) for further details. Both frequency and intensity clusters were extremely similar in content and could be placed under the following domain headings: (D1) Relationships, (D2) Lack of Confidence, (D3) Aimless Future, (D4) Work, (D5) Financial, and (D6) Socio-political. The five most representative items for each domain (i.e. the most commonly endorsed on the GWQ) were selected for inclusion on the WDQ. Domain (6), Socio-political, was omitted from the final version of the questionnaire. This contained items such as, I worry "That there are starving millions in the third world while food mountains exist elsewhere" and I worry "That human rights are being violated". Clearly, items such as these are associated with a considerable social desirability bias. It is extremely difficult for respondents to say that this type of item is not worrying.

The 25 items finally selected for inclusion on the WDQ were randomly ordered. Respondents are requested to tick one of five boxes for each item, reflecting amount of worry. These are headed: "Not at all" (scoring 0), "A little" (1), "Moderately" (2), "Quite a bit" (3), and "Extremely" (4). These headings are psychometrically sound and discriminative (cf. McNair, Lorr & Dropplemann, 1971). The final version of the WDQ is shown in Figure 12.1.

NORMATIVE DATA

In the following, normative data are reported for non-clinical and clinical populations. The non-clinical respondents are roughly divisible into two groups: those undertaking undergraduate courses in higher education and those in full time work. The student sample comprises mainly undergraduate psychology students and medical students. The working sample contains a broad range of individuals, both professional and non-professional, skilled and unskilled. All the data were collected over a period of approximately 2 years. The clinical normative data are for two

Worry Questionnaire

Please tick an appropriate box to show how much you **WORRY** *about the following:*

I worry . . .	*Not at all*	*A little*	*Moder- ately*	*Quite a bit*	*Extremly*
1. that my money will run out	❏	❏	❏	❏	❏
2. that I cannot be assertive or express my opinions	❏	❏	❏	❏	❏
3. that my future job prospects are not good	❏	❏	❏	❏	❏
4. that my family will be angry with me or disapprove of something that I do	❏	❏	❏	❏	❏
5. that I'll never achieve my ambitions	❏	❏	❏	❏	❏
6. that I will no keep my workload up to date	❏	❏	❏	❏	❏
7. that financial problems will restrict holidays and travel	❏	❏	❏	❏	❏
8. that I have no concentration	❏	❏	❏	❏	❏
9. that I am not able to afford things	❏	❏	❏	❏	❏
10. that I feel insecure	❏	❏	❏	❏	❏
11. that I can't afford to pay bills	❏	❏	❏	❏	❏
12. that my living conditions are inadequate	❏	❏	❏	❏	❏
13. that life may have no purpose	❏	❏	❏	❏	❏
14. that I don't work hard enough	❏	❏	❏	❏	❏
15. that others will not approve of me	❏	❏	❏	❏	❏
16. that I find it difficult to maintain a stable relationship	❏	❏	❏	❏	❏
17. that I leave work unfinished	❏	❏	❏	❏	❏
18. that I lack confidence	❏	❏	❏	❏	❏
19. that I am unattractive	❏	❏	❏	❏	❏
20. that I might make myself look stupid	❏	❏	❏	❏	❏
21. that I will lose close friends	❏	❏	❏	❏	❏
22. that I haven't achieved much	❏	❏	❏	❏	❏
23. that I am not loved	❏	❏	❏	❏	❏
24. that I will be late for an appointment	❏	❏	❏	❏	❏
25. that I make mistakes at work	❏	❏	❏	❏	❏

AGE: SEX:

Figure 12.1   The Worry Domains Questionnaire

groups: generalized anxiety disorder (GAD) and obsessive compulsive disorder (OCD). Data for these two groups were included for several reasons. According to DSM-III-R (American Psychiatric Association, 1987), the cardinal diagnostic feature of GAD is worry. It was necessary, therefore, to collect data that would reflect how chronic and extreme worry would affect WDQ scores. Data for obsessional patients was also considered to be of interest. Contemporary neurobiological theories of OCD have implicated worry in the context of "hyperfrontality", especially with respect to the orbital cortex (Insel & Winslow, 1990). In addition, some theorists have suggested that GAD might represent a variant of obsessional checking, where worry is construed as an attempt to check the future (Tallis & de Silva, 1992). Finally, morbid preoccupations (Rachman, 1973) are a close relative of extreme worry in GAD (Barlow, 1988; see Brown, Dowdall, Côté & Barlow, Chapter 9, this volume).

It should be stressed that the two clinical samples are included only to give a rough guide to clinical ranges; unfortunately sample sizes are relatively small. Both GAD and OCD groups were controlled in that they had all received diagnoses from at least two health professionals (e.g. general practitioner and psychiatrist or psychiatrist and clinical psychologist). The GAD group were entirely ummedicated and given the WDQ on their first session of cognitive–behaviour therapy. A small number ($n = 6$) of the OCD group were medicated with clomipramine or other trycyclic antidepressant medication. All scored 18 or over on the Maudsley Obsessive Compulsive Inventory (MOCI; Hodgson & Rachman, 1977). Sixteen were on a waiting list for behaviour therapy when they completed the WDQ. The remainder of the OCD group were given the WDQ on first or second therapy sessions.

The normative data for non-clinical subjects are reported separately, as student and working samples differed significantly from each other in a number of ways. A liberal test of significance (t-test) was employed in order to increase the likelihood of capturing differences. The student sample were significantly younger than the working sample ($p < .001$). Student and working samples differed also with respect to total WDQ scores ($p = .001$), and scores on domains 1 and 4 (i.e. Relationships and Work: $p < .001$). Student scores were elevated compared with the working sample scores.

Data are reported independent of sex. When WDQ scores between sexes were compared for all non-clinical subjects no significant differences emerged. Sample characteristics for clinical and non-clinical groups are shown in Table 12.1. Normative WDQ data for non-clinical and clinical groups are shown in Table 12.2.

Table 12.1   Sample characteristics

Sample	(n)	Age Mean (SD)	Range Min–Max	Sex M	F
Working	419	34.7 (10.7)	17–66	108	311
Student	261	21.2 (3.4)	18–32	126	135
GAD	29	37.8 (12.9)	18–71	12	17
OCD	22	36.1 (11.8)	18–74	12	10

Table 12.2   Normative data for the WDQ. D1 = Relationships, D2 = Lack of Confidence, D3 = Aimless Future, D4 = Work, D5 = Financial

	Mean (SD) for WDQ domains and total			
	Working sample	Student sample	GAD	OCD
D1	3.4 (3.0)	4.3 (3.1)	5.7 (5.6)	9.1 (5.3)
D2	5.2 (3.9)	5.7 (3.8)	10.2 (4.7)	12.7 (4.7)
D3	4.2 (3.3)	4.6 (3.3)	9.5 (5.1)	9.4 (4.8)
D4	4.9 (3.3)	6.9 (3.6)	7.7 (4.5)	11.6 (4.6)
D5	5.1 (3.9)	4.8 (3.8)	7.1 (5.0)	7.6 (5.5)
Total	23.1 (13.4)	26.6 (13.0)	40.03 (19.8)	50.7 (20.8

Elevated levels of worry in the student sample with respect to domains 1 and 4 can be explained when age and circumstances are considered. Concern about the formation of intimate relationships, parental approval, friends and appearance are likely to be of greater significance in a young student population. All these concerns are reflected in items under the D1 heading. Elevated worry with respect to work can be explained by the presence of exams. Several WDQ distributions would have occurred prior to written examinations and our medical student samples would have participated in relatively frequent oral examinations. Items subsumed under the D4 heading on the WDQ reflect concerns such as meeting deadlines and not getting behind with work.

As suggested earlier, normative data for clinical groups has been included to provide only a rough guide to how pathological worry might affect WDQ scores. The fact that the OCD group scored considerably higher than the GAD group is of some interest, especially since some of this group were medicated (cf. Molina & Borkovec, Chapter 11, this volume). However, these data must be interpreted with caution for several reasons. In general, the symptoms of OCD are more debilitating than those of GAD (Barlow, 1988), perhaps causing significantly more interference with respect to everyday functioning in areas of life reflected in the WDQ domains. The absence of severity and life interference ratings for both groups precludes the possibility of drawing firm conclusions with respect to the relative importance of worry in OCD and GAD. In addition, the fact that most of the OCD group completed their questionnaires while on a waiting list might possibly have elevated their scores. The large standard deviations for clinical groups is problematic insofar as these data cannot be used to determine a clear "cut off" level for non-pathological and pathological worry. Notwithstanding these problems, the fact that clinical groups produce means nearly double those of non-clinical groups bodes well for the potential discriminatory power of WDQ items.

RELIABILITY AND INTERNAL CONSISTENCY

Modest reliability statistics are reported by Tallis (1989). Sixteen subjects were given the WDQ on two occasions separated by 2 to 4 weeks. Data are shown in Table 12.3.

Using a large student population ($n = 136$), Davey (1993) reported that the WDQ has acceptable levels of internal consistency (Cronbach's alpha = .92).

THE WORRY DOMAINS: LEVELS OF ASSOCIATION

The five individual domains of the WDQ are all significantly associated ($p < .001$). Pearson's correlations were conducted on domain scores for both working and student samples used to generate normative data. These are reported in Table 12.4. Negligible differences in levels of association exist between groups. However, the working sample yielded slightly higher correlation coefficients overall than the student sample. In the working sample, "Lack of Confidence" (D2) yielded the highest levels of association with all other worry domains. For the student sample, "Aimless Future" (D3) yielded the highest levels of association with all other worry

Table 12.3 Test–retest correlation coefficients and significance levels for WDQ total and domain scores (d.f. = 14)

D1	Relationships	$r = .46$	$p = .05$
D2	Lack of Confidence	$r = .51$	$p = .05$
D3	Aimless Future	$r = .58$	$p = .01$
D4	Work	$r = .69$	$p = .001$
D5	Financial	$r = .86$	$p = .001$
WDQ	Total	$r = .79$	$p = .01$

Table 12.4 Correlation coefficients for worry domains. All are significant at $p <$ .001. D1 = Relationships, D2 = Lack of Confidence, D3 = Aimless Future, D4 = Work, D5 = Financial

Working sample (n = 419)

	D1	D2	D3	D4	D5
D1	1.00	.66	.54	.43	.41
D2		1.00	.61	.52	.37
D3			1.00	.48	.41
D4				1.00	.24
D5					1.00

Student sample (n = 261)

	D1	D2	D3	D4	D5
D1	1.00	.60	.56	.41	.30
D2		1.00	.47	.43	.26
D3			1.00	.52	.42
D4				1.00	.26
D5					1.00

domains. "Financial" worries (D5) were the least associated with all other domains for both working and student samples.

It is possible that the different worry domains have a differential impact on general mental health. Hodgson, Tallis & Davey (submitted), using a student population, have provided correlational data showing how the individual worry domains are associated with scores on the General Health Questionnaire (GHQ; Goldberg, 1972). All worry domains are positively and significantly ($p < .001$) associated with GHQ totals with the exception of D5 (i.e. Financial). The highest level of association was found to be between D1 (Relationships) and the GHQ (Table 12.5). This is consistent with phenomenological analyses (see Tallis, Davey & Capuzzo, Chapter 3, this volume), which suggest that worries about intimate relationships are experienced as the most unpleasant. However, it should be noted that the WDQ–GHQ relationship is mediated by trait anxiety (see below).

Table 12.5 The impact of individual worry domains on general psychological health as measured by the General Health Questionnaire: A correlational analysis ($n = 80$). All are significant at $p < .001$ with the exception of D5

		GHQ
D1	Relationships	.58
D2	Lack of Confidence	.50
D3	Aimless Future	.55
D4	Work	.47
D5	Financial	.21

VALIDITY WITH RESPECT TO DIFFERENTIAL COGNITIVE PERFORMANCE

Subjects designated high or low worry status according to WDQ scores perform differentially on cognitive and computer based tasks (Tallis, 1989; Tallis, Eysenck & Mathews, 1991a, 1991b) For example, when asked to form ego-relevant images prompted by words or phrases generic to primary worry domains, high worriers are able to produce more images and with shorter latencies compared to low worriers. This advantage is not apparent when word and phrase prompts are generic to domains of equal significance to high and low groups. These findings suggest that information congruent with active worry domains is more accessible in high worriers. Moreover, the specificity of the advantage with respect to particular domains is consistent with Eysenck's (1984) storage characteristics hypothesis.

Subjects designated high worry status on the basis of WDQ scores appear to exhibit elevated evidence requirements. This was demonstrated in two experiments, one employing the Zaslow figures (Zaslow, 1950) and the other a visual search paradigm. The Zaslow figures are a continuum of shapes varying with respect to their triangularity and circularity. When requested to select triangles and circles from the Zaslow continuum high worriers are significantly more likely than low worriers to restrict endorsement to perfect exemplars. Employing a computerised visual search task, high worriers were requested to make present–absent decisions with respect to a target letter. In the absent condition, high worriers showed significantly retarded response times. Increased search times show that high worriers require more evidence than low worriers when making a decision, particularly under conditions of high ambiguity. Alternative hypotheses relating to test-anxiety effects were eliminated in both the Zaslow and the visual search experiments. Finally, cognitive deficit measures were significantly and systematically correlated with WDQ scores suggesting a link between cognitive characteristics and everyday worry as measured by the WDQ.

ASSOCIATION WITH OTHER MEASURES

Davey (1993) reports that the WDQ is highly correlated with the PSWQ ($r = .67, p < .001$) and Trait anxiety (Spielberger, 1983: $r = .71, p < .0001$). The WDQ is also significantly correlated with the avoidance coping ($r = .51, p < ,.001$) and emotional discharge ($r = .39, p < .001$) subscales of the Health and Daily Living Form (Moos, Cronkite, Billings & Finney, 1986), a questionnaire which measures strategies for coping with stress. Emotional discharge reflects indirect efforts to reduce tension by excessive eating, drinking, or smoking. In addition, a significant association exits between the WDQ and the monitoring subscale ($r = .26$ $p < .001$) of the Miller Behavioural Style Scale (Miller, 1987). The monitoring subscale reflects an information-seeking coping style. Partial correlation analyses indicate that the WDQ is significantly associated with Active Cognitive Coping ($r = .26$, $p < .001$) and Avoidance Coping ($r = .30$, $p < .001$) independent of trait anxiety. Collectively, these data suggest that the WDQ is relatively unique, in that it captures both positive (e.g. problem-solving) and negative (e.g. avoidance) aspects of the worry process (see Davey, Chapter 2, this volume).

The relationship between the WDQ and the GHQ (Goldberg, 1972) was investigated by Hodgson, Tallis & Davey (1993). Scores on the GHQ-28 reflect general levels of psychological health. Scores on the WDQ predicted GHQ scores independently of daily hassles (de Longis, Folkman & Lazarus, 1988), negative life events (Sarason, Johnson & Siegel, 1978), depression (Beck et al., 1961) and somatic anxiety (Chambless, Caputo, Bright & Gallagher, 1984). However, the relationship between the WDQ and the GHQ was not independent of trait anxiety.

Tallis & de Silva (1992) report modest but significant levels of association between the WDQ and the MOCI ($r = .20$, $p = .001$). However, of greater theoretical interest was the finding that WDQ scores were significantly associated with the MOCI Checking ($r = .17$, $p = .01$) and Doubting ($r = .18$, $p < .01$) subscales, but not with the Washing and Slowness subscales. These data are consistent with other work suggesting a close relationship between worrying, checking and doubt (Steketee, Grayson & Foa, 1987; Tallis, Eysenck & Mathews, 1991a; cf. Molina & Borkovec, Chapter 11, this volume).

THE USES OF THE WDQ

Clearly the WDQ can be used to distinguish between high and low worriers drawn from a non-clinical population. The total WDQ score will give a general indication of worry frequency, and the subscales will provide information with respect to worry content. Scores on the WDQ are systematically associated with cognitive performance variables, and as such, the WDQ is primarily recommended as a research instrument. Unlike non-content based measures, WDQ scores are likely to reflect aspects of constructive or adaptive worrying. These sources of variance appear to be independent of anxiety (cf. Davey, 1993; see Davey, Chapter 2, this volume).

Employing the WDQ as a clinical instrument is questionable, in that elevated scores might reflect, at least in part, problem-focusing coping. However, the WDQ could be usefully employed as a companion measure to an instrument like the PSWQ in clinical settings. Scores on the five domains of the WDQ can provide a worry profile, facilitating the recognition of key areas for intervention. Moreover, specific items can be used as a starting point in clinical sessions.

CONCLUSION

The scientific study of worry is relatively recent, and existing measures will no doubt be superseded by others. However, future measures will more than likely retain indices of both frequency and content. The use of a content element is not only useful with respect to guiding clinical work, but necessary with respect to diagnosis. In DSM-III-R (American Psychiatric Association, 1987), worry is recognised as the cardinal feature of GAD. However, the focus of worry must not be on any symptom or group of symptoms associated with another Axis I disorder. Future instruments might include exclusion items (e.g. "I worry about getting contaminated") to strengthen diagnostic utility.

Unlike most other forms of repetitive and intrusive cognition, worry may be, at least in part, an adaptive process. Further measures might include items that reflect both the positive and negative consequences of worry. Moreover, consideration of the consequences of worry could provide a framework within which to distinguish pathological from non-pathological forms. Worry that motivates mental problem-solving and subsequently reduce stress could not be considered pathological. In principle, an adaptive worrier might show elevated scores on frequency and content measures; however, such elevated scores would be entirely misleading with respect to such an individual's clinical status.

In addition, pathological and non-pathological worry might coexist in the same individual with respect to different worry domains. For example, an individual might worry adaptively about work and subsequently engage in frequent and productive goal-directed problem-solving. This might in turn lead to promotion and professional success. However, the same individual might worry maladaptively about relationships, suffer sleepless nights, and subsequent mood disturbance. A useful worry measure therefore would be one that considered *specific* domains and the *specific* consequences of associated worry.

Finally, a further potentially useful index of pathological vs. non-pathological worry is perceived control. Two phenomenological studies

(Craske, Rapee, Jackal & Barlow, 1989; Tallis, Davey & Capuzzo, Chapter 3, this volume) have suggested that difficulty controlling worry reliably determines worry status.

In sum, the WDQ is a useful research instrument and one that can also be used with the PSWQ in clinical settings. The domains can serve to prioritise targets for therapeutic intervention. Further worry questionnaire development should retain frequency and content indices. However, these indices could be usefully supplemented with (i) exclusion items to assist diagnosis, (ii) negative and positive consequence items, and (iii) recognition of process variables such as controllability.

REFERENCES

American Psychiatric Association (1987). *Diagnostic and Statistical Manual of Mental Disorders*, 3rd edn. Washington, DC: American Psychiatric Association.
Barlow, D.H. (1988). *Anxiety and its Disorders*. New York: Guilford Press.
Beck, A.T. (1976). *Cognitive Therapy and the Emotional Disorders*. New York: International University Press.
Beck, A.T., Ward, C.H., Mendelson, M., Mock, J. & Erlbaugh, J. (1961). An inventory for measuring depression. *Archives of General Psychiatry*, 4, 561–571.
Borkovec, T.D., Robinson, E., Pruzinsky, T. & DePree, J.A. (1983). Preliminary exploration of worry: some characteristics and processes. *Behaviour Research and Therapy*, 21, 9–16.
Bower, G.H. (1981). Mood and memory. *American Psychologist*, 36, 129–148.
Chambless, D., Caputo, G., Bright, P. & Gallagher, R. (1984). Assessment of fear in agoraphobics: The body sensations questionnaire and the agoraphobic cognitions questionnaire. *Journal of Consulting and Clinical Psychology*, 52, 1090–1097.
Collins, A.M. & Loftus, E.F. (1975). A spreading-activation theory of semantic processing. *Psychological Review*, 82, 407–428.
Craske, M.G., Rapee, R.M., Jackel, L. & Barlow, D.H. (1989). Qualitative dimensions of worry in DSM III-R generalised anxiety disorder subjects and nonanxious controls. *Behaviour Research and Therapy*, 27, 397–402.
Davey, G.C.L. (1993). A comparison of three worry questionnaires. *Behaviour Research and Therapy*, 31, 51–56.
de Longis, A., Folkman, S. & Lazarus, R.S. (1988). The impact of daily stress on health and mood: Psychological and social resources as mediators. *Journal of Personality and Social Psychology*, 54, 486–495.
Eysenck, M.W. (1984). Anxiety and the worry process. *Bulletin of the Psychonomic Society*, 22, 545–548.
Goldberg, D.P. (1972). *The Detection of Psychiatric Illness by Questionnaire*. Oxford University Press.
Hodgson, R.J. & Rachman, S. (1977). Obsessional compulsive complaints. *Behaviour Research and Therapy*, 15, 389–395.
Hodgson, S., Tallis, F. & Davey, G.C.L. (Submitted). Worried sick: the relationship between worrying and psychological and physical health status.
Insel, R. & Winslow, J. (1990). Neurobiology of obsessive-compulsive disorder. In M. Jenike, L. Baer & W. Minichiello (Eds.), *Obsessive–compulsive Disorders: Theory*

and Management, 2nd edn. Littleton, Massachusetts: Year book medical publishers.

Janis, I. (1958) *Psychological Stress*. New York: Wiley.

Kovacs, M. & Beck, A.T. (1978). Maladaptive cognitive structures in depression. *Archives of General Psychiatry*, **135**, 525–533.

Liebert, R.M. & Morris, L.W. (1967). Cognitive and emotional components of test anxiety: A distinction and some initial data. *Psychological Reports*, **20**, 975–978.

McNair, D.M., Lorr, M. & Droppleman, L.F. (1971). *Profile of Mood States Manual*. San Diego, California: Educational and Industrial Testing Service.

Meyer, T., Miller, M., Metzger, R. & Borkovec, T.D. (1990). Development and validation of the Penn State Worry Questionnaire. *Behaviour Research and Therapy*, **28**, 487–495.

Miller, S. (1987). Monitoring and blunting: Validation of a questionnaire to assess styles of information-seeking under threat. *Journal of Personality and Social Psychology*. **52**, 345–353.

Moos, R.H., Cronkite, R.C, Billings, A. and Finney, J.W. (1986). *Health and Daily Living Form*. Social Ecology Laboratory. Veterans Administration of Stanford University Medical Centers.

Pinter, R. & Lev, J. (1940). Worries of school children. *Journal of Genetic Psychology*, **56**, 67–76.

Rachman, S. (1973). Some similarities and differences between obsessional ruminations and morbid preoccupations. *Canadian Psychiatric Association Journal*, **18**, 71–73.

Sarason, I.G., Johnson, J.H. & Siegel, J.M. (1978). Assessing the impact of like changes: Development of the Life Experiences Survey. *Journal of Consulting and Clinical Psychology*, **46**, 932–946.

Simon, A. & Ward, L.O. (1976). The Simon-Ward Response Survey. In O.G. Johnson (Ed.), *Tests and Measurements in Child Development*, Handbook II, 2, 597–599. San Francisco: Jossey-Bass.

Spielberger, C. (1983). *State-trait Anxiety Inventory*. Palo Alto, CA: Consulting Psychologist's Press.

Steketee, G.S., Grayson, J.B. & Foa, E.B. (1987). A comparison of characteristics of obsessive-compulsive disorder and other anxiety disorders. *Journal of Anxiety Disorders*, **1**, 325–335.

Tallis, F. (1989). Worry: a cognitive analysis. Unpublished Doctoral Dissertation. University of London.

Tallis, F., Eysenck, M.W. & Mathews, A. (1991a). Elevated evidence requirements and worry. *Personality and Individual Differences*, **12**, 21–27.

Tallis, F., Eysenck, M.W. & Mathews, A. (1991b). The role of temporal perspective and ego-relevance in the activation of worry structures. *Personality and Individual Differences*, **12**, 909–915.

Tallis, F. & de Silva, P. (1992). Worry and obsessional symptoms: A correlational analysis. *Behaviour Research and Therapy*, **30**, 103–105.

Tallis, F., Eysenck, M.W. & Mathews, A. (1992). A questionnaire for the measurement of nonpathological worry. *Personality and Individual Differences*, **13**, 161–168.

Wisocki, P.A. (1988). Worry as a phenomenon relevant to the elderly. *Behavior Therapy*, **19**, 369–379.

Zaslow, R. (1950). A new approach to the problem of conceptual thinking in schizophrenia. *Journal of Consulting Psychology*, **14**, 335–339.

AUTHOR INDEX

SUBJECT INDEX

THE WILEY SERIES IN
CLINICAL PSYCHOLOGY

Series Editors

Fraser N. Watts   *MRC Applied Psychology Unit,*
                            Cambridge, UK

J. Mark G. Williams   *Department of Psychology, University College*
                            of North Wales, Bangor, UK

continued from page ii